LANDSCAPES OF LONDON

ELIZABETH MCKELLAR

LANDSCAPES OF

THE CITY, THE COUNTRY AND THE SUBURBS 1660–1840

& LONDON

PUBLISHED FOR THE PAUL MELLON CENTRE

FOR STUDIES IN BRITISH ART BY

YALE UNIVERSITY PRESS · NEW HAVEN AND LONDON

Designed by Emily Lees
Printed in China

Library of Congress Cataloging-in-Publication Data

McKellar, Elizabeth.
Landscapes of London : the city, the country and the suburbs, 1660–1840 / Elizabeth McKellar.
pages cm
Includes bibliographical references and index.
ISBN 978–0–300–10913–9 (cl : alk. paper)
1. London Metropolitan Area (England) – History – 17th century. 2. London Metropolitan Area (England) –
History – 18th century. 3. London Suburban Area (England) – History – 17th century. 4. London Suburban Area
(England) – History – 18th century. 5. Suburbs – England – London – History. 6. Landscapes – England – London
Metropolitan Area. 7. Middle class – England – London Metropolitan Area – History. 8. London Metropolitan Area
(England) – In art. 9. London Metropolitan Area (England) – In literature. I. Title.

DA677.M43 2013
942.107 – dc23
2013007072

A catalogue record for this book is available from The British Library

Endpapers: Thomas Milne, *Plan of the Cities of London and Westminster* (detail of fig. 51).
Frontispiece: Jan Siberechts, *View of a House and its Estate in Belsize, Middlesex* (detail of fig. 126).
Image on p. v: John Seguier, *View of the Alpha Cottages near Paddington* (see fig. 178).

FOR ROGER

CONTENTS

(*facing page*) James Basire after William Jett, *Colonel Jack robbing Mrs Smith going to Kentish Town* (detail of fig. 25).

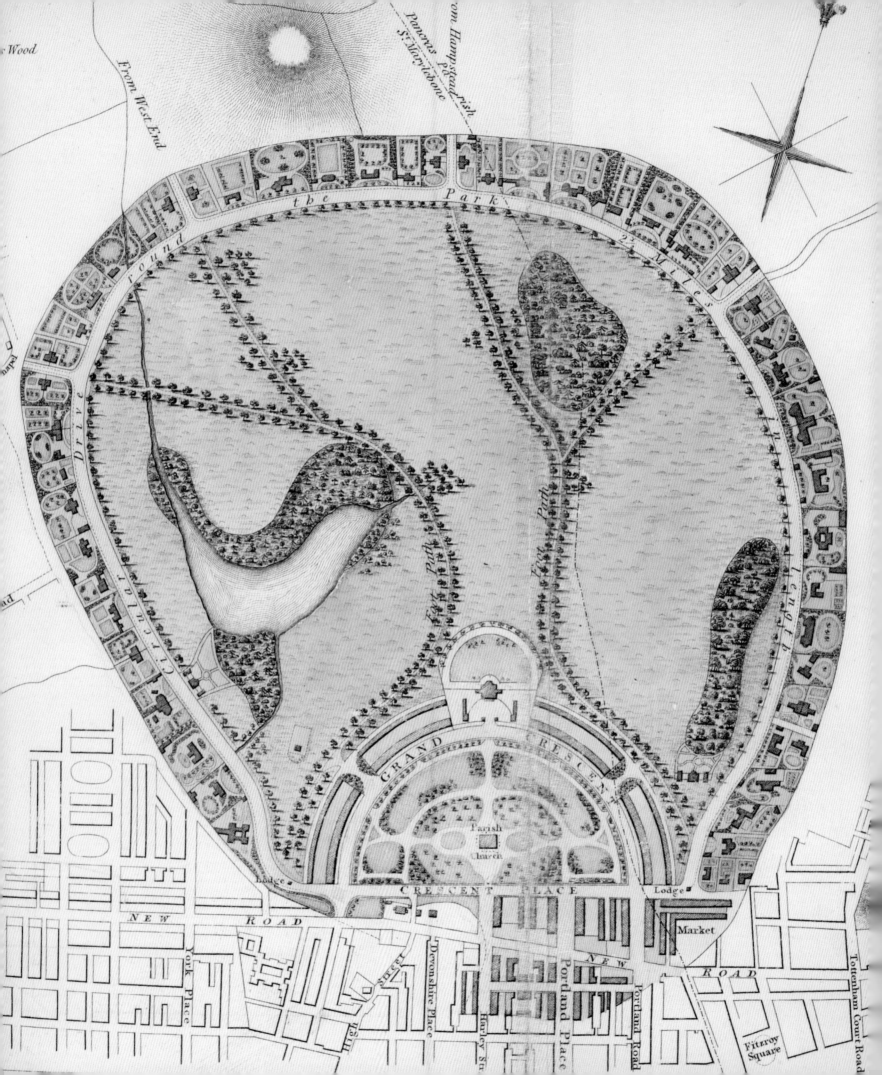

From West End

s Wood

From Hampstead
Pancras parish
St Marylebone

round the Park

Drive
round
Drive

2¼ Miles

Foot Path

Foot Path

in length

Foot Path

GRAND CRESCENT

Parish
Church

Lodge

CRESCENT PLACE

Lodge

Market

NEW ROAD

York Place

Devonshire Place

High Str

Harley Str

Portland Place

New Portland Road

NEW ROAD

Tottenham Court Road

Fitzroy Square

ACKNOWLEDGEMENTS

This book is the result of many years work, but it would never have seen the light of day without the awarding of a Research Fellowship by the Leverhulme Trust in 2011–12. I am enormously grateful to the Trust for providing me with the time and space to write and for being a truly delightful organisation to deal with, an unusual attribute these days. The Paul Mellon Centre for Studies in British Art has generously supported the publication, and the Open University has also contributed towards illustration costs.

I have naturally incurred many individual debts, and I must begin by singling out three colleagues for their unflagging encouragement, all of whom read at least parts of the text at various stages in its preparation. They are: Peter Guillery, with whom I have walked and talked many of London's peripheries; Geoffrey Tyack, who never forgot that there was a book buried somewhere beyond the demands of the day-to-day and whose knowledge of the later period has been invaluable; and last but not least, Bernie Herman, who has been a source of wise counsel and a tireless champion from across the Pond.

I am also most grateful to all the people listed below who have provided information, invitations to speak and help in many guises, with apologies, of course, to any who have been inadvertently overlooked: Glenn Adamson, Ian Archer, Barbara Arciszewska, Dana Arnold, Andrew Ballantyne, Paul Barnwell, Neil Burton, Timothy Clayton, Claire Gapper, Perry Gauci, Mark Hallett, Julian Holder, Valerie Holman, Derek Keene, Daniel Maudlin, Miles Ogborn, Leonard Schwarz, Christine Stevenson, John Styles, Michael Symes, Linda Walsh, William Whyte. Despite the input of others, responsibility for mistakes and mis-interpretations naturally rests entirely with myself.

I thank the staff of the many libraries and collections who aided my researches, particularly those of the Bodleian Library, the British Library and the National Archives. I am especially grateful to the creators of the many wonderful online databases that made my life so much easier in the latter stages of this project and that have truly transformed London studies. Hats off then to: the British Museum Department of Prints and Drawings; the Guildhall Library and the London

(facing page) John White junior, 'Plan of the Improvements proposed on the Marylebone Park Estate with the Contiguous Parts of the Parishes of St Marylebone and St Pancras by John White, 1809' (detail of fig. 181).

Metropolitan Archives and their Collage database; the National Maritime Museum; the RIBA on-line catalogues; the British Library's Crace Collection of Maps; and many others where references were checked and details magnified and verified.

At Yale University Press, Gillian Malpass lived up to her reputation as the finest art editor in the business, and I am profoundly grateful to her for pushing this publication through in time to meet a very tight deadline. The rest of the Yale team were also magnificent, especially Hannah Jenner, who did a sterling job in ordering and organising the illustrations, and Emily Lees, who produced such a stunning design.

My final thanks are to friends and family. I am especially indebted to Shona Brown, Michelle O'Callaghan and Jackie Wullschläger, all of whom provided essential support – intellectual, moral and practical – and helped me to persevere at critical junctures. My love and thanks go to my immediate family, four-legged and otherwise: to the late, lamented Walter and to Holly, with whom I shared many walks and explored the suburban landscapes of London and Oxford; and to my tribe – Gabriel and Roger – who lived through the whole process and provided distraction and delight in equal measure.

'BEYOND THE FRINGE'

'Begin at the beginning,' the King said gravely, 'and go on till you come to the end; then stop.'

Lewis Carroll, *Alice's Adventures In Wonderland*, 1865

This book is about cities, where they begin and where they end. And what happens in the space between the beginning and the end: how do you know when you have got there? Cartography suggests that towns end where the black lines on the map finish, but experience tells us otherwise. As Michel de Certeau writes, maps only refer 'to the absence of what has passed by ... the trace left behind is substituted for the practice'.[1] This is particularly true when there is no trace at all, when the map is blank, but where we know from other evidence that there was life 'beyond the fringe'. F. M. L. Thompson wrote of London's development pre-1800: 'This growth has not so much filled up empty spaces on the map as occupied particular districts which already had existences of their own'.[2] It is tracing the connections between 'spaces' and 'existences' that is at the heart of this book.[3] My work has been inspired by the concept of the post-modern global megacity, 'post-suburban or edge cities', as the post-metropolitan conurbation has variously been termed in the late twentieth and early twenty-first centuries.[4] As cities throughout the world have swelled

and expanded to unfathomable shapes and sizes, their perimeters have become ringed with a variety of alternative cityscapes, not just the familiar homely suburbs but out-of-town retail and industrial zones, cheap housing and containers for the new dot.com businesses, 'technoburbs' as Robert Fishman has labelled them.[5] It became increasingly apparent to me that London in the long eighteenth century had its edge city or exopolis also.

These ideas of new types of urban landscapes challenge classic centre-place theory, as expounded by Walter Christaller among others.[6] They overturn the normal centre–periphery paradigm in which the relationship between towns and the surrounding countryside or suburbs is taken as axiomatic, with the latter dependent on the former for goods, services and, most importantly for the purposes of this work, culture. Arguments against 'downtown-centric' theories of city growth were advanced as early as 1971 by Reyner Banham in his *Los Angeles: The Architecture of Four Ecologies*.[7] This offered a powerful argument for the non-traditional city with an interesting reversal of centre and periphery, whereby the latter becomes the former and the former ceases to exist in any meaningful sense: 'The growth of the metropolis . . . makes visible and final nonsense of any idea of regular centrifugal growth. To speak of "sprawl" in the sense that, say, Boston, Mass., sprawled centrifugally in its street-railway years, is to ignore the observable facts.'[8] Clearly, eighteenth-century London is not twentieth-century Los Angeles, but 'the observable facts' provide powerful and compelling evidence that outer London's growth was far more vigorous and complex than the normal catch-all term 'satellite development' conveys.

It is notable that Banham uses the term 'observable facts', and for him, like me as an architectural historian, the first form of evidence is visual. This is a book about seeing and visiting, about how an area was viewed, represented and experienced. As W. G. Hoskins stated, the best way to study a town is to walk around 'and we can really see its contours and bone structure'.[9] First, and most importantly for me then, there is the built and topographical evidence still visible today. The cliché of London as a collection of villages still holds considerable truth and resonates with the self-fashioning by Londoners of their individual neighbourhoods. To walk, drive or cycle around the outer areas is to experience a landscape of varied architecture and distinct local centres, with housing in decreasing density as one ventures further afield. Compare this to the endless repetitions of American or Australian suburbs, or closer to home those of Paris, and the contrast is clear. Second, there is the visual evidence from maps, plans and the plethora of prints produced for the home market from the mid-eighteenth century onwards. The huge volume of these printed views of the outskirts, little studied by art historians to date, testifies to their aesthetic interest and appeal at the time. Third, there are a large number of written accounts of the outer areas including travel and topographical guides, plays, poems and songs, which reveal them to be a significant strand in metropolitan literature. I have taken the interdisciplinary route in the belief that, as the author of a study on eighteenth-century tourism concluded: 'It is only through such an approach that we can appreciate the profoundly relational character of all cultural institutions and artefacts, and of the classes that create and "consume" them.'[10] The variety of built and unbuilt spaces, visual and

textual sources taken together provide a cornucopia of evidence for establishing the existence of what I am calling the outer London 'landscape' in the long eighteenth century. The chronological span of the book covering the period 1660–1840 has been adopted to suggest the continuities not only between the seventeenth and eighteenth centuries, which are now well established, but also between the latter and the nineteenth century. This is particularly important in relation to debates about the development of suburbs and notions of the suburban.

My use of the term 'landscape' demands some explanation here. Hoskins, in his classic work *The Making of the English Landscape*, included a chapter on 'The Landscape of Towns' in which he wrote: 'One studies them as landscapes, so to speak . . . to get behind the superficial appearances, to uncover the layers of the palimpsest . . . planned towns are the easiest kind of urban landscape to understand, and perhaps for that reason the least interesting to the curious traveller . . . they satisfy our curiosity too soon.'[11] The approach taken in this book is likewise to consider the environment of outer London as a totality – a terrain – of the built and the unbuilt, the man-made and the natural. It was quintessentially an unplanned landscape, in complete contrast to the eighteenth-century Westminster estates, and it is therefore elusive and fragmentary. It is almost necessary to consider it from a variety of angles in order to grasp its presence and make sense of the traces that it has left behind. A pioneer in this respect was Gillian Tindall's *The Fields Beneath: The History of One London Village* (1977), in which the intersections between the land, the buildings and the people in Kentish Town were mapped and explored. 'Landscape' is used in this work not just in this broad sense to indicate an inclusive concept of spatiality but also because of its particular resonances and significance in the period. In the eighteenth century the term landscape took on its current dual meaning of both the natural environment itself and ways of representing it, particularly visually, thus turning the neutral land into the culturally determined 'scenery' or 'prospect'.[12] Hoskins, writing of Wordsworth, observed, 'poets make the best topographers', a sentiment with which many in the eighteenth century would have agreed, as an increasingly urbanized society voraciously consumed poetic visions of an idealized countryside.[13]

While more attention will be given to artists and other forms of writing in the following chapters, the Romantic poet Keats's lines 'the poetry of earth is ceasing never' underlie my text.[14]

It is necessary to return to Banham's 'observable facts' one more time before sketching out a few other key influences on, and issues in, this book. In one way, as I have outlined, this is a book based on the identification and analysis of certain types of objects and texts. Through this process I have postulated the existence of something that I call 'the London region' or a 'Greater London' in the eighteenth century. The region I am concerned with extends to about 20–25 miles from the core, roughly the position of the current M25. The reasons for adopting this limit are set out in Chapter 1, although a glance at any of the maps there will provide an initial answer. The terms contemporaries used to describe this culturally constituted 'region' varied throughout the period, but from the second half of the eighteenth century the 'environs' was increasingly the most common terminology. Normally when proposing a new cultural construct of this type, the urban historian will look to social and economic history for corroborative evidence or at least to provide some quantitive data for such conclusions. But in this instance there are virtually no such accounts to draw on. There are plenty of detailed local histories ranging from the first antiquarian accounts in the eighteenth and nineteenth centuries, to stupendous series such as the Survey of London and the Victoria County History, to Thompson's pioneering account of Hampstead as a microcosm of change, and through to invaluable studies produced by local history societies on a vast range of topics.[15] All of these have proved essential sources, and I have relied on them hugely to inform myself about the different areas of London that I have covered. But there are no comprehensive population studies that tell us how many people lived in the outer areas, no studies of the social composition of these areas and how they changed over the period, very little information on business and industry and on what proportion of the population lived in retirement or were employed there. The two aspects we probably know most about are agriculture and transport networks, and these are both briefly covered in the Introduction. But for the most part this is a cultural history written in something of a socio-economic vacuum. For some of my more speculative statements I therefore apologize in advance. I am fully aware that some of my conclusions may later be overturned by subsequent geographical or social analysis, and indeed I hope that this study may help to promote further investigations.

I am also fully aware of the lacunae in my own research and coverage. For the most part I concentrate on domestic architecture, but if time and space had allowed I would have looked at parish churches as well. Although my impetus has always been to investigate a set of issues that span the metropolis, it has been impossible to research all locations in equal depth. In the chapters which make up the second part of the book I have used case studies, of necessity focused on different places, with which to develop my themes. As I worked on individual areas issues in neighbouring locations came to the fore, and so my exemplars began to interlink and thus mainly concentrate on the north of the built core. I make no apology for this, as the northern villages were one of the main centres for many of the trends that I discuss. At the same time, in selecting my examples I have steered away from the south-west Richmond area, which has dominated discussions of the eighteenth-century suburban pastoral to date.[16] I have also avoided east London, whose suburbs have received attention from a number of historians, including Peter Guillery as part of his account of 'Another Georgian London': the term being used to highlight the contrast with Summerson's great work.[17] However, as Thompson commented in his study of Hampstead, at the risk of simply providing 'another dimension besides that of the parish pump . . . the prospect [remains] that scrutiny of any one of the satellites may yield clues about the development of the whole system. However differentiated London districts may have become – or always have been – . . . all of them have by definition experienced in some form the impact of the general forces which created the expanding conurbation.'[18]

Does this lack of a concomitant conventional history matter? To a large extent the answer is no. Many of the questions I am asking relate to debates within architectural, urban and cultural history and may be answered within the discourses of those subject areas. Indeed, one of my aims in this book is to demonstrate how the visual and the material can provide the basis for opening up new areas of historical investigation.

I attempt to rise to the challenge posed by fellow architectural historian Daniel Abramson's question: 'What can architectural history teach history, that the latter might not learn by other means? How might architectural history – with its own particular methods, knowledge, and insights – fill some of the lacunae of history?'[19] Mark Girouard's *Life in the English Country House*, subtitled *A Social and Architectural History*, answered this question brilliantly and provided the essential starting point for what has become an entire subject area of 'country house studies'.[20] For no historical evidence is more immediate or more pervasive than that of the buildings which surround us and continue to form part of our twenty-first-century world. The problem with the surviving middling-sized buildings on which I concentrate is that they have often been remodelled, are engulfed by later developments and are often hard to read, even for experts. Even higher status buildings, lost among the suburban sprawl, have only recently been championed in Caroline Knight's *London's Country Houses*.[21] Of course architecture, like any other form of artefact, is never neutral, and the evidential base for any period, even the twentieth century, is always highly selective. Nevertheless, in filling in the 'lacunae' of the metropolis in the eighteenth century it can prove a powerful corrective. Peter Guillery has demonstrated this most persuasively, illuminating artisanal life in the city through a study of the fabric of their 'houses', as he rightly insists on terming them, rather than the abstract sociological 'housing'.[22]

One cannot examine the periphery of a city for long without getting drawn into thinking about suburbs and the suburban. There have been two particularly important studies, both of which propose that the very first suburbs were to be found in London in the eighteenth century. The earlier work is by Robert Fishman, whose *Bourgeois Utopias: The Rise and Fall of Suburbia* (1987) traces the history of the suburb in the Anglo-American world, while the more recent is John Archer's *Architecture and Suburbia: From English Villa to American Dream House, 1690–2000* (2005). Both of these works proposing London as the well-spring interestingly enough are by Americans, despite the fact that as Fishman comments, the United States embraced the model so decisively 'that ever since Americans have been convinced that it was they who invented suburbia'.[23] Fishman argues that in fact the first suburbs were formed in places like Clapham, where a heady mixture of an intense focus on the godly nuclear family by evangelicals, a separation of work and home, and bourgeois individualism came together to form peripheral suburbs of permanent dwellings for wealthy business people based on daily commuting. Archer traces a similar arc of influence across the Atlantic, but significantly he shifts the start of suburbia back to the late seventeenth century with the development of 'villadom' in elite riverside villages, such as Richmond and Twickenham. He links the development of the middling-sized suburban detached house to Enlightenment notions of self-determination and individualism, particularly as propounded by John Locke. This formed the basis of what later became the 'American dream house', which he argues has been and still remains one of the main instruments for realizing bourgeois selfhood.

This book takes a similar chronological stance to Archer, although I push the development of the suburb slightly further back into the seventeenth century. Like both these authors I see the 'villa' as being central to the development of new forms of dwelling on the metropolitan fringes, although unlike them I am not concerned with tracing its psychological or intellectual roots. Crucially, I conceive the villa rather more loosely than Archer in particular, and place it within the context of domestic architecture more broadly in order to consider the wider built landscape that might constitute these new environments. I also argue that the peripheral zone was defined as much by certain non-domestic activities as by residential dwelling. Unlike the planned suburbs of what later became known as the 'West End', this was an organic landscape of mixed uses and a variety of architectural typologies which consequently produced a diversity of types of suburb. In many ways this brings the outer suburbs closer to Fishman's 'technoburbs' or Garreau's 'Edge City' than their nineteenth- and twentieth-century dormitory-style successors. The issue of the birth of the suburbs is central to this book, then, but it is not *the* central issue, which is to establish the distinctive character of the urban fringes as part specifically of middle-class culture and consumption. The middle classes have been the focus of increasing amounts of attention by historians of the eighteenth-century metropolis, but there are still huge gaps in our understanding of their cultural expectations and agency.

In looking at the interrelationship of urban and rural no one can escape the gravitational pull that Raymond Williams's (1921–1988) classic work, *The Country and the City* (1973), still exerts. His central theme (hugely simplified) of the distinction between the pastoral ideal versus a corrupting urban environment was enthusiastically embraced by subsequent generations of scholars, leading to a bifurcation in cultural studies between urban and rural studies. In architectural history, for example, it led to sharp distinctions in methodology and ideology between histories of country houses and villas on the one hand and town houses and urbanism on the other (a distinction sharpened admittedly by the unlikelihood of the devotees of the former approach having ever paid much attention to Williams's work). But architectural history was unusual in this respect. His influence on the majority of scholars exploring the cultural construction of what had become in effect two 'separate spheres', to paraphrase the gender studies debate, could not be overestimated.[24] In fact, as Williams himself pointed out in an essay seeking to redress the balance called 'Between Country and City' (published in 1984 a few years before he died), the book was concerned with connections as much as oppositions between his two categories:

> My central case in *The Country and the City* was that these two apparently opposite and separate projections – country and city – were in fact indissolubly linked, within the general and crisis-ridden development of a capitalist economy, which had itself produced this division of modern forms. With the increasing development of a more fully organised agrarian capitalism, ever more closely linked with the general money market, this is clearly even more true now than then.[25]

Since then there have been a number of works which have begun to unpick these two binaries and explore the connections and interstices between city and country. An important collection of essays, *The Country and the City Revisited: England and the Politics of Culture, 1550–1850* (1999), is part of a growing body of scholarship that repositions Williams's famous text and suggests that his urban–rural dichotomy 'can be more satisfactorily grasped as a series of permeable boundaries'.[26] The refiguring of Williams's urban–rural binary has developed out of what has been characterized as 'the spatial turn' in the humanities: a post-structural scepticism about single-voiced historical narratives which recognizes that position and context are central to all constructions of knowledge.[27] Equally critically, such thinking positions 'spaces' of whatever type – architectural, landscape, print – as socially determined and the outcome of economic flows, social relations and cultural representations. In relation to early nineteenth-century London, Dana Arnold has offered an important reconceptualization of urban and rural as having a commonality of values rooted in land and its associated ideologies, arising from the practices of land ownership and development by the great estates.[28] This book by contrast suggests that middle-class practices and culture were central to the creation of a new urban–rural configuration in the environs, a zone with a far more fragmented pattern of land ownership and no history of large-scale estate development until the second quarter of the nineteenth century. This was a novel landscape arising not out of aristocratic ownership but out of the consumer society of the metropolitan middle classes in the long eighteenth century, which created something neither city nor country but rather in-between, a new suburban culture in which dwelling, leisure and commerce were all intertwined.

INTRODUCTION

LONDON – THE SUBURBAN CITY

Two chief types are distinguishable among large cities: the concentrated and the scattered. The former is more common on the Continent and is clearly represented in the big government seats of Paris and Vienna, which were the prototypes of European town-planning, at the end of the last century. The second type is represented by the English town, which now seems to many of us the ideal.

Steen Eiler Rasmussen, *London: The Unique City*, 1934

LOCATING THE LANDSCAPES OF LONDON:
DEFINING AND TRACING
'THE METROPOLIS'

Steen Eiler Rasmussen (1898–1990), the great Danish town planner and writer, in his classic work of 1934 characterized London in the opening chapter as 'The Scattered City'. The scattered town was the 'English' urban prototype in his account, consisting of a low-rise, low-density arrangement in single rather than multiple dwellings. He discussed how in London by the Middle Ages there was already considerable development outside the old Roman walls, known as 'the wards without [the walls]'. The walls themselves were too huge to move but too narrow in compass for growth. Paradoxically, therefore, because its confines were restricted, 'London became a greater and still greater accumulation of towns, an immense colony of dwellings.'[1] Rasmussen's book was dedicated to Raymond Unwin, one of the leaders of the English Garden City Movement of the early twentieth century. It was a cry against the new modernist high-rise urban

planning and a plea for a return instead to the English low-level tradition. In an essay on 'London New Towns' of 1978 subtitled 'A New and More Happy Ending But No End', he was able to portray his subject as 'London always the Scattered City'.[2] Rasmussen argued that the garden city ideas of Unwin and Ebenezer Howard lived on in Abercrombie's 1944 Greater London plan with its creation of the Green Belt around the inner and outer suburban rings, the whole encircled by an outer country ring stretching into the Home Counties.[3] *The Unique City* portrayed the building in the seventeenth century of the suburbs of Bloomsbury and Covent Garden – the 'little towns' as they were called by contemporaries – as the start of a process which ends with the building of the Greater London New Towns after the Second World War, such as Hemel Hempstead and Harlow and ultimately Milton Keynes (1967). However, as the second part of the title of the essay indicates – 'But No End' – he did not see this as a completed process. Just because London was the scattered city, it did not mean that it was in any way regressive; as Rasmussen wrote it was also 'The Commercial City', the home of free trade and the antithesis of Paris, the absolutist city.[4]

For Rasmussen, therefore, London's character as the scattered city had its roots in its earliest Roman formation, which was given a particular impetus and socio-economic underpinning by the introduction of estate development through leasehold speculative building in the seventeenth century.[5] This work similarly argues that both suburbs and a dispersed city, exemplified initially in the two centres of London and Westminster, have a long pedigree in the metropolis and that certain key developments in the seventeenth century consolidated the identity of London not just as the scattered city but as the suburban city. The multi-centred nature of the metropolis has received increasing attention from social and urban historians.[6] However, the history of suburban growth in the eighteenth century has received less attention, at least outside the well-documented elite estates of the West End.[7] For a long time the beginning of the middle-class suburb has been located in the late eighteenth or early nineteenth centuries, following the lead established by scholars such as Dyos and Summerson in their pioneering accounts.[8] In the latter's classic on the city's eighteenth-century growth, *Georgian London* (1945), Summerson mainly concentrated on the centre, but he did add a chapter on 'Greater Georgian London' to later editions. In it he elegantly sketched out various types of suburban development, the first of which – village development – he traced back to the late seventeenth century. This book suggests a similar periodization for modern suburban development, arguing that the suburbs began in the post-Restoration period as part of a broader transformation of the metropolis into a modern, decentred, commercial conurbation. Issues of modernization will not be addressed in relation to the familiar territory of the centre and its novel social spaces here, but rather will be reorientated towards debates about suburbanization, urban morphology and cultural plurality.[9]

In discussing the growth of the city Rasmussen was as alive to the importance of the open spaces between developments as to the built-up area itself. A consideration of the whole environment and its landscapes also underpins this work. Unlike Rasmussen I shall turn my back on the centre and focus solely on the outer areas of London, but like him I aim to show that the dis-persed nature of London was crucial to its character and identity. It will be argued that these 'outer' areas, although distinctive, were as much part of metropolitan life in the long eighteenth century as the West End and the City. At one time Rasmussen was dismissed as a nostalgic reactionary, but his reputation was rehabilitated following the rejection of modernist planning solutions and the reissue of *London: The Unique City* in the 1980s.[10] Many of the themes that Rasmussen wrote about have now achieved a central place in both historical and planning studies, such as the importance of open space in cities, the role of sport and leisure activities in the formation of cultural identity, the significance of communications networks, and the importance of the domestic in the creation of the political and urban realm. Indeed, as Georgian architecture used the same form for domestic and non-domestic buildings, the conception of the house to the typology of the Georgian city and suburb is paramount.

The growth of suburbs in London, then, dates back to the medieval period and the need for expansion beyond the old Roman walls. This decentring was increased by the fact that the capital by the Middles Ages consisted of two cities: London – the old Roman centre known as the 'City' – and Westminster. There was also Southwark to the south of the river, which was technically not a suburb but a separate self-governing borough (fig. 2). Over time extramural settlements grew up outside the walls and began linking the two cities. The term 'suburban' was adopted in the Middle Ages to define those areas outside the walls but contiguous with them and within the jurisdiction of the City of London. The early suburbs were the 'wards without', for example Farringdon Without and Bishopsgate Without. Then, as the built-up area spread, the term encompassed places like Smithfield just beyond Newgate to the north and Whitechapel just outside Aldgate in the east. William Fitzstephen in his description of London *c*.1174 wrote of 'suburbio frequente continuante' between London and Westminster – along Fleet Street and the Strand – with their 'horti spatiosi et speciosi' (spacious and beautiful gardens).[11]

The population of the built-up area of London and Westminster – based on the 'most plausible of current estimates' – was 200,000 in 1600, had risen to 400,000 by 1650, and reached 575,000 by 1700.[12] This extraordinary growth was fuelled by immigration both inter-

2

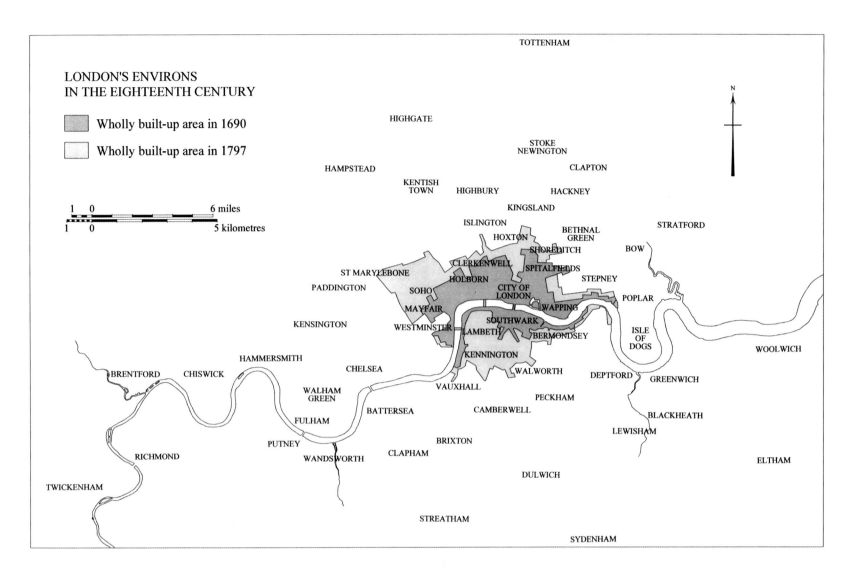

nal and international. Most 'Londoners', therefore, were born outside the capital. The areas of greatest growth were Westminster, Surrey and Middlesex, where the population increased eightfold between 1580 and 1695, compared to no overall increase at all in the City.[13] By the Restoration the territory governed by the Lord Mayor accounted for less than half of the capital's population. The outer areas continued to expand in the early modern period despite numerous proclamations against growth. Acts forbidding the building of new houses with less than four acres of ground were issued at regular intervals from 1580 to 1605 in the country around London at a distance varying between two and seven miles. However, this legislation was never properly enforced, and the pressure for new housing proved too great for it to be effective.[14] By 1605 it is estimated that 75,000 people

lived in the City, 115,000 in the immediately adjacent wards and liberties, and 35,000 in the out parishes.[15] City patriots and antiquaries, such as John Stow (1525–1605), lamented the continuous expansion of the City and its swallowing up of the surrounding open spaces. Stow wrote *The Survey of London* (1598), which is our main source on early modern London and its suburban growth. His description of Whitechapel provides a revealing account of the rubbish heaps, poor housing and makeshift smallholdings (inclosures) that blighted the entry to the Tudor City despite repeated attempts by the authorities to legislate against such sprawl:

But this common field, I say, being sometime the beauty of this city, on that part is so encroached upon by building of filthy Cottages, and with other purpressors [*sic*], inclosures and laystalls (notwith-

3

3   E. H. Dixon, *King's Cross, London: The Great Dust-Heap, next to Battle Bridge and the Smallpox Hospital*, 1837, watercolour, Wellcome Library.

The dust heap was finally removed in 1848 to make way for the new railway terminus. The mountain of ash was exported to Russia where it was mixed with clay to make the bricks that rebuilt the fire- and war-damaged Moscow.

standing all Proclamations and Acts of Parliament made to the contrary) that in some places it scarce remaineth a sufficient Highway for the meeting of carriages and droves of cattle; much less is there any fair, pleasant, or wholesome way, for people to walk on Foot: which is no small blemish to so famous a city, to have so unsavoury and unseemly an entry of passage thereunto.[16]

Stow is presenting the less appealing aspects of the suburbs here, particularly those contiguous to the City, as areas of low-grade housing and marginal and un-savoury activities such as laystalls. Laystalls were giant rubbish heaps of rotting offal, cinder and household waste which ringed the city and were a notable feature of its outer landscapes well into the nineteenth century, just as they are of the slums of rapidly expand-ing cities such as Mumbai today[17] (fig. 3). This zone of marginality, and often criminality, as Stow observed, made an uncomfortable entry point for a wealthy capital city. Stow portrays the outparts as the location for outcasts of all kinds: noxious industries which had long been sited outside the City walls, as well as hos-pitals, leper houses and lunatic asylums, and other disreputable activities such as theatres, brothels and bull and cock-fighting pits. However, he reflects the dichotomy in the suburban landscape, which at the same time was also the location for walks and recrea-

tion, gardens, summer houses and fine mansions for the aristocracy and wealthy City traders. Above all, Stow shows that in the late sixteenth and early seventeenth centuries the outer areas were a mixed environment of wealth and squalor, of recreational, residential, agricultural and commercial uses. They were also a contested area of conflicting uses and land pressures. Stow informs us that the issue of enclosure became a pressing one in the sixteenth century when the long-established custom of the citizens of London of using the adjacent fields for exercise and archery practice came into conflict with the expansion 'of the towns about London, as Iseldon, Hoxton, Shoreditch'.[18] The inhabitants of these places enclosed the common field with hedges and ditches, leading to a furious crowd digging them up in defence of their ancient rights. But now Stow writes:

> we see the thing in worse case than ever, by means of inclosure of gardens, wherein are built many fair summer-houses; and in other places of the suburbs, some of them like Midsummer pageants, with towers, turrets, and chimney-tops, not so much for use of profit as for show and pleasure, betraying the vanity of men's minds, much unlike to the disposi-tion of the ancient citizens, who delighted in the building of hospitals and almshouses for the poor, and therein both employed their wits, and spent their wealths in preferment of the common com-modity of this our city.[19]

Many of the issues to be discussed in this book are prefigured in Stow, who shows us clearly that suburban expansion was not a new process at the end of the seventeenth century. The diversity of the metropolis was evident from at least mid-century, as Michael Power has shown, as east and west increasingly bifur-cated in terms of economic wealth, social composition and prestige.[20] In the eighteenth century this pressure for expansion in the suburban ring intensified as the middling sort grew substantially both in terms of numbers and spending power.[21] The commercial revo-lution of the long eighteenth century created a newly confident urban middle class keen to spend its hard-earned wealth and leisure near the capital rather than on far-flung country estates of the aristocratic type. An expanding economy, improved transport links and new forms of middle-class cultural identity all accelerated

4

4 Leonard Knyff, *A View of Hampton Court*, *c.*1702–14, oil, Royal Collection Trust.

This bird's-eye view shows the palace after the transformation of the gardens by William and Mary in an imposing Franco-Dutch fashion radiating out into the surrounding landscape.

The marchants, have they fayre houses?

Fayre, and chiefly the Aldermen have houses, that you would thinke them able to lodge a king.[22]

By the beginning of our period Whitehall Palace was a warren of medieval buildings with only the Tudor Holbein Gate (1532) and Inigo Jones's Banqueting House (1619–22) as the architectural features of any note, alongside the Queen's Chapel by Jones (1623–5) at St James's Palace. Royal spending was targeted towards the suburbs and the Home Counties at places such as Wolsey's magnificent Hampton Court (1514 onwards) requisitioned by Henry VIII; Nonsuch (1538–41), the fairytale Surrey palace; and the Queen's House (1616–19, 1630–35) and new Charles II block (1664) at Greenwich, which were later taken over by the Royal Naval Hospital from 1694 onwards (fig. 4).

Following this royal migration, courtiers likewise began to build in the countryside around London from the sixteenth century onwards. These second homes – which were separate from their country estates – were normally, but not always, located near to the substantial number of royal palaces in the outskirts. Hackney was an exception where a number of houses were built or remodelled, notably Sutton House by Ralph Sadleir, private secretary to Thomas Cromwell, *c.*1535; Balmes House by Sir George Whitmore in the early seventeenth century; and Brooke House, to which Sadleir's master himself carried out major works, and further modifications were made by Lord Hundsdon, who owned the house until 1583 (fig. 5). Caroline Knight has drawn attention to the fact that Brooke House alternated between aristocratic and City owners, which illustrates the mixture of nobility and new men who inhabited the area.[23] The presence of City men and civil servants helps to explain the lack of a royal focus for Hackney's elite growth, and in the eighteenth century it became known as the City plutocrats' suburb par excellence. The gentry's penchant for south-west London, by contrast, does seem to have been largely connected to the royal palaces there, which continued to multiply along with the Hanoverians' large numbers of children, legitimate and otherwise. Maids of Honour Row was leased by the Prince of Wales from 1722 to house the maids of his wife, Caroline of Ansbach (fig. 6).[24] Daniel Defoe in his *Tour of Great Britain* (1724–6)

the processes of suburbanization and colonization of the environs through the long eighteenth century.

One of the unusual features of London was that although it was a capital city, it was not a royal city. From the thirteenth century onwards, the monarchy abandoned the Tower as a royal palace and instead based itself at Westminster. Over time other outer London palaces were built, such as Richmond, Eltham and Theobalds in Hertfordshire, and these were in fact generally more favoured than the cramped conditions of Whitehall and St James's. The reason for this regal and by extension courtier aversion to the City is made clear in the following dialogue from John Florio's *His firste Fruites*, a language primer of the late sixteenth century.

The queene, cometh she often to the citie, or not?

Seldome times, yea very seldom

Wherefore do you know it?

Because London is almost always infected with plage, and there dye many, and the queene feareth much.

But she doth not lye farre from the citie?

Not very farre about five, eight, or ten, and sometymes twentine myles. . . .

The nobles, dwel thei in the city?

Yea sir, in winter, but in somer they are abrode in the countrey, at their Farmes.

pital there, but also as a desirable suburb for both the gentry and the middling sort.[28]

Andrew Saint has written that until the mid-eighteenth century, 'The city core with few exceptions was a repository of banal domestic buildings; the suburbs were the location for the great architectural projects.'[29] Greenwich was perhaps the prime example of the architectural splendour of the hinterland. Hospitals might be banished to the outskirts and rely on charity for their functioning, but they were often magnificent creations. The Royal Naval Hospital (1699–1743) was designed by the elite architects of the Office of Works, Wren, Vanbrugh and Hawksmoor, using Jones's Queens House as a centrepiece (see fig. 81). Bethlem Hospital (1675–6) in Moorfields was another architectural show-stopper in a French style by Robert Hooke, while St Bartholomew's, Smithfield, was completely rebuilt by James Gibbs in the mid-eighteenth century[30] (fig. 7). Well into the 1760s architectural writers, such as John Gwynn, and other commentators bemoaned the lack of monumental buildings in the core while recognizing the need to integrate centre and environs in terms of planning and ornament. Joseph Massie, for example, in an essay on the embellishment of capital cities and their suburbs wrote:

> In a great, populous, and capital City like ours, all its *Grandeur*, Decorations, and Ornaments, are by no Means to be confined to, or near its Center only....In ours, true Taste and Judgment require a great Number and Variety of Ornaments to be dispersed at proper Distances, all over it. Neither if possible, ought even the meanest and remotest Suburb to be intirely without some Ornaments. ...Hereby...as before remarked of ancient Rome in its Glory...would spread our Fame to the uttermost Parts of the Earth.[31]

In terms of power, prestige and magnificence the monumental architecture of the outer areas held sway in the seventeenth century over the tightly packed City (both pre- and post-Fire) and the new suburbs to the west, which were hugely admired but domestic in scale and purpose. The trend for the monarchy to abandon the city escalated after the Restoration, with the later Stuarts and Georges increasingly favouring Kensington and south-west London as their metropolitan base. It

5 Sutton House, Hackney, first floor panelled Great Chamber with a portrait of its first owner, Sir Ralph Sadleir (1507–1587), *c*.1535, National Trust.

attributed the growth of the 'town' of Richmond to the presence of the Prince and Princess of Wales, who used it as their place of summer residence, so that, he wrote, it increases 'daily in ... nobles houses'.[25] By the mid-century the guidebook *London in Miniature* was reporting that the gentry resided there in both summer and winter due to its nearness to London, an increasingly common pattern of year-round residence in the suburbs throughout the region.[26] At Greenwich there was an early wave of aristocratic building centred on the royal palace and also the one at Eltham: for example, Charlton House, built by Sir Adam Newton, tutor to Prince Henry, *c*.1607–12. However, under the later Stuarts these south-easterly palaces were abandoned, the Queen's House surviving as a dower house and from 1690 as the Ranger's House for Greenwich Park.[27] Despite the withdrawal of royal patronage Greenwich continued to expand significantly through the seventeenth and eighteenth centuries, partly due to the presence of the Royal Naval College and Hos-

6 Maids of Honour Row, Richmond Green, 1717–21, Courtauld Institute of Art.

The urban terrace form is transposed here to a suburban location, indicated by the generosity of the plot width of five bays per house with centrally positioned doorways.

was for this reason that artists, in particular, featured the outer areas almost as strongly as the inner ones in their depictions of the metropolis, as we will see in Chapter 3. When Canaletto came to London in 1746 hoping to weave his Venetian magic in northern climes, he struggled to find monumental buildings of the conventional kind.[32] Once he had exhausted the river and skyscape potential of the Thames and the limited possibilities of Westminster, of which the building of the new bridge in 1746–50 proved the highlight, he turned his attention upstream to the bridge at Walton and the new suburban playgrounds of Vauxhall and Ranelagh (fig. 8). James Ralph in his *Critical Review* of 1734 had lambasted the lack of suitably magnificent building in the centre of the metropolis, and his words were echoed and indeed directly lifted by Robert Dodsley, in his *London and its Environs Described* of 1761, who quoted them to suggest that central locations lacked the space for suitably monumental architecture: 'A taste for elegance in architecture, and a desire to improve and adorn the city, have produced one of the finest bridges in the world at Westminster. . . . We are becoming sensible of the absurdity of building magnificent structures in holes and narrow passages, where they cannot be seen to advantage; and now resolve to make what is beautiful in itself, an ornament to the city.'[33]

London was not only the scattered city but also the elusive city. Contemporaries continuously commented on its vast scale and unknowability, unable to comprehend where it began and ended. The increased residence of the gentry in town plus migration into the capital by all social groups, combined with an economic boom, led to London's rapid and seemingly inexorable growth.[34] At the turn of the seventeenth century the built-up core stretched about two miles east to west and far less north to south; by the 1760s these figures were four miles and two miles; and by the 1830s it was nearly six miles and nine miles.[35] Deptford alone was as large as some capital cities abroad, according to the writer(s) of *London in Miniature*, while Chelsea was 'a town . . . near a mile in length'.[36] Between 1660 and 1743 eighteen new parishes were formed reflecting this pattern: seven in the eastern suburbs including Christ Church, Spitalfields, and St Anne, Limehouse; five in the west including St Paul, Covent Garden, and St John, Smith Square; three in the north including St Luke, Old Street; and three in the south including St John, Horselydown, and St Alfege, Greenwich.[37] These new parishes were extremely large and contained populations the size of a significant provincial town. By 1700 the older extramural suburban parishes had populations of 2,500– 10,000 while St Martin-in-the-Fields was in the tens of thousands and Stepney, the largest parish of all, contained 40,000 people.[38] This phenomenal expansion resulted in a characterization of London as 'the Monster' whose spread and size were seen as uncontrollable. Defoe was one of many who elaborated the theme, contrasting the wealth and power of 'the new Rome' with its lack of a concomitant classical harmony in its form: 'It is the disaster of London, as to the beauty of its figure, that it is thus stretched out in buildings, just at the pleasure of every builder . . . and this has spread the face of it in a most straggling, confused manner, out of all shape; whereas the city of Rome, though a monster for greatness, yet was in a manner, round, with very few irregularities in its shape.'[39]

Whereas we praise the harmony of the Georgian city, for many contemporaries it was simply not regular enough, particularly compared to European alternatives. The experience of the continual metamorphosing of the metropolis was a confusing one in a period of almost constant building activity. Until at least the

mid-eighteenth century the centre of the capital itself was unstable as it continually revolved westwards, creating a sense of spatial ambiguity fuelled by anxieties over the uncontrollable growth and sprawl of the city. Leonard Schwarz comments in the *Cambridge Urban History*: ' "London" had long been the built-up core of a diffuse region of satellite towns and villages; increasingly during the eighteenth century, and overwhelmingly during the nineteenth century the ever-expanding core took on the characteristics of an urban region in itself. . . . London can therefore be seen as a built-up area, itself a kaleidoscope of neighbourhoods, set amidst a large and amorphous urban region.'[40] As Schwarz has demonstrated, it was not just the core but

also the region itself that exhibited this multivalency. He has shown that rural Middlesex and Surrey had far more towns with large numbers of manservants in 1780 than any of the other counties in England, a good indicator of the prevalence of the wealthy in the outer areas. Many employers of manservants lived in the environs: 196 in Croydon, 66 in Clapham, 66 in Hampstead, 56 in Kensington, 58 in Leyton and 49 in Tottenham.[41] These figures should be set against those of 1,209 for the City and 1,939 for Westminster.[42] Peter Clark, also writing in the *Cambridge Urban History*, summarizes the situation from 1660: 'The majority of the population lived outside the civic limits and by the later Georgian period there was a penumbra of met-

ropolitan and suburban satellite communities, many of them larger than middle-rank provincial towns, frequently with distinctive identities. . . . As Britain became a modern urban nation the urban community was increasingly amorphous and elusive.'[43]

Definitions of centre and periphery therefore were neither stable nor absolute, but dependent on subtle shifts in the nexus of identity, power, time and place. If the image of the outparts was a shifting coalescence of the unwanted and the highly desirable, neither did the 'centre' have a fixed identity across the period. It too was characterized by the same paradoxical combination of the cultivated and the squalid. The new Westminster streets were celebrated for their regularity and spaciousness, but were as prone to congestion and street nuisances as anywhere else in the metropolis: 'The Streets and Highways in the City and Liberty of Westminster, and the Passages leading to both Houses of Parliament . . . are in such disorder, that a Man is toss'd about like a Gin Informer, before he can get to them.'[44] The western suburbs, far from being an instantly recognizable entity, as subsequent literature has tended to present them, were not identified as the West End until over a hundred years later, the term coming into use in 1807 according to the *Oxford English Dictionary*. As F. M. L. Thompson has written of the nineteenth century, but that could equally well be applied to the previous one: 'Men had no great difficulty in understanding what they meant by the larger London, which they usually called "the metropolis", even if it had no well marked boundary lines . . . it was this area of the future LCC which was already thought of as constituting "London" at the beginning of the century even if the major part of it was still empty.'[45] We might wish to substitute the expanded GLC boundaries for the LCC ones and drop the use of the term 'men' here, but nevertheless Thompson's main point about a conception existing of an urban area – one which paradoxically consisted largely of unbuilt land – is an important one.

A sense of the incomprehensibility of the metropolis is also reflected in its changing nomenclature as later accounts began to use 'the name of London . . . with latitude', as *The London and Westminster Guide* of 1767 put it, 'comprehending under that denomination all Westminster and the suburbs, with the whole range

9 Thomas Kitchin, *The Environs or Countries Twenty Miles Round London*, from Dodsley, *London and its Environs Described*, 1761, British Library.

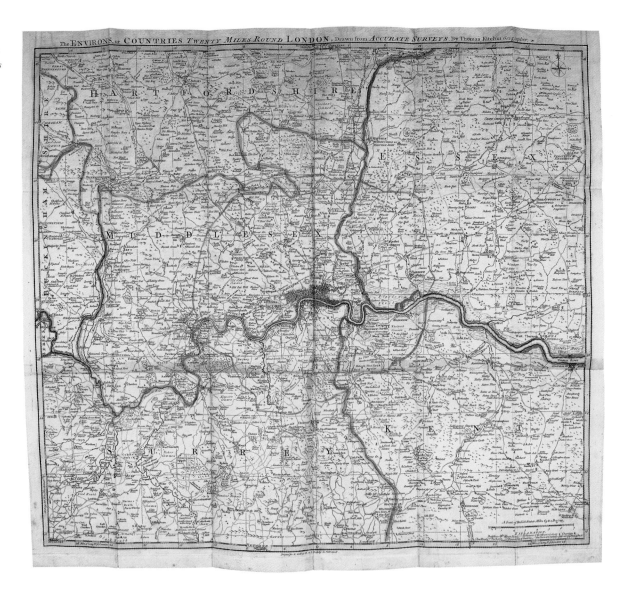

of buildings on the south side of the river'.[46] *The Foreigner's Guide* used similar terminology as early as 1729.[47] For others the burgeoning commercialization of the city was a source of pride not shame. William Maitland in his 1756 *History of London* proudly proclaimed that at present, 'This antient City has ingulphed one City, one Borough and 43 villages.'[48] In the map accompanying his book, the centre has become an anonymous mass surrounded by a carefully delineated rural landscape of villages and open spaces, suggesting that the urban core could only be defined by its outer extremities, any attempt at internal logic or coherence having been abandoned. An earlier version of the map creates the same effect (fig. 9). Maitland linked London's unregulated growth with its political

freedom, comparing the city favourably with ancient imperial Rome and eighteenth-century European absolutist states, remarking that it 'never had its Equal for Oppulency, and Number of Inhabitants, tho' not the Metropolis of an overgrown Monarchy'.[49] Nor did he see a problem, as so many did, with the spread of the city to take in the surrounding areas:

Some Authors have objected, that the Bounds of *London*, are extended far beyond what they ought to be, and wherein are included divers Villages at a considerable Distance, with no other View, as they imagine than the aggrandizing the City; wherefore I think myself obliged to acquaint all those that are of that Opinion, that Hackney is the only Parish

10

that ought not to be added, as lying at too great a Distance: But the other Places objected against viz Stepney, Lambeth, Newington and Rotherhithe, being all contiguous, they as justly belong to the Bill of Mortality, as any Parish in the Centre of the City.[50]

We should now address a few key words and definitions, notably the terms outparts or skirts, suburb, suburban and environs. The first term was one of the most commonly used at the beginning of our period to denote those areas outside the City walls. Daniel Defoe distinguished between 'the city, the Court and the outparts' in trying to make sense of 'the whole body of this vast building'.[51] James Howell in *Londinopolis: An Historicall Discourse* (1657) described the areas 'without the Gates' as 'the skirts of London'.[52] The term suburb is a far more ideologically freighted one. It derives from the Latin *suburbium* and stems from classical definitions of urban and rural as two cultural opposites in between which there exists some kind of hinterland. The word has consistently been used to denote the area lying immediately outside a town or city, but in the Roman empire and the medieval period it particularly referred to those parts outside the protection of the city walls. The word was commonly employed to describe the outparts of London, as for example by Fitzstephen in his twelfth-century 'Description of London', as we noted earlier. In the Middle Ages, although many noblemen built large houses in the countryside around London, the term suburb was generally confined to the extramural areas, many of them either industrial or housing the poor, and so the term began to take on pejorative overtones. In 1593 Thomas Nashe asked: 'London, what are thy Suburbes but licensed Stewes?'[53] In response to this a strand of low-life literature developed with authors such as Ned Ward (1667–1731) in the *London Spy* (1698–1700) exploring these noxious stews, often with a frisson of delight. However, as John Archer, who has studied the etymology of the term extensively, comments, 'Even in the sixteenth century the "suburbs" were regarded according to an emerging range of values, with vice and pollution at one end and the other embracing healthy and beautiful landscapes.'[54]

From the mid-seventeenth century with the development of the new polite suburbs of first Covent Garden (1631), then Bloomsbury Square (1661) and St

James's Square (1665), the more salubrious associations of the word began to dominate. Indeed, by the time Daniel Defoe was writing his *Tour* in the 1720s, he uses the term to describe a wide range of outer parish settlements. In the eighteenth century the term western or Westminster suburbs immediately connoted the most fashionable and desirable part of the metropolis, the forerunner of the West End. The existence of suburbs in London is clear; what is less obvious is how early one can identify an ideology of the suburban arising out of this intermediate pattern of settlement. According to the *Oxford English Dictionary* the term 'suburban' dates from the mid-seventeenth century. It was used descriptively at first but began to take on its modern meaning of a separate – primarily residential – enclave from the mid-eighteenth century. This new sense was exemplified in William Cowper's poem *Retirement* (1781). He writes of 'Suburban villas, highwayside retreats ...Tight boxes neatly sashed'. Cowper is discussed further in Chapter 6, where we see that he was one of the first to use the term suburban with its modern connotations of having a narrow viewpoint or limited horizons.

The term 'environs' first came into use in the 1660s denoting the areas surrounding a place, frequently an urban one, according to the *Oxford English Dictionary*. Its usage became far more frequent from the late eighteenth century onwards, perhaps in an attempt to distinguish between the genteel landscapes of the Home Counties and the ubiquitous middle-class inner suburbs. The word gained widespread currency with the publication of the Reverend Lysons's history of *The Environs of London* in 1792–6, which covered Middlesex, Kent, Essex, Hertfordshire and Surrey. The concept of the Home Counties, that is the counties surrounding London, may have derived from the Home Circuit. This was a judicial circuit with London as its centre comprising Middlesex, Kent, Essex, Hertfordshire and Sussex, the same counties included by Lysons with the exception of the latter in place of Surrey. To this list the counties of Buckinghamshire and Berkshire were often added, and all of these, as will be discussed in the following chapter, were seen as being very much in the purlieu of London right from the beginning of our period. Alan Everitt in thinking about regions in the eighteenth century dismissed the notion of the 'Home Counties' as having any meaning. There was no connection between Hertfordshire and Sussex or Essex and Kent, he declared. However, there was a link and that was London. 'The Great Wen', as Cobbett was famously to term it in the 1820s, was the hub of a transport, trading and cultural nexus that bound a disparate set of counties together through sheer proximity to the behemoth in their midst.[55] Everitt, who to be fair was not principally concerned with the south-east region in his essay, then rather undermined his previous statement by concluding that as towns expanded 'and as the scope of their facilities increased they also began to give rise to a new kind of region, the modern urban hinterland, and to impart to that region a growing sense of solidarity, a deepening consciousness of belonging together'.[56]

There is one more term that needs examining for the purposes of this study, and that is the contemporary one of the 'middling sort'. It is with the material and visual culture of the middling sort as they lived, played and memorialized the London environs that this book is principally concerned. Trying to define the 'middling sort' and indeed the other 'sorts' in the long eighteenth century is no easy task given the social fluidity and shifting conceptions of status across the period.[57] In terms of economic gradations Defoe, as ever, came up with a plausible division into seven groups: 'the great, who live profusely'; 'the rich who live very plentifully'; 'the middle sort who live well'; 'the working trades who labour hard, but feel no want'; 'the country people, farmers, &c., who fare indifferently'; 'the poor, that fare hard'; and the 'miserable, that really pinch and suffer want'.[58] For London in the 1700–1850 period Leonard Schwarz has estimated that the upper income group with an annual income of over £200 p.a. accounted for 2–3 per cent of London's male population. The middling groups with an income of £80–130 p.a. comprised 16–21 per cent and the working classes with an income under £80 p.a. 75 per cent.[59] The middling sort could range from wealthy merchants and bankers, through professional and artistic occupations, to the most successful tradesmen, wholesalers and manufacturers. There is still much we do not know about where precisely they were located, but it seems that by the late eighteenth century they were fairly evenly spread across the metropolis.[60]

This large and somewhat amorphous middling group did have some factors in common, the most important of which was that it was literate and thus able to participate in the new world of print culture, one of the key arenas for social formation according to Jurgen Habermas.[61] The new polite culture of the eighteenth century was forged in the cities and towns of the nation. Peter Borsay has termed this 'The English Urban Renaissance', and it was in this new realm of 'polite society' that the gentry and those of the middle classes willing to acquire the necessary social patina could engage on equal or nearly equal terms.[62] For although both the middling sort and the gentle-born might belong to the ranks of the polite, there were also many distinctions within that culture, and the term 'class' will be used here as it helps to suggest the particular middle-class identity that emerged in this period. In terms of the arts classicism is usually seen as the marker between polite and impolite or high and low culture, but as we will see there were many intermediate gradations and formations of the antique. Classicism formed the lingua franca for both high and middling culture as through the long eighteenth century traditionally elite art forms became democratized and modernized. As the century continued, other idioms became popular, particularly the exotic styles such as Chinoiserie and 'Hindoo' and the Gothic, which became increasingly important as a nostalgic means of figuring the past.[63] As this study reveals, a wide variety of artefacts, spaces and texts for a largely middle-class audience can be identified specifically related to the environs. This suggests that although the Urban Renaissance, by definition, had its roots in the town, we need to consider the extent of its influence on the surrounding countryside as well.[64] It is with the houses, books, prints and environment of this expanding and increasingly visible group of the middle classes in their suburban location that this work is primarily concerned.

THE ENTERPRISES OF THE ENVIRONS:
PURITY AND POLLUTION IN THE
OUTSKIRTS

Before we turn to the cultural history of the London environs and consider how it was represented and constituted in a range of material and other cultures, it is necessary to offer a brief guide to its main functions, commercial and otherwise. The first and most impor- tant of these was as an agricultural region providing food and other products for the metropolis. The Rev- erend Henry Hunter's *History of London and its Envi- rons . . . within twenty-five miles of London* (1811) provides an excellent summary of the agricultural structure around the metropolis which will be our guide for this purpose. Although the use of a single work may seem restrictive, in fact, as we will see in the following chapter, Hunter's analysis has been substantiated by con- temporary maps and by more theoretical works[65] (see fig. 51). Hunter outlined agricultural production as taking place in a series of belts around the capital related to the underlying geology and distance from the centre (fig. 10). The first ring was not actually agricultural at all but rather an industrial zone of clay-pits 'whence are dug the brick-earth used in the kilns which smoke all around London, to the great annoyance of the neigh- bouring inhabitants'.[66] Cruickshank's famous engraving of the brick fields of the Islington area, *March of Bricks and Mortar*, shows the environmental havoc that such activities created. Pollution could be just as much of a problem if not more so in the outskirts than it was in

the centre (fig. 11). The clay soil derived from the Taplow Terrace of the Thames and was excavated to a depth of four feet, according to Hunter, yielding one million bricks per acre in each foot. Once the clay had been exhausted the land was filled in with a mixture of rubbish and manure, after which it was either built on or became available for grazing. The first agricultural zone immediately contiguous to the town consisted of the old brick grounds converted into pasture, which created an early form of 'green belt' around the city. Hunter commented that it created 'a green and open tract round London, especially to the north of it, which is almost solely in the possession of the cow-keepers, who supply the metropolis with milk'.[67] This zone at its widest extended about three miles from the edge of the Taplow Terrace to the foot of the Hampstead–High- gate hills, the so-called 'Northern Heights'.[68] This was a sand-capped ridge of hills which ran to the north of the centre and from which numerous streams issued, such as the Fleet, which were critical for London's water supply for both drinking and leisure purposes. Islington sat just to the south of this ridge and within Hunter's green belt. It had been known since the six- teenth century as 'the dairy of London' where by 1810 the vast Laycock's Dairy kept 500–600 cows on 225 hectares of pasture.[69] An 1839 illustration of the dairy mentions 'cattle layers' (fig. 12). These were long rows of overnight accommodation for livestock en route to Smithfield, and it was estimated that 150,000 cattle and 460,000 sheep had been housed there between 1825 and 1827.[70] Islington was one of the main routes con- necting Smithfield with the north and east, and was an important stopping point for those taking sheep and cattle to slaughter. In 1754 29,000 oxen and 267,000 sheep passed through the Islington turnpike as well as other animals.[71] Hunter calculated that there were 7,200 cowkeepers in Middlesex and 1,300 in Surrey and Kent. This figure accords well with one of 8,500 given for a slightly smaller area in 1794.[72] The cows were fed on brewers' grains as well as turnips, grass and hay. Pigs also were fed on the waste from distilleries and starch manu- factures besides the by-products of the dairy industry.[73] The cost of carting the bulky waste from brewing was high and this helped to keep milk production close to the capital, as did the problems of transporting a perish- able food commodity over any distance. Generally the cows overwintered inside and were let out again in the

10 G. B. G. Bull, 'Land-Use Regions of the London Area from Henry Hunter 1811', from Bull, 1956b, pp. 26–7, Geographical Society.

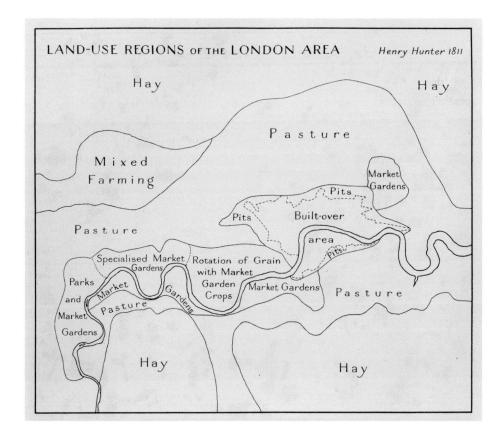

11 George Cruikshank, *London Going out of Town – or – The March of Bricks and Mortar!*, 1829, hand-coloured etching, British Museum.

The thick black pall of smoke from the brick kilns forms a powerful backdrop to this famous etching. It was made in response to a threat from Sir Thomas Maryon Wilson, the lord of the manor of Hampstead, to enclose and build on Hampstead Heath. Cruikshank shows the haystacks in the fields running away from the advancing artillery of bricks and builders' tools 'To Hampstead' as indicated on the signpost. On the hills of the Heath a few frightened trees announce: 'Our fences I fear will be found to be no defence against these Barbarians, who threaten to enclose & destroy us in all "manor" of ways.'

spring. However, ever more intensive systems of production began to be introduced, and in 1793 Arthur Young's *Annals of Agriculture* reported on five cowkeepers near the city, all of whom kept their animals indoors for six to seven months of the year[74] (fig. 13). This allowed for higher milk yields as did the practice of continually manuring the fields for those cows kept outside, by which, as Hunter wrote, they 'are preserved in almost perpetual verdure, and soon recruit themselves after being fed down'.[75]

The manure was also used on the next belt, which was that of the gardeners and market gardeners 'who cultivate the immense quantity of vegetables, both culinary and ornamental, with which this metropolis is so excellently supplied'.[76] This zone stretched for about fifteen miles from Bow to Hampton along both sides of the rich alluvial flood plain of the Thames. The underlying soil here was formed by the terrace gravels of the Thames and Lea Valley. Hunter wrote that such was 'the reputation of the English gardeners for exotics . . . that in time of peace a large exportation of these articles takes place . . . even to the more favoured climes of France, Spain and Italy'.[77] Exotic fruits such as pineapples, apricots and grapes were produced in hothouses. Pehr Kalm, a Swedish agriculturalist who visited the London region in 1748 and is another great source on its farming and much else besides, reported that the market gardens nearest the high road sold 'all kinds of flowers, which the passers by bought and carried away with them'.[78] Similar bunches of flowers were sold on the streets of London. As well as the main crops of fruit, flowers and vegetables there were important subsidiary crops in this

12 C. H. Matthews, *View of Laycock's Dairy and Cattle Layer*, 1839, drawing, British Museum.

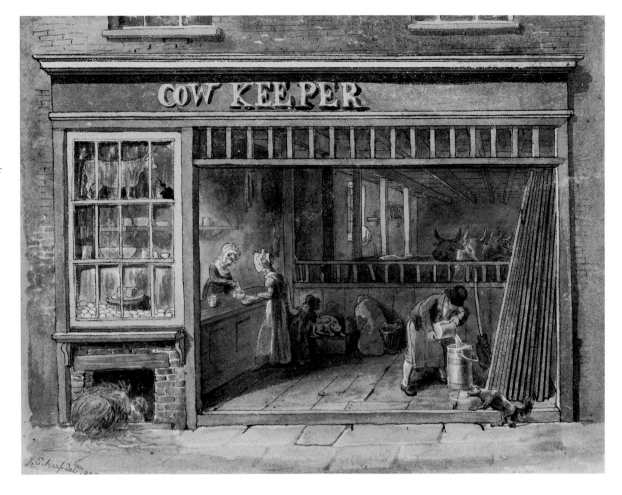

zone, such as the osier beds of willows between Fulham and Staines, which were used for basket and sieve making.[79] The flower girls that Kalm mentioned were one of the stock characters in the *Cries of London*, a series of representations of urban street sellers and their wares which were frequently reproduced in different guises in the 1660–1840 period.[80] Jacopo Amigoni's depiction of the apple seller makes clear the town–country nexus of food supply that such hawkers embodied (fig. 14).

Manure was a valuable commodity, not just cow dung but also horse droppings from the numerous stables around the city and even scraped off the street itself.[81] These deposits were collected in dung heaps just outside the centre in carts. Farmers who carried goods of any type into town would then use their empty cart to take a load of dung to the heap, where they would be paid a few pence per load. 'Those who sell this dirt are said to derive large incomes from it,' wrote Kalm.[82] He described the use of tip-carts of a

special design for carrying manure to the fields for spreading by itinerant gangs of Welsh and Irish labourers. In such fundamental and elemental ways were centre and periphery connected. This pattern of recycling was not just limited to the dung trade but also applied to the internal coastal trade with the capital, which made use of waste from the chalk pits used to create mortar for building work (fig. 15).

From Essex, Middlesex, Surrey, and very many other places in the English Provinces which either lie near the Thames, or else on the sea coast, all kinds of provisions, such as wheat, barley, oats, butter, cheese, …&c., are carried to London in small vessels. When the same small vessels return home from London, they will not go back empty; therefore they come to some one of these chalk pits, ballast their vessel with chalk which they can have here for a small price, and carry it home, where … they lay it on the arable fields.[83]

14 Joseph Wagner after Jacopo Amigoni, *Golden Pippins*, 1732–9, etching, British Museum.

The girl is shown in the Southwark fields with St Paul's and the City behind and a dawn sky heralding the early morning when fruit and vegetables were taken to market or sold on the streets for the day.

15 Paul Sandby, *Lime Kilns, Charlton, Kent, c.*1768–96, drawing, British Museum.

This drawing is one of many Sandby made of south-east London during his tenure as Drawing Master at the Royal Military Academy in Woolwich (1768–96).

The second circle was devoted to hay, which with the huge number of horses and cows to feed 'must ever be a very valuable article at the markets of the metropolis', as Hunter remarked.[84] The fields were heavily manured and the most economic produced two crops a year. Although rents on such land were high, Kalm reported that for the farmers 'the meadows alone are sufficient to earn for them and their households, food, clothes, and everything they require, and to give them power to pay their heavy rents without loss.'[85] Farming around London was a profitable business despite the high land values, and it was not until the 1820s that competition from house builders, in places such as Islington, made rents untenable for agriculture.[86]

The final zone consisted of a mixture of arable and pastural land combined with the rearing of sheep on heaths. This was the beginnings of more liminal forms of land usage, including common or unenclosed land. Hunter wrote dismissively that in Middlesex alone 20,000 acres 'are unprofitably occupied by wastes and commons' such as Hounslow Heath and Norwood Common.[87] It was in this belt furthest from the centre, Hunter noted, that there was the largest variation between the different counties in types of produce. In Surrey there was more arable than pasturage. Hertfordshire was 'a corn county' along with livestock of all sorts and timber, while in Essex the main focus was on pigs and grain. Kent was the most varied, specializing in (among other things) 'hops, fruit, pigs. &'.[88] The Kentish forests were used for 'much cord-wood, brush-wood, bavins, wheel and plough timber, hurdles, stakes, &c. [and] large navy timber'.[89] Hunter's belts are the first of a whole series of zones or circles around the capital which will be encountered in subsequent chapters. As we will see, this idea of the environs as a series of layers or indeed outer skirts in which each is independent but which together form a whole was to be one of the ways of figuring the metropolis in the period. In this way the centre–periphery relationship was established while at the same time suggesting the possible autonomy of the constituent parts.

London's situation on the Thames within this agriculturally productive and varied region provided it with many natural advantages, as William Maitland eloquently recounted in his *History and Survey of London* (1756):

London is not more happily situate in respect to Health and Commerce, than it is for many other great Advantages; a few of which I shall just mention.

16 Paul Sandby, *The City Conduit, Bayswater Fields*, c.1772–1809, watercolour, British Museum.

Sandby also produced numerous images of the Bayswater area, where he lived from 1772 and from where he commuted to his job at Woolwich.

For the Convenience of Building, we have Plenty of divers Sorts of Materials at hand, having seen in several Parts of the Suburbs (where new Buildings were lately erected) Clay dug up, made into Bricks, and built into Houses, upon the spot from whence they were taken. With which Matter the neighbouring Fields not only plentifully abound, but likewise with Abundance of choice Gravel, which not only serves to make our beautiful Terras-Walks in Gardens, but also to repair the Highways; Besides, in the Neighbourhood there's great plenty of Chalk for Mortar Whiting, and rich Manure; but Wood and Stone being scearce [*sic*] those defects are amply supplied by Water-Carriage. And for Firing, it probably surpasses all other great cities upon Earth for Plenty . . . notwithstanding the great Duty upon Pit-Coals. . . . And as for Water, the secondary Cause of all Things . . . it abounds with that precious Element, that there's scarce a House, which has it not brought into it by leaden Pipes.[90]

The natural abundance and fertility of the metropolitan region was a common theme in the rhetoric which presented London as a world metropolis. It was recognized that the city's economic prosperity was interde-

pendent with that of the surrounding land. Maitland's *History* was very much City-centric but he was still keenly aware of the critical role of the countryside in providing the essentials of life – earth, fire and water – that kept its inhabitants fed, warm and watered. This theme was also picked up by artists and writers who depicted the Thames Valley as an Eden in various guises over the course of the period. Paul Sandby's view of *The City Conduit, Bayswater Fields* unites the bucolic and the utilitarian in its celebration of the watery bounty of the London region (fig. 16).

These natural elements were used for other industries besides mining and construction. Along the water courses, not just of the Thames but also the river Lea to the east and the Wandle to the south, were located manufactories – as contemporaries termed them – requiring water power such as brewing, milling and dyeing. At Bromley-by-Bow on the river Lea Three Mills Island survives as a relic of this industrial past (fig. 17). Polluting industries, like glass or chemical works or those such as dyeing which created noxious by-products, tended to be situated well outside the centre or along the primarily industrial south bank (fig. 18). The Port of London in the City was the major generator of employment along the Thames, not just centrally but up and downstream as well. The river trade extended to shipbuilding, coopering, ropemaking and innkeeping among many others, and it has been estimated that a quarter of London's population depended on the port directly or indirectly.[91] The south-east bank was the great 'governmental-military-industrial' complex: with the Royal Ordnance producing armaments at Woolwich; the navy's dockyards at Deptford, Woolwich and Chatham; the Royal Naval College and Hospital at Greenwich; and the forts at Tilbury and Gravesend[92] (fig. 19). The Thames was a critical routeway not just for its links to the coastal and continental port but also for inland trade upstream westwards. Defoe wrote: 'All the bridges on the river, between London and Oxford, are of timber, for the conveniency of the barges.'[93] Henley and Maidenhead sent meal and timber to London, and its dependence on beech wood from the Chilterns could not be overestimated: 'without which the city of London would be put to more difficulty, than from any thing of its kind' for cart wheels, for 'billet wood', furniture and many

17 Three Mills, Bromley-by-Bow, mid-eighteenth century onwards.

18 Paul Sandby, *Lambeth Drug Mill*, c.1780, drawing, British Museum.

The mill was located from at least 1759 in what is now Lambeth Walk and was used for grinding materials for drugs.

other uses.[94] The river was also an important channel for heavy items such as stone for the building industry, which was sent to London from the Cotswold quarries in the Oxford–Burford area.[95]

According to Leonard Schwarz, aside from the two main central economic generators of the port and the court, the other key location for manufacturing was the suburbs: 'Silkweavers were concentrated in Spitalfields, watch makers in Clerkenwell.... Potters were in Chelsea, Lambeth and Bow, brewers were in South-

wark.'[96] He writes that examples could easily be multiplied, particularly for the suburbs nearest the centre and along the river. Some of these suburbs, such as Spitalfields, developed a distinctive industrial identity, which in its case is still visible today in the weavers' garrets at the top of its many surviving Georgian houses[97] (fig. 20). However, Spitalfields is the exception rather than the rule in the visibility of its commercial activity.[98] Most industrial enterprises were housed either in buildings indistinguishable from their domestic counterparts or in numerous sheds, outhouses and other wooden (often short-term) creations which have long since disintegrated or been demolished.[99] As Guillery has observed, the extensive use of the 'putting-out' system for organizing manufacturing, whereby much of the work was subcontracted to individual workers, encouraged the use of the domestic house as the focus of production.[100] A nineteenth-century photograph of a forge in Highgate housed in such a make-shift timber structure is illustrated in Chapter 5 and also a remarkable survival of a corn merchant's premises (see figs 138 and 139). The type of luxury goods given in Schwarz's list is typical of the many small-scale producers working to supply the elite London market with a never ending stream of new fashions in dress, design and furnishings of all types. Due to the high rents in London there were relatively few large-scale factories, and those there were, such as for wood-cutting, brewing or hat-making, were located on the outskirts.[101] Consequently, much of this commercial operation is invisible to us today in the built evidence, and significantly it did not feature prominently in representations of the environs, although there were exceptions such as Chelsea Water Works (see fig. 88).

This book will therefore have far more to say about the pastoral than the industrial in defining the London region, but that does not mean commercial activity, apart from the very evident agriculture, was absent. Of course, many of those employed in the environs, as throughout the metropolitan region, were working in the retail, service and professional sectors. The inflated land values produced a lively property market with a high turnover of rentals and sales. Pehr Kalm commented on this large service sector when writing of Chelsea. He observed that there were 'a frightful number of market gardens and nurseries' and went on to muse:

18

19 N. Pocock, *Woolwich Naval Dockyard*, 1790, oil, National Maritime Museum.

This is one of five paintings of the Royal Dockyards commissioned from Pocock and Joseph Farington by the Navy Board in 1785. The scale and complexity of the dockyard are displayed in this view with workshops, warehouses, timber yards, barracks and foundries as well as the nearby Royal Arsenal built around the waterfront.

The place resembles a town, has a church, beautiful streets, well-built and handsome houses all of brick, three or four stories high. I cannot 'just' understand what some of those who dwell here live upon. Some have small haberdashers shops, but that is not saying much. Publicans, innkeepers, coffee-house keepers, brewers, bakers, butchers, and such like, can here make a good living: because a multitude of people from London in fine weather, in the summer come out here, to enjoy themselves, when such people well know how to charge for what they sell. The principal livelihood of the others seems to be from houses and rooms, which they let to gentlemen, who in summer now and again, especially on Saturdays, Sundays, and part of Monday, come out here from London to stay and take the fresh air. Rooms are here considerably dearer than in London

itself, which is said to be due to this, that they have heavy taxes, and that they get no one in the winter time to lodge there, wherefore they are obliged in the summer time, as it were, to take for both at once to compensate for the loss.[102]

The two primary commercial functions of the environs, agriculture and manufacturing, created a dual environment: on the one hand green and healthy, but also polluted and suffering the effects of industrial by-products. London was notorious for its stench from both human and animal waste, particularly the open sewer of the Thames and the ubiquitous horse dung.[103] There was also the constant smog that hung over the city. This was due to the sea-coal, which from the mid-seventeenth century onwards was shipped round the coast from Newcastle, after it replaced wood as the

20 Wilkes Street, Spitalfields, with weaving garrets, 1720s.

major source of domestic fuel. John Evelyn gave a vivid account of the smoke and its effects in his *Fumifugium* of 1661:

> The City of *London* resembleg the face rather of Mount *Ætna*, the *Court of Vulcan, Stromboli* or the Suburbs of Hell, then an Assembly of Rational Creatures, and the Imperial seat of incomparable *Monarch*. For when in all other places the *Aer* is most Serene and Pure, it is here Ecclipsed with such a Cloud of Sulphure, as the Sun it self . . . is hardly able to penetrate . . . and the weary *Traveller*, at many miles distance, sooner smells, then sees the City to which he repairs.[104]

He told of a merchant whose constitution could not stand the effects of the smoke in the centre: 'Though he were a *Merchant*, and had frequent businesse in the City, was yet constrained to make his Dwelling some miles without it; and when he came to the *Exchange*, within an hour or two, grew so extremely indispos'd, that (as if out of his proper Element) he was forced to take horse (which us'd therefore constantly to attend him at the Entrance) and ride as for this Life, till he came into the Fields, and was returning home again.'[105] The traveller identifying London from afar by the cloud of vapours it emitted became a standard trope in late seventeenth- and eighteenth-century literature, although tellingly its effects were little explored in visual depictions. But what Evelyn's words convey above all is the contrast between the pure, unsullied nature of the countryside and the polluted hellish mess of the city, with an interesting twist on the use of the word 'suburbs' to apply to the disorder of the centre. Raymond Williams showed how notions of the purity of the countryside versus the corruption of the city have often been symbolized through images of environmental harmony or disharmony.[106] Pehr Kalm gave a vivid description of the virgin snow being slowly polluted by the all-encompassing smog. He created a memorable image of the inevitable defilement of purity by the contaminating embrace of the city: 'When the snow had lain a couple of days on the roofs, it began to acquire a black colour. The houses were all either blackish or grey from the coal smoke.'[107] In *Fumifugium,* as Mark Jenner has shown, aerial, spiritual and political pollution went hand in hand. Evelyn's proposals, which were dedicated to the newly restored Charles II, had a political and religious as much as an environmental agenda.[108] His solutions are interesting in the context of the environs, a word he uses several times in the text. Evelyn felt that the pollution was primarily caused by industrial not domestic coal consumption. He therefore proposed removing all the offending industries – such as brewers, dyers, soap and salt manufacturers, lime-burners – to a distance of five to six miles downstream from London, as the predominant winds were westerly not easterly. This distance was calculated to protect the royal palace at Greenwich to the south-east. He also suggested creating a green belt of 'plantations' around the centre. These would consist of 'invironing gardens' of shrubs, herbs, trees and flowers which would be both fragrant and useful 'for Health, Profit and Beauty'.[109] The 'suburbs of Hell' would be replaced by the garden suburb.

Laura Williams has shown how open space and greenery became associated with healthiness and purity as a result of contemporary ideas about circulation and disease.[110] She extends the association Richard Sennett explored, between William Harvey's work on the circulation of the blood and notions of the importance of movement to the public health, to the circulation of water and air in the city.[111] Williams observes that this discourse of movement operated both at the level of the individual body and for society as a whole. The outskirts, then, were the lungs

of London where air could flow more freely and city dwellers went to escape the smog and to purify their systems. William III, who was asthmatic, developed Kensington Palace to the west of the city to avoid the polluted air of the centre. The Earl of Shaftesbury, who also suffered from asthma, bought and extended a house at Little Chelsea *c.*1700 for his health. He wanted the house as a residence during parliamentary sittings. However, even here he was not safe from attacks when the wind blew in the wrong direction: 'He dreaded the smoke of London as so prejudicial to his health, that whenever the wind was easterly he quitted Little Chelsea.'[112] Consequently, he moved away entirely in 1706 and sold the house in 1710 to the property developer Narcissus Luttrell. It was eventually sold to the parish of St George, Hanover Square, for conversion into a workhouse in 1786, a typical cycle of reuse and adaptation for large houses in the suburbs.[113] Lord Shaftesbury grew fruits and vines in his garden, which flourished there due to the 'open air of this climate'.[114] Fruits and vegetables were also grown at Old Corney House along the river at Chis-

wick (fig. 21). Similar comments on the wholesomeness of the suburban air were made as late as 1828 of north Bloomsbury by J. T. Smith, who described Upper Gower Street as 'a part of the town, until very lately, so perfectly healthy and free from London smoke, that at No. 33 . . . grapes were ripened by the sun in the open air at the back-parlour window' and that 'an abundance of nectarines and celery were produced by William Bentham at No. 6'.[115]

THE INHABITED LANDSCAPE: MARGINALITY AND PROSPERITY IN THE ENVIRONS

The dualities that traditionally characterized the environs – arising out of their mixed agricultural and industrial environment – extended beyond the purity and pollution trope to incorporate their double nature as both bucolic retreat and repository for the unwelcome and even the downright dangerous. On the one hand, the environs were a realm of relaxation, retreat and rurality. They provided an arena for sports, military functions and leisure facilities such as tea gardens, inns and spas. They offered recuperation and relief from the tight confines of the city whether for an afternoon, a weekend, a summer or permanent retirement. These themes of the London countryside as a playground and residential retreat are explored extensively in the following chapters and do not need further elaboration here. However, the outskirts were not just a bucolic paradise; they were also a zone of marginality and displacement. It was not just noxious industrial waste that was disposed of in the margins; they were also a human dumping ground. As I have written elsewhere, the environs developed a number of distinctive and specialized functions which traded on their reputation for rurality 'for those wishing to educate, convalesce or incarcerate their relations there'.[116] According to John Gwynn, such exilement should extend to the dead as well as the living: 'The great number of hospitals and burying grounds or church-yards in this metropolis are extremely disagreeable, and ought by all means to be banished to proper places at a convenient distance from it.'[117]

Since the early medieval period hospitals, lunatic and orphan asylums, leper and pest houses had ringed the City. Indeed, the metropolis's shifting boundaries can be traced by the relocation of these institutions ever outwards, right down to the present day. Bethlem Hospital, popularly known as Bedlam, started just outside the City in Bishopsgate in 1247 close to St Bartholomew's Hospital in Smithfield (1123), London's oldest hospital. Bethlem Hospital then moved to a palatial new building in the tranquil surroundings of Moorfields in 1675; such out-of-town locations were thought to be preferable for the inmates due to their airiness (see fig. 7). Visiting the lunatics there became one of the sights of the town, as memorably depicted in Plate VIII of Hogarth's *Rake's Progress* (1735). In 1815 a further move to St George's Fields, Lambeth, took place and finally in 1930 to Beckenham, Kent (now the London Borough of Bromley), where the hospital remains at present. The old Lambeth building, with its imposing domed and porticoed central block by Sydney Smirke, became the Imperial War Museum in 1936. Nor were the mentally ill only confined in large institutions, which tended to be for the destitute. Better-off patients often lived with their families or were sent to smaller private asylums in the outer villages. Two of the most famous cases were Mary Lamb (1764–1847) and Samuel Taylor Coleridge (1772–1834).[118] Lamb, who killed her mother, was subsequently cared for by her devoted brother Charles in Edmonton and Islington, with periodic stays in private madhouses during her manic depressive phases. Coleridge, who became debilitated by the effects of his opium addiction, moved into The Grove, Highgate, at the house of the surgeon James Gillman, where he was cared for from 1816 until his death (see fig. 135).

Marginality was not confined to the insane or the dying – for hospitals at this date were essentially for incurables – it also embraced other groups, less immediately threatening but nonetheless still tangential to normal society: notably children and fallen women. The same mixture of public and private provision that pertained for the mentally ill was also to be found in relation to the housing of kept women and their offspring. The author of *A Trip Through the Town* (1735) noted: 'There is hardly a Village within twenty Miles round London, but affords a kind of Residence to one or more Widows who have had Husbands, to whom they had the Misfortune to be never Married, and who by being tied down to certain yearly Stipends (the wages of their youthful Labours,) are oblig'd to pass the latter Part of their Days in a retired manner.'[119] The riverine and eastern suburbs were notorious as the main area of low-class prostitutes, as Ned Ward's account of *A Frolick to Horn-fair* (1700) held at Charlton so graphically illustrates (fig. 22 and see fig. 1). Another long-standing red-light area was Southwark, shown in great detail in Hollar's panorama of 1675 (see fig. 31). However, of the numerous brothels and inns where the 'Bishop of Winchester's geese' (so-called due to the neighbouring bishop's palace) plied their trade, this view is silent. Although the visual evidence is scarce, all around London kept women could be found at all social levels. Some were happy to advertise and even solidify their presence in a neighbourhood. The most famous example was Henrietta Howard, mistress of George II, who built the exquisite Palladian gem Marble Hill, Twickenham (1724–9), using the income from her royal stipend (fig. 23). Most other women were forced to be far more circumspect, and the papers were full of advertisements, such as the one below from 1802, aimed at wealthy women wishing to hide

22　Jan Griffier the Elder, *London from Greenwich Park* (with Horn-fair at Charlton), oil, Muzeul National Brukenthal, Sibiu, Romania.

The Horn-fair was held annually on St Luke's Day, 18 October.
It involved a procession with horns, in reference to St Luke's ox and also to cuckoldery. According to Defoe, it was a licence for 'indecency and immodesty … such as ought to be suppress'd'.

the evidence of illicit liaisons by removing themselves quietly to the countryside. In order to be safe one would probably need to go at least to the outer limits of the London region to avoid detection.

> Ladies Temporary Retirement – Unexpected events sometimes rendering a concealed temporary retirement to Ladies convenient, an accommodation of this sort at present offers, in a genteel detached village, less than 20 miles from London, where every necessary and pleasurable comfort and assistance may be obtained … more need not be said in public. C.s. at Mr Barker's, Cheshunt-Street, Herts.[120]

Poorer women of course had fewer options. It was not until the mid-eighteenth century that municipal lying-in hospitals for the poor were established. The Queen's Lying-in Hospital was founded in 1752 for 'delivering poor pregnant women, married or not married'.[121] It was first housed in St George's Row near the Tyburn turnpike and subsequently moved to Bayswater. It later

formed branches across London – extending to Temple Bar and Holborn east, Hammersmith west, Fulham south and Hampstead north. The Westminster Lying-in Hospital was founded in 1765 near Westminster Bridge principally as an asylum for 'wives of poor industrious tradesmen, or distressed housekeepers … also for the wives of indigent soldiers and sailors, the former particularly being very numerous in and about the city of Westminster. It was afterwards resolved by the governors that unmarried women should be admitted in cases of real distress, but it was determined that such indulgence should be restricted to the first instance of deviation from the paths of virtue.'[122]

The Foundling Hospital (1741) for abandoned children, situated just beyond the northern edge of the city at Bloomsbury, was the most visible symbol of the outhousing of children on the edges of the city (fig. 24). Like Bethlem it became one of the fashionable sights of eighteenth-century London, not only to view the children, but also to hear fine music in the chapel

23 Roger Morris, Henry Herbert and Colen Campbell, Marble Hill, Twickenham, 1724–9, English Heritage.

– including annual benefit concerts – and to view the substantial picture collection donated by artists such as Hogarth, Hayman and Reynolds[123] (see figs 7 and 81). The separation of infants from their mothers took place at all social classes, voluntarily as well as under duress. The London villages were home to numerous wet-nurses who nurtured the offspring of the well-to-do. John Vanbrugh sent his children from his home in Greenwich to be nursed at Walton-on-Thames on the opposite side of London, where his younger son died just after his first birthday.[124] However, at the same time Greenwich itself was a wet-nursing location for less well-heeled artisans, as Ned Ward wrote: 'Here many Citizens in the Summertime keep their Wives at Board-Wages, purely because there's no manner of Dainties to incline them to Extravagence: here many of 'em also put up their Children to Nurse, because it's a Sharp Air, and fit for the Breeding up of a Young shop-keeper.'[125] Older children were sent to boarding schools, usually housed in domestic premises, and education was one of the main commercial activities of

the outparts. Schools abounded all around London. F. Colsoni in his *Guide de Londres* of 1693, for example, singled out the quantity and quality of good boarding schools in Hackney.[126] These establishments were frequently housed in large mansions in areas once salubrious where the march of bricks and mortar had driven out their aristocratic occupants. An example can be seen at Lauderdale House, Highgate, which was turned into a school in the later eighteenth century (see fig. 141).

Another significant group associated with the edge, particularly in the popular imagination, was criminals and outlaws, most notoriously highwaymen.[127] The newspapers were full of accounts of robberies on the roads and rewards offered for stolen property. The *Flying Post or The Post Master*, 14–16 December 1699, reported that the highwaymen had found a new kind of seasonal target: 'And we hear that they have committed several Robberies on the Oxford Road, upon Students that were coming up hither against Christmas.'[128] Thomas Pennant in his *Account of London* (1791) related that Oxford Street was 'the lurking-place of cut-throats: insomuch that I never was taken that way by night, in my hackney-coach, to a worthy uncle's ... but I went in dread the whole way'.[129] These mobile burglars, although justly feared, also became a central feature in the mythology of the outparts through their romanticization in popular hits such as John Gay's *Beggar's Opera* (1728) and numerous ballads, broadsheets and prints (fig. 25). This is not to say that there were not plenty of criminals and fear of crime in the centre, but the peculiar fascination with the figure of the outlaw introduces us to one of the central themes of this book: the imaging of the environs as 'the other', an alternative environment in which the normal social rules and conventions might on occasion be subverted or even disbanded. Nothing symbolized this more potently than the fascination with the paradoxical persona of the gentleman robber who literally inhabited the marginal, twilight zone between respectability and criminality.[130]

The medieval and early modern conception of the suburb tended to focus more on the institutions and markers of marginality and displacement than on the grand individual houses scattered slightly further out in the countryside. But the image and extent of the suburbs began to change as the London region under-

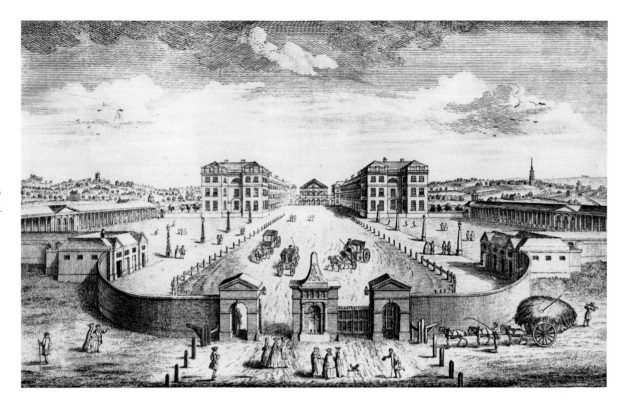

24 Anon., *A View of the Foundling Hospital*, c.1750, etching, British Museum.

Taken from outside the gates, the print emphasizes both the hospital's role as a place for fashionable promenade and its out-of-town location. A wagon of hay passes in front while the northern villages – and particularly their parish churches – feature prominently on the skyline.

25 James Basire after William Jett, *Colonel Jack robbing Mrs Smith going to Kentish Town*, c.1750, etching and engraving, British Museum.

The scene of the crime is set in front of St Pancras church, visible in the background, and is directly derived from the very carefully detailed drawing of the area shown in fig. 93.

went a period of prolonged and profound transformation in the period 1660–1840.[131] The outskirts, no less than the centre, were reconfigured by the impact of the new consumer economy and the rise of the middle class. As London became the economic powerhouse of the nation and drew more and more people to it to work in its industries – manufacturing, creative, knowledge, domestic service and retailing – the need for new areas of housing became acute, and new residential enclaves were formed to supply them.[132] The suburbs of Westminster were the largest, grandest and most evident of these, but there were also considerable numbers of new developments to the north and east of the City – in places such as Whitechapel, Hoxton, Shadwell and Spitalfields – continuing a long-established pattern of extramural development there.[133] The outlying areas became an urban playground for all types of city dwellers, a consumerist smorgasbord of delights finely calibrated to appeal to every taste and pocket (fig. 26). Alongside their leisure and important agricultural and industrial functions, the London counties increasingly became a residential zone. This took place in two ways: first, incrementally as the outer edge of London expanded

26 Thomas Rowlandson after Henry William Bunbury, *Cits airing themselves on a Sunday*, 1810, etching, London Metropolitan Archives.

Bunbury satirizes the taste of the urban middle class for venturing into the countryside at weekends while entirely oblivious to its true nature, symbolized here by the trampling of the two pigs underfoot.

constantly and exponentially; and, second, under a wave of gentrification and second-home ownership as commuting became commonplace for the wealthy from the late seventeenth century onwards. As transport and roads improved, it became possible to be based ever further from the centre, issues which are explored further in Chapters 1, 5 and 6. Defoe in his *Tour* outlined the social and economic impact that increased mobility produced:

> This improving of the roads is an infinite improvement to the towns near London, in the convenience of coming to them, which makes the citizens flock out in greater numbers than ever to take lodgings and country-houses which many, whose business called them often to London, could not do because of the labour of riding forward and backward, when the roads were but a little dirty, and this is seen in the difference in the rents of houses in those villages upon such repaired roads, from the rents of the like dwellings and lodgings in other towns of equal distance.[134]

As we will see at numerous points throughout this book, it was Defoe above all who identified and appreciated the profound social revolution – if that is not too strong a term – taking place in the villages, towns and suburbs around London. Many writers celebrated the lush landscape and architecture of the

environs, but Defoe, with his keen interest in commercial matters, was one of the few to place them so securely within their economic and social context. As he so rightly identified, this was a landscape of mobility, not just the obvious physical mobility, with increasingly good transport links and roads, but social mobility as well. The grand houses of London's hinterland as surely and prominently represented the unparalleled wealth of its citizens as the City church steeples and the gleaming suburbs of Westminster. Writing of the Thames Valley Defoe eulogized: 'In a word, nothing can be more beautiful; here is a plain and pleasant country, a rich fertile soil, cultivated and enclosed to the utmost perfection of husbandry, then bespangled with villages; those villages filled with these houses, and the houses surrounded with gardens, walks, vistas, avenues, representing all the beauties of building, and all the pleasures of planting.'[135] In Defoe's eyes the sight was the finest in Europe, finer than any in Paris, Rome or Vienna, such 'that nothing in the world can imitate it'.[136] The environs are incorporated as a central element into the discourse of the New Rome here. Defoe did not see a dichotomy between the city and the country around it; rather he viewed it as a whole in which the 'jewels' of the suburban houses shone within the 'rich coronet' of the overall metropolis. Country and city were united for him in producing the prosperity of the region. The bountiful inhabited landscape and its fine new houses were a marker of the new social mobility that trade had brought. He goes on to say that the Thames Valley has created a new national identity: 'Here they reflect beauty, and magnificence upon the whole country, and give a kind of character to the island of Great Britain in general.'[137] The peripheral has now become central, not displacing the centre, but joining with it to create a new image of the metropolitan region as not just a New Rome but a New Britain.

It is primarily these new style middle-class suburbs and landscapes that will form the focus of the following chapters. This does not mean that the more marginal elements of the outer zone can be made to disappear or are entirely ignored. The heterogeneous environments that surrounded the metropolis were naturally a product of this collision of the genteel and the criminal, the leisured and the indigent. The centre

(top) 27   Francis Jukes and
Robert Pollard after Robert
Dodd, *North View of Highbury
and Canonbury Places*, 1787,
etching, British Museum.

This print reworks George
Stubbs's famous paintings of
haymakers and transposes them
to the suburban setting of the

recently built Islington terraces
of Highbury (1774–9) and
Canonbury (1776–80) Places.
While the agricultural workers
are clearly idealized, the view
demonstrates very powerfully the
abrupt physical relationship
between the new housing in the
outskirts and the green fields on
which they were developed.

(bottom) 28   Anon., *Fleet River
near Bagnigge Wells*, early to
mid-nineteenth century,
engraving, private collection.

Temporarily stilled brick kilns
loom over a scene of
semi-rusticity.

itself, of course, was also a mix of the refined and the
raucous – architecturally, socially and culturally – but
there was a growing attempt to separate the polite
suburbs of Westminster from the areas around them.
With the exception of the controlled spaces of the
West End estates, what we would now call the zoning
of functions was far less evident elsewhere, and in
the outskirts startlingly contrasts could be found, as at
the *Great Dust Heap, King's Cross* (see fig. 3). Further
examples can be seen which demonstrate the collision
of the urbane and the pastoral (fig. 27) and the conjunction of the industrial and the leisured (fig. 28).

For a long time this outer region has been ignored
in architectural, planning and cultural histories. But
slowly it is beginning to be recognized as something
more than a marginal zone of little significance except
as a repository for the idle or the rich or both. *The
Cambridge Urban History* (2000) represented a major
shift in the historiography in acknowledging the multicentred nature of London and the links between
town and country. Jeremy Boulton, one of the con-
tributors, states: 'Many of London's economic and
social developments had their roots in its provincial
hinterland.'[138] He goes on to explore the ways in
which links were perpetuated through family visits, the
indenturing of apprentices from the countryside,
county feasts and bequests to the home area: 'Nor
should it be imagined that metropolitan inhabitants
were isolated from their provincial origins. London
was a revolving door in which not only people but
also capital, information, cultural contacts, goods and
services were exchanged regularly between the capital
and the rest of the country.'[139] *The Cambridge Urban
History* is notable for the amount of attention it gives
to the outer areas and for stressing the interdependence
of the various parts of the metropolis within the wider
region. This book is likewise concerned with exploring this new multivalent and spatially extended notion
of the metropolis, but from a cultural rather than a
socio-economic or political perspective. My means of
doing this is to take the environment of this outer area
as my base for exploring its identity in maps, prints,
books and buildings. What was the morphology of this
area, how was it represented and what did it mean in
terms of defining both city and country around the
metropolis? These are the questions with which the
following chapters will be concerned.

PART ONE

PAPER LANDSCAPES

A MAPP Containing the Townes Villages Gentlemens Houses Roads Rivers Woods and other Remarks for 20 Miles Round LONDON

1

MAPPING THE LANDSCAPES OF LONDON

By comparing this MAP with the celebrated MAP of Monsr. Roussel containing Les Environs, or the County round Paris; and with all other MAPS of the Countries round, all large Cities of Europe, it will plainly appear that no Country is so fruitful, so well cultivated, so much built upon and inhabited, and so beautiful as the Country round the Metropolis of the British Empire.

John Rocque, *Proposals . . . for Engraving and Publishing by Subscription A New and Accurate Map of the Country Adjacent to the Cities and Liberties of London, Westminster, and the Borough of Southwark,* 1741

INTRODUCTION: 'KNOWING ONE'S PLACE'

The publication of a major new city map was seen as an important event across the capitals of eighteenth-century Europe. Maps had a significant political agency in the histories of government, empire and improvement.[1] Their contribution to the processes of commercialization, rationalization and urbanization in the eighteenth century has been well documented as surveys were employed to create a new sense of an ordered and regulated nation.[2] The maps we will be considering in this chapter are not for the most part official ones concerned with tracing administrative boundaries, although of course such maps existed and helped to shape a sense of the London region (see fig. 185). Rather we will focus here on another tradition of mapping, one highlighted by David Matless and particularly relevant to topographical cartography, whereby maps are less a representation of power than a form of popular knowledge, pleasure and material culture. He writes that the topographical map was 'a

form of citizenship . . . whereby people could know their place – in all senses of that term'.[3] It is with these twin issues that this chapter will primarily be concerned: of mapping as a means of presenting a particular socially inflected metropolitan identity and as a form of democratizing engagement with the local. How were the environs mapped in the 1660–1830 period? How were they constituted and defined through that process? And what audiences did the map-makers seek to address? The shifting boundaries of the metropolis through the period will be traced in order to indentify spatially where the 'London region' was thought to be located in the long eighteenth century. The protean nature of mapping at the time will be considered and the variety of cartographical practices employed. Finally, maps will be examined as a product of the London print trade and the demand for new types of maps considered in relation to processes of modernization and popularization; as John Brewer writes, 'print was the bedrock on which British culture was built' in the eighteenth

(facing page) 29   Philip Lea, *A Mapp containing the Townes Villages Gentlemens Houses Roads Rivers Woods and other Remarks for 20 Miles Round London* (detail of fig. 34).

century.[4] Maps are the first of these 'paper landscapes' to be explored, while subsequent chapters will look at books and print images.

The problem with mapping the 'outskirts', as we saw in the Introduction, was that no one really knew where they began and ended or what they included and excluded, and this remained true even into the early nineteenth century. Maps are one of the best indicators we have of analysing the London region's shifting boundaries through the long eighteenth century as surveyors sought to wrestle its ever-expanding form into a comprehensible shape. They did this largely through manipulations in scale, albeit sometimes in an audaciously spectacular fashion. Such maps, of course, are naturally selective and contain lacunae. J. B. Harley has written about the notion of 'silences on maps', and the depiction of unbuilt land on topographical surveys is one such silence.[5] This is leaving aside for now the issue of the other type of silences in maps raised by de Certeau and alluded to in the Preface, of maps as 'procedures for forgetting' in relation to lived experience.[6] Given the centrality of estate land surveying in the eighteenth century, happily this silence was not one to which all surveyors were deaf in our period and we can build up a surprisingly good picture of the range of landscapes that formed the environs from maps, while still being alive to their representational and commercial contexts and constraints.

EARLY MAPS AND MAP-VIEWS

The earliest surviving maps of London date from the mid-sixteenth century, and one of the very first of these, by Frans Hogenberg of 1572, establishes an image of London as a green city – literally in this case, figuratively in other instances (fig. 30).[7] The title of the map translates as 'London Capital City of the Most Fertile Kingdom, England'. Hogenberg locates the urban core within a carefully delineated landscape of pasture land, pleasure grounds and outlying suburbs and villages. Field boundaries and hedgerows are marked along with orchards and even individual gardens, both inside and outside the City walls. The central area at this date consisted principally of the old Roman and medieval City, to which the 'Londinum' of the title refers. However, the title also includes the term 'Metropolis', indicating both its premier position in the country and the larger built-up area of Southwark and Westminster. The latter by this time was already joined to London by the procession of noblemen's residencies along the Strand mentioned by Fitzstephen in the twelfth century.[8] Westminster was the seat of the Court, the judiciary and Parliament, while on the opposite bank of the river the Archbishop of Canterbury had his seat at Lambeth Palace. In Southwark a 'beere house' can be seen to the far east in its walled garden and the bull and bear-baiting pits to the far west in the circular buildings. These are not to be confused with the Swan and Globe theatres, which were not built until 1595 and 1599 respectively, although they were housed in remarkably similar physical structures. Indeed, so much so that Wenceslaus Hollar mixed up the Globe and the bear-baiting pit in his panorama of 1675, a mistake which reveals much about their shared cultural identity as well as physical similarity (fig. 31). Hogenberg's map also shows a considerable amount of development outside the City walls to the north in Clerkenwell around Smithfield – the meat market for the City – and in Hoxton. The importance of the River Thames as a means of communication is evident in the amount of water traffic depicted and its centrality for commerce by the wharves that line its banks.[9] What is striking about the map is the dominance of the surrounding landscape as well as the extent to which this is presented as a fertile and populated zone with figures and animals shown in the fields around the City.[10]

The figures in the foreground of Hogenberg's map seem to be inviting us to share their view of the metropolis from some raised ground to the south of the city, which in reality did not exist. However, the map is typical of those up until the mid-seventeenth century in being not strictly a map but more of a view, what is generally known as a 'map-view', stemming from the fact that maps had an essentially decorative purpose at this date.[11] Related to such map-views are the panoramic or bird's-eye portrayals of the time. These provided a perspective down between buildings giving an impression of depth and became increasingly popular through the sixteenth and seventeenth centuries. They began with Agas c.1535, followed by Norden in 1600, and reached their apogee with the Bohemian Wenceslaus Hollar's work in the mid-seventeenth

LONDINVM FERACISSIMI AN-
GLIAE REGNI METROPOLIS

30 Frans Hogenberg, *Londinum
Feracissimi Angliae Regni Metropolis*,
1572, London Metropolitan Archives.

century. Hollar (1607–1677), like Hogenberg, was a foreigner, and the early maps and views of London derived mainly from Continental traditions. Hollar revelled in the technique, producing many panoramic 'prospects' including his famous *Long View* of 1647 made in exile in Amsterdam during the Civil War.[12] A similar panorama by Hollar was published in 1675 but depicting London before the Great Fire of 1666 (fig. 32). The map-view necessarily emphasized the linkages between centre and periphery through its adoption of a perspective point outside the city. In the case of Hollar's 1675 panorama this is taken from the tower of St George's church, Southwark. No less than 110 views were published using this vantage point or the nearby one of St Mary Overie between 1660 and 1666 alone.[13] This shows the popularity of the genre,

although most were copies of Norden and Hollar. The interesting aspect of panoramas is in the representativeness rather than the accuracy of the view. As such, what appear as breaks in the black lines of an orthogonal map appear as spatial continuities within the sweep of the aerial viewpoint. Some historians and theorists have characterized the bird's-eye view as panoramic and controlling in a Foucauldian sense.[14] However, as Michael Charlesworth has argued, there are major differences between panopticism and panoramic seeing, particularly in relation to those under observation and the intensity of the gaze to which they are subject.[15] I would further argue that map-views such as Hollar's and Hogenberg's actually diminish the centrality of the city by emphasizing its essentially dependent nature on the agricultural landscape around it. Maps emphasize

33

1 Worcester house,   2 Temple Church,
2 Savoy.   8 Black Fryars.
3 Somerset house.   9 Baynards Castle.
4 Arundell house.   10 Queenehythe,
5 Essex house.   11 three Cranes,
6 The Temple,   12 Stiliard.

31 Wenceslaus Hollar, *Prospect of London as it was flourishing before the Destruction by Fire*, 1675, etching, British Museum.

This section shows the pre-Fire City and old St Paul's with the hills of Highgate and Hampstead behind. The foreground concentrates on the wharves and riverside development along both banks of the Thames and particularly the suburban landscape of Southwark set among pleasant gardens and tree-lined fields, as shown in figure 32.

breaks and draw definitive black lines of demarcation between built and unbuilt. Map-views create continuity and give context; as such, they are emblematic of a way of seeing the relationship between city and country as a connected continuum rather than as a binary opposition. Panoramas underwent a revival in the early nineteenth century when they were exhibited in the round in purpose-built circular exhibition spaces which allowed for a truly kinaesthetic viewing experience. A preparatory drawing for the *Eidometropolis* by Thomas Girtin, exhibited in 1802, has a viewpoint further west than Hollar's, but it is interesting to see how

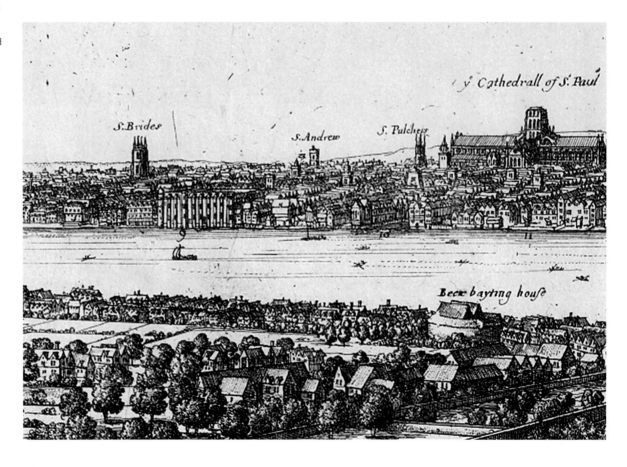

32 Detail of fig. 31.

34

13 Cold Harbour,   19 S. Edmunds
14 Old Swan,   20 S. Laurence.
15 Belins Gate   21 S. Martine in Thames street,
16 Custom house,   22 S. Augustine.
17 Tower wharfe   23 S. Andrew Wardrobe
18 S. Magnus,   24 ȳ Waterhouse.

comparable the two views are in terms of the relatively small amount of development which is visible, despite being produced a century and a half apart (fig. 33).

MAPPING THE 'COUNTRYSIDE AROUND'

In the seventeenth century the traumatic events of the plague outbreaks and the Great Fire led to more precise attempts to trace the metropolis and its boundaries. The Bills of Mortality began to be produced in London weekly from 1603 following an outbreak of plague. The bills included births and deaths, and in the words of Dorothy George 'stood for the greater London of the seventeenth century'.[16] They covered a wide area encompassing not just the City, Southwark and Westminster, but also all the adjacent parishes in Middlesex as far as Islington, Hackney and Stepney as well as Lambeth and the eastern riverside areas such as Rotherhithe and Bermondsey, although not Marylebone and St Pancras. The bills were produced in a tabular form, but the Fire in 1666 led to more

33   Thomas Girtin, *Westminster and Lambeth*, 1801, watercolour, British Museum.

This study for Girtin's *Eidometropolis* looks towards Westminster Abbey and St John's Smith Square. The windmills on the horizon are equally prominent, while the red tiled roofs of a jumble of non-classical buildings dominate the foreground.

specifically cartographic innovations. The subsequent regeneration sparked an intense interest in charting the central areas, initially the City of London where the destruction had taken place, and then the rest of the urban core as the capital expanded east and west. The map-view was abandoned as a surveying tool although it survived as an influential pictorial device, as is discussed in Chapter 3 (see fig. 71). It was replaced by accurate two-dimensional plans, such as Ogilby and Morgan's 1676 map, whose title makes clear the new concern with measurement: 'A New and Accurate Map of the City of London, Distinct from Westminster and Southwark, Ichnographically describing All the Streets, Lanes . . . Churches, Halls, Houses &c'. Ogilby and Morgan were the official surveyors to the City after the Fire, and such orthogonal mapping was necessary for their work 'in order to have a true record of property boundaries for the settlement of claims after the devastation and planning of new buildings'.[17] At the same time the scientific renaissance, led by the Royal Society, generated a new approach to mapping based on accurate surveying techniques and an interest in empirical measuring and recording, exemplified by Sir William Petty's statistical work. Petty was one of the few to argue for a new administrative grouping for London to be extended to include Westminster and 'so much of the built ground in Middlesex and Surrey whose houses are contiguous huts, or within call of those aforementioned'.[18] This was not to happen until the twentieth century, but it did become increasingly common as the eighteenth century progressed to use the term 'London' to refer to the three entities of the City, Westminster and Southwark.

However, if Petty's call for the City and Westminster authorities to amalgamate was politically inconceivable at this date, due to the Court–City split in the recent Civil War, the idea of a London area was already evident in maps of the time. The first known map of the environs was Ogilby and Morgan's *The Country about 15 Miles any Way from London* (1683) drawn by Hollar in 1670. This was closely followed by a map of 1686 by Robert Morden covering a twenty-mile radius from the capital. It is to a version of this map produced by Philip Lea that we shall now turn. At this date there was no copyright in existence, and hence many copies were made of existing maps, including a French edition of Morden's map. Maps were traded and consumed by

a pan-European market, and foreign editions of city maps were common, particularly in the first half of our period. Samuel Pepys's copy of Philip Lea's *A Mapp containing the Townes Villages Gentlemens Houses Roads Rivers Woods and other Remarks for 20 Miles Round London* (c.1690) is labelled in contemporary handwriting as 'The general Site and Environs of the City' (fig. 34 and see fig. 29). The map is divided into squares each containing three miles and stretches from Hatfield and Hemel Hempstead in Hertfordshire in the north to Rickmansworth, Uxbridge and Chertsey to the west; Guildford and Reigate to the south (with Tunbridge Wells marked as '3 miles further'); and Gravesend and Brentwood to the east. This provides an outline remarkably consonant with the present-day M25, suggesting that the current London orbital motorway follows some much older and well-established mental and natural boundaries delimiting London's outer edges.[19] As we saw in the Introduction, the word 'environs' first came into use in the 1660s to refer to the adjacent and interdependent localities around the metropolis. Lea's map begins to give us our first real picture of its terrain with its careful delineation of parish churches, villages, gentlemen's and ordinary houses, roads and rivers, each marked with their own symbol. The map is astonishingly detailed, and even market towns are distinguished typographically from villages and hamlets. Without a doubt the map underestimates the number of ordinary houses while on the other hand presenting a landscape rich with the dwellings of the gentry. Enclosed parkland estates are shown around some of the more major houses such as Hatfield, Wanstead, More Park and Kenton Park. This emphasis on the genteel partly arose out of the methods of funding such maps through subscriptions from local landowners, a means of financing that was to continue throughout the period. This can be seen even more clearly in John Warburton's *A New and Correct Mapp of Middlesex, Essex and Hertfordshire with the Roads Rivers Sea-Coast Actually Surveyed* (1724), which included the 850 coats of arms of its subscribers besides listing them individually (fig. 35). This topography of gentility symbolized by armorial shields, and impaled parks in particular, was to become a major strand in one aspect of the image of 'the environs': as a desirable and refined landscape.

Lea's map thankfully extends beyond the genteel in its coverage, and the commercial also forms a prom-

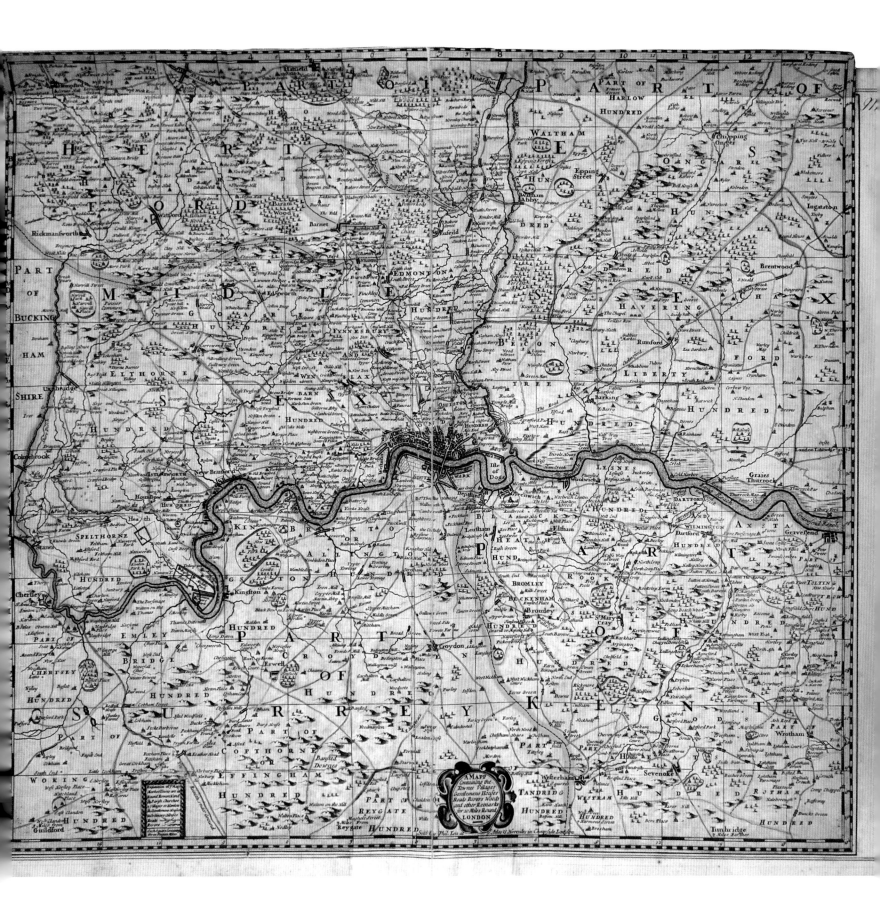

A Mapp Containing the Towns Villages Gentlemens Houses Roads Rivers Woods and other Remarks for 20 Miles Round LONDON

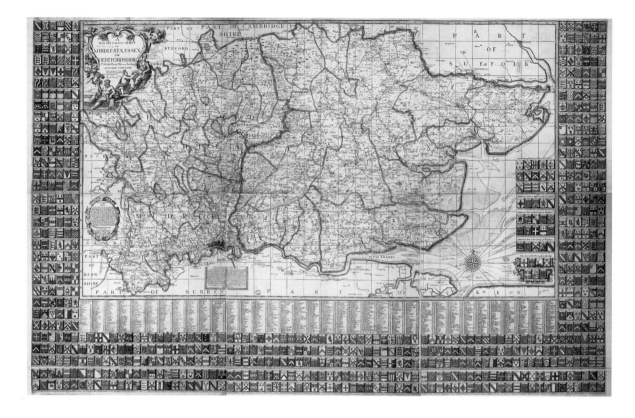

inent part of his terrain. 'Market towns' are indicated on the map and are shown in the index by a roman hand, as opposed to the italic used for villages and houses. An analysis of their distribution and location across the region, although necessarily impressionistic, is informative in suggesting how far one needed to be located from London to require an alternative servicing point for food and other provisions and entertainment. There are thirty-five market towns listed in the index to the map, including London, Westminster and Southwark. The listing of these 'towns' provides a useful reminder that the central cities might be conceived as market towns as well as those in the countryside further out (Table 1).

Table 1 contains market towns perhaps surprisingly close to the core. The cluster to the south-east along the river at Greenwich, Woolwich, Deptford, Lewisham, Eltham, Dartford and Gravesend – with Thurrock the sole representative on the north bank – reflects the density of population and employment there. It is also noticeable that the 'markets' identified are not evenly spread across the region, although this is probably due to a somewhat arbitrary system of categorization as much as anything more considered. The

Table 1   Market towns from Philip Lea, *A Mapp Containing the Townes Villages Gentlemens Houses Roads Rivers Woods and other Remarks for 20 Miles Round London, c.*1690 (spelling has been modernized but original counties are given)

St Albans, Herts	Hoddesdon, Herts
Barnet, Herts	Ingatestone, Essex
Barking, Essex	Kingston, Surrey
Brentwood, Essex	Lewisham, Kent
New Brentford, Middx	London
Bromley, Surrey	Rickmansworth, Herts
Chertsey, Surrey	Romford, Essex
Colnebrook, Middx	Southwark
Croydon, Surrey	Staines, Middx
Dartford, Kent	Thurrock Grays, Essex
Deptford, Kent	Uxbridge, Middx
Edgware, Middx	Waltham Abbey, Essex
Eltham, Kent	Watford, Herts
Greenwich, Kent	Westminster
Gravesend, Kent	West Ham, Essex
Hatfield, Herts	Woolwich, Kent
Hemel Hempstead, Herts	Wrotham, Kent
Hounslow, Middx	

north-east area above the Thames in Essex and the south-east area of Kent have the fewest settlements due to their being flat, marshy land which was good for grazing 'marsh mutton', as Defoe called it, but little else.[20] The most populous counties are Kent to the south-east and Middlesex and Hertfordshire to the west and north-west. Many of the market towns were situated on the major arterial roads running to and from the capital, linking it not just with the rest of the country but also with the ports on the south and east coasts and Europe beyond. The significance of water-borne trade is indicated by the frequency with which maps, and indeed other forms of 'mapping' such as guidebooks, often included tables of watermen's fares (see fig. 57). Other industrial areas and activities visible on the map are centred on the rivers Lea (the bound-ary between Middlesex and Essex) and Wandle, which joins the Thames at Wandsworth. The banks of both of these tributaries are shown lined by mills, some with their function indicated by name of place or owner. Along the Wandle and its tributaries one can find iron, copper and powder mills among others. Along the Lea more powder mills are marked, as well as the lock at Enfield and 'Abraham' Ferry near Tottenham.

The map also bears witness to another major role of the environs: as an urban playground and leisure retreat from the dust and congestion of the centre. This is primarily indicated through the detailing of wells or mineral spas on Lea's map, and such resorts are the focus of Chapter 4. What is remarkable in Lea is the sheer number that are indicated as early as 1690. They can be found all around the capital, and he includes some well-known ones such as Dulwich Wells and Highbury Barn, as well as some more obscure establishments including Roges Well in Bromley-by-Bow and Browns Well in Colny Hatch (near Finchley). The marking of Tunbridge Wells as being '3 miles further' on the map is significant in this context. Tunbridge and the slightly closer Surrey resort of Epsom were usually presented as being within the London orbit, unlike the more distant Bath, for example. Indeed, Defoe in his *Tour* of the 1720s wrote that in the summer: 'Tis very frequent for the trading part of the company to place their families here, and take their horses every morning to London, to the Exchange, to the Alley, or to the warehouse, and be at Epsome again at night.'[21]

However, unlike Hampstead and Richmond, he wrote, the place closed down in the winter when the roads were 'unpassable'.

Lea's *20 Miles Round London* is remarkably detailed considering its scale. The natural topography of the landscape is not its primary concern, but rivers, hills, windmills, woods and parks, both those of the gentry and royal enclosures such as at Bushey and Greenwich, are all carefully indicated. Individual natural landscapes including Bansted Downs in Surrey, Woolwich Com-mon and Hounslow Heath are also named. However, the major activity of the region, farming and market gardening, is not represented for the most part. The outskirts were subject to two conflicting forces in the long eighteenth-century stasis and movement. Lea's map represents this tension perfectly; on the one hand, we have the traditional obeisance to the gentry and nobility through the depiction of a landscape of park-land and country seats; on the other, we have the sinews of change carving through that landscape in the form of roads, industrial rivers, expanding villages and new leisure attractions that were to change the Home Counties for ever.

Samuel Pepys (1633–1703), the owner of the Lea map, merits some discussion as an early example of a collector of material relating to the metropolis and as a citizen not just of London but of Greater London as well. John Aubrey in his *Natural History and Antiqui-ties of Surrey. Begun in the year 1673* (1718–19) comment-ing on Pepys's collection related: 'In compiling matters relating to the City of *London* he spared no Cost, as Books, Prints, Ground-Plots, Maps, Views, Palaces, Churches, great Houses, Coronations, Funerals, Publick Shews, Habits and Heads of famous Persons, and all that could be collected relating to this *Metropolis*.'[22] The title page to his prints and drawings collection was labelled 'the Citys of London & Westminster and their Environs' (fig. 36). His collection on the 'Environs' included two maps and views of Hoxton, Islington, Kensington, Lambeth, Wapping, Hampton Court, Windsor, Richmond and Greenwich. Pepys is always thought of as the archetypal self-made City dweller spending his wealth on new luxuries such as maps, prints, dancing lessons and Parmesan cheese, to name but a miscellaneous few. But his employment regularly took him downriver to the navy bases at Deptford and elsewhere. He spent most of 1665 living in Greenwich

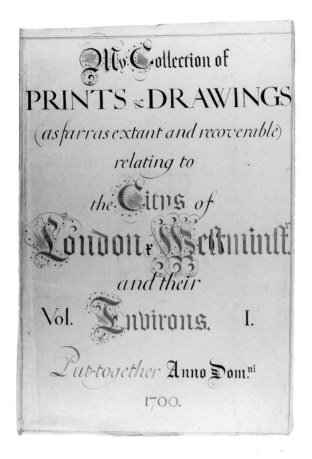

This functioned, along with the markers in degrees down the side of the map, as a substitute for latitude and longitude to some extent, which were not systematically used until the founding of the Ordnance Survey in 1791. His approach had two merits: first, its more consistent use of measurement equated to modern ideas of method and order; and second, and more critically for the present study, it introduced the idea of movement as a means of defining the city. At this date such circulatory bands were primarily used to calculate travelling distances, particularly for regular commuters, of whom there were considerable numbers. But over time they took on other functions and meanings which would increasingly come to define the capital as a series of concentric rings in which different activities and modes of living occurred. Such ideas have been thoroughly explored for nineteenth-century London by Lynda Nead, among others.[25] However, they were also central to a broader public understanding of the metropolis in the preceding period as maps and mapping became a key means of making sense of an ever-expanding city. As Robert Dodsley wrote in relation to the City, but of issues which applied throughout the metropolis:

> The citizens are particularly interested in knowing the extents and limits of the wards in which they reside . . . and as every inhabitant of the kingdom may, at one time or another, have occasion to visit or write to their friends or relations residing in this great city, the names and situations of all the several streets, lanes, row, courts, yards and allies could not be omitted. With regard to these an ingenious gentleman has furnished us with a key, which has let us into the origin of many of their names; and this part of our work is farther illustrated by a new and correct plan.[26]

where he and his staff had moved during the plague in 1665, while his wife went to Woolwich. His amorous adventures resulted in furtive forays all over the capital, both centrally in places such as Drury Lane and as far afield as Acton and Lambeth.[23] He paid regular visits to his family in Brampton, Huntingdonshire, and in his final years lived in a villa in Clapham.[24] Pepys clearly had a need for a map of the environs and not just as a collector's item.

The next map under consideration owes a clear debt to Lea and Morden but at the same time introduces one of the key means of configuring the London area, and that was as a flattened globe. It is Charles Price's *A Correct Map shewing all Towns, Villages, Roads, the Seats of ye Nobility and Gentry . . . within 30 Miles of London* (1712) (fig. 37). Price extended his coverage to a thirty-mile radius and introduced the idea of using concentric circles as a way of managing a large land area spread over four counties. The global presentation, albeit in two dimensions, offered the possibility of conceiving the environs as a world of its own: a coherent entity defined by a series of bands at half-inch intervals measured from the central point of St Paul's.

Price's map was the first of many subsequent wholly circular maps (which excised the corners of his rectangle) and was quickly followed by two different versions by Henry Overton and George Willdey, both *c.*1720. James Howgego cites these copies, plus three subsequent ones, as 'the most blatant example of pirating afforded by maps of London', and it was as a result of such practices that a protection of copyright law was passed in 1734.[27] Although the Act was a major step forward, enforcement was weak and copying

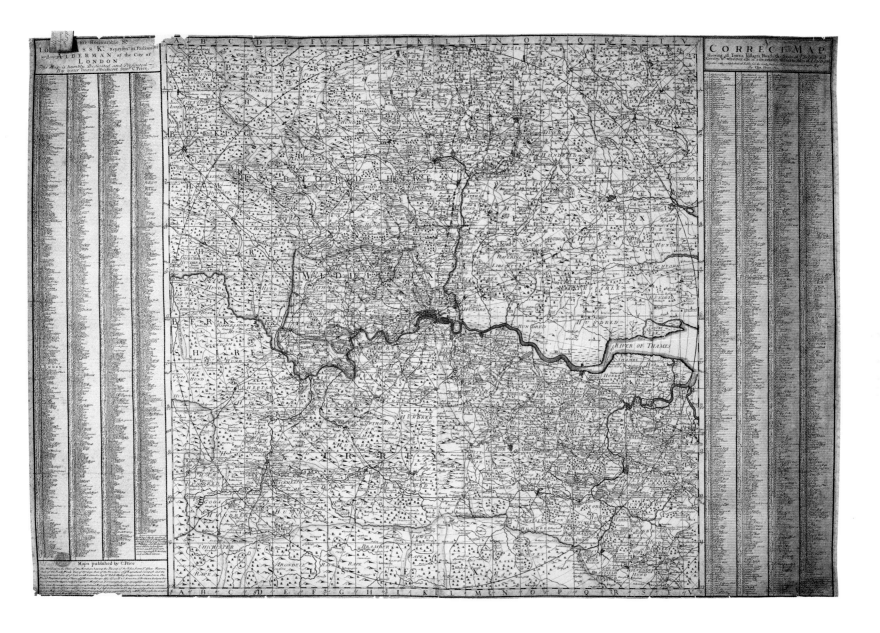

37 Charles Price, *A Correct Map shewing all Towns, Villages, Roads, the Seats of ye Nobility and Gentry . . . within 30 Miles of London: Together with an Alphabetical Table for the ready finding all Places mentioned in the Map*, 1712, British Library.

continued throughout the eighteenth century. This resulted in many map titles that stressed claims to be 'a new and exact survey' or the 'latest survey' in an attempt to establish their credentials and current relevance.[28]

The best known of the outer city maps of the eighteenth century is John Rocque's *An Exact Survey of the City's of London, Westminster ye Borough of Southwark and the Country Near Ten Miles Round* (1746). Rocque's map is one of the few in this chapter to have been extensively reproduced and discussed elsewhere, and so it will only be touched on briefly here. His map extended to a mere ten miles, but what it lacked in distance it more than made up for in preci-

sion of detail, at a scale of five and a half inches to the mile. Rocque (*c.*1709–1762) was a Huguenot refugee who came to London in the 1730s along with his brothers. He started his career as a 'dessinateur des jardins', or land surveyor, while one of his brothers, Bartholomew, became a market gardener in Fulham.[29] With this horticultural family background his maps are remarkable for their careful delineation of natural features (see figs 39, 104, 110 and 127). The technique of two-dimensional orthogonal mapping adopted in the late seventeenth and early eighteenth centuries necessarily flattened and homogenized the landscape. Rocque introduced a range of devices, pioneered in France, to overcome this deadening effect, most

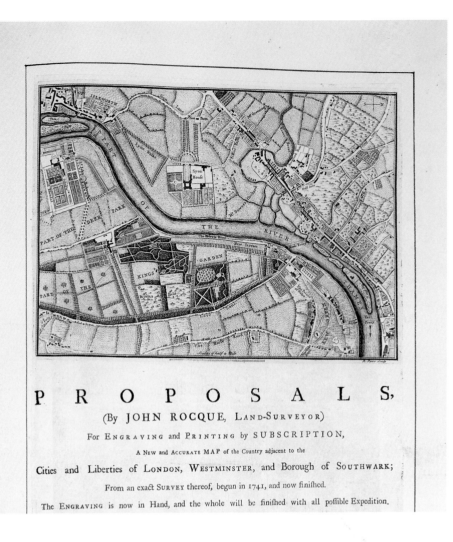

P R O P O S A L S,

(By JOHN ROCQUE, LAND-SURVEYOR)

For ENGRAVING and PRINTING by SUBSCRIPTION,

A NEW and ACCURATE MAP of the Country adjacent to the

Cities and Liberties of LONDON, WESTMINSTER, and Borough of SOUTHWARK;

From an exact SURVEY thereof, begun in 1741, and now finished.

The ENGRAVING is now in Hand, and the whole will be finished with all possible Expedition.

38 John Rocque, *Proposals . . . for Engraving and Publishing by Subscription a New and Accurate Map of the Country Adjacent to the Cities and Liberties of London, Westminster, and the Borough of Southwark*, 1741, Bodleian Library, University of Oxford.

notably through the use of fine shading and hatching and by the inclusion of elaborate decorative devices, such as cartouches, around the borders. By utilizing an elaborate system of stippling and broken lines Rocque was able to distinguish between market gardens, fields, woods, heath, ploughland, orchards and pasture. His *Ten Miles Round* map not only provides a vivid guide to agriculture but also shows the gravel pits, lime and brick-kilns and timber yards that ringed the capital. As he wrote in his *Proposals* for the project: 'This MAP will admit not only an exact Description of all the main and cross Roads, Lanes, Paths and bye Ways; where the Buttings of all the Walls, Pales and Hedges will be set down, but all the Hills, Vallies, Rivers, Bridges, Ferries, Brooks, Springs; Ponds, Woods, Heaths, Commons, Parks, Avenues, Churches, Houses, Gardens &c. and in short all that can be desired in so particular a Survey' (fig. 38).[30]

Rocque's *Ten Miles Round* map with its lists of gentlemen's parks and seats, which could be 'inserted . . . upon Terms which no Gentleman . . . will think unreasonable,' was still partially aimed at the traditional audience of the landed gentry and international collectors.[31] It was extremely large, consisting of sixteen sheets of 'best Imperial paper' of $c.19\frac{1}{2} \times 25\frac{1}{2}$ inches. The size and number of sheets posed some significant problems in handling, particularly for private collectors (fig. 39). Rocque, ingenious as ever, suggested some strategies for containing his master work in domestic situations: 'These Sheets may be preserved loose in a Book, like other MAPS, or pasted all together on Cloth: – And tho' this MAP is of so large a Size, when put on a Roler, to the Cornish of a Room, it will not interfere with any of the furniture, and yet by means of a small Pully, may be let down for Examination at Pleasure.'[32] The problems of depicting the ever-expanding metropolis at a usable and reproducible scale for a domestic audience are dramatically highlighted here, and the development of new formats for maps suitable for markets beyond the connoisseurial was to prove essential.

Rocque in his *Proposals . . . for Engraving and Publishing by Subscription A New and Accurate Map* (1741) indicated that he was aware of the need for such adaptation and expansion into new markets among commercial and official bodies. He wrote: 'Such a Map will be of great use to all Directors of Insurance Offices, and Commissioners of Turnpikes, to all Church-Wardens and Overseers, to all Persons who have Occasion to travel round this Metropolis for Business, Health or Pleasure; and lastly to curious persons at Home and Abroad.'[33] Mapping the city for a wide range of governmental and business purposes, including the tourist trade, became increasingly important through the eighteenth century. As Rocque's remarks quoted at the head of this chapter also demonstrate, mapping the metropolis was seen as part of a wider discourse intended to highlight national achievement and prosperity in an imperial context. According to this Huguenot immigrant there was no country 'so fruitful, so well cultivated, so much built upon and inhabited, and so beautiful as the Country round the Metropolis of the British Empire'.[34] Rocque was echoing Defoe's transference of the New Rome metaphor from the centre to the periphery in this quote, a theme which

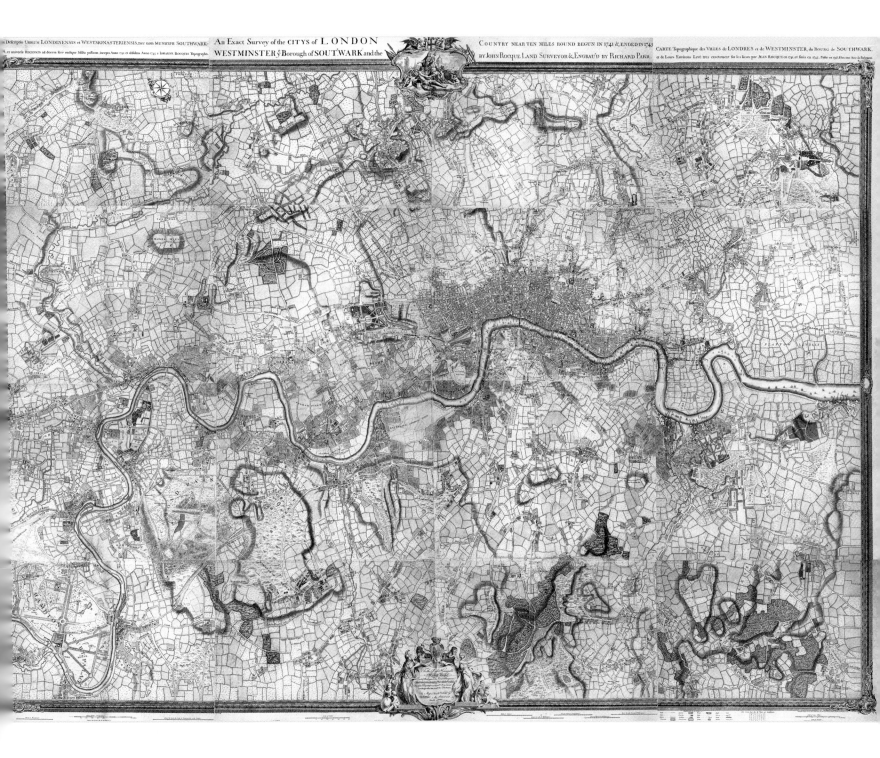

An Exact Survey of the CITYS of LONDON
WESTMINSTER ʸ Borough of SOUTWARK and the

COUNTRY NEAR TEN MILES ROUND BEGUN IN 1741 & ENDED IN 1745
BY JOHN ROCQUE LAND SURVEYOR & ENGRAU'D BY RICHARD PARR.

CARTE Topographique des VILLES de LONDRES et de WESTMINSTER, de BOURG de SOUTHWARK,
et de Leurs Environs. Levé très exactement sur les lieux par JEAN ROCQUE en 1741 et finia en 1745. Publié en 1746 Elise une Acte de Parlement.

39   John Rocque, *An Exact Survey of the City's of London, Westminster ye Borough of Southwark and the Country Near Ten Miles Round*, 1746, British Library.

was to become a notable strand in the emerging identity of the environs.

In the second half of the eighteenth century, in response to the need for greater compression and commercialism, maps took on a wider variety of forms and types. One important genre for the environs was that used in histories or guides to London, which are discussed more fully in Chapter 2. Pocket maps for tour-

ists were developed, sometimes folded into slipcases, and suitable for carrying on trips. As traffic increased from the mid-century by both private and public means, maps were produced showing the fare stages for public coaches, goods wagons and hackney carriages. The problem with determining the validity of such rates was eloquently expressed by Joseph Massie in 1754: 'The vast Extent of the Town makes it difficult

43

EXPLANATION.

Roads open and Close............

Rivers....................

Parks and Hills............

Heaths and Commons.............

Towns &c....................

Note

The GENERAL MAP being given to shew the junction of the pages, it is divided into the same Number of Squares as there are pages in the Book; by which means the connection which one page has with another will be immediately seen, by referring from any of the pages, to the same figure in the General Map, & the continuation of the roads by connecting the pages agreeable to the Squares will be immediately traced as

40 John Cary, 'Explanation', from Cary, *The Country Fifteen Miles Round London*, 1786, Bodleian Library, University of Oxford.

for Strangers (as well Natives as Foreigners) to judge exactly of the just Rates or Fares of Hackney-Coaches and Chairs; so that People are often imposed on, and great and frequent Disputes happen in the Streets.'[35] Such information could be made more usable through mapping rather than by textual presentation. It was the improvement in the roads funded by the turnpikes that made such an increase in traffic possible, and this increased circulation created a new psycho-geography for the metropolis based on embarkation locations, fare stages and toll collection points in a series of concentric rings from the centre echoing the configuration of Price's early 1712 map.

MAPPING MOBILITY

The next figure we are going to look at, John Cary (1755–1835), exemplifies this new age. He produced a vast number of canal plans, road maps, road books and itineraries, totalling approximately six hundred in his lifetime.[36] He started life as an engraver and then became a publisher and surveyor. Like many in his trade his business was based centrally, first in the City and then the West End, but his home was in the outskirts of the western suburbs, initially at Chelsea and then at Mortlake (see fig. 75).[37] He would therefore have been a regular user, as well as a chronicler, of the new road networks and transport systems. In 1786 he produced a map of *The Country Fifteen Miles Round London*. It consisted of a series of individual sheets, each measuring 6 × 3½ inches, which could be adapted to a variety of formats. Following more traditional models they could be 'pasted together for Roll & Ledge &c. / if preferred may be fitted on canvas for the pocket'.[38] Or more innovatively they might be bound together to create a pocket-sized volume, a portable atlas in other words. An index was supplied for this purpose and detailed instructions given for its use so that journeys could be plotted accordingly. The main emphasis was on circulation around the increasingly complicated and congested environment of the outskirts, which now required detailed mapping in its own right. The roads were extremely carefully delineated, with those open to general traffic and those which were private and closed being distinguished (fig. 40). The maps reveal the mixed landscapes to be found in the outer London territory. Figures 41 and 42 show the Enfield area to the north-east of the city. The latter of these depicts a fairly settled landscape with long-established villages, fields and farms and the old royal palace of Theobalds, which was sold during the Commonwealth, now shown as a park (fig. 42). There is new arterial development along the high road to Ware but also the remnants of 'highway waste', common land used for grazing droving stock. Two important water courses are visible: the New River, an artificial cut which brought drinking water to the city, and the fringes of the Lea where a number of mills and a 'water turnpike' are marked (fig. 43). The other plate (fig. 41) reveals a rather different environment and a far more contested landscape of the type discussed in Chapter 6. The northern half of the map shows an environment which was widespread on the outer fringes of London up until the late eighteenth century. It consisted mainly of common land plus traditional activities for fringe areas such as brick fields and a house for 'medicinal waters'. However, the southern half reveals that a great deal of enclosure for gentry seats has taken place, particularly

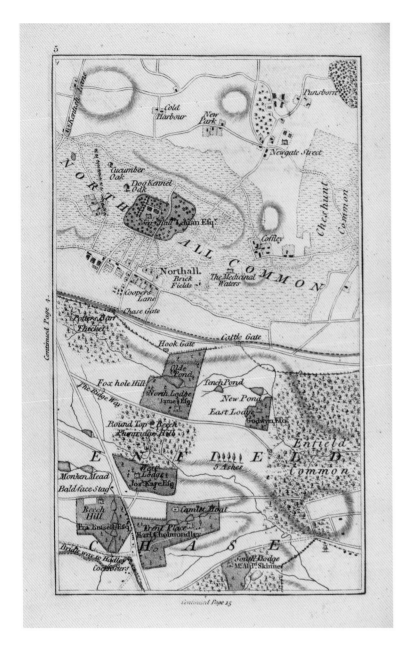

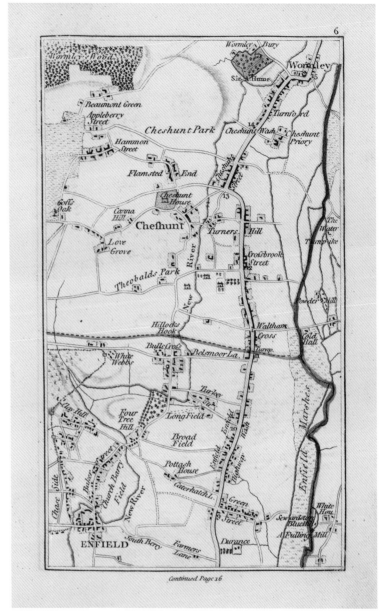

Continued Page 15

Continued Page 16

(left) 41 John Cary, 'Enfield', Plate 5 from Cary, *The Country Fifteen Miles Round London*, 1786, Bodleian Library, University of Oxford.

(right) 42 John Cary, 'Enfield', Plate 6 from Cary, *The Country Fifteen Miles Round London*, 1786, Bodleian Library, University of Oxford.

below the turnpike road, into which a cattle gate has been inserted to allow for movement of stock in what would previously have been a totally open area. J. T. Smith chronicled the architecture and inhabitants of these marginal wastelands in the Enfield area in the 1790s (see figs 84 and 85).

Cary's *Fifteen Miles Round London* map of 1786 also included the postal limits taken from a previous map of his, *An Accurate Map of the Country Twenty Miles Round London . . . with the Circuit of the Penny Post* (1782) (fig. 44). The Penny Post was initiated by William Dockwra in 1680 covering the City, Westmin-ster and the suburbs within ten miles. He established seven sorting offices and hundreds of receiving houses. Letters cost a penny if within the central area and an extra penny if delivered to the London countryside. Thomas De Laune writing in 1681 praised the new innovation, stating that now the circumference of London was above twenty miles: 'This extraordinary Length though it adds to its Splendor and Beauty, yet it renders speedy Communication and Intercourse in Business very uneasie. . . . Now to keep up a necessary Correspondence, the way formerly used, was to hire Porters at Excessive Rates to go on Errands . . . but

now all these Inconveniences are remedied by the Penny-Post.'[39] In 1682 the Post Office took over the running of the service. Defoe noted that the Penny Post had greatly shrunk old notions of London as 'letters are delivered at the remotest corners of the town, almost as soon as they could be sent by a messenger, and that from four, five, six, to eight times a day'.[40] *The Foreigner's Guide* (1729) put this astounding development – as it would be were it the case even today – in an international context, boasting that 'here is such a convenience as is not found in Paris, Amsterdam, or any other City in Europe'.[41] In 1794 Cary was appointed Surveyor of the Roads to the General Post Office and became the first person to map the highways systematically for government since Ogilby in 1675. He employed five surveyors who measured the streets by pushing perambulators with revolving wheels in front of them. This was the closest any survey came to achieving something near to geographical accuracy using pre-Ordnance Survey methods.[42] The result was his *New Itinerary* (1798 and numerous later editions), which was dedicated to the Post Masters General and provided the official measures for all mail coach routes and for the postage due on letters, which until 1840 was charged by distance carried. A later map, *Country Districts of the TwoPenny Post*, by Arrowsmith shows the districts into which the metropolis was divided, within which there were fixed 'walks' that the post carriers followed each day (fig. 45).[43] By this date prices had risen to 2*d.* in the centre and 3*d.* or 4*d.* to the suburbs. There were 224 urban and 165 suburban letter carriers who did six walks a day, three to collect and three to deliver, so that it was possible to send a letter and receive a reply on the same day. The postal maps not only superimposed another layer of psycho-geographical circles around the capital, to add to those created by the hackney coaches and watermen's fares, but at the same time also led to more accurate charting and maintenance of the road system. In 1840 a uniform Penny Post was introduced, and such complex mapping of the region by postal zones became redundant; although it survives in the postcodes by which each London district is still defined.

The other major transformation in the period was the improvement of the road system funded by tolls.[44] From the early eighteenth century turnpikes were erected around the capital (fig. 46a and b). Defoe wrote

(top) 43 Gentlemen's Row, Enfield, with the New River, built early eighteenth century onwards but here with nineteenth-century housing.

(bottom) 44 John Cary, *An Accurate Map of the Country Twenty Miles Round London: From Gravesend to Windsor East and West, and from St Albans to Westerham North and South with the Circuit of the Penny Post*, 1782, British Library.

The title of the map alone, reinforced by the red line of the postal service limits, demonstrates how the London region extended far beyond the central built-up areas.

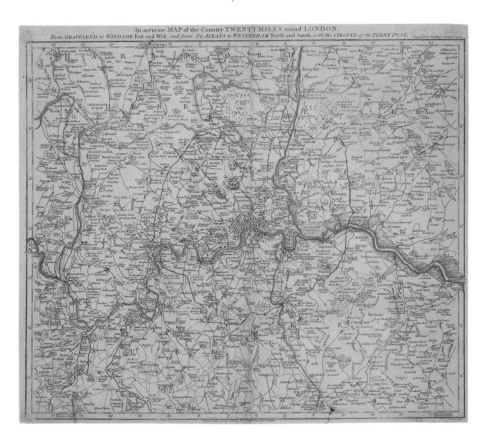

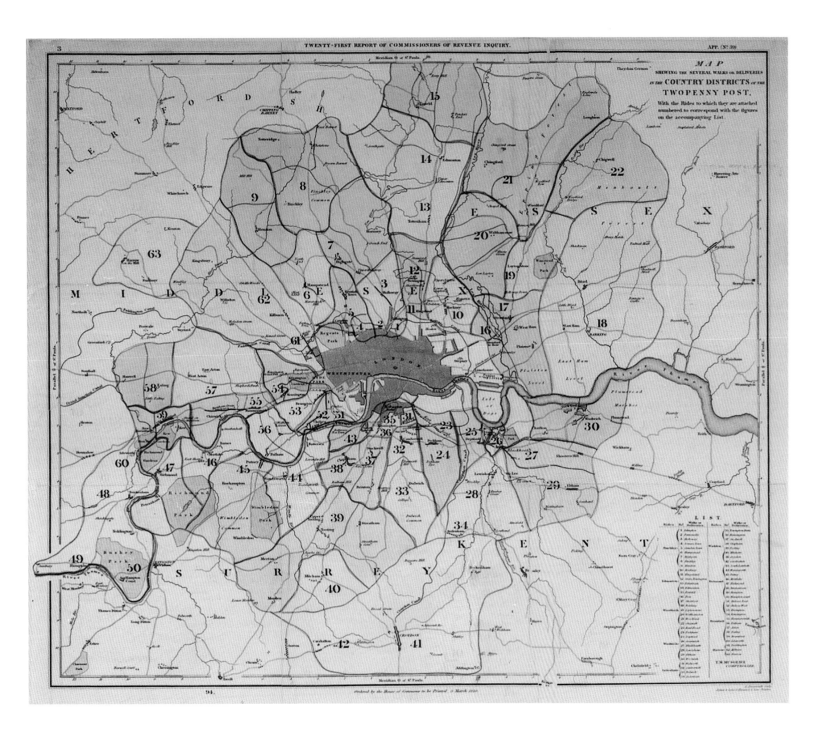

45 Aaron Arrowsmith, *Map shewing the Several Walks or Deliveries in the Country Districts of the TwoPenny Post*, 1830, British Postal Museum and Archive.

Produced for the Parliamentary Twenty First Report of the Commissioners of Revenue Inquiry.

that the roads previously had been 'a scandal to the city of London'.[45] The charges, he related, were normally in the region of 1*d.* for a horse, 3*d.* per coach, 4–8*d.* per cart, 6–12*d.* per wagon, and livestock by the score or by the head.[46] The higher charge for commercial carriages was due to its much heavier impact on the roads and thus on maintenance costs. The funds from tolls led to staggering improvements in the road network across the country both for private traffic and

'our inland commerce'. Goods, particularly perishable ones, could now be moved more rapidly and cheaply and livestock driven up to London even in the winter. Defoe hailed this remarkable transformation as one of his hallmarks of modernity and progress, although the process was not as smooth as he presented it. There was opposition to the erection of turnpikes from various interests throughout the eighteenth century.[47] However, the improved roads were to his eye an

47

(*this page*) 46a and b   Dulwich
tollgate, rebuilt 1995, and board.

The first turnpike was opened here
in 1789 on a private road belonging
to the Alleyn Estate. It is now the
last historic tollgate in use in
London.

(*facing page, top*) 47   John Cary,
'Explanation', from Cary, *Survey of
the High Roads from London*, 1790,
Bodleian Library, University of
Oxford.

(*facing page, bottom*) 48   John Cary,
'Buckhurst Green and Epping', Plates
39–40 from Cary, *Survey of the High
Roads from London*, 1790, Bodleian
Library, University of Oxford.

important signifier of the nation's status as the New
Rome: '[We] may see the roads all over England
restored in their time to such a perfection, that travelling ... will be much more easy, both to man and
horse, than ever it was since the Romans lost this
island.'[48] These developments resulted in the south-east
having the best developed road system in the country
and further reinforced the links between London and
its surrounding region.[49] Eric Pawson, who mapped
the clustering of turnpike trusts around the capital,
concluded: 'Nearly a quarter of all new trusts established before 1720 were located within 10 miles of
London, half were within 30 miles, and two-thirds
within 40 miles.'[50]

In 1790 John Cary produced a *Survey of High Roads
from London* which sought to provide travellers with all
the information that might be required to plan their
journeys (fig. 48 and see fig. 164). The need for such
information is illustrated by the following anecdote
from J. T. Smith's book on *Nollekens and His Times*:

> He would frequently, on a Sunday particularly, order
> a hackney-coach to be sent for, and take Taylor,
> Bonomi, Goblet, and sometimes his neighbour, the
> publican's wife from the 'Sun and Horse-shoe', a
> ride out of town of about ten or twelve miles before
> dinner. Now and then, however, in consequence of
> his neglecting his former cautious custom of bar-
> gaining for the fare before he started, he had a
> dispute with the coachman, on his return, as to the
> exact distance.[51]

As the 'Explanation' to the *Survey* showed, each individual map covered the location of inns, milestones,
parks, commons and turnpikes (fig. 47). With regard to
the latter, as the title page stated, the key feature of
turnpikes was 'the connection which one trust has
with another', for by this date movement in and
around the capital necessarily meant negotiating not
just one but often several turnpike gates. To this end
Cary included a 'General Plan for explaining the Different Trusts of the Turnpike Gates in the Vicinity of
the Metropolis' (1790) (fig. 49). The turnpikes were
controlled by different trusts who between them
divided the city into various zones. The fare structures
this created, allowing for usage within each trust's
patch, engendered certain patterns of behaviour and
the carving of pathways through the city, just as the

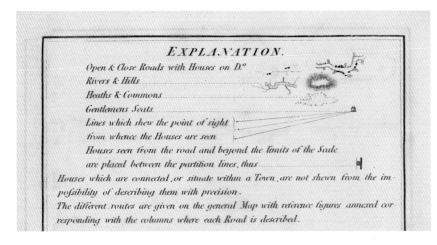

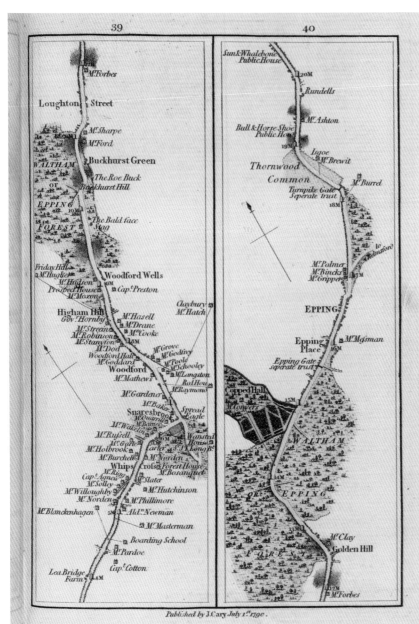

Tube and congestion charge zones do today. It certainly helped reinforce north–south and east–west divisions, and contributed to a process whereby travel between the different outer areas was rendered problematic while travel between the centre and the periphery was encouraged. This in turn bolstered the circular conception of the metropolis as a series of concentric layers connected by radial threads. The turnpikes themselves became transition points marking the intersections of the different layers of the metropolis. Rowlandson depicted these edge locations as social melting pots in a series of prints for Ackermann in the 1790s (fig. 50). The geography of transport thus extended the notion of the zoning of the metropolis – which had long existed between the City, Westminster and Southwark – into the outer suburbs. In this way the mapping of London contributed to a new sense of the metropolis as an agglomeration of parts, visually, spatially and kinetically. It was a modern conurbation, in other words, defined by commercial and organizational boundaries among which the arbitrary and essentially abstract geography of the turnpike system played a key role in constructing new temporal and spatial boundaries.

THE TERRAIN AT THE TURN OF THE CENTURY

In the later eighteenth and early nineteenth centuries it became increasingly common for maps to extend as far as sixty-five miles from London, as its perceived boundaries pushed further and further out. Andrews and Drury's 1807 map, for example, expanded beyond the normal four adjacent counties to include Bedfordshire, Oxfordshire, Berkshire, Hampshire and Sussex as well. As the scale of the environs grew, in an interesting inverse of the normal centre–periphery relationship, the space allocated to the core shrank. As was discussed in the Introduction, as maps of the environs got larger and larger the representation of the centre decreased proportionately (see fig. 9). At the same time that the concept of the London region seemed to steadily enlarge, there was also a counter trend towards producing detailed maps of individual parishes (see fig. 185). This formed of part of a wider reassertion of local identity evident from the turn of the nineteenth

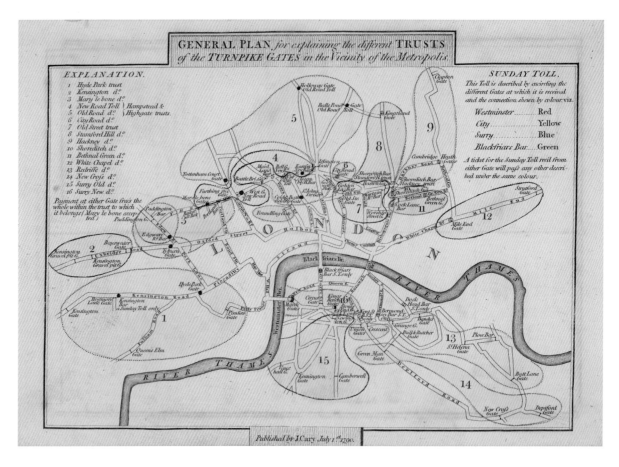

century which is also reflected in the new parish histories of the outer areas, the lists of subscribers indicating their local appeal.[52]

The next map for consideration brings us firmly back to the world of land surveying and its fundamental role in documenting agricultural patterns in the countryside. Milne's *Plan of the Cities of London and Westminster, circumadjacent Towns and Parishes &c, laid down from a Trigonometrical Survey taken in the Years 1795–99* (1800) was one of the first to be based on accurate trigonometrical observations and to show longitude (fig. 51). It covered an area of about seventeen miles west to east and about fourteen miles north to south. It was hand coloured and coded to show the usage of every parcel of land, a veritable Booth for the Environs.[53] Milne's key of land types alone is informative with twelve different categories including market gardens, nurseries, orchards and osier beds along the Thames. Half the map is taken up with meadow and pasture land, including the hayfields which fed the multitude of horses stabled in mews in the centre. The map also shows the preponderance of common land

that was soon to disappear under the General Enclosure Act of 1800. One-third of the agricultural land of the London area still remained unenclosed in 1800.[54] Milne's map aligns nicely with the 'zones' of agriculture that Henry Hunter identified in his *History of London and its Environs* (1811), as is shown in George Bull's diagram (see fig. 10). Hunter identified four zones of clay pits, cattle pasture, market gardens and hay. The combined total of these was 240 square miles: almost identical with Milne's map. Half this area was meadowland and pasture, one-fifth was arable, one-fifth consisted of market gardens, nurseries and pleasure grounds, and the last tenth was 'unprofitably occupied' by wastes and commons.[55] As George Bull has pointed out, Hunter's zones accord remarkably closely with Von Thünen's location theory formulated in 1826–63.[56] Von Thünen proposed that the intensity of land use decreases as the distance from large settlement increases.[57] He argued, like Hunter, that this resulted in a series of rings of decreasingly intensive agricultural production with very similar patterns of crops and livestock. The interesting feature of both Hunter's and

50 Thomas Rowlandson for Rudolf Ackermann, 'Entrance of Tottenham Court Turnpike, with a View of St James's Chapel', from *Views of London*, 1798, hand-coloured aquatint, British Museum.

The chapel is to the left of the gate through which a stage coach has just passed heading into town. The print shows a range of types of transport, from carriages – including a children's one – to a donkey, horses and Shank's pony as well.

Von Thünen's systems is that they both postulate an agricultural region of approximately thirty miles in diameter as surrounding each town. Von Thünen described such towns as 'Isolated States' dependent on their agricultural hinterland for supplies, while the surrounding region relied on them for their market. Von Thünen has been criticized for underestimating the impact of modern transportation systems – he ignored canals and industrial production, for example – but it is striking how closely his model fits London and the sense of a London region in the period.

Thomas Moule's map of the 'Environs of London' (1837) brings us to the culmination of the circular map tradition in our period while at the same time indicating new trends of the future (fig. 52). Moule (1784–1851) had worked for the Post Office and as a bookseller, and was an authority on architecture, heraldry and genealogy.[58] These interests are reflected in his maps, which were among the last in the pre-Ordnance Survey tradition, blending geographical and decorative features. The Ordnance Survey had in fact begun surveying the Home Counties around this time, with a map of Essex appearing in 1805 and one of Surrey in 1816. Moule's maps did not follow the new cartographically accurate trend, but rather they formed an equivalent to the picturesque approach of late eighteenth-century publications such as Boydell's *A Collection of Views in England and Wales* (1790) (see fig. 88). However, if Moule's approach was traditional, the technology used to produce his maps was completely up-to-date. They were printed using the new machine-made paper and steel engraving techniques which, along with lithography, had replaced copper plates in the 1820s.[59]

Moule's 'Environs' map comes from his series *The English Counties Delineated*, which was issued in monthly parts between 1830 and 1837, a means of spreading the cost for both publishers and purchasers. Unlike earlier county volumes, Moule's output was not aimed at wealthy collectors. Rather his purpose was to produce a work 'published at a price so low as to place it within the attainment of every class; they confidently

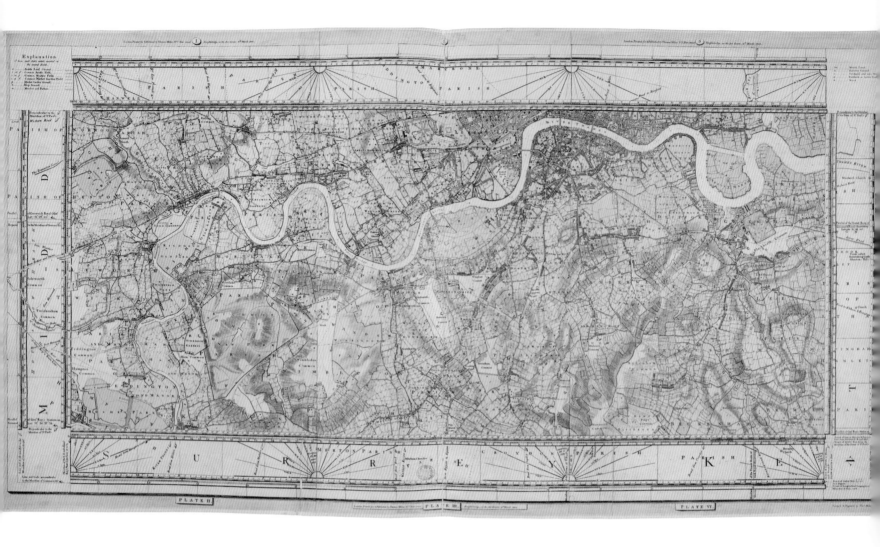

51   Thomas Milne, *Plan of the Cities of London and Westminster . . . from a Trigonometrical Survey taken . . . 1795–99,* 1800, British Library.

Just after this map was made, the land uses shown here were altered irrevocably through the impact of two different types of enclosure: first, the creation of enclosed docks in the east indicated by the preparatory channel cut across the Isle of Dogs; second, the General Enclosure Act of 1800 which led to many of the surviving commons disappearing.

rely upon the liberal spirit which now pervades all ranks of society, to repay them for the great expence they have necessarily undergone.'[60] The maps cost 1*s.* plain or 1*s.* 6*d.* coloured. In the Preface to the bound volume Moule reported that he had been praised by the Society for the Diffusion of Useful Knowledge for the work's 'cheapness and utility'.[61] His aim, he wrote, was 'to combine accuracy with commodiousness of size, and above all to obviate the inconvenience of folding'.[62] Moule saw the series as contributing to 'the Topographical History of the Kingdom'. Other books he wrote in this vein included works on the antiquities of Westminster Abbey, catalogues of books on heraldry and genealogy, a description of Elizabethan architecture, and the text for Westall's *Great Britain Illustrated* (1830) and *The Illustrations of the Work of Walter Scott* (1836). As he wrote in his Prospectus: 'Topography is a species of literature peculiar to England. . . . The

intrinsic merit and usefulness of Provincial History have always been acknowledged . . . and in the present state of national taste, works of this description are regarded with increased attention.' He saw his publications as following in the footsteps of the great antiquaries. He cited as influences Leland, Dugdale and Ashmole among others, as well as more recent authors such as Clutterbuck, Hunter and Lysons. His object, he wrote, was to combine 'the most interesting and picturesque objects . . . as well as . . . antiquities worthy of notice'.[63] The issue of the balance to be struck between artistic considerations and historical accuracy was a crucial one in representing the outer landscapes, as the following chapters on textual and visual representations of the environs will explore.

Ashley Baynton-Williams wrote of Moule's *English Counties* series: 'The maps speak of a rural paradise of seamless continuity with the past, of prosperity, but above all of a sense of calm and stability.'[64] The 'Environs' map is perhaps the anomaly in this respect, so it is interesting to compare it with a county map which is perhaps more typical of the atlas as a whole, that of 'Middlesex' (fig. 53). The decorative architectural border to the 'Middlesex' map is typical of the county maps, which were framed in an astonishingly inventive repertoire of styles, including Gothic and Tudor. Moule's use of non-classical imagery puts him in the vanguard of Gothic popularizers pre-Pugin and developed out of his historical and topographical interests. The counties surrounding London are included both in the 'Environs' map and individually with classical motifs prevailing, with the exception of the map of Kent. The inclusion of heraldic shields in the 'Middlesex' map and the archaic land boundaries of shire hundreds is typical of Moule's nostalgic historicizing approach. Riverine imagery dominates the plate and the two rivers that define the county, the Thames to the south and the Lea to the east, provide the essential threads between the rural countryside and the urban core. The continuities between these two are emphasized by the choice of buildings to represent the county, Westminster Bridge and Abbey and Buckingham Palace. Moule wrote in his notes accompanying the plate: 'The whole county may be considered as a demesne to the metropolis, the land being laid out in gardens, pastures and enclosures of all sorts for its convenience and support. London is its chief place and county town.'[65]

The 'Environs' map, by contrast, at first glance is dominated by symbols of modernity in the form of four very recent metropolitan buildings: New London Bridge – 1831 (top left); Suspension Bridge at Hammersmith – 1827 (top right); Triumphal Arch, Hyde Park Corner – 1828 (bottom left); and fittingly given its importance to cartography, the New Post Office – 1829 (bottom right) (fig. 52). These were archetypical symbols of metropolitan improvement in the early nineteenth century, which were reproduced in countless prints and publications. However, the cartouche at the bottom of the map depicting Old Father Thames with a cornucopia as a mythical river god speaks to an older tradition. The cornucopia itself, thanks to its dual structure, is able to represent both Agriculture and Commerce simultaneously: fruit, flowers and wheat to one side and ivory, gold chains, pearls, jewels and coins

to the other. The latter signified international trade in particular, and thus we see emblematized the national importance of the environs now expanded to a wider imperial and international context. Moule stressed the significance of London both as 'the great Emporium of Nations' and as a centre for inland commerce: 'More than 40,000 waggons, vans and other vehicles, arrive and depart annually, occasioning a traffic of goods worth more than £50,000,000.'[66] Of all the parts of London by this date, it was perhaps the outer areas that best embodied this mix of old and new, and it was the map's oval form that best encompassed and expressed it visually. The circularity of the map also masks the impossibility of assessing London's limits, as Moule wrote: 'Such has been the rapid enlargement of this vast metropolis . . . that it is by no means an easy task to determine its extent or assign its boundaries.'[67] In the bound volume of 1837 Moule added a map of 'The Metropolitan Boroughs as Defined by the Reform Bill' of 1832. This Act increased the limits of the existing boroughs to form a new official boundary for London in recognition of its expanding girth. The new boroughs extended out as far north as Tottenham and Highgate, east to Stratford and Forest Hill, south to Norwood and Wandsworth, and west to Kensington and Kilburn: a distance of approximately seven miles east to west and two to four miles north to south. By the 1830s, then, the edge where centre and periphery met was beginning to take on its own identity as an ever-expanding and infilling zone of suburban development. Maps were one of the ways in which a concept of 'the environs' became established through the long eighteenth century. Mapping helped to turn the incredibly varied and amorphous 'outskirts' – a rather vague term at the beginning of the period – into 'the environs', a recognizable and understood entity by its end. Maps defined the area through charting its towns, villages, countryside and industry and by using the notion of concentric circles to overlay a visual and geometrical template on the diverse landscapes below. They also imposed order through utilizing modern bureaucratic systems, notably those of the postal service and the turnpikes, to introduce a new social geography for the region arising out its rapid urbanization and commercialization. The presentation of a genteel vision of the environs in some of the maps which have been discussed introduces a theme which will run

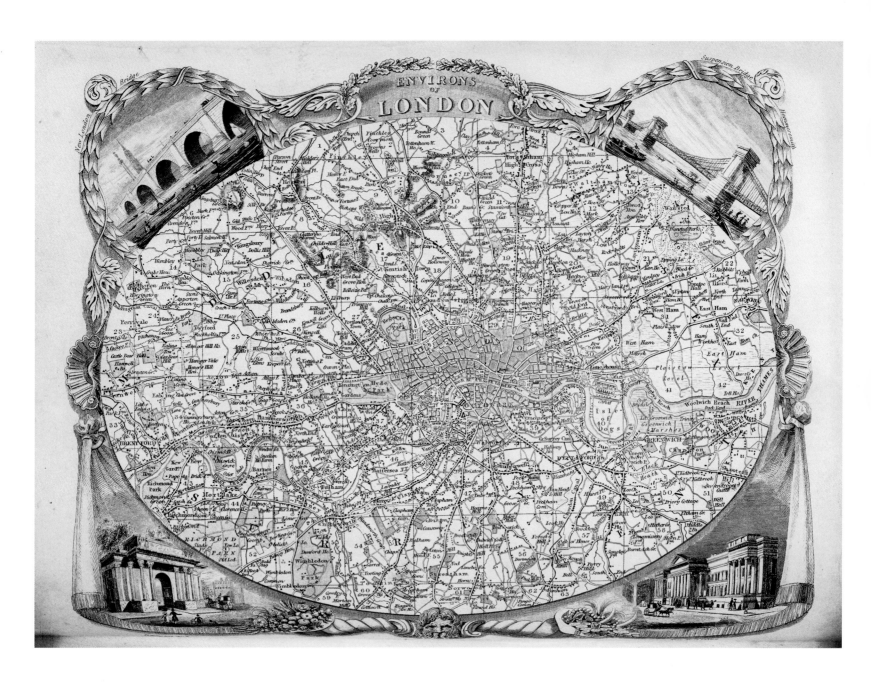

52 W. Schomollinger (engraver), 'Environs of London', from Moule, *The English Counties Delineated: or, a Topographical Description of England*, 1837, British Library.

throughout the following chapters. Given that the audience for maps and other cultural products increasingly included the middle classes as well as the gentry, it is possible that this stable image of rusticity was a version of an idealized 'London countryside' that the bourgeoisie identified with as well as the upper classes. This was almost certainly true around the turn of the nineteenth century, when the pace of development increased dramatically, and this 'timeless', traditional image continued to be perpetuated, masking the actual processes of modernization and rapid change. Neither was this middle-class incorporation of the pastoral

necessarily emulative of a land-based lifestyle but rather an appreciation by the bourgeoisie of the rusticity which they valued and increasingly sought in a suburban environment.[68] Without further research into the social composition of the Home Counties it is impossible to know how far the image of the environs as a stable, gentry-dominated zone reflected the proportion of the gentle-born as an actual presence on the ground. On the other hand, maps also reveal the morphing of the environs into a metropolitan region throughout the period and its modernization. The outer London areas had no governmental or adminis-

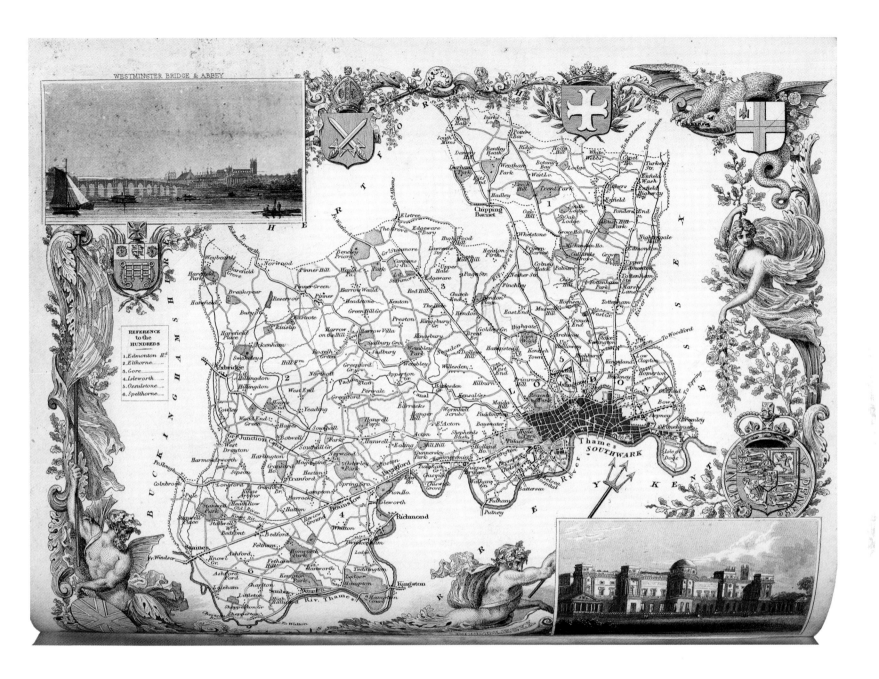

WESTMINSTER BRIDGE & ABBEY

REFERENCE
to the
HUNDREDS
1. Edmonton Hd.
2. Elthorne
3. Gore
4. Isleworth
5. Ossulstone
6. Spelthorne

53 'Middlesex', from Moule,
*The English Counties Delineated: or, a
Topographical Description of England*,
1837, British Library.

trative coherence; indeed, they crossed county boundaries and in so doing they challenged one of the
fundamental bases of traditional hierarchies. This was
not a region defined primarily by governmental
borders or by noble families and great estates, but
rather a landscape created by commerce, consumer
leisure activities, the arrival of the urban middle classes

in the countryside and rapid transport systems. Map-
makers might still pay deference to the older world of
county families, partly from commercial necessity, but
essentially theirs was a geography which exemplified
the modern age and modern society, a topography of
consumerism and suburbanization.

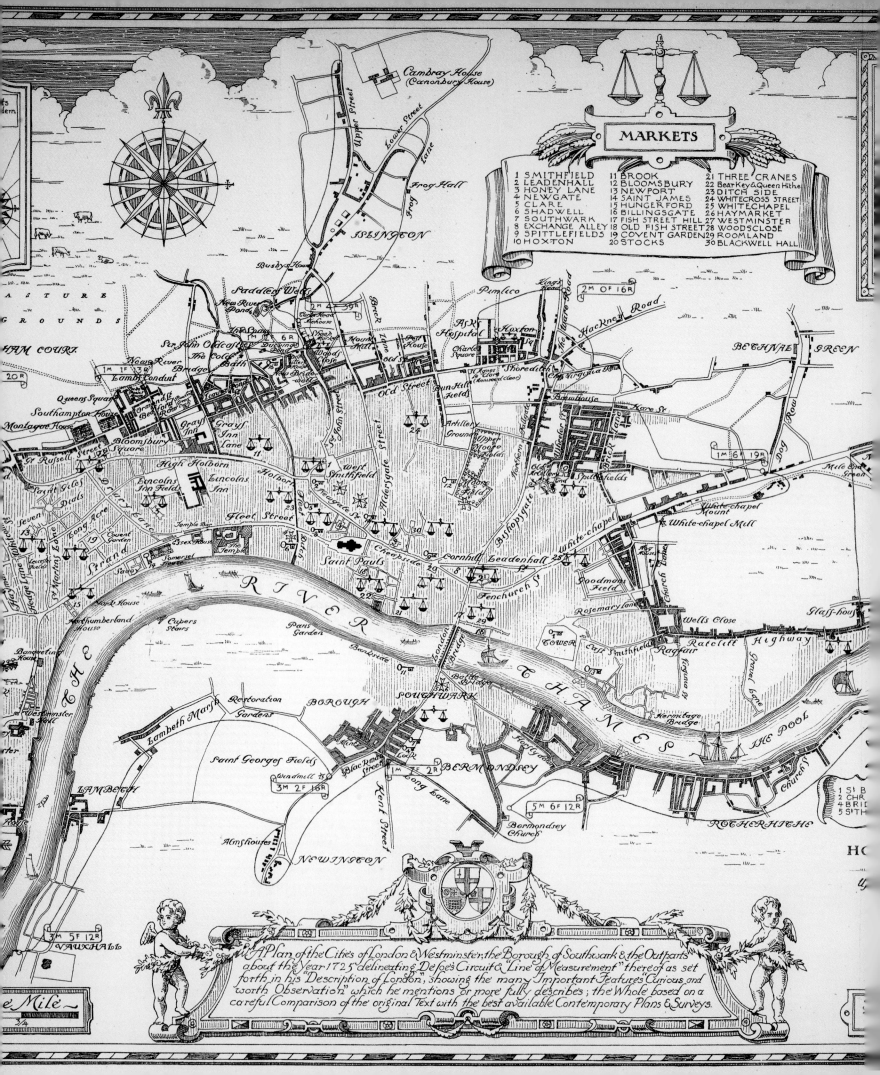

1 SMITHFIELD   11 BROOK   21 THREE CRANES
2 LEADENHALL   12 BLOOMSBURY   22 Bear Key & Queen Hithe
3 HONEY LANE   13 NEWPORT   23 DITCH SIDE
4 NEWGATE   14 SAINT JAMES   24 WHITECROSS STREET
5 CLARE   15 HUNGERFORD   25 WHITECHAPEL
6 SHADWELL   16 BILLINGSGATE   26 HAYMARKET
7 SOUTHWARK   17 FISH STREET HILL   27 WESTMINSTER
8 EXCHANGE ALLEY   18 OLD FISH STREET   28 WOODSCLOSE
9 SPITTLEFIELDS   19 COVENT GARDEN   29 ROOMLAND
10 HOXTON   20 STOCKS   30 BLACKWELL HALL

A Plan of the Cities of London & Westminster, the Borough of Southwark & the Outparts about the Year 1725 delineating Defoe's Circuit & "Line of Measurement" thereof as set forth in his "Description of London", showing the many "Important Features" Curious and worth Observation" which he mentions or more fully describes; the Whole based on a careful Comparison of the original Text with the best available Contemporary Plans & Surveys.

2

WRITING THE LANDSCAPES OF LONDON

An Historian may be compared to one walking in a Garden, and making a posie of Flowers, which he culs and plucks from divers beds and banks; now, though the Flowers be none of his, yet the choyce of them, and twisting them together, to give the fuller fragnancy, and not to thrust in any unsavory vegetal, is solely his own work.

James Howell, *Londinopolis: An Historicall Discourse*, 1657, 'To the Reader'

This chapter considers the treatment of the environs in metropolitan literature in the long eighteenth century. The main focus will be on city guidebooks, a genre which first developed in Europe in the seventeenth century.[1] Urban histories were established slightly earlier with the first London example, John Stow's *Survey of London*, being published in 1598. This seminal work became the ur-text for subsequent histories of and guides to London. Its influence lives on through the *Survey of London*, founded by C. R. Ashbee and others in 1894, which continues to produce the most authoritative guides to the historical development of the capital to this day.[2] Stow was mined by subsequent authors well into the nineteenth century, who often included long verbatim sections from the Tudor historian in their own works. He was a religious conservative whose nostalgia for the pre-Reformation period became intertwined with his negative attitudes towards urban change and growth.[3] He formed part of a group who founded the Society of Antiquaries, which included the topographer John Norden, one of the first cartographers of London and Middlesex, and William Lambarde, whose Kent perambulations provided the

model for the *Survey*.[4] As a passionate antiquarian he amassed a large collection of medieval documents which he used as the basis for his historical account.

However, Stow was not just looking back to the past; he was also interested in and wrote about contemporary London. This mixture of historical and current information was to become the hallmark of the later London guides, albeit in varying proportions depending on the intended audience. The tradition of mixing historical and contemporary information makes it difficult to distinguish in any clear-cut fashion between London histories and urban guidebooks. What both genres took from Stow and shared in common was a primarily topographical approach rooted in the buildings and monuments of the city. The latter, such as funerary monuments, were discussed primarily in terms of their associated biographical and topographical narratives rather than their sculptural forms or artistic merits. In this way the physical structures of the city became the prime texts for conveying its histories. They provided a palimpsest in which could be located themes of the civic, the popular, the local, the institutional and the individual. The

(*facing page*) 54 'A Plan of the Cities of London and Westminster etc., about the Year 1725: Delineating Defoe's "Circuit" and "Line of Measurement" Thereof' (detail of fig. 61).

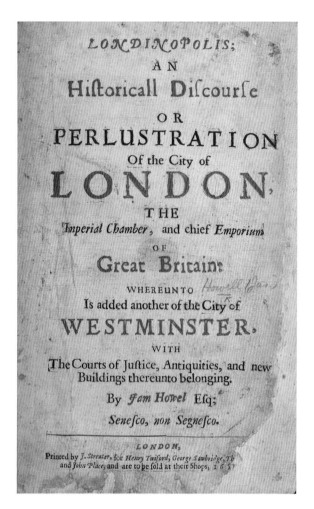

LONDINOPOLIS;
AN
Hiſtoricall Diſcourſe
OR
PERLUSTRATION
Of the City of
LONDON,
THE
Imperial Chamber, and chief *Emporium*
OF
Great Britain:
WHEREUNTO
Is added another of the City of
WESTMINSTER,
WITH
The Courts of Juſtice, Antiquities, and new
Buildings thereunto belonging.
By *Jam Howel* Eſq;
Seneſco, non Segneſco.

LONDON,
Printed by *J. Streater*, for *Henry Twiford, George Sawbridge, Th*
and *John Place*, and are to be ſold at their Shops, 1 6 5 7

architecture and terrain of the city thus provided the key to decoding its past and present.

However, if there were overlaps between histories of London and guidebooks in terms of content and format, there were clear distinctions in their intentions, tone and audiences. Urban histories aspired to be sober and scholarly and to appeal to a well-informed antiquarian audience. Guidebooks, by contrast, were aimed at Londoners and visitors requiring an up-to-date gazetteer of the sites of the capital, including both historic attractions and new developments. City guidebooks as a form have been less well studied than contemporary urban histories, although there is still much work remaining to be done on the latter as well as the former. The main reason for selecting the guidebook genre as the focus for this chapter is that it more closely reflects the contemporary understanding and use of the expanding metropolis than official histories, which were often rooted in the City for historical and institutional reasons. The countryside around the

centre, as a key part of Londoners' recreational milieu, featured more fully in guidebooks than in historical accounts, which were slower to cover the outer parishes and counties. The London guidebook to a considerable extent therefore lies outside and exists in contradistinction to the Stow tradition. The metropolitan guidebook with its emphasis on the fashionable and the ephemeral, as well as the traditional and the historical, provides a new and modern form of urban writing and experience in its own right.

THE BIRTH OF THE MODERN LONDON GUIDEBOOK

City guidebooks in England did not appear until the second half of the seventeenth century, with works such as James Howell's *Londinopolis: An Historicall Discourse* (1657), which despite its title also included much coverage of what he called 'modern Occurrences . . . contemporary with my self'[5] (fig. 55). Howell acknowledged his debt to his predecessors fulsomely: 'So, concerning this present Treatise, although the trace, and form of the Structure be mine own; yet, I am so much the Child of modesty, as to acknowledge to have fetch's most of my Materials from others, who preceded me in the same Subject; as from Mr Stow, and those industrious persons, who have made Additionals unto him.'[6] Howell (1594?–1666) was primarily a historian and political commentator, but having travelled widely on business in Europe from an early age, he also became known as a travel writer with works such as *Familiar Letters* (1645 onwards) and *Instructions for Forreine Travel* (1642).[7] In what will become a familiar career pattern for a number of figures in this chapter, he also worked as a translator and lexicographer. He revised a French dictionary in 1650 and produced his *Lexicon Tetraglotton*, a more ambitious English–French–Italian–Spanish dictionary, in 1660.[8]

Howell included the outlying areas of the City in his account, which he defined as 'heterogeneal, or *Suburbian* parts, which are yet contiguous, and make one entire continued peece'.[9] He painted a vivid picture of the eastern and north-eastern suburbs – 'the skirts of London' as he referred to them – as a dynamic zone fuelled by the expansion of trade and shipping.[10] At Wapping, he wrote, 'There is a continued street

'London is like a Laurel Leaf
May She be radiant still and
flourish like the Tree.' *Hatton 1708.*

towards a mile long . . . all along the River . . . which proceeded from the encrease of Navigation, Mariners and Trafique.'[11] *Londinopolis* also covered Westminster and the rapidly developing areas between it and the City such as Holborn, the Strand, St Giles and Lincoln's Inn Fields. But already at this date, as Howell shrewdly observed, the shape of London was changing from round to broad like 'a laurel leaf', as he put it, due to the shifting balance between centre and periphery (fig 56):

> 'Tis true, that the Suburbs of *London* are larger than the Body of the City, which make some compare her to a *Jesuites Hat*, whose brims are far larger then the Block, which made Count *Gondamar* the *Spanish* Ambassador to say, as the Queen of *Spain* was discoursing with him . . . of the City of *London*. Madam, *I believe there will be no City left shortly; for all will run out at the Gates to the* Suburbs; *and for the* Men, *I think they are gone by this time into the Country, for I left them all booted and spur'd when I came away.*[12]

Two other important early publications, both dating from 1681, were Nathaniel Crouch's (published as R. B. – Richard Burton) *Historical Remarques and Observations of the Ancient and Present State of London and Westminster* and Thomas De Laune's *The Present State of London: Or, Memorials, Comprehending a Full and Succinct Account of the Ancient and Modern State Thereof.* These works, as their titles indicate, adopted the usual Janus-like chronological perspective. However, in trying to address the present as well as the past, they

evolved some important features that were to become standard in later guides. First, they both used the pocket-book format, suggesting that they were intended to be portable. De Laune included a small number of illustrations and information on the rates for coachmen and watermen and the Penny Post. As Julia Merritt in her account of Stow's successors points out, the provision of practical information in an easily consultable, tabulated form was one of his most important innovations, which was embraced enthusiastically in subsequent publications (fig. 57).[13] Such tabulation also reflects the contemporary concern with political arithmetic, which is seen most markedly in the often tortuous attempts to calculate the number of inhabitants and dimensions of a town with which nearly every urban guide opened.

It has already been suggested that the new London guidebooks, although indebted to Stow for their historical frame of reference, also drew on alternative traditions and forms. We can see this most clearly in what might be called the first modern London guidebook, F. Colsoni's *Le guide de Londres* (1693, 2nd edn 1697, reprinted 1710). Colsoni's book is the antithesis of the Stow tradition and as such has largely been dismissed as a picaresque period piece of no great significance. To serious-minded scholars of London, Colsoni's focus on the fun and the fashionable is reductive and frivolous. However, a close examination of the genesis and content of Colsoni's work shows that, far from being marginal in London literature, he was a key figure in introducing a new type of urban writing in England. Colsoni was a teacher of languages and a lexicographer living in St Christopher's Alley in Threadneedle Street, near the Royal Exchange. We know this from the title page of his *The New Trismagister* (1688), one of his prodigious published output. The *Trismagister* was one of the first multilingual grammars to appear in English, following on from Howell's pioneering publications. It offered a trilingual primer, in French, Italian and English, which unlike most earlier works did not use Latin as an intermediary between them.[14] Other works in his eclectic oeuvre included a French and Italian grammar, a book of kings and queens, *The Royal Almanack, Peace and War in the Field*, and *Ladies of Europe at the Conclave of Juno* – the last two being described as 'Historical Dialogues'.[15] Colsoni, like Howell, made his living trading

WAT   265

	Oars.		Skul.	
	s.	d.	s.	d.
From Whitehall to Lambeth, or Vauxhall	0	6	0	3
From the Temple, Dorset-stairs, Black Friars stairs, or Paul's wharf, to Lambeth	0	8	0	4
Over the water directly, from any place between Vauxhall and Limehouse	0	4	0	2

Rates of oars up and down the river, as well for the whole fare as company.

Up the River.

	Fare.		Comp.	
	s.	d.	s.	d.
To Chelsea, Battersea, and Wandsworth	1	6	0	3
To Putney, Fulham, or Barn-elms	2	0	0	4
To Hammersmith, Chiswick, or Mortlack	2	6	0	6
To Brentford, Isleworth, or Richmond	3	6	0	6
To Twickenham	4	0	0	6
To Kingston	5	0	0	9
To Hampton Court	6	0	1	0
To Hampton Town, Sunbury, or Walton	7	0	1	0
To Weybridge, and Chertsey	10	0	1	0
To Stanes	12	0	1	0
To Windsor	14	0	1	0

5   Down

266   WAT

Down the River.	Fare.		Comp.	
	s.	d.	s.	d.
From London to Gravesend	4	6	0	9
To Grays, or Greenhithe	4	0	0	8
To Purfleet, or Erith	3	0	0	6
To Woolwich	2	6	0	4
To Blackwall	2	0	0	4
To Greenwich, or Deptford	1	6	0	3

Rates of carrying goods in the tilt boat from London to Gravesend.

	l.	s.	d.
For ever single person in the ordinary passage	0	0	9
For a hogshead	0	2	0
For a whole firkin	0	0	2
For half a firkin	0	0	1
One hundred weight	0	0	4
One sack of corn, salt, &c.	0	0	6
An ordinary chest, or trunk	0	0	6
An ordinary hamper	0	0	6
The hire of the whole tilt-boat	1	2	6

Any waterman who takes more than the above rates is liable to forfeit 40s. and to suffer half a year's imprisonment, and if he sets up a sail between Lambeth and London-bridge, upon complaint being made, as hereafter mentioned, forfeits 5s.

However any person going by water, need not make any bargain with the waterman, but only let him know at what

on his language skills and taking advantage of the possibilities for reaching broader audiences that the new markets in print offered. The third edition of his London *Guide* states that he also kept a chocolate house and had two 'Good Billiard Tables'. He says that he himself will guide foreigners round the city and that besides French, English and Italian he understands German and Dutch; elsewhere he includes Spanish among his main languages.[16] Unlike Howell Colsoni was an immigrant, from a dual French–Italian Protestant background, which possibly points to a background in Switzerland.[17] The initial F for his first name is variously given as Francesco, Francis or François.[18]

Rosemary Sweet has highlighted the presence of teachers as a significant group among those writing urban histories, but the significance of foreign language specialists to the genre – particularly in the London context – is only now beginning to be recognized.[19] *The New Trismagister* can itself be seen as continuing a strand of urban writing stemming from the Elizabethan language-lesson dialogue manuals such as John Florio's *Florio His Firste Fruites*, an Italian–English primer of 1578. Florio developed the language textbook tradition to incorporate sample dialogues which related everyday activities to recognizable London scenes. The continuing legacy and absorption into city literature of the language guide can be seen in later eighteenth-century works where 'conversations' are one of the main forms of urban discourse along with 'trips or tours', 'accounts' and 'descriptions'. In the 1744 *A Trip from St James's to the Royal-Exchange* the topics include 'Conversation betwixt several Gentlemen at an Ordinary', 'The Use of a Diamond-Ring in Conversation' and 'Of saying nothing in Conversation' – the latter apparently being a particularly necessary art.[20] The anonymous author of the *Trip* stresses the cosmopolitan character of the city and presents an unforgettable image of London as an international honeypot for crooks and chancers:

> London is the grand Reservoir, or Common-Sewer of the World . . . this City receives all the Scum and Filth, not only of our own, but of all other Countries: *Italian, French, German, Dutch. . . . France* furnishes *Cooks, Valets de Chambre, Dancers*, and *Teachers of French*, who seldom understand a Sentence of *English. Italy* supplies us with *Fidlers* and *Eunuchs. . . . Scotland* sends us *Pedlars, Beggars* and *Quacks*; and *Ireland, Evidences, Robbers*, and *Bullies*.[21]

Urban guidebooks, particularly to capital cities with their large numbers of foreign visitors, were part of a pan-European market and audience. Colsoni's *Guide* was obviously intended for a European audience, and not just a French one, as French was the international language of the time. Colsoni drew upon Continental models for his book, which was structured by perambulations around neighbourhoods, an approach used in the sixteenth-century Roman guides. From these he also took the idea of establishing a five-day itinerary.[22] Stow had also used the perambulatory approach, but unlike him and his more conservative successors Colsoni dispensed with the traditional municipal boundaries, in order to create itineraries determined solely by their interest for tourists. This firmly grounded his account in the contemporary physical realities and preoccupations of the metropolis; even the primary distinction between the cities of London and Westminster was not made explicit.

The Fifth Tour included a section on 'Les Dehors de Londres' which suggested outings to the following 'beaux Villages': Islington and Epsom were recommended for their mineral spas; Greenwich and Chelsea for their military hospitals; Kensington, Hampton Court and Windsor for their royal palaces; Chatham for its warships; and Stepney for its Sunday preachers, both Anglican and Nonconformist.[23] The longest entry is reserved for the Spring Garden at Vauxhall and the nearby Cupid's Garden in Southwark. These are less wholesome destinations, and although he recommends the former as the most suitable and charming of the many pleasure gardens around London, frequented by those with taste, he also has to warn his readers of the

dangers of contracting 'Le Mal de Naples appellé *the French-Pox*' from some of the women there.[24] It is not clear from Colsoni's outraged tones whether he is more offended by the behaviour of these loose women or the fact that the clap should be given a French title. Colsoni, like his contemporary Ned Ward, author of *The London Spy* (1698–1700), was one of the first to reflect the truly multifarious nature of 'the London experience', which included the liminal zones around the capital as much as the built urban core itself.[25] Despite emphasizing the role of these areas as a pleasure ground, Colsoni did not employ the notoriously lewd and scabrous tone of Ward's *Spy*. Indeed, he warns his readers against the danger of corruption from 'Harpies' in England where debauchery is 'álamode' at present.[26] Ward and Colsoni offered two of the most radical accounts of turn-of-the-century London, both structured through perambulations around the varying parts of the city, through which the visitor is introduced to its multicentred and multilayered complexities. The main difference is that in writing a guidebook Colsoni attempted to make the metropolis knowable and manageable, while Ward's literary account presented London's attraction as lying in its dangerous, labyrinthine impenetrability.

In 1708 another modern-style guidebook appeared, Edward Hatton's *A New View of London* (fig. 58). Hatton's work, which was described on the title page as '*A Book Useful not only for Strangers, but for the Inhabitants*', again reflects the close relationship between English and French tourism and travel literature in the period. Hatton referred in his Preface to a Parisian volume on which his book was based. This was almost certainly Germaine Brice's *Description nouvelle de ce qui'il ya de plus remarquable dans la Ville de Paris* of 1684, which was translated into English in 1687 and 1688.[27] Hatton turned the traditional explanation of the need for guides for natives to their own cities on its head by saying that the work would be useful 'for English Noble and Gentlemen, as intend to Travel, whereby they may be enobled, when in Foreign Countries, to give a satisfactory Account of the Metropolis of their own'.[28] Although Hatton's was a pocket book, it was arranged not as a series of walks but rather alphabetically and thematically under headings such as churches, streets, public statues and so on. This format was increasingly adopted in later eighteenth-century pocket

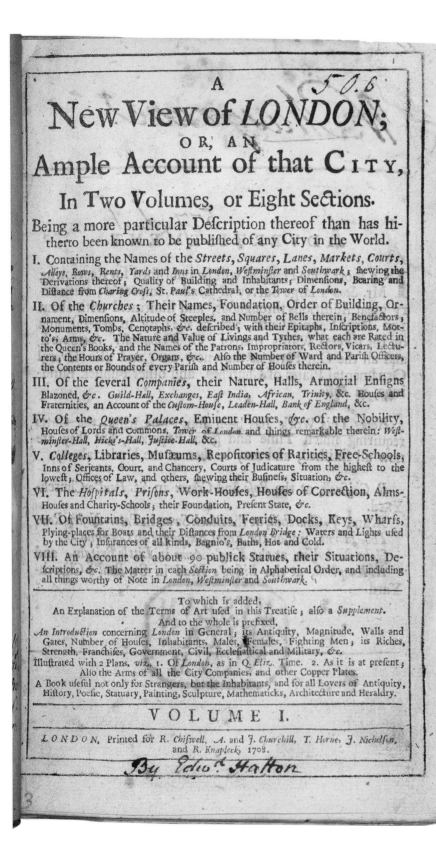

A

New View of LONDON;

OR, AN

Ample Account of that CITY,

In Two Volumes, or Eight Sections.

Being a more particular Description thereof than has hitherto been known to be published of any City in the World.

I. Containing the Names of the *Streets, Squares, Lanes, Markets, Courts, Alleys, Rows, Rents, Yards* and *Inns* in *London, Westminster* and *Southwark*; shewing the Derivations thereof; Quality of Building and Inhabitants; Dimensions, Bearing and Distance from *Charing Cross*, St. *Paul's* Cathedral, or the *Tower of London*.

II. Of the *Churches*; Their Names, Foundation, Order of Building, Ornament, Dimensions, Altitude of Steeples, and Number of Bells therein; Benefactors; Monuments, Tombs, Cenotaphs, &c. described; with their Epitaphs, Inscriptions, Motto's; Arms, &c. The Nature and Value of Livings and Tythes, what each are Rated in the Queen's Books, and the Names of the Patrons, Impropriators, Rectors, Vicars, Lecturers; the Hours of Prayer, Organs, &c. Also the Number of Ward and Parish Officers, the Contents or Bounds of every Parish and Number of Houses therein.

III. Of the several *Companies*, their Nature, Halls, Armorial Ensigns Blazoned, &c. *Guild-Hall, Exchanges, East India, African, Trinity,* &c. Houses and Fraternities, an Account of the *Custom-House, Leaden-Hall, Bank of England,* &c.

IV. Of the *Queen's Palaces,* Eminent Houses, &c. of the Nobility, Houses of Lords and Commons, *Tower of London* and things remarkable therein: *Westminster-Hall, Hicks's-Hall, Justice-Hall,* &c.

V. *Colleges,* Libraries, Musæums, Repositories of Rarities, Free-Schools, Inns of Serjeants, Court, and Chancery, Courts of Judicature from the highest to the lowest; Offices of Law, and others, shewing their Business, Situation, &c.

VI. The *Hospitals, Prisons,* Work-Houses, Houses of Correction, Alms-Houses and Charity-Schools; their Foundation, Present State, &c.

VII. Of Fountains, Bridges, Conduits, Ferries, Docks, Keys, Wharfs, Plying-places for Boats and their Distances from *London Bridge*: Waters and Lights used by the City; Insurances of all kinds, Bagnio's, Baths, Hot and Cold.

VIII. An Account of about 90 publick Statues, their Situations, Descriptions, &c. The Matter in each *Section* being in Alphabetical Order, and including all things worthy of Note in *London, Westminster* and *Southwark.*

To which is added,

An Explanation of the Terms of Art used in this Treatise; also a *Supplement.*
And to the whole is prefixed,

An Introduction concerning *London* in General; its Antiquity, Magnitude, Walls and Gates, Number of Houses, Inhabitants, Males, Females, Fighting Men; its Riches, Strength, Franchises, Government, Civil, Ecclesiastical and Military, &c.

Illustrated with 2 Plans, *viz.* 1. Of *London,* as in Q. *Eliz.* Time. 2. As it is at present; Also the Arms of all the City Companies, and other Copper Plates.

A Book useful not only for Strangers, but the Inhabitants, and for all Lovers of Antiquity, History, Poesie, Statuary, Painting, Sculpture, Mathematicks, Architecture and Heraldry.

VOLUME I.

LONDON, Printed for R. *Chiswell, A.* and *J. Churchill, T. Horne, J. Nicholson,* and R. *Knaplock,* 1708.

By Edwd Hatton

58 Edward Hatton, title page, from Hatton, *A New View of London,* 1708, British Library.

guides, such as the long-running *Ambulator* series of 1774 onwards. Hatton followed Brice in his architectural interests and his focus on the modern, while referring his readers to Stow if they required a historical source.[29] In his Preface he listed the different audiences he hoped to interest, and at the end of the book he provided an Explanation of the 'Terms of Art' covering architecture, sculpture, painting, mathematics and heraldry. Hatton even echoed Brice in an appreciation for the Gothic, which was generally disparaged at the time. His interest may have arisen more from historic than aesthetic interests; nevertheless, he valued monuments such as Henry VII's chapel at Westminster Abbey that were often ignored in contemporary discourse. This appreciation of the non-classical was extended to the suburbs more broadly by Hatton and other writers, where vernacular and traditional architecture continued to form a substantial part of the environment until the late eighteenth century. Guidebooks presented themselves as primarily concerned with the experiential rather than the aesthetic, and in this way they could incorporate elements of the non-polite, such as the Gothic, within the genre while at the same time remaining part of urbane literate culture.

Before we finish this section on the pioneers of the guidebook in the later seventeenth and early eighteenth centuries, we should pause briefly to consider a new edition of Stow which appeared in 1720 produced by John Strype, a well-known ecclesiastical historian. Strype (1643–1747) was the vicar at Low Leyton and Rural Dean of Barking, Essex, and therefore the first of many London writers and artists we shall encounter who lived in the environs. The new edition of the *Survey* was never intended as anything other than a comprehensive updating of Stow's work.[30] However, Strype, like his predecessor, embraced the contemporary, and he expanded the coverage of Westminster as well as including other suburbs such as Stepney, Clerkenwell and St Giles-in-the-Fields. Following Colsoni he added a 'Perambulation, or Circuit-Walk' of four or five miles around the City as an appendix. His treatment, however, follows Hatton rather than Colsoni's racier account of the outskirts in concentrating on churches and their monuments, for, as he matter-of-factly remarked, as they were places of retirement, 'many of our eminent Citizens having Country Houses in those Towns, happened to dye, and be interred

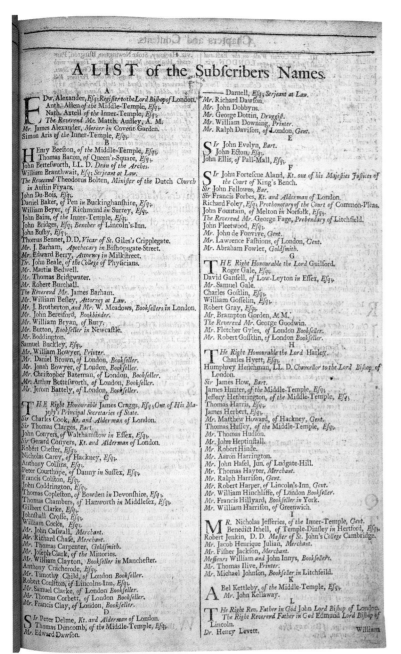

59a and b 'A List of the Subscribers', from Strype, *The Survey of London*, vol. 1, 1720, British Library.

there'.[31] He was alive to the expansion of London, which was creating a new kind of many-headed hydra of a city. He wrote of Stepney that it might be considered 'rather a Province than a Parish, especially if we add that it contains in it both City and Country.... And were it not eclipsed by the Lustre of the neighbouring city, it would appear one of the Considerable Towns of the Kingdom, and would give place to very few Cities in England.'[32] Strype's book was a large, expensive folio production in two volumes

costing six guineas. Despite this it proved a very popular work and went through three further editions within the space of the following thirty years.[33] In the light of this it might be worthwhile analysing the 'List of Subscribers' given at the beginning of the first edition to see who was buying such works and where they were based (fig. 59a and b).

✳

Table 2 Subscribers to Strype's edition of Stow, 1720, by occupation

Titled Gentry	19
Esq or Gent	64
Lawyers	33
Clergymen	11
Academics	7
Booksellers/Printers	42
Other Trades	29
'Mr'	35
Total	240

Excluding a handful of miscellaneous and smaller categories, e.g. doctors.

The list (Table 2) includes a significant number of subscribers giving addresses in the Home Counties and the environs in places such as Hackney, Richmond, Greenwich, Walthamstow and Hanworth. It also reveals the diversity of potential readers, who included well-known figures such as John Evelyn and Narcissus Lutterell; many gentry (mainly knights); some ministers and academics, principally from Gresham College and Oxford and Cambridge; a large number of City merchants and other trades; plus forty-two booksellers and printers, the latter group spread across the country. There are certainly more unidentified tradesmen on the list, for example Edward Strong from the dynasty of masons, whose name but not occupation is given. The other largest single group is lawyers and judges, who number thirty-three. This shows that even for an expensive two-volume folio work such as Strype's, the number of gentry subscribers was less than the number of businessmen and professionals. It also reveals, as one would expect given London's dependence on immigration, that there was a market for books on London beyond the immediate confines of the capital itself.

DEFOE AND THE TOPOGRAPHICAL NARRATIVE

No account of the London area in the eighteenth century can dispense with Defoe; indeed, we have already encountered him many times already. Daniel Defoe (1660?–1731) provided the perfect modern complement in the 1720s to Strype's historicism in chronicling the metropolis. The nature of Defoe's great journey is well captured in its full title: *A Tour thro' the Whole Island of Great Britain, Divided into Circuits or Journies. Giving A Particular and Diverting Account of Whatever is Curious and Worth Observation, Including Descriptions of Towns, the Customs, Diversions and Employment of the People, Trade and Manufacture and Public Edifices and Seats of the Nobility and Gentry* (1724–6). In his depiction of London he eschewed both conventional antiquarian and classical urban tropes, and instead presented the city as a commercial machine and imperial powerhouse. He wrote in the Preface, 'here is the present state of the country described' and 'the looking back into remote things is studiously avoided' as scholars have covered the ground well enough already.[34] Defoe came from and wrote for the new urban middle classes. His method as a journalist (and previously as a government agent) was to employ the direct observational approach to contemporary life. In the battle between the ancients and the moderns he was firmly on the modern side, as were his readers, who for the most part would not have received a classical education.[35]

Defoe undertook trips from 1722 specifically to research his *Tour* but also made use of his previous extensive travels around the country, including to Scotland spying for Lord Harley. He drew on earlier literature such as William Camden's *Britannia* (1695) and John MacKay's *Journey through England* (1722). The metropolitan sections are generally held to be the most directly observed in the book, forming as they did Defoe's everyday milieu.[36] He was, like so many writers and Nonconformists, resident in his self-designated 'outparts'. He had trained as a minister at Charles Morton's famous dissenting academy in Newington Green, and although he did not enter the ministry he later settled in the area (fig. 60). As the full title of the *Tour* indicated, the book was intended to provide something for everyone: a traditional focus on historical sites and country seats, new urban histories of towns large and small, accounts of contemporary trade and agriculture, and plenty of social observation and anecdotes. Defoe, as someone who wrote novels as well as non-fiction, brought some of his literary sensibilities to the hitherto more prosaic genre of travel writing. His *Tour* uses the landscape, both urban and rural, as the major structuring device of the text so that the

60 81–87 Stoke Newington Church Street, 1733–5.

Defoe lived just along the road from here in a house which is now demolished but whose existence is indicated by a plaque and through the naming of the adjacent Defoe Road.

topography becomes an unfolding narrative, imbued throughout with a strong social purpose.

As befitted the author of the contemporaneous *The Complete English Tradesman* (1726) and a businessman himself, Defoe was fascinated by the new British entre- preneurialism.[37] His aim in the *Tour* was to show 'the situation of things . . . not as they have been but as they are; the improvements in the soil, the product of the earth, the labour of the poor, the improvement in manufactures, in merchandizes, in navigation . . . not forgetting the general dependence of the whole country upon the City of London, as well as for con- sumption of its produce, as the circulation of its trade'.[38] Defoe has been accused of overestimating the impact of London in the national and global econo- mies by critics from the proud Scotsman Tobias Smollett onwards.[39] But what his account reveals is not just a dominant capital but the existence of an entire metropolitan region: 'The villages round London partake of the influence of London, so much, that it is observed as London is increased, so they are increased

also, and from the same causes.'[40] Defoe realized that it would be impossible to stop the growth of London, but he wanted to see it take a more regular form to produce a rounded rather than a ragged shape. 'Whither will this monstrous city then extend?' he asked.[41] He proposed as a solution an Act of Parliament to call the entire metropolis 'London', rather than just the City, and for a means of regulating building to even out the variations in line around the edge of the city.[42] He suggested, for example, 'particularly stopping the running out of the buildings at the east and west ends, as at Ratcliff and Deptford, east, and at Tyburn and Kensington roads, west, and encouraging the building out at Moor-fields, Bunhill-fields, the west side of Shoreditch, and such places'.[43]

We will return to the ongoing issue of the edge of the city in Chapters 6 and 7. For now it is sufficient to note that Defoe was but one of a long line of writers and theorists concerned with how to control and mould the rampant forces of speculative develop- ment in order to produce urban forms in concordance

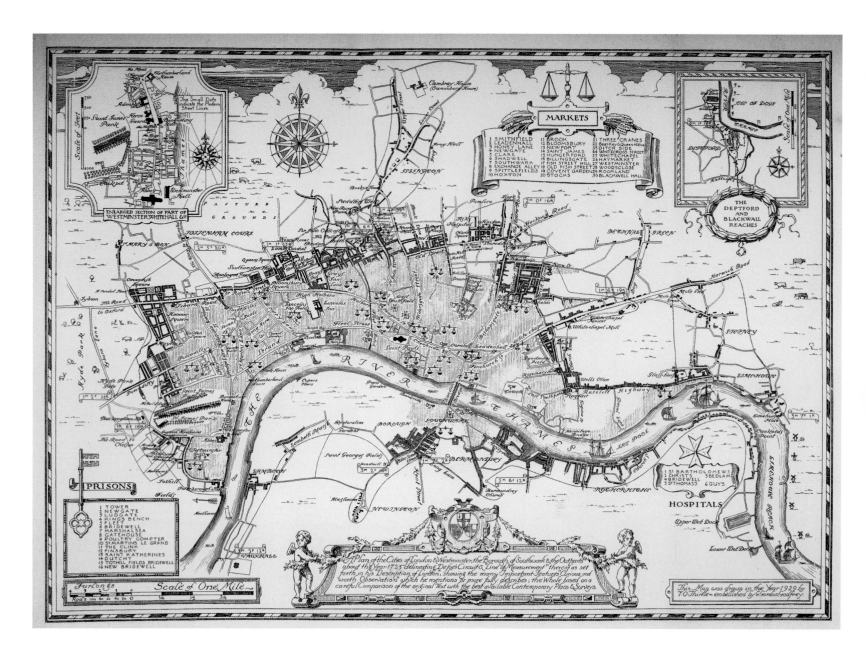

61 'A Plan of the Cities of London and Westminster etc., about the Year 1725: Delineating Defoe's "Circuit" and "Line of Measurement" Thereof', Plate LVII from Chancellor and Beeton, *A tour thro' London about the year 1725*, 1929, British Library.

with classical architectural ideals.[44] Howell had compared London to a cardinal's hat, but increasingly the metaphor used was of a monster whose swollen head (London) would outgrow the body (nation). Defoe shared these fears but also celebrated the new greater London and the polite company now to be found widely distributed around the adjacent counties. Defoe's text is remarkable for the sense it creates of a vastly enlarged and multi-dimensional notion of London.[45] He extended the coverage of earlier writers, such as Colsoni and Strype, to provide a picture of an interconnected region with London's tentacles reaching far out into the surrounding countryside. The rural

zone in turn feeds its produce and wares into the city, sustaining the great beast. The centrality of 'landscape' as a structuring device has already been commented on, and the *Tour* displays a new sensitivity for Defoe to the natural world. His interest in the agriculture of the London region was intensified by his purchase in 1722 of a large amount of land in Colchester. He bred cattle and raised corn there besides owning woodland.[46] His frequent diatribes about the sufficiency of English forestry to meet the nation's needs stem from his own first-hand experience, combined with a distaste for the navy's reliance on Baltic and Scandinavian rather than native timber.

66

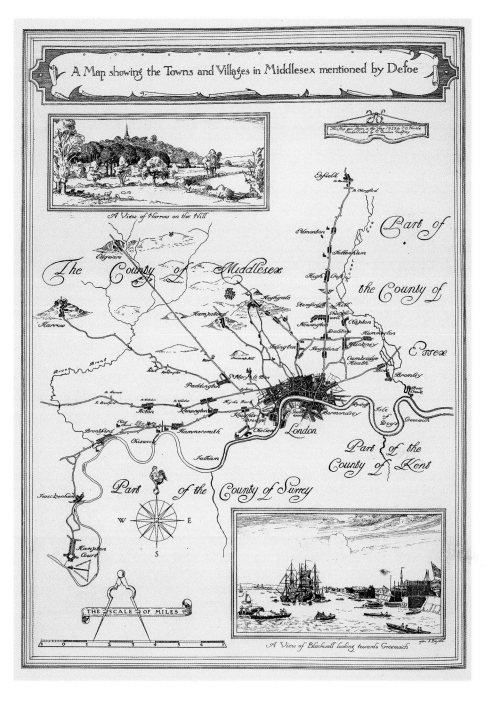

62 'A Map showing the Towns and Villages in Middlesex mentioned by Defoe', Plate XLIX from Chancellor and Beeton, *A tour thro' London about the year 1725*, 1929, British Library.

The *Tour* is epistolary in form and letter Five contains the central account of the City, Westminster, Southwark 'and the buildings circumjacent'. It was defining the latter that caused Defoe most problems. In order to make sense of the ever expanded city, in true Royal Society fashion he drew a 'Line of Measurement' around it totalling thirty-six miles two furlongs and thirty-nine rods.[47] By Defoe's reckoning this covered the area 'from Black-Wall in the east, to Tot-Hill Fields in the west . . . or river, in the south to Islington north . . . and all the new buildings by, and beyond, Hannover Square', or in modern terms from the Isle of Dogs to Westminster (fig. 61 and see fig. 54).[48] However, even in drawing this line he was aware of its inadequacies, and he inserted various notes justifying his inclusions and exclusions: for example, Deptford is included but Greenwich excluded, even though he admits they are contiguous. One of the most novel and perhaps the most significant features of Defoe's *Tour*, in terms of London writing, is the amount of space he gives to covering the 'outparts', which as he said 'partake of London' (fig. 62).[49] Defoe is the first writer after Colsoni to recognize the significance of the London hinterland. His focus, as ever, was on the contemporary and the secular, thus expanding on Strype's and Hatton's ecclesiastically dominated accounts, although some of his entries are indebted to the former.[50] Defoe, as was discussed in the Introduction, defined the outer areas as a new zone of suburban residence for the wealthy middle class. He began and ended Circuits 1–7 in London and provided a detailed account of the villages and suburbs lying along the major arterial routes as he travelled in and out of the capital. From the start of his first circuit through Essex and East Anglia he is alive to the economic transformation that the region has undergone: 'The first observation I made was, that all the villages that may be called the neighbourhood of the city of London are increased in buildings to a strange degree, within the compass of 20 or 30 years past at the most . . . but the increase of the value and rent of the houses formerly standing, has . . . advanced to a very great degree, and I may venture to say at least a fifth part; some think a third part, above what they were before.'[51]

He went on to note not just the social but even the gender transformations that such increases in population had wrought in the Essex villages: 'For now people go to them, not for retirement into the country, but for good company; of which that I may speak to the ladies . . . there are in all these villages . . . excellent conversation, and a great deal of it.'[52] Whereas at Eltham, he observed, although there was a plenitude of ladies there was a dearth of young men, as they were all either working abroad as merchants or at court or in the army. 'The ladies will abandon the place', he commented, 'unless the scene alters in a few years.'[53] Defoe had an acute antenna for the nuances of suburban growth and, even more presciently, decline: 'We see several villages, formerly standing, as it were, in the country, and at a great distance, now joined to the streets by continued buildings, and more making haste to meet in the like manner: for example, Deptford.'[54] Richmond had likewise seen a great increase in building, but it was vulnerable to royal caprice. Many noble houses for courtiers had been lately raised, 'but 'tis feared should the prince come, for any cause that may happen to quit that side of the country, those numerous buildings must abate in the value which is now set upon them'.[55] Defoe chronicled the dramatic rise in the status of the environs and the new and significant role they now played as centres of fashionable residence and leisure, alongside their longer standing function as places for retirement and retreat. He also had, arguably, as big an impact as Stow on subsequent London guides, which plagiarized him and indeed lifted huge chunks of his text shamelessly.

Two examples from the many who 'borrowed' from Defoe's *Tour* will suffice. *The Foreigner's Guide: Or, a Necessary and Instructive Companion Both for the Foreigner and Native, in their Tour through the Cities of Westminster and London* of 1729 was the most direct and popular successor to Colsoni for a French audience. It was a pocket book which went through a number of editions up until the 1750s and was the first to employ a facing-page dual-language format in English and French (fig. 63a and b). The author lamented in the Preface that there had been a previous attempt to introduce visitors to the city, 'but in every respect so imperfect, that as I have heard it express'd by many, It does Shame to the Title it bears'.[56] This must be a reference to Colsoni, as *The Foreigner's Guide* is a far more sober and measured account than Colsoni's whistle-stop tour. However, the facing-page format could have been inspired by the *Trismagister*, or other linguistics texts, which employed mirror pages. The book begins with 'A Description of London in general' which is largely dedicated to outlining the growth of the city and the new buildings which had gone up in the past fifty years or so. The author writes of the 'many thousand Houses, large and beautiful Streets, Squares &'. In its adoption of a relativistic historical perspective *The Foreigner's Guide* displays a greater

sense of the fluidity and mutability of the city than Colsoni, whose view is very much a snapshot taken at one point in time. The opening general description is followed by the now familiar format of perambulations arranged by neighbourhood, pointing out the principal sights. In the 1740 revised edition the outlying parts form one of the four sections of the book, the others being a description of the two cities; palaces, noblemen's houses, churches, streets, etc.; and rates of coaches and watermen and roads to Dover and Harwich. The contents list indicates the elasticity of the concept of the London area, in accordance with the likely interests of visitors: 'A Description of the several Villages in the Neighbourhood; as Chelsea, Kensington, Richmond, Greenwich, Woolwich &c. As also others more remote, viz. Hampton-Court, Windsor, Oxford, Cambridge, Bleinheim, Newmarket, Epsom, Tunbridge, Bath &c'. The rhapsodic account of the racing at Newmarket is seemingly the highlight of the entire book.

The constant enlargement of what might be constituted as London and the emphasis on peregrination continued in later works, such as the anonymous *London in Miniature* (1755), another of Defoe's progeny. The title *London in Miniature* nicely encapsulates the novel features that guidebooks pioneered in the late seventeenth to mid-eighteenth centuries in London. These were, first, a fine balance between the need for a concise format in conjunction with the provision of as much information as possible: the difficult juggling act of every tourist guide ever since. Second, there was an emphasis on the sensory and the experiential (as opposed to knowledge and improvement) which embraced high, low and middling culture. Third, they presented a highly malleable and regionalized notion of an ever-expanding London both physically and conceptually. As the subtitle of *London in Miniature* stated, such books provided 'A Concise and Comprehensive Description of the Cities of London and Westminster, and Parts Adjacent, for Forty Miles Round ... Intended as a Complete Guide to Foreigners, and All Others Who Come to View this City, or Travel for Pleasure to any of its Circumjacent Parts ... The Whole Collected from Stow, Maitland, and other Large Works on this Subject; with Several New and Curious PARTICULARS'. *London in Miniature*, due to its forty-mile circumference around London, is arguably the first comprehensive guide to the environs. Its outer London

THE

Foreigner's Guide:

Or, a neceſſary and inſtructive

COMPANION

Both for the

Foreigner *and* Native,

IN THEIR

TOUR through the CITIES of LONDON and WESTMINSTER.

GIVING

I. A general Deſcription of theſe two Cities, with an Account of their reſpective Governments.

II. A Deſcription of the Royal Palaces, Noblemen's Houſes, publick Buildings, Churches, Streets, Squares, and the moſt remarkable Places in and near this famous *Metropolis* : With an Account of the Inns of Court, Royal Society, Publick Walks, Diverſions, Remarkable Days, Court Days, Poſt Days, &c.

III. A Deſcription of the ſeveral Villages in the Neighbourhood ; as *Chelſea, Kenſington , Richmond , Greenwich, Woolwich, Hampſtead,* &c. As alſo others more remote, *viz. Hampton-Court, Windſor, Oxford, Cambridge, Bleinheim, Newmarket* Horſe-Races, *Epſom, Tunbridge, Bath,* &c.

IV. An Account of the Rates of Coaches, Watermen, &c. Alſo the Rates of Poſt-Horſes ; with the Roads to *Dover* and *Harwich.*

Very Uſeful and Entertaining both to the *Foreigner* and *Native :* And done in *Engliſh* and *French.*

LONDON:

Printed for JOSEPH POTE, at Sir *Iſaac Newton's* Head, near *Suffolk-ſtreet, Charing-Croſs.*

Where may be had, Books in all Languages, both Antient and Modern, at the loweſt Prices. 1729.

LE

Guide des Etrangers:

OU LE

COMPAGNON

Neceſſaire & inſtructif à

L'*Etranger* & au *Naturel* du *Pays,*

En faiſant le

TOUR des Villes de LONDRES & de WESTMINSTRE.

CONTENANT

I. La Deſcription générale de ces deux Villes & de leurs Gouvernemens differens.

II. La Deſcription des Palais Royaux, Hôtels, Edifices publics, Egliſes, Rues, Places ou Quarrez, & des Lieux les plus remarquables de cette fameuſe *Métropole* , avec une Relation des Colléges des Juriſconſultes, de la Societé Royale, des Promenades publiques, des Divertiſſemens , des Jours ou Fêtes remarquables, des Jours de Cour, Jours de Poſte, &c.

III. La Deſcription de pluſieurs Places aux Environs, comme *Chelſea , Kenſington, Richmond, Greenwich , Woolwich, Hampſtead,* &c. Avec d'autres plus eloignées, *ſavoir, Hampton-Court, Windſor, Oxford, Cambridge, Bleinheim,* la Courſe de Chevaux à *Newmarket, Epſom , Tunbridge , Bath.* &c.

IV. Le Prix des Fiacres, Bâteaux, &c. Le Prix des Chevaux de Poſtes, avec la Route de *Londres* à *Douvre* & *Harwich.*

Ouvrage très utile & divertiſſant à l'*Etranger* & au *Naturel* du *Pays :* En *Anglois* & en *François.*

A LONDRES:

Chez JOSEPH POTE Libraire à l'Enſeigne du Chevalier *Iſaac Newton,* proche de *Suffolk-ſtreet, Charing-Croſs.*

Chez qui l'on trouve auſſi un Aſſortiment général des Livres tant vieux que nouveaux à juſte prix. 1729.

63a and b   Facing title pages in English and French, from Anon., *The Foreigner's Guide,* 1729, British Library.

coverage ranged from the immediate suburbs of Clerkenwell, Lambeth and Paddington as far out as Totteridge and Edgware to the north, Tilbury and Newmarket to the east, Tunbridge Wells to the south and Windsor to the west.

London in Minature owed nothing to the Stow/ Maitland antiquarian tradition and instead effectively revived and reorganized Colsoni's brief individual entries into separate typographical blocks as a gazetteer (fig. 64). The text is a formalization of Defoe's continuous prose into sections arranged under the headings of 'The Villages, Gentlemen's Houses and Places of Entertainment'. From this very particular mix there developed a new type of guide which rejected antiquarianism as being irrelevant for its more generalized audiences. These guides grew out of London's position as the

[253]

to *Charles Hedges*, Efq; and the other to *John Allen*,
Efq; Two Miles from hence is

TOTTERIDGE,

On the Border of the County of *Hertford*. Here
are two fine Villas, the Refidence of Sir *Peter Meres*
and Mr. *Da Cofta*, a wealthy *Jew* ; alfo a handfome
Seat, with a fmall Park, and fine Gardens, belonging
to the late Sir *William Lee*, Knt. Lord Chief-Juftice
of the Court of *King's-Bench*.
   At about ten Miles from *London*, and fix from
Hampftead, is

EDGWARE,

A little Town, going on what was anciently the
main Road from *London* to *St. Alban's*; being the
famous high Road called *Watling-ftreet*, which reached
from *London* to *Shrewfbury*, and on towards *Wales*.
Here was a Market kept formerly, but has been dif-
ufed for fome Years paft, and the Market-houfe is
now converted into a School.
   At the upper End of this Town was, within thefe
few Years, a moft magnificent Seat, called

CANNONS,

Belonging to the late Duke of *Chandos*, by whom it
was built. But though this noble Palace is now
taken down, and the fine Gardens laid open, we
imagine that a fhort Defcription of the former
Splendor of this beautiful Place will not be unen-
tertaining to our Readers.

The

European epicentre of the new commodity culture,
but in themselves also contributed to the creation of
the metropolis as an object of consumption in its own
right. Thus, a genre of guidebooks emerged which, in
parallel with various literary strands, developed new
approaches to writing about the city which stressed its
visual consumption, geographical diversity, and multifarious and protean character.

HANDBOOKS TO THE ENVIRONS

London in Minature deviated from Defoe in one important respect which represents a significant shift in
approach. The 1755 guidebook eschewed Defoe's coverage of trade and production, and instead focused on
the environs as primarily a domestic and leisure arena.
One of the few manufacturing features to be men-

tioned is the Chelsea Water Works, which maintained
its fascination as a symbol of industry throughout the
period (see fig. 88). The exclusion of the impolite and
the commercial became increasingly common across
all genres and media in the second half of the eighteenth century. From the mid-eighteenth century, as
representations of the environs became increasingly
selective and genteel, they also became increasingly
aestheticized and romanticized under the impact of the
picturesque. We can see this trend in the first book to
use the term 'environs' explicitly in its title. This was
the anonymous *London and its Environs Described*,
known to be by Robert Dodsley (1704–1764), a fascinating character who once again demonstrates the col-
ourful backgrounds from which writers of guidebooks
seem to have been drawn.[57] He began life as a liveried
footman in domestic service and took to writing plays
and poetry. His first poem, *Servitude*, on the master/
servant relationship, came out in 1729 and in 1732 he
published by subscription *A Muse in Livery, or, The
Footman's Miscellany*. Dodsley was taken up by Defoe
and later Pope. The latter helped him get his play *The
Toy Shop* put on at Covent Garden in 1735. The
venture was such a success that with the proceeds
Dodsley set up as a bookseller in the same year, in
partnership with his brother James. He became a
hugely important and prolific publisher and purchased
a house in Richmond, where he commissioned a
garden from the designer and theorist Joseph Spence
in 1753.[58] He was one of the six booksellers who commissioned Dr Johnson to produce his *Dictionary of the
English Language* and was even credited by Johnson as
having given him the idea for the work. In 1759 he
handed over the running of the business to his brother
in order to concentrate on his own writing, including
London and its Environs, which he appears to have
compiled himself.[59]

   Dodsley's was the first account in which the balance
shifted from a concentration on contemporary attractions, as with *London in Miniature*, to a more self-
conscious presentation in which historical and artistic
associations took precedence. He stated that although
the environs 'contain many of the most remarkable
seats and places in the kingdom, [they] have never
before been included in any account of that metropolis'.[60] This was an exaggerated boast, but Dodsley could
claim to be the first to cover the adjacent areas in

70

greater depth. For example, his was the first London guide to feature in any detail the country seats that had featured so prominently on maps of the region. For some of these he was able to procure descriptions of the properties and lists of their paintings and contents, which the Preface stated 'have greatly enriched and added a value to our work; and being entirely new, cannot but be acceptable to the public'. Royal residences were another staple ingredient in the touristic conception of London, and Dodsley also provided information about them wherever possible. He included a detailed plan of Windsor Castle 'shewing alphabetically at one View the several Appartments in the Royal Palace as shown to the Publick' to aid their appreciation and understanding of the visiting experience (fig. 65). *London and its Environs Described* was pioneering in its use of integrated visual imagery by Samuel Wale, the illustrator of the volume. His plate of Windsor Castle shows it as seen from the meadows below as a scenographic element in a tourisitic landscape dominated by leisured visitors (fig. 66). Wale therefore depicts this royal residence primarily as an object of tourist consumption reflected back to its intended audience through the medium of the guide.

Although the presentation of the environs from the mid-century was increasingly as a rural arcadia, drawing on classical notions of the pastoral landscape, in guidebooks such as Dodsley's these idealized images were still firmly situated within contemporary consumerist society. Visiting villas and their gardens, for example, was a firmly established practice by this date, the most popular being Chiswick, Kenwood, Alexander Pope's villa, Marble Hill and Strawberry Hill – the last three all at Twickenham. At Strawberry Hill Horace Walpole was forced to impose increasingly strict procedures to moderate the flow of visitors to his Gothic villa, whom he termed 'the plague'.[61] These began with the production of a written note; then from 1774 dated printed tickets were produced, and finally a printed page of rules for admittance was issued in 1784. These were necessary, they state, 'as the villa is situated so near to London and in so populous a neighbourhood'.[62] In order to aid such visitors Dodsley's book included two maps, a feature that became standard from this date. One of the maps was of the central area, and the other showed 'The Environs or Countries Twenty Miles Round London' by Thomas Kitchen (see fig. 9). These

maps could be used to locate the seats, and other attractions, described in the text.

The move towards a more polite form of domestic tourism initiated by Dodsley was escalated in subsequent works such as the anonymous *The Ambulator: Or, the Stranger's Companion in a Tour Round London, within the Circuit of Twenty-five Miles Describing Whatever Is Remarkable, either for Grandeur, Elegancy, Use, or Curiosity; and comprehending Catalogues of the Pictures by Eminent Artists*, which went through thirteen editions between 1774 and 1820. This was the first work in which the relation between the outskirts and the centre is completely reversed. In *The Ambulator* the 'prefix' on London, Westminster and Southwark takes up a mere twenty-seven pages while the 'Tour' of the outskirts takes up 219 pages in an A–Z gazetteer format. As the author or authors wrote: 'As the principal design of this Work is to serve as a companion ... in excursions into the country round London ... we shall mention the principal remaining objects in the Metropolis in a very cursory way.'[63] In keeping with its title the book was intended to be taken on visits and, unlike Dodsley's six-volume account, the author states that they were determined 'not to exceed the limits of a pocket-volume'.[64] It was presumably for this reason that illustrations were omitted from the first edition in 1774, although subsequent editions did include them as the series inexorably expanded in scope and ambition.

The Preface to *The Ambulator* established the purpose and tone of the text and is worth quoting at length:

No part of the kingdom, perhaps, can present more attractive scenes than the environs of London; in which the man of leisure may find amusement, and the man of business the most agreeable relaxation. With respect, indeed, to rural scenery, the country described in the following Tour, does not exhibit Nature in her more sublime and stupendous views; it presents no savage mountains crowned with perennial snows, no vast extent of uncultivated wilds, no tremendous cataracts, no wonderful expanse of waters. But rural elegance and rural beauty here appear in their most fascinating forms. Royal palaces, magnificent seats, and elegant villas interspersed, afford inexhaustible gratifications for curiosity; in some, the finest collections of paintings, inestimable

65 'A Plan of Windsor Castle
shewing alphabetically at one View
the several Appartments in the Royal
Palace as shewn to ye Publick with
sundry other Appartments belonging
to the Officers of State &c. &c.,
1760', from Dodsley, *London and its
Environs Described*, 1761, British
Library.

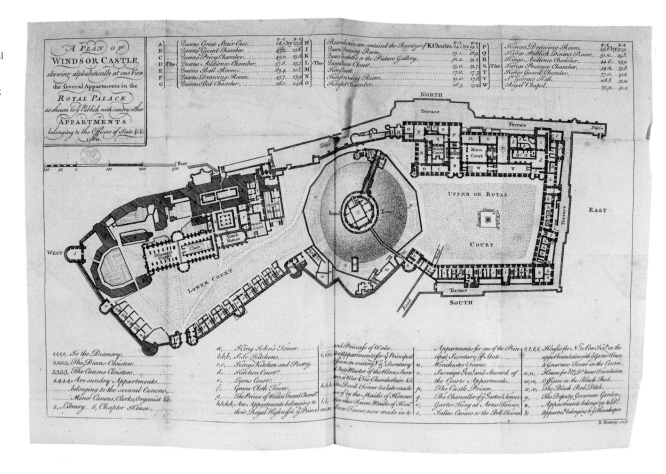

66 'Windsor Castle', from Dodsley,
London and its Environs Described,
1761, British Library.

antiques, venerable decorations of ancient splendour, or all the exquisite embellishments of modern art. Extensive prospects charm the eye with undescribable variety: the landscape, less extensive, invites the pensive mind to contemplation; or the creative powers of Art exhibit an Elysium, where Nature once appeared in her rudest state.[65]

The presentation of the environs as a nationally important landscape was in place from the early eighteenth century. What is new here is the taste for the Burkean 'sublime' which was creating new tourist attractions in the hitherto neglected mountainous and wild areas of Britain. Wales, Scotland and the Lake District became the focus for nature and art lovers for the first time in search of the type of rugged scenery which had hitherto only been appreciated in the Alps.[66] The London environs, by contrast, offered a more sedate environment in which the man-made was as seductive as the natural in constituting 'beauty': beauty being the antithesis of sublimity according to Burke.[67] These themes are developed more fully in the next chapter, but it is worth noting that it is the particular combination of landscape, architecture and art that were thought to comprise the unique attraction of the Home Counties in this late eighteenth-century guide.

The Ambulator combined the concise format of *London in Miniature* with the increased emphasis on the artistic and the genteel of Dodsley. There is a more blatant appeal to the aspirational element among its readers than in Dodsely's connoisseurial rhetoric. The Preface stated: 'To assist the inhabitants of the Metropolis, or its occasional visitors, in the choice of their excursions, is a principal object of this publication; to be an entertaining companion in these excursions is another.' *The Ambulator* positioned itself as an authoritative and indeed definitive guide, noting: 'Places that appear in the Map, without being noticed in the Tour, are supposed not to contain any thing very remarkable.' The middle-class audience for the work is explicitly addressed when the author suggests that the guide will also aid their participation in polite society: 'Where any place has been distinguished by some memorable circumstance, he has not forgotten how much the incidental recollections of it may improve the fources [*sic*] of conversation'. A list of the nobility and gentry – 'The present Proprietors or Occupiers of the

Seats mentioned in this Tour' – was appended to aid conversation, no doubt, for those not personally acquainted with dukes and baronets. The Preface to the fourth edition of 1792 announced that many of the entries had been rewritten, with 100 new entries included and 200 plus 'more seats and villas noticed' than in previous editions. 'New catalogues of the pictures in the best collections have likewise been obtained.' This is perhaps the closest we come to a modern guidebook series to the environs, one which was continually updated and reissued. Previous guides had been released in new editions, with or without the same title depending on the degree of plagiarism involved, but *The Ambulator* was the first to establish what we would now term a brand. In the late eighteenth and early nineteenth centuries, as guidebooks increasingly came to compete with the more authoritative histories, they had to stake their claims to comprehensiveness, portability and up-to-dateness as their principal selling points.

THE NEW HISTORIES: PENNANT, LYSONS AND HUNTER

In the late eighteenth century, alongside the greater aesthetic appreciation of the environs, a parallel and related interest in local history and archaeology developed. With the creation of vast new suburbs in the outer areas, the issue of the recording of historic artefacts before they were lost in a tide of development became a matter of pressing concern. Numerous individual parish histories began to be produced – such as the Chelsea bookseller Thomas Faulkener's accounts of Chelsea (1810) and Fulham (1813) and the lawyer William Robinson's of Tottenham (1818), Edmonton (1819) and Stoke Newington (1820). Antiquarians, as well as commercial publishers, began to discover that the newer suburbs had their own narratives and identity. In this last section of the chapter we move away from guidebooks per se to look at three important histories produced at the turn of the century which bring together many of the strands of eighteenth-century urban writing we have considered so far as well as introducing some new ones.

The first publication that must be mentioned is Thomas Pennant's *Some Account of London* (1791), a book which spans the genres of urban guides and antiquarian histories.[68] Pennant (1726–1798) was best known as a natural history writer, and his metropolitan guide was inspired, he wrote, by his 'numberless walks taken in and about our capital'. Pennant's remarks in the 'Advertisement' suggest the artful arbitrariness typical of the ambulatory tradition; he claimed that the work's irregularities sprang from the materials being collected 'according to the course of the walk of the day'.[69] He was also keen to have 'condensed into it all I could' while at the same time keeping its price and size down to 'a quarto volume' so that it should not become 'a guinea book'.[70] Pennant's format and lively polemical style tended more to the guide-book approach, and he did discuss contemporary buildings and developments at times in his account. He wrote of St George's Fields, Southwark, as being 'the wonder of foreigners approaching . . . our capital, through avenues of lamps, of magnificent breadth', while next door Lambeth was summarily dismissed as having 'very little remarkable in it'.[71] But his subject matter and interests were for the most part antiquarian, and in his rambles around different neighbourhoods he tended to focus on when they were first built rather than their current state. Devonshire Square, for example, was of interest not as an unusual example of a classical City square but as the site of Old Devonshire House.[72] Like many urban narratives Pennant's was structured around individual buildings – churches, houses, palaces, hospitals and inns – but what he called 'heroic and benevolent characters' also featured prominently.[73] In focusing on individual people Pennant may have been inspired by the Reverend James Granger's *Biographical History of England* (1769), a very popular volume which was highly influential for other reasons as well. Granger's work inspired the practice of extra-illustration which was to become a central feature of subsequent metropolitan imaging. Extra-illustration was a fashion for pasting additional material into volumes in a similar way to an album. As Bernard Adams writes: 'Thus was born the hobby of "grangerizing", a clipping, matching and pasting operation which must have helped many a Regency family circle to pass winter evenings.'[74] Pennant's early editions contained relatively few illustrations – seventeen mostly etched by John Carter in the 1791 volume – but the tome quickly became adopted by the grangerizers,

and later editions were produced with blank pages where extra material could be inserted. This in turn prompted the publication of topographical prints produced 'with an eye to the needs of such collectors who continually sought fresh engraving to swell the corpulence of their ever expanding interleaved sets'.[75] J. T. Smith, a printmaker who will be discussed in the following chapter, published several sets of prints for this purpose, beginning with *Antiquities of London* (1791) followed by *Ancient Topography of London* (1810), which included individual page references from Pennant for ease of matching the prints to the text. One of Smith's clients was William Crowle, whose magnificent fifteen-volume extra-illustrated set of Pennant now resides in the British Museum, a monument to the print mania of the period.

The most authoritative publication on the London region of the late eighteenth century was by the Reverend Daniel Lysons, *The Environs of London, Being an Historical Account of the Towns, Villages and Hamlets, within Twelve Miles of that Capital with Biographical Anecdotes* (1792–6). Lysons (1762–1834) was a noted antiquarian who, along with his brother Samuel, went on to produce many county histories in their *Magna Britannia* series (1806–22). At the time he started writing the London volumes he was chaplain to Horace Walpole, to whom the work is dedicated. The brothers were renowned for their meticulous research and stamina in fieldwork. Walpole wrote of their strong legs while another contemporary recorded that Daniel 'spent seven hours up to his knees in water in the vaults of Stepney Church copying epitaphs'.[76] Lysons's *magnum opus* was the first scholarly historical work on the environs, following on from recent county histories such as Philip Morant's *The History and Antiquities of the County of Essex* (1762–8). He wrote in the 'Advertisement' to the first volume: 'Whilst a taste for local history so generally prevails, it is somewhat singular that the counties adjacent to London should not have had their due share of illustration.' The persistence and popularity of the historical tradition within metropolitan literature show how central an appreciation of the past was to creating an identity and sense of place, not just for the county gentry, but for the urban and suburban middle classes as well.[77] There were originally four volumes covering the counties of Surrey, Middlesex, Hertfordshire, Essex and Kent within twelve miles of London. A further volume on those parts of Middlesex outside the twelve-mile limit was produced in 1800, while in 1811 a *Supplement* to the first edition appeared, which updated the previous entries in relation to new social and environmental developments.

'Lysons', as the work became known eponymously, combined picturesque nostalgia with the antiquarian diligence of a Stow. Its folio size alone indicated its serious historical intent in comparison to the lightweight pocket-book guides and maps. His careful acknowledgement of sources with quotation marks and footnotes also immediately distinguished him from the more populist touristic accounts. Illustrations, however, were central to Lysons's antiquarian method, and the later editions which allowed space for extra-illustration became hugely popular. *The Environs of London* was the first attempt to establish a serious historical pedagogy for the Home Counties, returning to a parish-based account covering both natural and human history. In the 'Advertisement' for the 1800 additional volume, in answer to critics of the previous volumes, he outlined his methodology more explicitly. He thanked the landed gentry and clergy for their help, stressing their importance in providing 'information as none but a resident inhabitant could have supplied'.[78] He asserted his authorship of the volumes and his active role in researching and interpreting such information, by implied contrast to those demotic guides that were primarily compilations of the work of others. He also took the side of Richard Gough, Director of the Society of Antiquaries 1771–91, who had argued for the maintenance of antiquarian scholarship in a debate against some who thought they should modernize and offer more accessible history.[79] Lysons wrote: 'He had another object in view than merely to furnish an entertaining narrative, and intended that his work should answer the same ends of useful reference as County Histories.'[80] Lysons in fact, besides the county approach, was also indebted to the urban history tradition of Stow through his incorporation of contemporary as well as historical material. Lysons showed that the environs were an entity worthy of a serious history in their own right and not just an anonymous hinterland. At the same time he provided the best guide to the London suburbs in the late eighteenth and early nineteenth centuries just as they were beginning to

undergo a period of substantial expansion. We will return to his account when we consider that period in Chapters 6 and 7.

In 1811 Lysons's publisher, John Stockdale, a prolific producer of urban histories including ones of Manchester and Liverpool, brought out a populist successor to Lysons's great work at a cost of £4 4s. to subscribers and £5 5s. to non-subscribers. This was *The History of London and its Environs . . . within Twenty-five Miles of London* by the Reverend Henry Hunter (1741–1802), which reduced Lysons's final six volumes to a mere two and provided, if not quite a pocket-book, a more accessible narrative history of the metropolitan region. Hunter was a Church of Scotland minister for the congregation at London Wall and well known as a translator of French and German texts, as well as the author of the seven-volume *Sacred Biography*. His history of the environs has been subject to much criticism as purely a plagiarized version of Lysons. The *Gentleman's Magazine* wrote that he had 'no talents or research for a work of this description'.[81] However, if the bulk of the text draws on Lysons, this is to miss some of the novel features of the overall concept and the introductory chapters, such as those on agriculture. The diagram that accompanied the 'Proposals' for the book's publication graphically exemplifies how Lysons's sprawling work has been distilled to a containable and comprehensible format, represented in a novel rectangular format (fig. 67). The 'Proposals' shed an interesting light on the subscription process, informing readers:

No money will be taken in Advance, nor will any Subscriber be desired to take the work unless it fully answers his expectation. Should any Gentlemen be inclined to contribute towards the Expence of engraving any particular Portrait, View of his Seat, Monument, Church &c. it will be acknowledged in the Work. Any Information relative to the History or Situation of Gentlemen's Seats, Towns, Villages, &c. within the Compass of Twenty Miles Round the Metropolis will be esteemed a Favor. At the same Time, should there appear any particular Object worthy of Notice, though at a Short Distance beyond our limits, it will readily find a place.[82]

An 'Advertisement' for undertaking just such views of gentlemen's seats demonstrates perfectly the intersec-

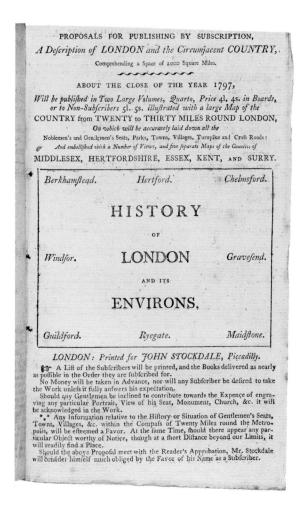

PROPOSALS FOR PUBLISHING BY SUBSCRIPTION,

A Description of LONDON and the Circumjacent COUNTRY,

Comprehending a Space of 2000 Square Miles.

ABOUT THE CLOSE OF THE YEAR 1797,

Will be published in Two Large Volumes, Quarto, Price 4l. 4s. in Boards, or to Non-Subscribers 5l. 5s. illustrated with a large Map of the
COUNTRY from TWENTY to THIRTY MILES ROUND LONDON,
On which will be accurately laid down all the
Noblemen's and Gentlemen's Seats, Parks, Towns, Villages, Turnpike and Cross Roads:
And embellished with a Number of Views, and five separate Maps of the Counties of
MIDDLESEX, HERTFORDSHIRE, ESSEX, KENT, AND SURRY.

Berkhamstead.	*Hertford.*	*Chelmsford.*
	HISTORY	
	OF	
Windsor.	LONDON	*Gravesend.*
	AND ITS	
	ENVIRONS.	
Guildford.	*Ryegate.*	*Maidstone.*

LONDON: Printed for *JOHN STOCKDALE*, Piccadilly.

☞ A List of the Subscribers will be printed, and the Books delivered as nearly as possible in the Order they are subscribed for.
No Money will be taken in Advance, nor will any Subscriber be desired to take the Work unless it fully answers his expectation.
Should any Gentlemen be inclined to contribute towards the Expence of engraving any particular Portrait, View of his Seat, Monument, Church, &c. it will be acknowledged in the Work.
• Any Information relative to the History or Situation of Gentlemen's Seats, Towns, Villages, &c. within the Compass of Twenty miles round the Metropolis, will be esteemed a Favor. At the same Time, should there appear any particular Object worthy of Notice, though at a short Distance beyond our Limits, it will readily find a Place.
Should the above Proposal meet with the Reader's Approbation, Mr. Stockdale will consider himself much obliged by the Favor of his Name as a Subscriber.

metropolis, and takes its general character from that connection.'[85] Hunter begins with general accounts of each county, and these unusually focus primarily on the geology and agriculture of the region, rather than on artistic or recreational pursuits as the previous generation of writers had done. In this Hunter was reflecting the output of the newly formed Boards of Agriculture, whose reports on the various counties appeared from the 1790s onwards, the first two being on Middlesex in 1793 and Kent in 1796.[86] Hunter's novel approach to defining the agriculture of the region in terms of a series of concentric belts has already been discussed in Chapter 1, and this is the most innovative part of his account. He also included a section on the Thames, the New River and the new canals in his Introduction, emphasizing the centrality of natural features, as Maitland had done, to the region's viability and prosperity.

Hunter's text brings together the increasing knowledge of the past, derived from Lysons and the new parish histories, with the accessible formats pioneered by guidebooks and gazetteers. This was to be the approach that dominated for the rest of the nineteenth century as publishers and authors sought to extend the formula in ever new directions. One very popular genre was the combined map and tour exemplified by publications such as David Hughson's *Walks Through London* (1817). Walks for the young were introduced by the prolific children's author Priscilla Wakefield with her *Perambulations in London and its Environs ... Designed for Young Persons* (1809) and *A Visit to Uncle William in Town: Containing a Description of the Most Remarkable Buildings and Curiosities in the British Metropolis* (1824), published by John Harris in his 'Juvenile Library'. Dictionaries and handbooks also became common, such as James Elmes, *A Topographical Dictionary of London and its Environs* (1831). This was a follow-up to his hugely successful *Metropolitan Improvements* (1827–30), which is discussed in Chapter 7. These innovative formats are indicative of the vitality and flexibility of the guidebook genre, whereas the more traditional histories of London struggled to break out of the Stow mould and find a new identity. Peter Clark writes: 'During the Georgian period, however, one has a growing sense that the old format was on its last legs, unable to cope with the scale and complexity of the capital.'[87] Even as early as 1720

tion of the new commercialism with the longer-established tradition of the country house prospect in the London print trade (see fig. 69).

However, there was no getting away from the fact that Hunter's account was derived almost exclusively from Lysons.[83] Indeed, so heavily did Hunter draw on his predecessor that he took great pains to point out those few instances where he thought that Lysons had made an error.[84] In structuring the text Hunter maintained Lysons's primary organization by county, but broke down the individual parishes into the much more manageable format of alphabetical entries. He included Hertfordshire as well as the familiar four counties contiguous with the centre, in line with most maps of the period. In Hunter's text the centre and periphery are presented as a mutually self-sustaining regional entity. As he wrote of Middlesex: 'A small district, containing within itself a metropolis of immense magnitude, must necessarily be principally devoted to the wants and conveniences of that

Strype struggled to fit the diversity of contemporary London into the format that he had inherited from Stow.[88] Guidebooks, free from the obligations of antiquarianism, were able to fill the gap, eschewing comprehensive coverage and increasingly breaking the metropolis down into manageable parts, of which the suburbs – where more and more of the population was located – was one of the most significant. By the 1820s the environs had become well-charted territory in metropolitan topographical literature. They had lost the edge quality evident in seventeenth- and early eighteenth-century works and become transformed first into an artistic landscape and then into a safe suburban environment. This history of representation will be explored further in our next paper landscape: printed visual images of the environs.

3

PICTURING THE LANDSCAPES OF LONDON

The prospects which in Italy pleased me most, were that of Rome, and the Mediterranean from the mountains of Viterbo; of Rome at forty, and the Mediterranean at fifty miles distance from it; and that of the Campagne of Rome from Tivoli and Frescati. . . . But from an hill which I passed in my late journey into Sussex, I had a prospect more extensive than any of these, and which surpassed them at once in rural charms, in pomp, and in magnificence. . . . I saw a sight that would transport a stoic; a sight that looked like an inchantment and vision. Beneath us lay open to our view all the wilds of Surry and Sussex, and a great part of that of Kent, admirably diversified in every part of them with woods, and fields of corn and pastures, every where adorned with stately rows of trees. . . . This beautiful vale is . . . terminated to the south by the majestic range of the southern hills, and the sea: and it is no easy matter to decide whether these hills . . . seem more aweful and venerable, or the delicious vale between you and them more inviting. . . . And that which above all makes it a noble and wonderful prospect, is, that . . . at the same time as you behold to the south, the most delicious rural prospect in the world; at that very time, by a little turn of your head towards the north, you look full over Box Hill, and see the country beyond it, between that and London; and over the very stomacher of it, see St. Paul's at twenty-five miles distance, and London beneath it, and Highgate and Hampstead beyond it.

Mr Dennis, Letters, on the view from Leith Hill, in Robert Dodsley, *London and its Environs Described*, 1761

This chapter is about how the London countryside was depicted, viewed and appreciated over the course of the long eighteenth century. It takes printed images of the environs as its main focus for discussion, but it also draws on a little-studied strand of metropolitan topographical literature, especially poetry, to consider how the despised outparts became an internationally recognized and indeed celebrated landscape. We will begin by outlining the significance of the London print trade and its output, much of it produced in sets or in bound publications such as would have been affordable by those of middling incomes and above. The distinction between book illustration, prints and maps is a somewhat artificial one in this period. The

current chapter, therefore, carries on from the previous two in considering aspects of print production but focuses specifically on a new trade in visual images produced in greater numbers and quality than ever before. Together this vast printed output formed a critical part of the 'bourgeois public sphere', as Habermas defined it, in which polite society participated in the interchange of knowledge and ideas to create a new metropolitan public culture.[1] Print activity was centred on London and took both the inner city and its surrounding landscapes as one of its major subjects for audiences at home and abroad. The topic of the visual representations of the environs is a vast and hugely under-researched one, with the notable exception of Bernard Adams's *London Illustrated 1604–1851*, which provides an indispensible catalogue of topographical books and their plates.[2] Research to date has tended to focus on painted depictions of the metropolis, which I will not touch on here, and on individual areas or artists.[3] However, as Julius Bryant has pointed out: 'The relative anonymity of illustrative engravings, acquired for their subject matter rather than as the work of a particular artist, makes them a potentially more direct mirror of their market's interests.'[4] In the light of a lack of synthetic accounts, this chapter can hope to do no more than attempt to outline some of the major themes among a plethora of printed images and to establish the novelty of the aesthetic approach that underlay them. Key figures will be identified at different points across the course of the long eighteenth century to illustrate shifts in the treatment of the environs ranging from Wenceslaus Hollar's wholesome early images, through the establishment of an English topographical tradition by pioneers such as J. C. B. Chatelaine, and on to a self-consciously picturesque approach by artists including Joseph Farington and J. T. Smith at the turn of the nineteenth century.

The pioneering commercial enterprises of the London printmakers have been outlined in compelling detail by Louise Lippincott in her study of the print-seller Arthur Pond, and by Timothy Clayton in his book *The English Print 1688–1802*.[5] They show that there was a well-established and substantial market for prints from the early eighteenth century among both the gentry and the middle classes. Clayton discusses the problems of assessing the social classification of prints, and concludes that the wealthier middling groups brought 'original' prints while the bulk of the middle class bought smaller and cruder versions of the same. There were also cheaper woodcuts available for those on even more limited budgets.[6] Arthur Pond counted a substantial group of City merchants and government office-holders among his regular customers, to whom he acted as a mentor and advisor for their print purchases.[7] As with maps and books, some prints were published by subscription, and this was particularly effective where there might be a local or personal interest, as in topographical views. A print by Henry Winstanley (1644–1703), an engineer, eccentric and engraver, shows a fascinating attempt to enter this market by offering individual house prospects (fig. 69). One of his other enterprises was the design for the Eddystone Rock lighthouse off Plymouth.[8] As far as is known no one took up Winstanley's offer, but his 'Advertisement' graphically illustrates the new commercial market within which topographical views were both produced and consumed.

From the beginning of our period to the 1740s, French and foreign-trained artists dominated the London print trade, and large numbers of Continental prints were imported.[9] There was very little print production in the provinces before the mid-century, and the English market was essentially the London one.[10] Topography was arguably the most dynamic area of printmaking in the first quarter of the eighteenth century as part of the rhetoric of national achievement, allied to a growing recognition of the distinctive natural beauty and history of England from the 1740s. Peter Clark's analysis of the prints of the Guildhall Library and Art Gallery in the Collage database demonstrates the increasing representation of the suburbs and London periphery against those of the City, Westminster and Southwark. According to his figures, in 1640–60 84.7 per cent of topographical images were of the central areas and 3.6 per cent of the outer areas (plus 11.7 per cent panoramas – statistically insignificant for later periods); in 1700–20 it was 86.8 per cent and 13.2 per cent respectively; in 1760–80 65.4 per cent and 34.6 per cent; while by 1820–30 the balance was 61.5 per cent and 38.5 per cent.[11] He concludes: 'Overall, the pattern of visual representation provided by the Collage images illustrates a metropolitan picture of increasing fragmentation, localisation and commercialisation.'[12] Topographical prints, including those of the London area, sold in all markets – provincial, colonial and overseas – and were one of the most successful genres of prolific publishers such as the Overtons and the Bowleses.[13] The British born and trained painter and printseller John Smibert (1688–1751), for example, who emigrated to America, reported from Boston to Pond: 'Ye View from Greenwich & Antiquities by P. Panini please more here than ye others and I hope a number of them will sell.'[14] Many prints, such as those by John Rocque of Chiswick House and its grounds (1736), included a parallel French text for foreigners, a familiar technique from maps and guide-books. By the end of the period London dominated

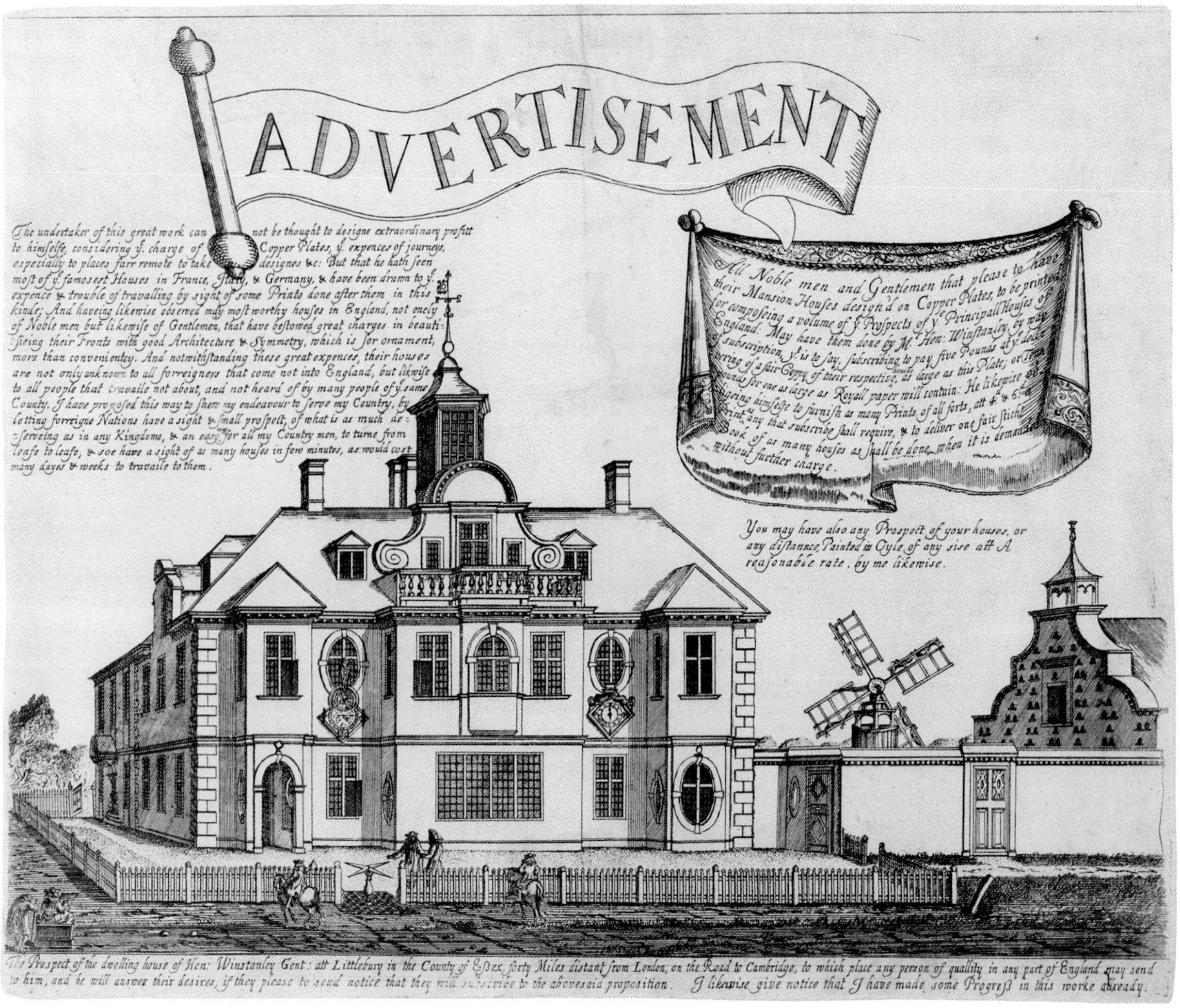

69 Henry Winstanley, *Advertisement with a View of his Own House at Littlebury, Essex*, 1670s, etching, British Museum.

The advertisement gives Winstanley's proposals: 'All noble men and gentlemen that please to have their mansion houses design'd on copper plates, to be printed for composeing a volume of the prospects of the principall houses of England, may have them done by Mr Hen. Winstanley by way of subscription, that is to say, subscribing to pay five pounds at the delivering of a fair coppy of their respective houses as large as this plate; or ten pounds for one as large as royall paper will contain. He likewise obligeing himselfe to furnish as many prints of all sorts, att 4d and 6d a print as any that subscribe shall require, & to deliver one fair sticht book of as many houses as shall be done, when it is demanded without further charge.'

His intentions are explained on the left: 'The undertaker of this great work can not be thought to designe extraordinary profitt to himselfe, considering the charge of copper plates, the expenses of journeys, especially to places farr remote to take designes &c. But that he hath seen most of the famosest houses in France, Italy & Germany & have been drawn to the expence & trouble of travalling by sight some of prints done after them in this kinde. And haveing likewise observed many most worthy houses in England, not onely of noble men but likewise of gentlemen, that have bestowed great charges in beautifieing their fronts with good architecture & symmetry, which is for ornament more than convenientcy. And notwithstanding these great expences, their houses are not only unknown to all forreigners that come not into England, but likewise to all people that travaile not about, and not heard of by many people of the same county. I have proposed this way to shew my endeavour to serve my country, by letting forreigne nations have a sight & small prospect of what is as much deserveing as in any Kingdom, & an easy way for all my country men to turne from leafe to leafe, & soe have a sight of as many houses in few minutes as would cost many dayes & weeks to travaile to them.'

Along the bottom is: 'The prospect of the dwelling house of Hen. Winstanley Gent. att Littlebury in the County of Essex, forty miles distant from London on the road to Cambridge, to which place any person of quallity in any part of England may send to him, and he will answer their desires, if they please to send notice that they will subscribe to the abovesaid proposition. I likewise give notice that I have made some progress in this worke allready.' Another smaller text reads: 'You may have also any prospect of your houses, or any distance, painted in oyle of any sise att a reasonable rate by me likewise.' (Text from Griffiths, 1998, cat. 171.)

70 Wenceslaus Hollar, 'By Islington', from *Views near London*, 1665, etching, British Museum.

the European and world market in prints, while at the same time many publishers and printsellers had become established in the provinces.[15]

HOLLAR AND EARLY VIEWS

Wenceslaus Hollar was not only the most important surveyor of mid-seventeenth-century London, he was also one of its most important artists.[16] He most clearly exemplifies the intersection between the map-survey tradition and the topographical print tradition, but he was also one of first to step down from the lofty vantage point of the panorama to draw his immediate surroundings.[17] He portrayed London's outer landscapes as places of lonely retreats and solitary contem-

plation in his six *Views of London* (1665), all taken near the waterhouse on the New River at Islington (fig. 70). Hollar shows the area just before it was developed at the end of the seventeenth century into an urban playground of spas and pleasure gardens. This transformation and its impact on the image of the area will be discussed more fully in the following chapter. The Hollar tradition of representations of Islington as a healthy open space for family outings and sporting activities, particularly fishing and walking, continued through the eighteenth century. Bernard Lens's views of the area around the New River Head of 1730–31 perpetuate Hollar's air of rural tranquillity while at the same time introducing a far more populated landscape in terms of both people and buildings (see fig. 91). Lens (1682–1740) was one of a family of Flemish artists who settled in London and produced topographical works while also active as a well-known miniaturist and drawing master.[18]

The aerial vantage point of early maps and surveys left another – and perhaps more important – legacy in contributing towards the appreciation of the city in its landscape. The panoramic tradition had an impact on both how the metropolis was viewed as a totality and what were deemed the significant landscape features of the capital. The bird's-eye view was abandoned for maps and map-views from the early eighteenth century as the city expanded and panoramic views became increasingly difficult to contemplate, as Peter Clark's Guildhall study confirms.[19] Nevertheless, the aerial viewpoint continued to provide an important perspective for studies on a smaller scale, until at least the 1730s. A good example of the genre is *London Described* (1731) published by John Bowles, which consisted of engravings by Sutton Nicholls, particularly of the London squares, as well as notable buildings in the centre.[20] Nicholls's prints gave a detailed account of the new domestic environment of the centre but care-

fully situated it within the context of the broader landscape, thus establishing a rapport between outer and inner open areas. The use of the distinctive and aptly named swallow-tailed banderole, shown in the print of Soho Square and pioneered in Bowles's *British Views* (1723–4), provides a further echo of the avian theme (fig. 71). Bird's-eye views continued to be used in many London histories well into the eighteenth century. The 1754 edition of Strype's updating of Stow's *Survey*, for example, was illustrated with a large number of reproductions of Nicholls's engravings from *London Described*.[21] In this way what were by then historic views of the city were reanimated and given new life as quasi-documentary artefacts.

The interest in trying to depict the relationship between periphery and centre led to the creation of scopic corridors connecting different parts of London.[22] The main viewing points around the capital consisted of hill-top views. The principal ones were Greenwich Park and Shooters Hill in the south-east; from along the northern ridge, particularly at Highgate and Hampstead; and finally from Richmond Hill across the

71 Sutton Nicholls, *Sohoe or Kings Square*, 1754, etching, British Museum.

The alternative title of Kings Square (built 1677 onwards) derives from the statue of Charles II in the middle of the railed garden. In the plate this centrepiece is seemingly aligned along the main axis of Charles Street with a windmill, underneath the Hampstead ridge.

Thames landscape of the south-west (see figs 22 and 130). These three effectively formed a triangulated skyscape from which to view not only the centre below but also each other and the broader countryside beyond. Subsidiary views were to be found all along the Thames and from smaller eminences such as Denmark Hill to the south (see fig. 145).

WAYS OF VIEWING

> Who is there who would not chuse with me
> To read his Poem than the Forest see?

> Edward Howard, *Greenwich-Park* (1728) on
> Alexander Pope's *Windsor Forest* (1713)

Before we turn to the key figures in the development of topographical prints of London in the eighteenth century, we need first to consider some ideas underpinning a new conception of landscape in the early eighteenth century. The development of what is now known as the English picturesque landscape tradition is a well-known story which we do not need to rehearse here.[23] It is sufficient to note that from the 1720s onwards a new conception of landscape developed, based on an appreciation of natural scenery best summed up in Pope's famous lines from *An Epistle to Lord Burlington* (1731):

> In all, let *Nature* never be forgot.
> Consult the *Genius* of the *Place* in all,
>
> .   .   .   .   .   .
>
> Now breaks, or now directs, th' intending Lines;
> *Paints* as you plant, as you work, *Designs*.

However, as Pope demonstrates, the *genius loci* was of a strongly aestheticized nature influenced by particular pictorial references (notably those of Claude Lorrain and Salvator Rosa), and this led to a conflation between natural landscape and its representation in the eighteenth century. The passion for gardening by the elite became a more widely shared interest in landscape as an artistic genre, spread through the medium of print.[24] What is of particular interest in relation to London's countryside is how the discourse of 'the natural' was applied in the most intensively farmed and inhabited region of the country. The metropolitan environs became famous as one of the paradigmatic landscapes

of the early picturesque movement in their own right, independent of the many famous individual landscape gardens – such as Chiswick, Pope's own garden at Twickenham and Painshill in Surrey – that the outskirts contained.

In 1739 the architectural writer and theorist Robert Morris (1703–1754) published *An Essay Upon Harmony: As It Relates Chiefly to Situation and Building*. The essay was published anonymously and was subsequently mistakenly attributed to John Gwynn, author of the considerably later *London and Westminster Improved* (1766), who features prominently throughout this book.[25] Morris's writings are an interesting, if ultimately doomed, attempt to apply Shaftesburian morality to the competitive arena of building practice. In the *Essay Upon Harmony* he focuses on the relationship between architecture and landscape using Alexander Pope's notion of the coming together of nature and art in the genius of design; indeed, he cites both Shaftesbury and Pope at the beginning of the *Essay*. Morris, like Pope, had lived in Twickenham, although by 1740 he had moved to Hyde Park Street on the Grosvenor Estate.[26] Morris's approach, as Eileen Harris points out, is essentially pictorial not proportional, and his main interest in *An Essay Upon Harmony* is the harmony between the building and its situation.[27] For Morris, therefore, topography and the specifics of locality were paramount, echoing Pope's insistence on respecting the *genius loci*. This interest in topography and the combination of architecture and landscape was to be critical in the new appreciation of the landscapes of the environs. What Morris did in effect was to extend the appreciation of landscape gardens with their attendant buildings, by now well established, to the wider public landscape. In his *Essay* the landscapes that he chose to illustrate this harmony of the natural and man-made were all metropolitan: Shooters Hill in Blackheath, Richmond Hill and Windsor. He wrote: 'I have chosen to mention those three remarkable Places of Situation; because, as they are more beautiful, are more generally known, and being situate so near the Metropolis of the Kingdom.'[28] As John Barrell has pointed out, panoramic views were typically seen as public and idealized: 'the anologue of the social and the universal, which is surveyed, organised and understood by disinterested public men'.[29] In selecting specifically London prospects Morris was following in a tradition of political

84

topographical poetry established by the Royalist poet Sir John Denham in his *Cooper's Hill* (1642), in which he surveyed London from the Surrey hills at Egham. Denham chose a site which encompassed many important historical locations: Windsor Castle, Runnymede (where Magna Carta was signed), a ruined abbey (symbol of the Reformation), and linking them all the River Thames. Denham created the metaphor of the hill-top as a vantage point from which to survey the political and moral pulse of the nation, especially the progress of liberty within the context of a constitutional monarchy. The trope was continued by Alexander Pope in his poem *Windsor Forest*, in which he figured the Thames as both an imperial waterway and a sylvan refuge. Matthew Craske writes: ' "Cooper's Hill" was a prime influence upon the tendency to equate the viewing of Thames-side England with taking a dose of enlightening historical medicine.'[30]

Morris began his account of his three London landscapes by asserting their national significance as well as asserting their right to equality with foreign examples: 'As we can claim a Share of equal Propriety and Graces, in several Villa's and Seats in our own Country: It were needless to trace foreign Climates for Example.'[31] He then went on to outline the significance of his three chosen examples, which exhibited the characteristics of three particular types of situation: the grand, the charming and the remote:

> Prospects of Extent have various Excellencies, which differently affect us; *Shooters* Hill, beyond *Black Heath*, has the noble, the grand, and magnificent, the populous, and busy Prospect: The Images are moving, or great, the River Northward, with so many Vessels of Magnitude, which almost every Tide displays; the great City, and Town and Buildings, Westward; The Vale of *Essex* and contiguous country have all a Sameness of Grandeur, the ideas impressed on us are great and singular: Trade, Commerce, Government, Show, and external Pomp possess the Imagination: Till we turn Eastward, which has a kind of blended Pleasure mingled with its Magnificence; a Nobleness mix'd with Solitude; and to the South something still more *rural* and entertaining.[32]

Morris attempts to present the metropolitan environs here as a site for a new definition of landscape and national self-imagery.[33] The multi-faceted view from Greenwich, for Morris, encapsulated the nation in all its various aspects – governmental, commercial and agricultural – through a single rotational viewpoint (see fig. 22). What is particularly striking is the emphasis on viewing and on the active engagement of the spectator in constructing the prospect through their movements and sensations.

The full implications of what viewing and writing about this landscape might mean are developed further in Edward Howard, the Earl of Suffolk's poem quoted at the beginning of this section, *Greenwich-Park* (1728), dedicated to Lord Montagu, a resident of the area.[34] He asks at the beginning of the poem in relation to Pope's *Windsor Forest*, 'Who is there who would not chuse with me / To read his Poem than the Forest see?' The representation of the scenic, Howard suggests, is now as powerful – if not more so – than the actual physical landscape itself. This is the key to understanding the proliferation of texts of all types, written and visual, concerning the metropolitan landscapes in our period. The Thames, Windsor Forest, the views from Richmond, Greenwich and Hampstead became well known as national icons and were constantly recirculated in a variety of media and styles. Poems, plays, prints and paintings all gravitated to the same intertextual subject matter. As Thomas Baker (b. 1680/81), the author of the play *Hampstead Heath* (1706), wrote in relation to an earlier version of the work which had been banned in Oxford:

> One Dispensation he does humbly pray,
> To borrow from his late forbidden Play;
> The Ladies on his Side he dares ingage,
> Since Patchwork is the Fashion of this Age.[35]

This patchwork of references and images created, as John Brewer observed, a deliberately modern form of pastiche which drew attention to its borrowings from other sources: sources furthermore that might come from anywhere across the whole cultural spectrum from high to low to middling and all points in between.[36]

Greenwich, like Hampstead, inspired numerous poems and songs along with a comedy produced at the Theatre Royal, *Greenwich-Park* by W. Mountfort (1691). It also featured in less reputable works such as Ned Ward's *A Frolick to Horn-fair with a Walk from Cuckold's-point thro' Deptford and Greenwich* (1700) and

The Romance of a Day: Or an Adventure in Greenwich Park (1760) by John Cleland, the author of Fanny Hill. Of these Suffolk wrote in his Greenwich poem, with Ward in mind no doubt: 'Here shameful Men our shameful Authors quote / Obscenity, that Scum of Wit is wrote.' The genre of London topographical verse became so well established that a poem of 1747, Hounslow-Heath, was able to satirize the genre with a plaintive mock lament:

> Assist ye sacred Nine, the Sports rehearse
> Of Hounslow-Heath – a Word not seen in Verse!
> Hounslow – unknown to all the tuneful Throng,
> A Place ne'er mentioned in descriptive Song,
> With Boldness now puts in a Right to claim
> With any Plains an equal share of fame.
>
> Pure is the Air, the Prospects unconfin'd,
> And numerous the Sports, t'unbend the Mind.
> No more let Hounslow then be lost to Fame,
> No more let dull Oblivion blast the Name.
> We from the sacred Nine Advice receive,
> That in their Records Hounslow's Name shall
> live.[37]

This poetic and dramatic literature drew in turn on the multitude of visual images of Greenwich ranging from oil paintings to satirical prints depicting the park, the river, the town, Blackheath and, above all, the prospects in all directions. Indeed, Cleland's 'adventure' displayed a dramatic use of imagery in charting the locale and progress of this outdoor seduction in which the architecture and landscape of Greenwich are transformed into a setting simultaneously genteel and sinister for young Frederic, a gentleman in disguise as a 'Jemmy-prentice or journeyman just out of his time [his apprenticeship], escaped from behind a counter to holiday-making' (fig. 72).[38] In common with guidebooks, such a combination of textual and visual material became increasingly common in topographical works of all types from the mid-eighteenth century onwards.

Morris's two other landscapes at Richmond and Windsor were both further upstream. This section of the Thames Valley was already well known as a landscape of national significance through Cooper's Hill and Pope's Windsor Forest. Morris wrote of Richmond as follows, comparing it with the view from Blackheath:

(facing page) 72 Greenwich town, from J. Cleland, *The romance of a day: or an adventure in Greenwich Park*, 1760, etching, British Library.

The illustrations in the book present the classical streets of Greenwich, here with the gates of the Royal Hospital, on the right, as a place of deception and disorder in which the regularity of the architecture is counterpoised by the animated, off-balance male figures observed with alarm by the women on the balcony above.

RICHMOND Hill, though advantageous for Prospects of Beauty, has less of Grandeur, is less popular, busy, and extensive, the Images are fewer, more retreated, more separate and rural than the former; though from the North and West Views, the same River glides along, to cheer the Eye: The Vessels are of another Form, infinitely diminitive [*sic*] in Proportion; fewer Towns, Villages, and Seats, and fewer Objects, to dwell upon the Fancy; from hence a Storm view'd, with all its fatal Consequences, would hardly affect us, while one from *Shooters* Hill would fill us with Tenderness and Surprize; and even there the Images would have no Tincture of that Horror which would arise in us from the View of one from *Dover* Cliff. In short on *Richmond* Hill, the Scenes are more still and silent . . . the windings and Turnings of the River, the Woods, Villages, and Seats, scatter'd in that kind of accidental arrangement make it very agreeable.

WINDSOR may claim an equal Share, of extensive Images, to attract the Eye and Admiration; the same agreeable River, and Prospects equally beautiful, but *here* the Beauties are such, which more nearly approach to Solitude, and retirement; they are still Images of Picturesque Romance, of silent Retreats; *rural*, and poetick.[39]

Morris uses the term 'picturesque' in the quote above in a generalized sense to mean pleasing or like a picture, as was common in early to mid-eighteenth-century usage. In the later eighteenth century it began to be associated with more naturalistic scenery, but it was not until the 1790s, when Payne Knight and Uvedale Price sought to define the term more precisely, that it became a specific aesthetic category alongside Burke's beautiful and sublime.[40] Morris aligned these metropolitan landscapes with his three 'classes' of architecture: the Dorian or the grave; the Ionian or the jovial; and the Corinthian or the charming.[41] The Shooters Hill view was Dorian 'by its robustness', Richmond Hill Ionian and Windsor Corinthian. In each case the particular idioms 'thus mutually compose that joint *Harmony* of *Art* and *Nature* . . . that at once charm the Soul, and fill us with unspeakable delight'.[42]

Defoe had described the Thameside landscape as epitomizing the wealth of the nation in its villas and mansions. However, more surprisingly, he also addressed the theme of perceptions of landscape in his *Tour*, demonstrating how far the approach to landscape advocated by writers such as Addison, Shaftesbury and Pope had become popularized by the 1720s:

> But I find none has spoken of what I call the distant glory of all these buildings. There is a beauty in these things at a distance, taking them en passant, and in perspective, which few people truly value, and fewer understand; and yet here they are more truly great, than in all their private beauties whatsoever. . . . Here they reflect beauty, and magnificence upon the whole country, and give a kind of character to the island of Great Britain in general. . . . Take them in a remote view, the fine seats among the trees as jewels shine in a rich coronet; in a near sight they are mere pictures and paintings; at a distance they are all nature, near hand all art; but both in the extremest beauty. . . . It is impossible to view these countries from any rising ground and not be ravished with the delightful prospect. For example, suppose you take your view from the little rising hills about Clapham, there you see the pleasant villages of Peckham and Camberwell, with some of the finest dwellings about London; with all the villages mentioned above, and the country adjoining filled with the palaces of all the British nobility and gentry already spoken of; looking north behold, to crown all, a fair prospect of the whole city of London.[43]

Defoe's appreciation, as with Morris, is of the inhabited landscape, the combination of art and nature. This sense of habitation also comes through strongly in Howard's *Greenwich-Park* where he writes of 'How Friendship is emblematiz'd in Trees'. He goes on to itemize the individual seats in the locality in a remarkably similar fashion to the maps marked with the seats of the gentry discussed in the first chapter; indeed, he may well have had one open before him as he composed his work. Writing of the dedicatee Montagu's neighbours, he conjures up an image of a residential enclave: 'And here a View of *PAGE'S* mansion take . . . / Here *Vanbrugh's* House, for Novelty excels / And there the Hospitable *Wither's* dwells / The brave, the well-bred friendly Soldier's Seat.'[44] Howard depicts a landscape of habitation, gentility and sociability, a recognizable community of the affluent.[45]

The interesting point about Greenwich and the lower reaches of the Thames, as Morris and Howard explored in their poems, was its intersection of gentility with industry and militarism. Interesting architectural manifestations of this relationship could be found at Vanbrugh Castle off Greenwich Park, from where the great architect could view the Thames east and west as well as the Royal Hospital, for which he was Surveyor 1716–26. Just downstream Brigadier General Michael Richards (1673–1722), an engineer and Surveyor General to the Board of Ordnance, occupied a hill-top house in Charlton situated above the Ordnance base at Woolwich. From his eyrie he could survey the surrounding countryside, the Thames and the Ordnance complex itself; he led the rebuilding of the latter in a robust Vanbrughian English baroque idiom from 1716 to 1722.[46]

The extent to which the eastern industrialized River Thames was incorporated into the polite figuring of the environs in visual representations has been explored by Sarah Monks.[47] She concludes that 'downriver' was incorporated within the discourse of the Thames as a symbol of national power and wealth up to the mid-eighteenth century. She argues that from 1760, for reasons relating both to the internal structures of the art world and a new attitude to imperialism, the industrial Thames vanished from polite view. It was never again a major subject at the Royal Academy exhibitions after its brief artistic appearance in the mid-eighteenth century in the works of artists such as Samuel Scott, John Cleveley the Elder and John Hood. However, there were exceptions, particularly the royal dockyards and naval bases, which continued to receive considerable attention due to their national significance. Richard Paton and John Hamilton Mortimer produced five views of royal dockyards – Sheerness, Woolwich, Chatham, Portsmouth and Deptford – in 1770–75 for the king, who according to Horace Walpole was pleased to 'express satisfaction at his performance'.[48] Nicholas Pocock (1740–1821) was another artist who produced a number of similar views such as *Woolwich Naval Dockyard* (1790, see fig. 19). He was a naval captain who took up painting maritime scenes in mid-career and enjoyed considerable artistic success, including exhibiting annually at the Royal Academy 1782–1812.[49] However, in this view, which was painted for the Navy Board, the Kent landscape features almost

as prominently as the dockyard in the foreground, suggesting that some softening of the industrial scene might have been desirable by this date, even in a commission of this type. Indeed, Joshua Reynolds advised him to unite landscape and maritime painting in his work if he wished to achieve success.[50]

The situation with regard to mass market prints, as opposed to paintings, seems to have been more mixed. There was a fairly steady stream of representations of the eastern river reaches, albeit in fewer numbers than for the western Thames, largely due to the lack of a similarly high density of both settlements and gentry villas along its banks. The eastern riverscape featured prominently in the Buck brothers' *Town Prospects* (1728–53). Their London views in the series comprised four views of Westminster and the City; one of Greenwich; one each of the naval bases at Woolwich and Deptford; plus the Medway towns of Gravesend, Rochester and Chatham – all taken from the river and thus foregrounding industrial and maritime activity.[51] In the early nineteenth century the building of the London docks proved a popular subject with topographical artists such as William Daniell, who produced *Views of the London Docks* (1801–8) and *Six Views of the Metropolis* (1805), the latter predominantly also of the docklands area.

The appreciation of the particularities of topography and the interplay of the built and natural outlined in this section created an audience for images of the architecture and landscape of the environs. As it was the totality and specificity of the topography that was to be admired, this allowed for a figuring of the everyday as well as the grand, the modern and the historic. It was the perfect sensibility with which to approach the heterogeneous environment of the outskirts in which the vernacular, the contemporary, the elite and the plebeian all existed side by side. Furthermore, this primarily visual and kinetic appreciation of the suburbs as a landscape allowed for the inclusion of generally despised elements, for example the Gothic, to be included within the whole in the same way that such elements were permitted in landscape parks but not in polite interiors. The most important Gothic buildings to be incorporated into this way of seeing were the medieval parish churches, which remained the primary locus for local histories and memorialization throughout the period; as James Stevens Curl writes, they

'represent the collective memory of the English people'.[52] We have seen in the previous chapter the important role they played in antiquarian histories and guidebooks, and they were also a prominent subject in visual images of the London countryside, particularly in the earlier eighteenth century (see figs 76–8). At the same time the Gothic began to be used as a self-conscious historicist style for new designs, most famously at Strawberry Hill, Twickenham (1753 onwards), the creation of Horace Walpole (1717–1797). Here Walpole and his 'Committee of Taste' conjured up a medieval fantasy in which antiquarianism and artistic creativity were fused into a compelling vision of the Gothic. One of the most important aspects of Strawberry Hill was its wide dissemination, as James Macaulay writes: 'Its chief influence was not in architectural, nor in planning [matters] . . . but in the publicity accorded the house both in Walpole's time, and after his death . . . and also by its close proximity to London.'[53] Walpole wrote that 'my castle is of paper', suggesting both the material truth of its papier mâché decorations and the fictive truth of its power as representational icon.[54] Through visits, prints and by its

owner's and others' literary accounts, Strawberry Hill popularized a new approach to the Gothic as a romantic form of nostalgic otherness, embedded in its context as a suburban Thames-side villa (fig. 73).

The pluralistic conception of landscape which embraced the Gothic rested on theories advanced by writers such as Roger de Piles. His *Cours de Peinture* (1708) was influential in England even prior to its translation as *The Principles of Painting* in 1743. De Piles discussed landscape painting extensively and developed a theory of 'situation' as 'the view, prospect or opening of a country': in other words, the visual identity of a place.[55] He wrote that buildings contributed to the creation of landscape 'even when they are Gothick, or appear partly inhabited and partly ruinous', and thus in this way the objects of aesthetic appreciation could be expanded to incorporate an increasingly wide range of building types and styles.[56] It was this shift in viewing that transformed the environs into an aesthetic experience for the viewer – an experience furthermore that was primarily visual and mediated through the all-pervasive print culture. It is notable that this development first took place in the environs of London, where a substantial urban middle class had developed seeking to embrace a new cultural identity that reflected their suburban lifestyle.

THE NEW LONDON LANDSCAPE: CHATELAIN AND DODSLEY

In the mid-eighteenth century the Dutch-influenced landscape tradition espoused by Hollar gave way to new French and Italian influences introduced largely by émigré artists. Jean Baptiste Claude Chatelain (1710–1758) was one of a number of European artists who were satisfying a demand for landscapes in the manner of Poussin and Claude in the 1740s.[57] He was the son of Huguenot parents, and although probably born in London, his style was indebted to French influences so he may have received training in his homeland. He was used by Samuel and Nathaniel Buck, along with Gravelot, another French artist, for their town panoramas when they switched from a Dutch-influenced to a French look from 1743,[58] and he worked for Arthur Pond around the same time in making a series of landscapes after Claude and Gaspard

74 Samuel Hieronymus Grimm, *Man Sketching at Barnes*, 1760s/70s, drawing, British Museum.

This is possibly a self-portrait of Grimm at work sketching in a backyard area with sheds and a water pump to the left.

Dughet.[59] The latter proved to be an important collection that helped spread an appreciation of classical landscapes just as an interest in English picturesque gardens was becoming widespread. Lippincott calls Chatelain 'the best of the French landscape specialists'.[60] However, she relates, his drinking, casual work ethic and eccentric belief that Oliver Cromwell's treasure was buried in his house – which led to him blistering his hands pulling up floors and panelling searching for it – made him an unreliable employee.[61]

He was in the vanguard of those who began to use the classical style not just for foreign but also for native views, transforming the existing Dutch-derived topographical tradition. He engraved *Six Views in the North of England* (1754) for William Bellers, which included some pioneering views of the Lake District, but his most numerous commissions were to be found depicting the outskirts of London, reflecting the enormous demand for prints of the suburbs. He himself lived at Chelsea, and he must have known of Thomas Preist's etchings of the river there and at Wandsworth and Chiswick of 1738, which were among the few landscape views around London to have preceded his own.[62] He developed a strong personal involvement with the Thames Valley, a tradition which was continued by later artists such as the Swiss émigré Samuel Hieronymus Grimm (1733–1794), who produced many sketches of Barnes, Mortlake and East Sheen as part of his prodigious topographical output in the 1760s and 1770s (figs 74, 75 and see fig. 83).[63]

Chatelain used his sketches to form the basis for a pocket book of 1750, *Fifty Small Original, and Elegant Views of the most Splendid Churches, Villages, Rural Prospects and Masterly Pieces of Architecture adjacent to London*, engraved by J. Roberts and sold by Henry Roberts. It was reported that he had devoted four years to making the drawings, travelling around the capital sketching.[64] The frontispiece to the work stated that it was 'Design'd for the Improvement of Such Gentlemen and Ladies as have a Taste for Drawing, and Colouring, or are Delighted with the several Exhibitions of the Diagonal Mirror'. Chatelain, like many guidebook authors, also found employment as a teacher, and the didactic purpose of the volume is echoed in another of his publications, *A New Book of Landskips Pleasant and Useful for to Learn to Draw without a Master* (1737). Chatelain produced the illustrations, while the text

75 Samuel Hieronymus Grimm, *View of Mortlake*, 1760s/70s, drawing, British Museum.

Grimm's sketchbook with his minutely detailed and meticulously observed drawings is one of the best unpublished guides to the everyday riverside landscapes mid-century. This view is remarkably similar to Knyff's painting of Chiswick (see fig. 21) made 100 years earlier and shows how little the architecture and layout of the less fashionable Thameside villages had changed during that time.

was by his fellow Huguenot, John Rocque.[65] The pocket-sized format of the *Fifty Views* made it suitable for carrying around to the sites illustrated. In this way Chatelain brought together two current vogues: for sketching and for viewing perspectives through concave glasses, which developed after *c*.1745 and led to a huge expansion in the market for prospects (fig. 76).[66] The minute size of the prints – only *c*.4 × 6 inches, less than half the norm of 10 × 15 inches for such views – must have made using a glass extremely tricky. The work's true novelty lay in the use of a bound book format for topographical prints, its reduction to a manageable size and its consequent portability and price.

The *Fifty Views* provides a remarkable picture of the environs mid-century. Unlike in some of Chatelain's other work, such as his *Prospects of Highgate and Hampstead* (1745) discussed in the following chapter, there is no attempt to conceal the workings of contemporary life (see figs 108, 109, 129). The collection reflects the very wide-ranging concept of 'London' that existed at the time, echoing contemporary guidebooks such as *The Foreigner's Guide* and *London in Miniature*. The

Thames Valley, Chatelain's base, featured strongly as well as the Northern Heights which his previous series had covered. The south of the capital is fairly well represented, but to the east the only inclusion is Hackney. The title indicates the balance of subjects among the sketches: churches predominated with thirty views, followed by fourteen general views – eight of villages and six of the riverscape – besides one inn, one hospital, two houses and one spa. The ecclesiastical theme is fairly conventional and echoes Strype and Hatton; however, in the *Fifty Views* the churches are shown very much in their village context, and therefore many other buildings and activities also come into play. Nor are they solitary places; the graveyards surrounding them are often crowded with a throng of people, presenting them as 'new social spaces' or possibly simply a convenient arena for staffage. The churches themselves are for the most part depicted before the major wave of rebuilding and refurbishment which took place from the mid-eighteenth century onwards (fig. 76).[67] The plates are thus a valuable record of the accretive parish church just before the modernizing and classicizing programme really hit its stride, bent on turning medi-

76 J. B. C. Chatelain, 'A View of St Mary's Church, Islington', from *Fifty Views*, 1750, etching, British Museum.

The print shows the old medieval church (with interesting accretions) demolished the following year.

eval Catholic structures into plain Protestant preaching boxes. Some new churches, such as the one at Hampstead (1745–7), are included, but for the most part these are images of stability and continuity rather than of change and progress.

The *Fifty Views* concentrated on the specifics of the village environment, both its historic buildings and its contemporary life, suggesting a need to cater for antiquarian as well as local and artistic interests. The plates included scenes of agricultural activities as well as polite pastoral pursuits featuring finely dressed ladies and gentlemen. The 'South View of Barnes', for example, showed a windmill, a building that may be a farmhouse, livestock and workers in the fields, the latter also being prominently foregrounded in the equivalent view of Willesden (fig. 77). The river views echo Preist in showing the upstream Thames as an active landscape in which small working boats as well as pleasure craft make their way past the jetties on which men are fishing and hauling nets, boats and goods. This was in stark contrast to another series that Chatelain produced in 1750, *Six Views and the River Thames*. It provided more conventionally picturesque views using a distant viewpoint to construct the scene, resulting in an emphasis on the landscape rather than

on human activity. The contrast can be seen in Chatelain's views of the bridge at Fulham from the two series. The first is depicted close-to and concentrates on the built structure of the bridge and Fulham town (fig. 78). The second shows Putney on the other side of the river as a distant feature in which the buildings have become simply a punctuation, marking the transition in the landscape between the vast stretch of water in the foreground and the huge sky above (fig. 79). Topographical verisimilitude rather than an idealized version of the environs seems to have been Chatelain's purpose in the *Fifty Views*. The series crossed boundaries between the polite and the plebeian, and as such can be taken as one of the best representations of the mid-century environs that survives. Although the physical environment of the outskirts, with its emphasis on churches and villages, is represented as stable, there are signs of the tremendous changes that they were undergoing socially. This is no longer Hollar's landscape of lonely retreat, but rather these are spaces of sociability and society, principally shown in the numbers of the bourgeoisie strolling in the outdoors. There are also indications of new leisure arenas in the prints of the pleasure gardens at the Spaniards Inn at Hampstead and at Saint Pancras Wells

(see fig. 93). These landscapes of pleasure are the subject of the following chapter.

The early date of the *Fifty Views* and the *Six Views* – and indeed Chatelain's career overall – confirms Timothy Clayton's analysis that an interest in landscape imagery, and associated activities such as sketching and perambulations, were far more widespread in the mid-eighteenth century than has previously been thought to be the case.[68] Well before Gilpin's *Picturesque Tours* of 1782, people were both visiting and appreciating the London environs for their scenery, as well as other attractions, and were buying depictions of them in significant numbers. Clayton attributes the misdating of the interest in romantic scenery to the 1760s rather than the 1740s to both an over-reliance on literary sources and the misattribution of many works from the earlier period to the London printseller John Boydell. He and his nephew dominated the London trade in topographical views in the second half of the eighteenth century and reissued many earlier prints under their name. In Chatelain's case the confusion may have been exacerbated by the practice Bryan reports of being superseded by his erstwhile pupil François Vivares, who, 'being more appreciated by the public, his name was often placed on plates

engraved by Chatelain alone'.[69] Many of the prints were subsequently reproduced as individual sheets or re-engraved by others, such as the 'View of Fulham Church from Putney Bridge', which became a well-known image but lost the connection with Chatelain.[70] Henry Overton and Robert Sayer reissued twelve of Chatelain's plates as *Vues Diverses des Villages pres de Londres* as early as 1752, proclaiming: 'The great Call for, and Success foreign Views have met with, occasioned the Proprietor to publish these English landscapes and Villages, which are equal if not superior, to any Foreign ones of the Size and Price, ever published in England.'[71] From the 1740s onwards, 'these English landscapes' provided an alternative democratic urban topographical model to the rural prospect centred on the great estate. The metropolitan view represented a known and accessible landscape which could be widely consumed both graphically and in person by the polite. Its ideology and practices were widely embraced by both the middle and upper classes as a modern form of art in which 'the experience of uniqueness and individuality co-existed with an experience of conventionality and conformity'.[72]

Further evidence of the significance that Chatelain's output was accorded by contemporaries is shown by

78   J. B. C. Chatelain, 'A View of
Fulham Church from Putney
Bridge', from *Fifty Views*, 1750,
etching, London Metropolitan
Archives.

The wooden river crossing was
erected in 1729 and funded by tolls
payable at the Bridge House visible
to the right of the picture.

79   J. B. C. Chatelain, 'A View of
Fulham Bridge and Putney', from
Six Views of the River Thames, 1750,
etching, British Museum.

the posthumous selection of substantial numbers of his works for the famous Frog Service for Catherine the Great. This was a vast dinner and dessert service of around 1,100 pieces commissioned by the empress from Josiah Wedgwood in 1773 to be decorated with monochrome prints of British scenes. It was reported that she wanted only British views 'to contain all that could be of Gothic Remains, of Natural Views, & of Improved Scenes and Ornaments, Parks & Gardens'.[73] Catherine's interest in scenery arose from her passion for English landscape gardening, while the emphasis on the Gothic derived from the destination of the service, the Kekerekeksinensky Palace (1774–7), one of the first Gothic buildings in Russia. The images were chosen from the wealth of existing black and white or sepia prints, including works such as Samuel and Nathaniel Buck's *Antiquities* (excluding town prospects) and Thomas Smith of Derby's views of the Peak District

and Yorkshire. Chatelain featured strongly in the service with every one of his sixteen prints of the gardens at Stowe reproduced as well as some of his Lakeland views after William Bellers. At the same time, details of many of the Stowe views, particularly the garden buildings, proved ideal for the smaller images required for the sides of dishes or covers of tureens.[74] A considerable number of Chatelain's London views were also selected, principally from his *Six Views* (1750) showing the Thames and his *Prospects of Hampstead and Highgate* (1745) as reissued by Overton and Sayer in 1752.[75]

These outer London views formed a significant part of wider national images of prosperity, taste and progress centred on landscapes and their representation. Other topographical prints were transferred to pottery by the Bow, Chelsea and Derby manufacturers around the same time.[76] A pair of porcelain guglets (long-necked vessels for holding water) of *c*.1755 survive in the British Museum made by Derby with Chatelain's view of Cambray (Canonbury) House, Islington, on the larger taken from the *Fifty Views*.[77] Through publication, exhibition and copying in numerous formats, such images were reproduced in different editions and media not just nationally but internationally as well. The Frog Service reached a far broader audience than simply the Russian aristocracy. It was exhibited in London in 1774 before travelling to Russia, and once there it was displayed in the palace as a spectacle for visitors.[78] Here we see Morris's and Pope's vision of the London landscape as a national symbol dramatically embodied in a British dinner service, destined for one of the most flamboyant courts in Europe, which became a public event discussed and debated across Europe. Such images were not just intertextual but intermaterial as well i.e. across media, as the example of the Frog Service so powerfully demonstrates (fig. 80).

If Chatelain represents the evolving identity of the London region in the 1740s and 1750s, the same is true for the subsequent decades of Robert Dodsley's *London and its Environs Described* (1761), the first fully illustrated guidebook to the 'environs', as they were now designated. Dodsley, as was discussed in the previous chapter, presented his work in the language of the Grand Tour as 'a guide and instructor to the travelling Virtuosi … in their little excursions to any part of these delightfully adorned and richly cultivated environs'.[79] The copper plate illustrations were seen as

being an integral part of the whole: 'We imagine they will not only be considered as an ornament, but that they will be found of use in illustrating the verbal descriptions.'[80] The Preface stated: 'The prints with which the whole is decorated, are all engraved by the best hands, after original drawings which were taken on purpose for this work . . . at a very great expence.' The six volumes which made up the publication were available either as sixpenny individual numbers or as a whole. In total they contained two maps, three plans and seventy-six plates of views, all attributed to Samuel Wale, bar four anonymous ones.[81] There were eight engravers: Benjamin Green, J. Green, Edward Rooker,

Charles Grignion, W. Elliott, François Vivares (Chatelain's pupil), J. Fougeron and J. Taylor. All were well-established engravers who regularly contributed to Dodsley's illustrated publications.

Samuel Wale (1721–1786) is thought to have been taught by Francis Hayman, possibly at the St Martin's Lane Academy. He was one of those, along with Hayman, Haytley and Hogarth, who contributed to the early display of London topographical painting at the Court Room at the Foundling Hospital with his roundels of St Thomas's, Greenwich and Christ's Hospitals, all *c*.1748 (fig. 81). However, these paintings are exceptional in Wale's oeuvre and he was better known

82 Samuel Wale, 'Belvedere House', from Dodsley, *London and its Environs Described*, 1761, etching, Bodleian Library, University of Oxford.

Wale has included himself sketching in the bright sun in the foreground.

an invaluable record of little-known houses or those that were later destroyed, such as Sir Gregory Page's Wricklemarsh, Blackheath, mentioned in Howard's poem *Greenwich-Park*. Although many of the properties described and illustrated in the work were inaccessible in person to a middle-class audience, Fabricant suggests that their very inclusion in such touristic works 'rendered ... pieces of privately owned land accessible – and in a vicarious sense possessable – by their often middle-class audience....Such literature helped reinforce...the dispersion of ownership, as psychological and aesthetic (or more precisely tourist) experience, through widening areas of society.'[83]

as a watercolour and drawing specialist. He was one of the founders of the Royal Academy in 1768 and the first Professor of Perspective there. He shared a house in Leicester Fields with the architect and writer John Gwynn, the well-known polemicist on London's planning and development. Wale specialized in book illustration and was the artist for such key works as Pope's *Works* (1751), Walton's *Compleat Angler* (1760) and the first illustrated *Clarissa* (1768). The approach taken in the illustrations for *London and its Environs Described* was overwhelmingly architectural (fig. 82). All the plates are of buildings or their monuments, with the exception of a few landscape views such as the 'Cascade at Ham Farm', 'A Scene in Wooburn Farm', 'View from the Terrace at Oatland' and 'A Scene in the Gardens at Pains Hill' – notably all private not public landscapes. There is only one interior depicted, that of St Stephen Walbrook; rather, it is the architectural scenography of both the centre and the outskirts that is displayed. Unlike Chatelain's *Fifty Views*, the depiction of the environs by Wale is overwhelmingly genteel, with country seats predominating along with royal palaces such as Hampton Court and Windsor plus the occasional historic building such as Eton College (see figs 65 and 66). Only two more contemporary attractions creep in: Ranelagh and Vauxhall Gardens. Bernard Adams comments: 'The quality and number of the illustrations make this an unsurpassed guide to the appearance of mid-eighteenth century London.'[82] The illustrations also provide

The concentration on domestic secular buildings, in contrast to Chatelain's parochial approach in the *Fifty Views*, reflects both a new emphasis in Dodsley's work on the country seats of the London area and the increasing suburbanization and density of population there. From the 1760s onwards, retreat to the outskirts became a more self-conscious process – as is discussed in Chapter 6 – in which a desire for architectural differentiation in the form of 'the box' or villa became widespread. The individual house in *London and its Environs* has replaced the village as the signifier of settlement, reflecting the increasing architectural separation of the ideal and everyday – the villa and the village. Wale's images perfectly capture this shift in representation of the environs mid-century from a landscape of scenery which incorporated the human to a landscape of settlement which included the natural: in other words, from a rural to a suburban landscape. The suburbs necessarily created a new perception of landscape in which, as Anne Bermingham argues, land 'was both capital *and* scenery – scenic capital and capital scenery'.[84] The paradox of suburbia was to develop the land and maximize its value while at the same time maintaining its rusticity and scenic charms.

LATE PICTURESQUE VISIONS:
J. T. SMITH AND THE BOYDELLS

While the kind river wealth and beauty gives;
And in the mixture of all these appears
Variety, which all the rest indears.
John Denham, *Cooper's Hill*, 1642

In the late eighteenth century there were further shifts in the way that the London countryside was envisaged and reproduced in topographical prints. This was due to the increase in domestic tourism to the remote and rugged regions of the British Isles and the new tools for aesthetic differentiation between landscape types. The categories of the 'sublime' and the 'beautiful' had been introduced by Edmund Burke in his *Enquiry into the Origin of our Ideas of the Sublime and the Beautiful* (1757), while the portmanteau term of the 'picturesque' was theorized in the writings of Gilpin, Payne Knight and Uvedale Price in the 1780s and 1790s.[85] It was the Reverend William Gilpin's picturesque tours through different parts of the country in the 1780s which had the most profound impact in popularizing the concept.[86] He introduced the distinction between the beautiful – those objects that please in their natural state – and the picturesque: those that please from having some quality capable of being illustrated by painting. This allowed for the qualities of the rough, the irregular and the varied to be deemed picturesque as against the smooth and the harmonious of the beautiful.[87]

With the realities of the variety of landscapes across the country now far better known, it was much harder to maintain the notion of the London landscape as representative of the entire nation. Instead, it began to be defined more as a particular southern form of terrain in which the Thames Valley took centre stage. At the same time the Romantic interest in history, the vernacular and the Gothic led to an intense fascination with the relics and remnants of the past in a far more direct form than earlier antiquarian engagements. We will begin by looking at the impact of this new sensibility in the work of J. T. Smith, who introduced what he called a 'low-comedy landscape' to the metropolis, and then go on to consider the career of the Boydells, the most important London printsellers in the second half of the eighteenth century.

Under the aesthetic categories of the picturesque and the sublime, rougher elements began to intrude. In the late eighteenth century the notion of landscape was expanded to embrace the plebian, the workaday and even the downright dilapidated. The ruined and the ramshackle became fashionable, and views of cottages, inns and peasants (fig. 83) came to be set alongside Wale's country villas and the genteel pastoral of

Boydell's river views (see figs 88 and 89). In the London region no publication marks this shift better than J. T. Smith's *Remarks on Rural Scenery* (1797). Here we will concentrate on the destabilizing representation of the London margins provided by Smith, while the issues of enclosure and subsistence dwelling which his images inevitably raise will be explored further in Chapter 6.

John Thomas Smith (1766–1833) was one of the great anecdotalists and writers of the London art world in the late eighteenth and early nineteenth centuries. He produced two highly entertaining books, *Nollekens and his Times* (1828) and *A Book for a Rainy Day: Or, Recollections of the Events of the Years 1766–1833* (1845). His father was the printseller and sculptor Nathaniel Smith, who had been an assistant to the sculptor Joseph Nollekens. John too entered the Nollekens studio at the age of twelve, which he went on to immortalize in his entertaining biography of his master. He abandoned sculpture after three years and transferred to engraving, for which he showed far more talent. He became a successful printmaker and draughtsman, partly thanks to the opportunities for distribution that his father's shop in St Martin's Lane afforded him. He made his name capitalizing on the vogue for extra-illustration, bringing out *Antiquities of London* in 1791–1800, which he promoted as ninety-six prints 'to be bound up with Mr Pennant's *London*'.[88]

His career provides yet another example of the mixture of outer and inner London living which seems to have been the norm for many artists during the eighteenth century. He began married life in Edmonton, where he settled in 1788, and came into regular contact with a group of antiquaries centred around one of his patrons, Sir James Lake, who employed him as a drawing master. He moved back to Soho in 1797 and later became Keeper of Prints and Drawings at the British Museum. 1797 was also the year in which he produced *Remarks on Rural Scenery: With Twenty Etchings of Cottages from Nature and Some Observations and Precepts relative to the Picturesque*, published by his father. This was comprised primarily of views around Edmonton and Enfield but also included more distant cottages in Surrey, Battle Bridge (Middlesex), Hampstead, Chelsea and even one on Millbank, Westminster, then still an undeveloped area popular with artists. Smith claimed of the cottages depicted that 'they are all from

83 Samuel Hieronymus Grimm,
Cottages at Mortlake, 1760s/70s,
drawing, British Museum.

This is a good representation of
the unplanned development and
traditional architecture that
predominated in London's outer
areas, albeit drawn with other
interests in mind.

Nature, and indeed some of them were etched on the spot' (figs 84 and 85).[89]

Smith's opening 'Remarks' made a strong case for the inclusion of the cottage among picturesque objects:

> Of all picturesque subjects, the *English cottage* seems to have obtained the least share of particular notice and appropriate discrimination by modern *tourists*. . . . It seems not to have been sufficiently considered that the landscape-painter's beauty does not necessarily exist in grandeur, *exclusively* or *alone*; but equally pervading *every* department of Nature, is found not less perfect in the most *humble* than in the most *stately* structures, or scenery.[90]

However, Smith was anxious that 'one unvarying and uniform idea has served to describe every *cottage* in the kingdom' and that whereas he was 'by no means *cottage-mad* . . . am content that rural and cottage-

scenery shall be considered no more than a sort of *low-comedy* landscape'.[91] Smith wanted to reclaim the cottage for the category of the picturesque and rescue it from the prettification that viewing it through the rose-tinted spectacles of the genteel variant of the *cottage ornée* had produced:

> Cottage-scenery may be divided into two classes, namely the *neat*, and the *neglected*: It is a maxim that in poverty, nothing will more easily excite the attentions of benevolence, than the appearance of neatness and cleanliness: The regular, white-washed or new brick wall – the glaring red chimney-pot – the even-thatch'd roof – the equi-distant group of sweet pea. . . . But it is nothing to the artist. . . . We then turn from this neatness and regularity, to what we must esteem a far more profitable subject – the neglected fast-ruinating cottage – the patched

plaster . . . the weather-beaten thatch . . . the mutilated chimney top . . . the fence of bulging workmanship – the wild unrestrained vine.[92]

He rounded off this section by concluding: 'Nothing perhaps claims a greater share of attention from the artist than *propriety* of *place*.'[93] The best spots to find his 'neglected' subjects, Smith wrote, were 'the remote wild common – or the straggling undetermined borders of the forest – or in the silent sequestered dell, you shall find . . . the antient, feeble, roof-oppressed hovel'.[94] This search for the 'wild' in the London countryside established a fashion for expeditions to places such as Epping Forest for walks and picnics, a new word coined in the early nineteenth century. C. R.

Leslie's *Londoners Gypsying* (1820) shows such a scene, on which the artist commented: 'I am at present painting a picture of a party spending a day in the woods, which is a very common thing with the people of the middle class in the summer' (fig. 86 and see fig. 68).[95]

Smith's work shows an awareness of an edge landscape coming under increasing pressure from suburban development. He sketched the ramshackle habitations of the poor subsisting on the margins of waste or common land, stretching the picturesque taste for ruins to its very limits to embrace even the hovels of the indigent poor. One plate is ironically titled 'Lady Plomer's Palace, on the Summit of Hawke's-Bill Wood, Epping Forest'. The subscribers to the volume included William Blake, John Constable (two copies), Sir James

Lake, Joseph Musgrave and Benjamin West, President of the Royal Academy. This impressive list shows how far the art of the margins had been brought within the purlieu of the artistic establishment. The young John Constable had just come to London and was being encouraged by Smith to pursue his artistic interests in the face of family opposition.[96] By this date notions of centre and periphery were in constant flux, and Smith's views were produced just at the point that the itinerant poor were being neutralized and dispossessed by enclosure and increasing suburbanization on the London fringes.[97]

Let us move on now to consider another type of later landscape, that produced by John Boydell (1720–1804) and his nephew and partner, Josiah Boydell (1752–1817), who dominated the London trade in topographical views in the second half of the eighteenth century. John Boydell trained under W. H. Toms

86 Charles Robert Leslie, *Londoners Gypsying*, 1820, oil, Geffrye Museum.

for six years while attending drawing classes at the St Martin's Lane Academy in the evenings.[98] He opened his own shop in 1751, from which he began to build a print empire. At that date the demand was still principally for foreign prints, and so Boydell astutely taught himself French (the international language) so that he could 'speak and write the Language which enabled me to Correspond with Foreigners – which was of great service to me'.[99] He earned a fortune through buying up and reissuing earlier prints under his own name. He bought the entirety of Pond's collection as well as plates by Toms, William Bellers, Robert Pine and many others.[100] He was known as the 'Great Leviathan' and became the leading

87 John Boydell, 'Catalogue of Prints', from Boydell, *A Collection of Views in England and Wales*, 1790, British Library.

The list demonstrates the appeal of London views for an international market even at this late date.

merchant-printseller of his day.[101] He was elected an alderman of London in 1782, served as master of the Stationer's Company 1783–4 and became Lord Mayor of London in 1790.[102] He deserves ranking with Wedgwood and Boulton, according to Lippincott, as one of the great entrepreneurs of the eighteenth century.[103]

By the end of the period in which Boydell was operating, the European print market had reversed. Britain went from being a net importer of prints to primarily an exporter as the taste for modern English art, including landscapes, became widespread. It has been estimated that in the 1800s the total value of the sale of English prints abroad, including the colonies, was in the region of £250,000.[104] The Anglophilia of Catherine the Great's Frog Service was by no means unique but was widely shared by an international audience. They took a keen interest in English art and design, including landscapes of the Greater London region, fuelled by their accessibility and abundance in print form.[105] Boydell himself displayed the Frog Service at his Shakespeare Gallery in Pall Mall, which opened in 1789 as a venue for English art. He also published the Walpole Collection from Houghton prior to its purchase by Catherine the Great. He wrote in the 'Advertisement' to his *Collected Views* in 1790: 'He flatters himself, [that he] has somewhat contributed to bring the Art of Engraving to that wonderful State of Perfection in England, which at present gives its Artists so decided a Superiority over all the rest of Europe. Few men have had the Happiness of seeing in a single Lifetime, such a Revolution.'[106]

Boydell's output continued to maintain the prominence of London views in the national scenography, initially in his *Collection of 100 Views* (1770), which were largely of the Thames and reproduced plates mainly dating from the 1750s. He continued the subject in *A Collection of Views in England and Wales* (1790), in which the first section is 'Views In and About London' while then moving on to Oxford, Blenheim, Derbyshire, Wales, 'Sea Pieces' and 'Landscapes' (the latter being a mixture of old masters and new works).[107] The international nature of the intended market is indicated by the catalogue at the beginning, which lists all the works in both English and French in two parallel columns of text (fig. 87). The *Collection of One Hundred Views* maintained the varied depiction of the Thames adopted by earlier engravers, showcasing both its working and leisured aspects. The naval bases and dockyards to the east featured prominently, as well as notable industrial landmarks such as the Chelsea Water Works (fig. 88). Rural tranquillity is shown in both east and west with a mixture of rustic scenery in the villages, gentry seats and prospects, such as that from

88 John Boydell, 'A View of Chelsea Water Works', 1752, from Boydell, *A Collection of Views in England and Wales*, 1790, etching and engraving, British Museum.

The works were established in 1723 using a tide mill to distribute Thames water to the City and Westminster via a series of reservoirs and pipes.

'Wandsworth Hill towards Fulham'. Boydell's publications on the Thames came out of the long-standing artistic interest in its landscapes. Peter Clark in his study of the Guildhall topographical images analysed the number of views of the river, and gives the following figures as a percentage of all London images of the period: 1640–60 1.2 per cent; 1700–20 1.4 per cent, 1760–80 3.3 per cent; and 1820–30 5.5 per cent.[108]

Boydell's next project on the river was even more ambitious in its scope. He commissioned a two-volume account written by William Combe, *An History of the River Thames* (1794–6), covering not just its London section but its complete length. This interest in the entirety of the river's course inevitably extended the notion of the London region both eastwards and particularly westwards into Oxfordshire and Berkshire in line with contemporary guidebooks such as Henry Hunter's *History of London and its Environs* (1811). Hunter had featured the Thames and other metropolitan water courses prominently in his account. By this date the Thames Valley itself was becoming perceived as almost a separate region in its own right, at least in its western stretches. Hunter traced its course back to the Thames head in Cotes, Gloucestershire, although modern geologists more commonly give Lechlade as its source. The Thames region distorted the conception

of perfect concentric circles around London, forming a spur to the west which usually extended at least as far as Oxford, taking in Henley, Reading and Windsor on the way. In seeking to do justice to his subject, Boydell decided to employ other artists and engravers for the work rather than undertaking the drawing himself. He was aware of his limitations, as he wrote: 'He began to learn the Art of Engraving too late in Life, to arrive at a great Perfection, being within a few Months of Twenty-one years of Age, when he put himself Apprentice to the Art.'[109] The *History of the River Thames* was entrusted to the artist Joseph Farington, who used a softer, more picturesque style to wash the Thames in a soft-focus glow (fig. 89). This effect was partly due to Farington's more Romantic sensibility but also the result of the production of the prints in coloured aquatint by J. C. Stadler, one of the new techniques being pioneered in the late eighteenth and early nineteenth centuries.[110]

The Preface outlined the approach of the volumes and suggested that it was the diversity of the Thames-side landscape that was most to be cherished: 'In short, the history of a river, is the history of whatever appears on its banks; from metropolitan magnificence to village simplicity; from the habitations of kings to the hut of the fisherman; from the woody brow, which is the

pride of landscape, to the secret plant that is visible
only to the eye of the botanist.'[111] The Thames for
Combe was a microcosm of both the natural and man-
made worlds. However, Farington's illustrations mask
this diversity in an all-encompassing cloak of tranquillity. This river, following Burke's principles, was now
firmly in the category of the beautiful rather than the
sublime.[112] The Thames, which for Morris had been
capable of multiple moods and characters – including
characteristics that would later be termed sublime – was
now viewed as a tame landscape compared to the
dramatic scenery elsewhere in the British Isles. As
the Preface stated: 'Though the characteristic of the
Thames be beauty, I may be frequently found to
employ epithets that are suited to the more sublime
features of nature: they must therefore be taken in a
comparative sense: for Clifedon, which is a magnificent

scene on the Thames, would hide its diminished head
were it placed on the lakes of the North, or on the
rivers of Scotland.'[113] Henry Hunter wrote that the
Thames's beauties lay in the elegant rather than the
sublime of 'the rivers of alpine regions': 'In no part
of its course does it force its way through opposing
rocks, or struggle in pent-up bed amid over-hanging
crags.... Hence, in the estimate of picturesque beauties, the romantic is almost entirely to be left out of
the catalogue: the sweet, the soft, the sequestered, the
rich, and the majestic, compose the list of its distinguishing charms.'[114]

In Boydell's *History* the Thames becomes a bucolic
landscape of scenic views, many of them referencing
previous sources that would be known to the viewer.
Thus, we have a 'View of Windsor Castle from
Cooper's-hill', referencing Denham's famous poem,

and 'Garrick's Villa' shown after his death but its power still derived from its association with the great actor. Such an associative presentation of the sights along the river's banks was commonplace from the 1760s, as Julius Bryant has shown. Literary connections were evoked at Marble Hill, which was presented as a classic villa immortalized by Swift, Gay and Pope (with rather less mention of Henrietta Howard, George II's mistress, who built the house). Views of Pope's own villa continued to be made even after the house had been torn down in 1807 by Lady Howe, exasperated by the constant stream of day-trippers and unwelcome visitors.[115] The Thames by now was a great intertextual stew of associative images presented for its audience to enjoy in ever more self-referential and synecdochal terms. The *History*'s author, William Combe – who went on to write the Dr Syntax satires for the *Poetical Magazine* from 1809 to 1811 – was aware of the tensions between the particular and the general that this could engender.[116] He apologized for any unevenness in treatment: 'On approaching the metropolis, particular description must give way to a more comprehensive narration. Artificial objects continually multiply; property becomes infinitely divided; and instead of the family mansion, which commands respect from surrounding domain, historical circumstances and hereditary possession, we now meet with groups of villas, that change their owners with the season.'[117] Farington produced just such a view of a cluster of villas on top of Richmond Hill (fig. 89). The problem with this landscape for Combe and Farington was that it depicted modern mass housing that was anonymous and essentially ahistorical. It was thus hard to assimilate into national and pastoral narratives which relied on an integration of easily recognizable but distinctive forms to create a synergy between past and present.

Seventy years earlier Defoe had praised the Thames Valley as a symbol of the nation's new social mobility and commercial prosperity, but such irrefutable evidence of new wealth was now seen as disruptive of the pastoral image that Boydell and his collaborators sought to project. Farington's views, while not ignoring the working river, depicts it as a stream of tranquillity along its entire length. There is no change in register from the rural stillness of its upper reaches through Westminster and the City and on to the eastern industrial heartland. All is calm and remarkably unpopulated with the exception of artfully spread strolling gentry and respectful workmen, the latter usually shown at some distance to mask the true impact of their labour. The linear course of the Thames offered the opportunity to construct narratives for all levels of society from the royal to the plebeian, but increasingly the emphasis was shifting from the lower tidal reaches of the Thames to its upper parts where the pastoral idyll could be more easily and plausibly sustained. While the *History of the Thames* sought to offer a comprehensive account of the waterway along its whole course, the primary focus was on the residential, domestic river rather than the maritime imperial seaway. Henry Hunter asserted that it was indeed the man-made elements which made the greatest contribution: 'The artificial ornaments of villas, edifices, and pleasure grounds, must be allowed to contribute greatly to formation of some of the most admired landscapes of the Thames, which without them would only display the common beauties of a fine county.'[118] The great hub of industry that Defoe and Morris had praised had vanished in such works, to be replaced with a more sanitized version of a great working river transformed into a picturesque composition. But at the same time around 1800 it must be remembered that Daniell and others were producing their views of the recently built London docks, and the 'industrial sublime' became a popular genre for images of other new industrial features such as roadways, canals and factories, as is discussed in Chapter 7 (see figs 179 and 180).

The increasing idealization of the environs in topographical prints through the long eighteenth century does not in any way diminish their significance in what has been termed 'a middle class territorialisation of landscape'.[119] The lowly status of topographical representations within the art establishment was precisely due to their modernity, accessibility and increasing use of self-generated references, a semiotic system only partially dependent on established classical canons of art.[120] Topography might be despised by the Royal Academy, but its popularity with both domestic and foreign audiences remained undimmed and indeed increased as part of the interest in the native and the local inspired by the picturesque. As Lippincott and Clayton have shown so vividly, prints were the most innovative part of the English art market in the eighteenth century.[121] They broadened both the audience and the subject matter for art far beyond the traditional limits of aristocratic portraiture. In the specific genre of London topographical prints, artists created a new identity for the suburbs as a major feature of the metropolis. These were the first consumed landscapes, as Brewer writes, in the modern sense, available to a broad mass of the public who became familiar with a repertoire of sights and sites through their constant reproduction in print, quite independent of actual visits to the places depicted.[122] This is not to say that the actual visiting of sites was not an important feature in the creation of the 'environs'; it too played a central part. In the following chapter we shall move beyond paper landscapes to consider the creation of a 'greater London' landscape through the social practices and lives of its inhabitants – to concentrate on ways of being rather than ways of seeing.

PART TWO

INHABITED LANDSCAPES

4

LANDSCAPES OF PLEASURE
1660–1790

MODERN MORALITY TALES FROM THE EDGE

As the nobility and gentry go to Tunbridge, the merchants and rich citizens to Epsome; so the common people
go chiefly to Dulwich and Streatham; and the rather also, because it lies so near London, that they can walk
to it in the morning and return at night.

Daniel Defoe, *A Tour Through the Whole Island of Great Britain*, 1724–6

The identity of the environs was not just inscribed in the realm of print but was equally the creation of the thousands of visitors who flocked to its attractions, traversed its highways and walked its fields each weekend. As de Certeau argued, the urban is defined by the experiential as well as by 'graphic representations'. He identified circulation and particularly 'pedestrian movement' as one of those 'real systems whose existence in fact makes up the city'.[1] This was particularly true for the open areas around the city, in which one of the major activities was simply strolling, walking and taking the fresh air (fig. 91). On maps the open spaces of the outskirts, with the notable exceptions of the surveys of Rocque and Milne, often appeared as blanks beyond indications of the occasional footpath or field boundary. Yet as numerous topographical views show, these were landscapes thronging with life, as well known and familiar to many city dwellers as the streets

in which they lived and worked. Thomas Pennant wrote of Moorfields: 'It was the great *Gymnasium* of our capital, the resort of wrestlers, boxers, runners, and foot-ball players, and every manly recreation.'[2] The leisure facilities and functions (in their broadest sense) of the environs is a vast subject which would require several chapters, if not books, to do it justice. This chapter therefore focuses mainly on pleasure gardens and spas in three areas – Islington, Hampstead and Marylebone – to consider the type of locale that existed in such leisure resorts and the extent to which these were new spaces which generated new forms of behaviour. In the writing on eighteenth-century culture a great deal of attention has been given to the coffee houses, assembly rooms and open areas of the inner city (such as squares) as the quintessential Habermasian spaces of sociability. These spaces have been trumpeted as the harbingers and forgers of the public

(*facing page*) 90   A. C. Pugin and Thomas Rowlandson, 'Vauxhall Gardens' (detail of fig. 98).

91 Bernard Lens, *A View of ye New River Head and Water Mill at Islington near London*, 1730, drawing, British Museum.

The New River Head is in the middle with the Water House and in front of that is the reservoir known as the Round Pond. To the right are various buildings for pumping water, including a disused windmill, minus sails, which was abandoned as inadequate in 1720. Sadler's Wells music house is on the far left. The drawing was 'Taken by the Life' and shows the popularity of this mixed industrial and rural landscape for visitors from the City, seen in the background.

sphere, along with the realm of print.[3] Peter Borsay has also discussed the importance of promenading and outdoor socializing in provincial towns as indicators of a new urban sensibility.[4] But little attention has been paid to the equally important outer London suburban playgrounds with the notable exception of one of the most visible and fashionable, Vauxhall Gardens.[5] There are invaluable works on London pleasure gardens, particularly by Wroth and Wroth and more recently by James Stevens Curl, but few attempts to situate such places within the social and cultural milieu of the capital more broadly (fig. 92).[6] This chapter considers the impact of the commodification of the environs as a realm of tourism and leisure in the long eighteenth century for the middle classes, for whom they came to represent a recreational realm similar to that of the country estate for the landed gentry and nobility.[7] As Carole Fabricant writes: 'We can see in eighteenth-

century tourism the distinct beginnings of what it has developed into today: a collective, institutional force, a profoundly social and socializing ritual.'[8]

Londoners had long used the hinterland as a place for outdoor sporting activities, military exercises and repose and relaxation. Stow in the late sixteenth century noted: 'There are near London, on the north side, especial wells in the suburbs, sweet, wholesome, and clear. Amongst which, Holy-well, Clarkenwell, and St. Clement's well, are most famous, and most frequented by scholars and youths of the city in summer evenings, when they walk forth to take the air.'[9] Stow's commentary introduces us to several of the key features of the open spaces contiguous to the city. First, they combined both solitary pursuits for scholars and others of a reflective cast with sociable activities for the young and others in search of excitement and adventure. Second, he characterizes such spaces as masculine, and although this was never entirely the case they appear to have been predominantly so prior to the seventeenth century. Besides the wells and walks, as we saw in the Introduction, there were other less wholesome activities on offer all around the capital's fringes such as bear-baiting, cock-fighting and hunting – particularly of ducks, an activity which will feature prominently in a cautionary tale at the end of this chapter. Most of these field sports predated Stow's time and continued unabated through the long eighteenth century. The theatres of the south bank were one of the major out-of-town attractions in Stow's day, but by the early eighteenth century playhouses were being built in the centre for the first time which came to dominate over their extramural rivals. The Queen's Theatre opened in the Haymarket in 1705, for example, designed appropriately by Vanbrugh, nicely combining his theatrical and architectural expertise.

The outer fringe's purpose as an urban playground was greatly enhanced from the late seventeenth century onwards by the development of a range of establishments catering for all sectors of society, in which pleasure grounds, spas, inns, and tea and assembly rooms all vied for the custom of pleasure-seeking city dwellers. As Peter Clark writes of the transformation of the old-style drinking houses: 'Premises became larger, more lavish and commercial, acquiring specialist facilities including club rooms and assembly rooms, while their landlords became energetic social and cultural entrepreneurs, organising, hosting and marketing many of the new entertainments.'[10] As the types of activity on offer broadened, women began to participate in the consumer culture of these new recreational spaces. At the same time, in a reverse pattern from many other types of leisure pursuits, the gentry and aristocracy also came to patronize the outer London

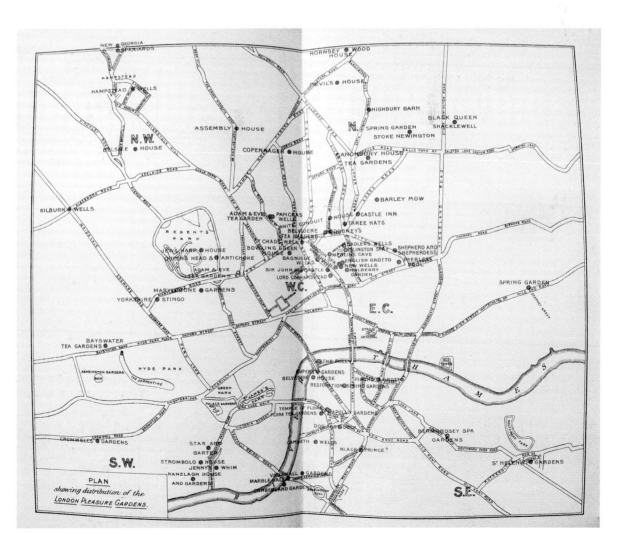

92 'Plan of London Pleasure Gardens', from W. and A. E. Wroth, *The London Pleasure Gardens of the Eighteenth Century*, 1896.

spas and inns, which had been hitherto the almost exclusive domain of the artisan and merchant classes of the City. Visits to outer London resorts became popular with all sections of society, as Defoe observed in the opening quote of this chapter. The 1751 Act for 'Regulating Places of Public Entertainment and punishing Persons keeping Disorderly Houses' shows how widely distributed such premises might be and yet still considered within the purlieu of London. The Act required licensing of all public places of entertainment within twenty miles of London and Westminster, including every 'house, room and garden'.

A flavour of these resorts can be gleaned from an answer in a play on Tunbridge Wells to the query 'What are the chief Diversions?': 'Beaus, Raffle and Dance – Citts play at Nine-Pins, Bowls and Back-gammon – Rakes scoure the Walks, bully the Shop-Keepers, and beat the Fiddlers – Men of Wit rally over Claret and Fools get to the Royal-Oak Lottery where you may lose Fifty Guinea's in a moment.'[11] The first and most essential feature to transform a village into a 'resort' (with a few exceptions) was a mineral spa, which offered the possibility of combining medical and leisure facilities. *The Foreigner's Guide* of 1740 advised: 'Near London also are several mineral and salutary Springs ... where in the fine Season People of all Ranks and Conditions resort either for Health or Pleasure.'[12] There were some 'baths' that were only medical, such as the 'Cold Bath' at Islington, but on the whole the bathing in and ingestion of the waters was combined with other refreshments and entertainments (fig. 93). It is with the pleasure aspect that we are going to be concerned here rather than the medical side of the resorts' operations.[13] As Stow had noted, the geological structure of London made the Thames basin a mass of watercourses and springs. These were created by the streams of the higher sandy areas, including the Bagshot sands of the Hampstead–High-gate ridge and the Surrey sands, flowing down to meet the gravel terraces of the Thames below, where they emerged as rivers such as the Westbourne, Wandle and Fleet. The centre was surrounded by a ring of mineral wells where these came to the surface, many of them chalybeate springs with a high iron content.[14] The two most popular waters, according to Defoe in the 1720s, were at Hampstead and Islington, and it is on these two resorts that we will concentrate along with Mary-

lebone to the south. The focus here will be on sociable pursuits and spaces which embraced both the gentry and the middle classes, with a concentration not so much on individual leisure genres, but on the identity of such areas which created a new kind of environment, the 'resort' or leisure arena, distinguished by its landscape, architecture and attractions. These were surprisingly varied in topography and tone. As with the early suburbs they were not the outcome of any systematic planning or development, but rather the result of the colonization and consumption of their spaces and activities by polite society.

ISLINGTON: RURALITY AND LIBERALITY ON THE CITY FRINGE

In the afternoon I walked out on the North side of the town to see the country on that side. The land here was mostly divided into grass fields. Beautiful and very well-built villages, farm-houses, and buildings were scattered here and there amongst them. These villages and houses were commonly surrounded with beautiful gardens. A multitude of people streamed out here from all sides of London to enjoy their Sunday afternoon and take the fresh air. In all the aforesaid villages there was a superfluity of beer-shops, inns, and such-like houses, where those who came from the town rested. There were also small summer houses, built in the gardens, with benches and tables in them, which were now all full of swarming crowds of people, of both sexes.
Pehr Kalm, *Kalm's Account of his Visit to England: On his Way to America in 1748*, May 1748

Defoe described Islington as being 'joined to the streets of London, excepting one small field', a not entirely accurate assessment, but one intended to convey its proximity to the centre.[15] As *The Foreigner's Guide* reported in 1740, 'The Neighbourhood of the City makes it very much frequented.'[16] John Swertner's *A View of the Cities of London and Westminster* (fig. 94) shows that even in 1789, on the eve of Islington's major period of expansion, it was still several fields' walk away from the ever-encroaching northern suburbs.[17] Two years earlier, the still predominantly rural aspect of the area, even allowing for the pastoral idealism of the image, was depicted by Robert Dodd (see fig. 27). This was after the arrival of the New Road in 1756 created to connect Islington and Paddington and extended eastwards in 1761 to the City. Dodd's print presents two

93 Anon., *Saint Pancras Wells*, copy of drawing of *c*.1750, British Museum.

This drawing provides a wonderful guide to the layout and operations of the spa, emphasizing the interdependence of the grounds, the buildings and the waters in providing a variety of entertainments for all types of visitors. The first panel outlines the illnesses that may be treated: 'These Wells are Situate about a Mile Northward from London The Mineral Waters of which are Surprisingly Successful in Curing the most Obstinate Scurvy, King's Evil, Leprosy & all other breakings out & defilements of the Skin: Running Sores, Cancers, Eating Ulcers, the Piles ... Corruption of the Blood and Juices of Rheumatism and all Inflamatory Distempers'. The middle panel shows five stones voided by various patrons of the spa which 'may be seen of Mr Bristowe Goldsmith' in Fleet Street, where the waters were sold in the City.

The right-hand panel provided an explanatory key to the drawing: 1 The New Plantation; 2 The Old Walk; 3 The Long Room; 4 and 5 The Two Pump Houses; 6 The House of Entertainment; 7 The Ladies Walk and Hall; 8 Two Kitchen Gardens; 9 Coach Road to Hampstead and Highgate; 10 and 11 Coach Ways to the Wells; 12 Foot Way from Red Lyon St Southampton Row and Tottenham Court; 13 A Foot Way from Grays Inn Lane and the City of London; 14 Foot Way from Islington; 15, 16 and 17 Pancras Church with ye Old and New Church Yds; 18 Kentish Town; 19 Primrose Hill; 20 Hampstead; 21 Highgate.

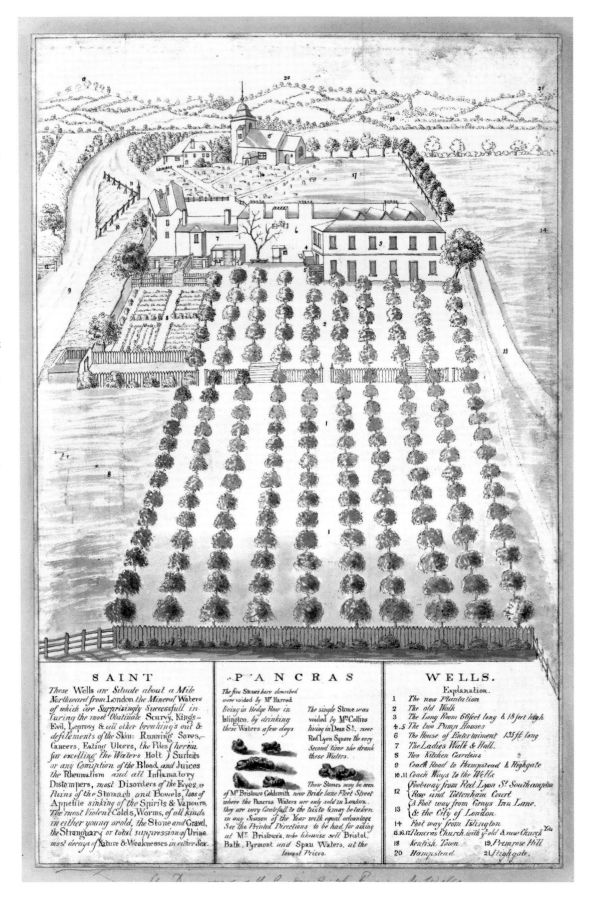

A VIEW of the CITIES of LONDON and WESTMINSTER with the SUBURBS and CIRCUMJACENT COUNTRY.
Shewing the steeples of all the Churches and as many of the Public Buildings as are seen from the gallery of the steeple of Islington which Town appears in the fore ground 1789

94   John or Johannes Swertner,
*A View of the Cities of London and
Westminster with the Suburbs and
Circumjacent Country*, 1789, aquatint
etching, British Museum.

The view was taken when the
steeple of St Mary's, Islington, was
undergoing repairs and was
enveloped in a wicker-work
structure which enabled the Dutch
artist to access the spire.

of the newly built fashionable Georgian terraces out in
the fields to the north, Highbury and Canonbury
Places of 1774–9 and 1776–80 respectively. By contrast,
the elevated view shows that the character of the old
area of settlement was very different, even in the late
eighteenth century. Swertner's panorama, taken from
the steeple of the parish church of St Mary's, presents
an image of semi-rusticity in the village set against the
metropolis on the horizon. We can see that the polite
architecture of Highbury Place was by no means universal, although some classical terraces are visible
snaking along the main roads. The foreground shows
the area behind Islington Green where the Upper and
Lower Roads met, and is dominated by the irregular
groupings, gables and pitched roofs of a variety of
structures and spaces of varying dates. Residential, commercial and agricultural buildings existed side by side
and are interspersed with gardens and low shed-like

structures. Even the brand new chapel which can be
seen being roofed in the centre of the picture seems to
be remarkably unassuming, notwithstanding that it was
a Nonconformist edifice and unfinished. Islington's role
as the dairy of London is represented by some cows
and pigs in the centre of the view, while evidence of
market gardening is visible in the right foreground.

The predominantly rural and historic character of the
village was captured by John Nelson in his *History of
Islington* (1811), where he was admiring of 'the prospect
down the Lower-street' in which 'the irregular disposition of the houses, intersected and enlivened by the
variegated foliage of the different sorts of trees gives the
scene a very agreeable and picturesque appearance'.[18]
Islington's open aspect and the course of the artificially
cut New River through its fields had long made it
popular as a place for fresh air and exercise, as Wenceslaus Hollar had so poignantly portrayed it (see fig. 70).

The area was transformed at the end of the seventeenth century with the discovery by Edward Sadler *c.*1674–84 of a medicinal spring in the gardens of his music house, which he opened as a spa.[19] This was followed in quick succession by the establishment of its rivals: the New Tunbridge Wells or Islington Spa, the Royal Oak, the White Conduit House and the London Spa. The Islington pleasure houses' fortunes waxed and waned during the long eighteenth century, reaching their peak of fashionability in the 1730s, but throughout they maintained a reputation for an exceptionally socially mixed clientele. In response to this diversity, a dual mode of depicting the Islington resorts developed which veered between the wholesome and the licentious. The Hollar tradition continued with representations of the area as a healthy open space for family outings and sporting activities, particularly fishing and shooting (fig. 95). Scenes showing the urban middle classes in their semi-rural playground, the poor man's equivalent of the country estate, were common and frequently satirical in nature (fig. 96). James Elmes, a writer who will feature strongly in the final chapter, wrote that the true gentleman 'would carry his fowling propensities farther a field than the cockney counties of Middlesex or Surry'.[20] It was one of these citizens or so-called 'cits' whom Hogarth depicted in his print *Evening* of 1738, in which the pretensions of the mercantile City elite to the aristocratic pastoral are portrayed through the pathetic figure of a cuckolded dyer strolling with his overbearing wife and children along the New River past Sadler's Wells and the Hugh Myddleton Tavern (fig. 97). The work was commissioned as part of the series *The Four Times of Day* for the rival attraction of Vauxhall Gardens by Jonathan Tyers, in an attempt to differentiate his more refined riverside grounds from the plebian establishments to the north.

The dichotomy between the health-giving and the hedonistic aspects of the spas' operations was also reflected in their gardens, ornamentation and architecture. Some gardens, such as those at Sadler's Wells, sought to create an atmosphere of tranquil rurality with its fruit trees and naturalistic planting (see figs 91 and 102). Others took a different more flamboyant approach, and if Sadler's Wells offered naturalism, the alternative was fantasy and whimsicality writ large. Nearby Bagnigge Wells used a collage of architectural styles, including Chinese and Gothick, to create a modern exotic fantasy image in direct contrast to the vernacular stability of the ancient inns and their orchards (see fig. 100). Such establishments offered a world of make-believe with their fairytale architecture, illuminated gardens, trellis work and exotic pavilion-type architecture. The exemplars par excellence were Vauxhall and Ranelagh Gardens where a cornucopia of ephemeral architectural delights formed one of the main attractions. At Vauxhall there was a Chinese Pavilion for the orchestra, Gothick supper boxes and Rococo triumphal arches along the walks, while the Music Room was a wonderfully eclectic confection of all three. The slightly later Ranelagh took the architectural crescendo to its utmost pitch, featuring the stupendous central Rotunda building (1741) with its circle of boxes and outside a Chinese Pavilion positioned on the canal set in extensive grounds. The essential razzmatazz is perhaps better captured in Ackerman's view from *The Microcosm of London* of the gaudily illuminated orchestra box at Vauxhall rather than the more often reproduced sanitized scenes of Canaletto (figs 98 and 90 and see fig. 8).

While small suburban tea houses and inns could not compete with the Rotunda at Ranelagh or the pavilions at Vauxhall, they did copy smaller features such as the coloured glass lamps and the private supper boxes which began to appear elsewhere from the 1730s onwards (fig. 99).[21] Bagnigge Wells had a colonnade with individual boxes, and many establishments built them in a circular or inward-facing arrangement so that performances could be put on in the centre. Bagnigge Wells's grounds adjoined the River Fleet and made full use of this waterside location, providing walks and seats along its banks as well as rustic bridges over the stream. In the centre of the gardens were a pond, the boxes or arbours, a rustic cottage and a Gothick grotto 'decorated in cockney fashion with shells, fossils, and fragments of broken glass'.[22] The stylistic melange is epitomized in one of Carington Bowles's prints of *Mr Deputy Dumpling and Family* (1781) on an afternoon visit to Bagnigge Wells, which draws on Hogarth's earlier satire of Sadler's Wells for its composition (fig. 100). Hogarth's lampooning of the City family bringing their urban manners and tastes to the countryside established a stock type for later eighteenth-century satirical prints. Here Bowles reprises many of the familiar features, such as the group's (*top*) 95   Jefferyes Hamett O'Neale, *Copenhagen House, Islington*, 1780–83, drawing, British Museum.

This was a tea house to the west of the village; the game of skittles in the background was a speciality of the place. Note the simple weatherboarded 'long room' which has been added to the existing building to house new entertainments. O'Neale was a leading British porcelain painter who worked at the Chelsea porcelain factory as well as an illustrator.

(*bottom*) 96   John Jones after Henry William Bunbury, *City Foulers – Mark!*, 1785, intaglio print, British Museum.

The suburban location of this hunting scene is indicated by St Paul's in the background; two City men with guns take aim at the quarry their dog has smelt out: 'Against the Wind he takes his prudent way, / While the strong Gale directs him to the prey; / Now the warm scent assure the covey near, / He treads with caution & he points with fear.' The prey is in fact a man squatting behind a bush defecating, echoed by a dog doing likewise on the right. Bunbury satirizes the impossibility of replicating rural pursuits in such a crowded location with people literally behind every bush.

(*facing page*) 97   William Hogarth, *Evening*, from *The Four Times of Day*, 1738, engraving, Victoria and Albert Museum.

Hogarth's image of overfed and overdressed City dwellers, often in family groups, playing at being country folk spawned many imitators in the 'cit' satire genre, such as fig. 100.

(facing page) 98   A. C. Pugin and
Thomas Rowlandson, 'Vauxhall
Gardens', from Ackerman's
The Microcosm of London, 1808–10,
aquatint etching, collection of
David Coke.

99   Anon., *The Devil reproving Sin*,
1804, handcoloured etching, British
Museum.

The view shows a dining box at
Bagnigge Wells complete with a
patriotic illustration of British troops
repelling the French on the wall.
A servant opens a bottle of wine
while a kettle can be seen on a
stand to the right.

overfed physiques indicative of a sedentary lifestyle devoted to business; their unsuitable clothing and general air of discontent; and above all the lampooning of the 'family outing', suggesting the enslavement of the hen-pecked husband to bourgeois domestic life.[23] Such comments are paralleled by other contemporary satires on 'cit's taste', particularly their deployment of an uncouth mixture of architectural styles, which will be explored in Chapter 6. This type of eclecticism could be found in the gardens of the elite as well as the plebeian – the Gothic folly was a staple of great landscape gardens such as Rousham and Stowe – but the reduction in scale bringing such heterodox items into unseemly proximity seems to have excited particular ire (see fig. 150).

The spas around London promoted themselves for their health-giving purifications, fresh air and open countryside, but they were also known as venues for drinking and gambling and gained a more ambiguous reputation as places of sexual immorality. From Colsoni's *Le guide de Londres* (1693) and Ned Ward's *The London Spy* of 1698–1700 onwards, the less respectable inns and

pleasure grounds, particularly those of Islington, became a staple of sex tourism guides and low-life accounts of the city. Indeed, Ward (1667–1731), perhaps inspired by his literary adventures, opened an ale house in 1712, the Bacchus Tavern in Clerkenwell, which he used as the setting for *The Delights of the Bottle* (1720).[24] This alternative tradition of licentiousness informs the view from George Bickham's songbook *The Musical Entertainer* (1733) of New Tunbridge Wells, produced at the height of the spa's success when it was patronized briefly by the princesses Amelia and Caroline (fig. 101). The accompanying song is a risqué ditty by John Lockman, a well-known composer of songs for pleasure gardens, entitled 'The Charms of Dishabille' in which the potential risks and misalliances of mixed company, in both senses of the word, are titillatingly celebrated.[25]

Whence comes it that ye shining Great
To Titles born and awful State,
Thus condescend thus check their Wills,
And scud away to Tunbridge Wells,
To mix with vulgar Beaux & Belles?

100 Carington Bowles after Robert Dighton, *Mr Deputy Dumpling and Family enjoying a Summer Afternoon*, 1781, mezzotint, British Museum.

The quixotic architecture of the Wells, here showing its Gothic ogee-arched entrance canopy with Chinese fretwork doors that contrasts with the sober brickwork and classical canted bay window, is used to symbolize the social and cultural confusion that the enterprise embodied.

Ye Sages your fam'd Glasses raise,
Survey this Meteors dazzling Blaze,
And say, portends it Good or Ill?

.   .   .   .   .   .

Behold the Walks, a checquer'd Shade,
In the gay Pride of Green array'd;
How bright the Sun! the Air how still!
In wild Confusion there we view,
Red Ribbons groop'd with Aprons blew;
Scrapes, Curtzies, Nods, Winks, Smiles & Frowns.
Lords, Milkmaids, Dutchesses and Clowns,
In all their various Dishabille.

The depiction of the healthy pleasures of the taking of the waters and the enjoyment of the attractive grounds are juxtaposed in the image with the more equivocal message of the song, which asks whether such behaviour 'portends . . . Good or Ill?' 'Dishabille' in this context referred to informal or even negligent dress, or 'undress' as it was called at the time, not nakedness. Ladies and gentlemen were said to be in a state of undress while at their toilette, before they had donned the formal attire deemed suitable for the time of day. Normally they would only be seen by others in such a state during their morning levée when intimates might gather in their bedroom, as is famously depicted in the *Countess's Morning Levée* in *Marriage à la Mode* (Plate IV) by Hogarth. To appear in public so attired or unattired was a daring undertaking, and it is open to question how far people really attended the spa in such a manner. It is known to have been open from the early morning, and the satirical publication *Islington: Or, The Humours of New Tunbridge Wells* (1733) opens with 'A Company of Sober Sots' arriving at the place at '5 i'th Morn' for 'a Cooler' after a night's male drinking, followed by at '7 a-Clock 700 Persons of Both Sexes' descending for breakfast.[26] The 'dishabille', then, was part of the artlessness or rusticity that these resorts encouraged, making the potential for social elision even more possible. The image itself, with the languorous poses of those shown positioned round the stairs drinking from the spa – particularly that of the woman in the foreground – speaks of the possibilities of unorthodox encounters in an intermediate space. It is a space neither town nor country, wholly occupied neither by the polite nor by the impolite, an ambiguous arena in which it is suggested the normal moral and social codes of conduct might be suspended.

However, it was not just sexual morality that was at stake here, but the moral health of the nation as well. This forms part of a broader concern with the dangers of leisure, or more specifically an excess of leisure and its necessary concomitant, luxury. The 'luxury debate' has become a mainstay of eighteenth-century studies, as Paul Langford comments: 'A history of luxury and attitudes to luxury would come very close to being a history of the eighteenth century.'[27] From urban guides to poems and ballads, metropolitan literature both celebrated and deplored the duality of

42
The Charms of Dishabille, or New Tunbridge Wells at Islington.
Whence comes it that ye shining Great, To Titles born & awful State, Thus condescend thus
check their Wills, And scud away to Tunbridge Wells, To mix with vulgar Beaux & Belles? Ye
Sages your fam'd Glasses raise Survey this Meteors dazling Blaze, And say, portends it Good or Ill?
Soon as Aurora gilds the Skies,
With brighter Charms ye Ladies rise,
To dart forth Beams that save or kill.
No Homage at the Toilette paid,
(Their lovely Features unsurvey'd)
Sweet Negligence her Influence lend,
And all ye artless Graces blends,
That form ye tempting Dishabille.
Behold ye Walks, a chequer'd Shade,
In ye gay Pride of Green array'd;
How bright ye Sun! ye Air how still!
In wild Confusion there we view,
Red Ribbons groop'd with Aprons blew;
Scrapes, Curtzies, Nods, Winks, Smiles & Frowns,
Lords, Milkmaids, Dutchesses and Clowns,
In their all various Dishabille.
Thus, in the famous Age of Gold,
(Not quite romantic tho' so old)
Mankind were merely Jack & Gill.
On flow'ry Banks, by murm'ring Streams,
They talk'd, walk'd, had pleasing Dreams,
But dress'd indeed, like awkward Folks;
Not Steeple Hats, Surtouts, short Cloaks;
Fig-leaves the only Dishabille.
For the Flute.
G. Bickham junr. Sculp.
The Words by Mr. Lockman Written in 1733.
To ye Tune of ye Black Joke.

101 George Bickham the Younger, 'The Charms of Dishabille, or New Tunbridge Wells at Islington', from *The Musical Entertainer*, 1733, etching and engraving, British Museum.

the outer London pleasure round. The pursuit of leisure (and pleasure) had become constituted as a positive virtue and a central tenet of the elites' claim to legitimacy for leadership. The foundations of the 1688 political settlement rested on the assumption that only those independent of the ties of commerce could truly represent the interests of the nation disinterestedly.[28] The nobility and gentry claimed social superiority not just on the grounds of birth but through the benefits for self-improvement and cultivation that their non-working status bestowed. However, as moralists from the earliest times onwards had cautioned, leisure could be a double-edged sword. An excess of leisure could be as dangerous as its opposite, so that gentlemen in the eighteenth century were enjoined to spend less time in town and take more of an interest in their estates.[29] The reality was that they spent increasing amounts of time in London, due to the extension of the parliamentary, court and social seasons, where an ever-expanding array of social pursuits in and around the capital presented themselves for their delectation. As the author of the *Tricks of the Town Laid Open: Or, a Companion for Country Gentlemen* (1747) argued, in seeking for relief from the tedium of the countryside the metropolis was the last place that sensible young men should search for distraction: 'Idleness is a very dangerous Thing, and the fertile Seminary of almost all other Vices; but then I cannot grant that London is a proper Place to remove you out of the reach of it.'[30]

The *Tricks of the Town* was a vade mecum or portable conduct guide for country dwellers arriving in the capital. This was a genre which stretched back to the early seventeenth century and reached well into the nineteenth century, with cautionary tales such as Pierce Egan's *Life in London* (1821), to which we will return in the final chapter. The *Tricks of the Town* dwelt at length on the dangers that the quasi-rural pursuits of the metropolitan fringes might provide: 'Tis the very same in all the rest of our pretended Diversions, *ie.* Bowling-greens, Cock-pits, Tennis-courts, ordinaries, Balls, Musick-Entertainments, *&c.* tho' the Recreations in themselves may most of 'em be innocent, and harmless enough; yet they are generally so vitiated and corrupted, and the Pleasure they Pretend to, is so interwoven with Danger, as well as Vexation of Spirit.'[31] These seemingly innocent pastimes were in fact the haunts of what he termed the three 'Idle Companions – Sots, Beaus and Gamesters', who would seek out and corrupt any innocent young gentlemen fresh from the country. Even a healthy activity, such as tennis, is exposed as a site of gambling and fleecing from which 'there are several in Town that live purely upon the Tennis-Courts (and live well too)'.[32] In part this was a long-established discourse against vice and dissipation, but the rhetoric was also directed against the commodification of culture which turned leisure into a business: 'I am not entirely advising you against the Play-house, Tennis-court or Bowling-Green, or any other innocent and harmless Recreation. . . . But that which I would reprehend is the Excess and Inordiancy of them; the making that a set and formal Business and trade, which should be only used as a Diversion.'[33] Furthermore, such commodification allowed for hitherto excluded groups such as women and the non-leisured to participate in its offerings. It was the degree of social ambiguity and the inclusion of respectable women (as well as disreputable ones) in these outer London venues that made such spaces both dynamic and dangerous, in contrast to the all-male coffee or alehouse:

> by what Steps and Variations the *British Ladies* have arrived at the excessive Politeness they now enjoy. . . . Our *Great-Grandmothers* they said their Prayers in their Closets, and seldom went to *Play-Houses*, or Places of Diversion; such as *Vaux-Hall, Ranelagh-Gardens*, &c. where as much Money is spent in one Evening, as would keep a Family a Week formerly. The very Thoughts of *Masquerades*, would have put them into a Swoon; and the sight of *Heydegger* [John Jacob Heidegger (1666–1749) was manager of the King's Theatre, Haymarket and a successful promoter of masquerades], would have terrified them. . . . They never insisted on that wicked Innovations, call'd *Pin-Money*, for they had no other Expences, than what were supplied from the Husband's Purse.[34]

Masquerades were particularly dangerous as women attended unescorted, and the use of masks allowed men to pose as women and women as men.[35] Commercialized leisure and its economic imperatives are presented in the quote above as having familial as well as social and moral repercussions. In Thomas Baker's play *Hampstead Heath* (1705), the merchant husband (Deputy Driver) of the main protagonist (Arabella) asks: 'What Business has a Tradesman's Wife at the Wells. Has she not her Family concerns, and a Shop to look to when I'm gone to Change?' He feels instead that she should 'rest contented with my Country-

House at Hogsdon [Hoxton], instead of fluttering through the Walks at Tunbridge . . . where you are laugh'd at by People of Quality and despis'd by People of Sense.'[36]

The ambiguity created in class and gender relations in the outer pleasure resorts was also the hallmark of the area's architecture. Islington's metamorphosis into an urban pleasure ground was not matched by any equivalent physical transformation. As the illustrations show, activities took place in the fields which had ringed the capital for centuries, among which were dotted cottages, inns and other structures largely vernacular in feel and only semi-classical in style at most (see fig. 91).[37] The various spas were largely housed in existing buildings, which could generally be characterized as rustic until at least the latter half of the century, as can be seen at Sadler's Wells (fig. 102). The spring there in fact dried up in 1697, after which the entertainments became the main attraction, along with a tea house. The entry in *The Foreigner's Guide* of 1740 states: 'Here you have all the Summer, Rope-Dancing, Vaulting, Singing, Musick &c. and every Evening there is a farce acted, which every Body may see, drinking and paying for one Bottle of Wine.'[38] The print published by Robert Wilkinson in 1814 provides two views of the building in its pre- and post-1764 state, before and after rebuilding. The earlier view is by George Bickham junior and was published in his *The Universal Harmony* of 1746. As with his 'New Tunbridge Wells' print, the depiction of the wells was originally placed above a song, a format he also used in his *Musical Entertainer* (1737–9), which bought together the sheet music sold at the different pleasure gardens – sometimes in the form of fans – into one volume. This is a good example of the cycles of reproduction and inter-materiality which surrounded the promotional goods of such venues.

There is a striking difference between the two depictions of Sadler's Wells in Wilkinson's print, for whereas the later view presented an image of sophisticated, worldly pleasures for knowing urbanites, in the earlier image the pretence of rural innocence is maintained. The song celebrates the bucolic setting of the resort beside the New River with its opportunities for healthy activities such as fishing as well as the other attractions, concluding with a paean of praise for the sweet air for which it was renowned:

There pleasant streams of Middleton,
In gentle Murmurs glide along:
In which the sporting Fishes play,
To close each weary'd Summers day:
And Musicks Charms in lulling sounds,
Of Mirth and Harmony's abounds:

.   .   .   .

And Zephyrs with their gentlest Gales,
Breathing more sweets than flow'ry Vales,
Which give new Health and Heat repells,
Such are the Joys of Sadlers Wells.

It is likely that this print and the poem were commissioned by the spa's owner at the time, Francis Forcer, as part of a commonly employed marketing strategy under which the semi-rural attractions of the hinterland were continuously promoted within the metropolis through the sale of prints and other souvenirs, and in due course tickets as well. The 1733 publication *Islington: Or, The Humours of New Tunbridge Wells*, for example, was advertised as being sold by 'the Pamphlet Shops of London and Westminster, and Miss Reason at the Wells'. Miss Reason was the principal character and 'Mistress of the Wells' in the story and in reality Mrs Reason, who managed the spa with her husband in the 1730s. The exaggerated pastoral and mythological allusions of the song create an atmosphere of sylvan refinement. However, the picture itself shows that far from taking place, as one might expect, in a suitably classical environment, the entertainments were housed in a pre-Georgian semi-vernacular building. The view foregrounds the natural setting of the secluded walled garden with its mature trees and the river with the two swans. Water remains a powerful presence, but its health-giving qualities are now imparted through the senses rather than being consumed in any more direct fashion. A central seven-bay building is shown with a subsidiary wing to one side, both with pitched roofs and dormer windows plus various attached outhouses. The empty landscape, devoid of people apart from a solitary figure at the window, contributes to the air of serenity and rurality. The irregularity of the windows on the building to the left indicates that it was an earlier or unaltered structure, possibly the Wells-house itself. The main building has a more regular disposition, but the presence of both casement and sash windows suggests that the right-hand side may have been an extension to an existing edifice which was possibly refaced at the same time.[39] The Survey of London suggests that the extension was for a dwelling house for Forcer and his family.[40]

This block was the music house, the end of which is visible, with its old casement latticed windows, in Hogarth's *Evening*. Seclusion had its pitfalls, however, and Forcer had to shift the programme to begin at 5 p.m. and finish before nightfall after the City Marshal was robbed by three footpads on entering Spa Field in 1733.[41] The perils of journeying to Islington and even more so to Hampstead, a notorious highwayman's haunt, remained a perennial problem, and various remedies were tried over the years including armed escorts and specially chartered coaches. When Thomas Rosoman, a local promoter, took over Sadler's Wells in 1746, the lease described the premises as 'the Brewhouse Storehouse Stables Granary Sheds Yards Walls Gardens Walks Trees Outhouses & other Buildings together with the Stage Benches & Galleries thereunto belonging and also all Ways Passages, Lights Pavements Water Springs Wells Watercourses Cellars Vaults Fixtures etc'.[42] In this list none of the structures are described in terms of their entertainment purposes, although other functions are clearly delineated, emphasizing the extent to which the enterprise was housed in converted buildings which retained their previous character and associations. Rosoman resurrected its fortunes as a palace of entertainments, following a period when it had been closed down for immorality. His first major intervention on the site was to build a large wooden theatre in 1748–9. This formed the basis of the large new brick theatre built in 1764, along with a house for himself (also possibly incorporating an

earlier building), which can be seen in the upper print by Andrews (see fig. 102).[43] This was the place Wordsworth recalled visiting in *The Prelude* in his youth, in the years 1788–1802, calling it 'Half-rural Sadlers Wells', where he saw 'giants and dwarfs, Clowns, conjurors, posture-masters, harlequins'.[44] The final and most dramatic development in the early nineteenth century was the aquatic dramas staged on a specially constructed metal tank to display naval battles complete with ships, fireworks and volcanoes – an astonishingly similar list to the attractions on show today at the various aquatic entertainments in Las Vegas. Pugin and Rowlandson included one of these watery pageants as one of the sights of the city in Ackerman's *Microcosm of London* (1808–10) (fig. 103).

Although the second building incorporated classical features and proportioning, it retained a rustic feel in Andrews's view with its steeply pitched roofs, the weather-vane on top of the theatre building and the dormer windows above the house. The illusion of absolute isolation was no longer sustainable, however, and new terraces and buildings are visible in the background. The surroundings were also updated with the addition of lamps and railings along the river in the grounds. By this date urban nuisances were beginning to intrude, and in *c*.1775 a wall and iron railings were placed along the Wells walk on the other side of the river to prevent passers-by 'throwing in their dogs, etc'.[45] Despite its proximity to the capital Islington maintained a rural aspect and vernacular buildings until the end of the eighteenth century. In the village this was probably more a matter of lack of need and opportunity rather than anything more conscious: survivalism rather than revivalism to employ Howard Colvin's useful distinction.[46] But with the vastly expanded number and range of entertainment venues which dotted the fields, this was survivalism of a different order. Given the competition to provide novelty and even excess, the image projected by the buildings of Sadler's Wells of stability and permanence may seem puzzling. It seems likely that the failure to transform the attendant architecture into the polite classicism of the town was not a matter of oversight or neglect but a deliberate ploy to help provide a country feel. The spas adjacent to London marketed themselves as a more convenient alternative to those further afield, particularly Epsom and Tunbridge Wells. To emphasize

103 A. C. Pugin and Thomas Rowlandson, 'The Ocean Fiend or The Infant's Peril', from Ackerman's *The Microcosm of London*, 1808–10, aquatint etching, English Heritage / Survey of London.

In 1801–2 the auditorium was revamped in line with the latest developments in theatre design, notably the introduction of a Circle and galleries supported by slim cast-iron columns, thus improving sight-lines.

the purity of their product the spa owners sought to perpetuate a rustic environment redolent of healthiness and tranquillity, even, paradoxically, as this was being undermined by the large number of townspeople who flocked to them. New forms of social interaction and entertainment were being housed here, but this does not mean that new forms of architecture were necessarily deployed to do so. Modernity, urbanity and the classical did not form an indissoluble holy trinity, and in the case of the outer London spas new forms of entertainment and social engagement were accommodated within an environment constituted predominately by the traditional and the rural.

HAMPSTEAD: THE HILL-TOP RETREAT

Within, thine every-shifting looks surprise, –
Streets, hills, and dells, trees overhead now seen,
Now down below, with smoking roofs between, –

A village, revelling in varieties.
Then northward what a range, – with heath and pond,
Nature's own ground; woods that let mansions through,
And cottaged vales with pillowy fields beyond.

Leigh Hunt, *Description of Hampstead*, 1815

Let us turn now to Hampstead, which, like Islington, first became fashionable in the late seventeenth century with the opening of several spas and associated assembly rooms, shops, taverns and pleasure gardens. This initial phase of popularity was short-lived, and by the 1720s Belsize House to the south was enjoying most of the custom from Hampstead Wells. Its fortunes revived in the 1730s, and it remained a genteel resort for the rest of the eighteenth century.[47] Hampstead, like all spas, had a dual aspect, catering for both the sick who came for rest and recuperation and the healthy who came for a round of sociability and amusement within which the taking of the waters formed just one part. Unlike Islington, where there were a number of rival spas, Hampstead presented a far more unified face to its clientele due to the fact that the wells were situated on land which had been gifted to the parish in 1698, known as the Wells Estate.[48] This enabled a much more systematic approach to be taken to the operating of the spa, including the appointment of a resident doctor whose house formed a prominent part of the complex. The first medical man there was a Dr Gibbons, who wrote an *Experiment on the Hampstead Waters*. He was succeeded by others keen to promote their services in written accounts, following the example of the famous Dr Oliver at Bath, who produced his *Practical Dissertation on Bath-Waters* in 1707. John Soame, the resident doctor in the mid-eighteenth century, modelled his *Hampstead Wells: Or, Directions for the Drinking of those Waters* (1734) on Oliver's text, stressing that his was a practical guide for the layperson rather than an obscure scientific account. Soame naturally extolled the virtues of Hampstead's air and position, and obviously intended his tract as an attempt to win back custom from his Islington rivals. The taste of the Hampstead waters – 'the Fountain of Health', he wrote – is 'much stronger and better than the New Tunbridge Wells at Islington that have been frequented so much of late'.[49] He cautioned against excessive alcohol consumption with a limit of no more than 'three or four glasses at dinner'.[50] The new menace of tea presented even greater dangers: 'I hope the inordinate Drinking of Thea will be retrenched, which, if continued, must bring a thousand Ills upon us.'[51] The spa was structured around the intake of these three liquids, although often in inverse proportion to that recommended by the doctors. Taking the waters was a

greater isolation plus its spectacular position led to the creation of a particular identity, a hill-top *urbs in rure*. It is situated on the slopes of one of the highest hills around London, at its summit 443 feet above sea level. The Northern Heights sit on a bed of clay from the lower slopes of which issue numerous springs and ponds, where the water-bearing sand runs out, some of which can be seen in John Rocque's map (fig. 104). However, its position slightly further from the centre put it at a disadvantage against other nearby places such as Islington and Bayswater. Complaints about the expense of staying at resorts were commonplace, and as Dr Soame related, 'Our provisions are full as good as those of *London*; but I can't say altogether as cheap.'[52]

Hampstead's spectacular growth and transformation from just another outlying Middlesex village was commented on by Defoe in the 1720s:

> Hampstead indeed is risen from a little country village, to a city, not upon the credit only of the waters, though 'tis apparent, its growing greatness began there . . . nor could the uneven surface, inconvenient for building, uncompact and unpleasant, check the humour of the town, for even on the very steep of the hill, where there's no walking twenty yards together, without tugging up a hill, or straddling down a hill. . . . But it must be confessed, 'tis so near heaven, that I dare not say it can be a proper situation, for any but a race of mountaineers, whose lungs have been used to a rarified air, nearer the second region, than any ground for thirty miles round it.[53]

In Baker's play *Hampstead Heath* the resort is presented as a social melting pot for all classes: 'Assemblies so near the Town, give us a Sample of each Degree. We have Court Ladies, that are all Air and no Dress; City Ladies, that are over-dress'd and no Air; and Country Dames with broad brown Faces like a *Stepney* Bun; besides an endless number of *Fleetstreet* Semstresses that dance Minuets in their Furbeloe Scarfs, and their Cloaths hang as loose about 'em as their Reputations.'[54] One of the play's heroines, Arabella, 'a modern City Lady', has run away to Hampstead to escape her boring 'Old Citt' husband, Deputy Driver. The outer London location, as with Islington, allows her a freedom not available in the close confines of the City: 'Well, this *Hampstead's* a charming Place, – to dance all

104 John Rocque, *An Exact Survey of the City's of London, Westminster ye Borough of Southwark and the Country near Ten Miles Round*, 1746, Guildhall Library.

morning activity, while the tea table dominated the afternoon and alcohol the evening's entertainments. This liquid economy and the constant circulation of fluids through the body was echoed by the circulatory round in which they were consumed; as the fluids circulated the body so the visitors perambulated around the resort, moving from one attraction to another in a set fashion through the day.

Hampstead, in contrast to its southern neighbour, was approximately four miles from the centre, and its night at the Wells, and be treated at *Mother Huff's* [a tavern on the Heath]; – to have Presents made one at the Raffling-Shops, and then to take a Walk in *Cane-Wood* [Kenwood] with a Man of Wit, that's not over rude; – but to be five or six Miles from one's Husband, Marriage were a happy State cou'd one be always five or six Miles from one's Husband.'[55] Arabella may love the Wells, but as her husband points out, her enthusiastic embracing of the social round lays her open to ridicule and worse. As Driver complains at the spa, where flirtatious behaviour was the norm, she may be approached by and dance with anyone: 'Why shou'd any Man speak to my Wife, he may as well come and dine with me without an Invitation?'[56]

Arabella mentions the different parts of Hampstead, which, according to the guidebook *London in Miniature* (1755), consisted of three distinct locations: the Village, the Wells further up the hill, and the Heath.[57] The village was the existing settlement centred around the pond and the green – the area marked Pound Street on Rocque's map – and then continuing up the High Street. The area to the east of the High Street was the new development around the Wells. The waters from the spa could be purchased on site and also in the centre, transported every day by a wagon to be sold in both the City and Westminster.[58] By 1700 flasks were available for threepence with a home delivery service provided for a penny extra.[59] Further north and west large individual mansions can be seen. These began to be built from the late seventeenth century onwards as out-of-town residences by the 'citizens and merchants of London', who were the 'chief inhabitants' of the place according to Dodsley.[60] The 'varieties' of landscape which characterized the village, as Leigh Hunt put it in his poem, were a major part of the appeal of the resort. Mrs Nollekens expounded on these in her usual theatrical style:

Towards the latter part of her life, she expressed a wish to go once more to Hampstead, a spot considered by most physicians and landscape painters as the most salubrious and beautiful of all the Montpeliers of England; but she could neither make up her mind as to the enormous expense of its accommodations, nor as to the peculiar fragrance of its seven sort of air, which of them she ought then to prefer. The latter perplexity afforded her at times

much conversation; and when she was requested to name the seven airs, she, in an elevated voice, stated them thus. 'My dear Sir, there are the fours sides of the hill, each receiving freely the air from the four quarters. There is the hill itself, very clear, but certainly often bleak. Then there is the 'Vale of Health', as it is called, in a stagnate bottom; a pit in the heath, where, if a bit of paper is whirling in the air, it can never rise above the high ground above it. And is there not also the mild air of the centre of the town [i.e. Hampstead], where the situation, though high, is entirely sheltered by surrounding buildings.'[61]

The Heath at this date comprised the area of common land to the east and north of the settlement. The village was made up of a similar mix of buildings to those found in Islington (see fig. 109). For the most part it consisted of cottages, alleys and courts designed and arranged in a traditional fashion. A nineteenth-century description from James Thorne's *Handbook to the Environs of London* (1876) conveys both its essentially cramped conditions and labyrinthine layout when viewed with a robust Victorian eye: 'The "Town" straggles up the slopes of the hill, towards the Heath on the top, in an odd, sideling, tortuous, irregular and unconnected fashion. There are the fairly broad winding High Street, and other good streets . . . and alongside them houses small and large, without a scrap of garden, and only a very little dingy yard; narrow and dirty byways, courts and passages, with steep flights of steps, and mean and crowded tenements.'[62] The lack of regular arrangements in the town, even in the newly developed area around the Wells, was partly due to its hilly topography, as Defoe thought, which discouraged regularized planning. It also arose out of the more individualistic nature of development in the outlying areas, which resulted in a greater variety of arrangements than in the centre. There were only two attempts to adopt formal layouts: Hampstead Square (1700–20), which for many years only consisted of a single terrace, and Church Row, begun in the early eighteenth century but not finished until the 1770s (fig. 105). The Row was intended for subletting to visitors to the Wells, and the lack of individual mews behind it suggests that the houses were never envisaged as more than short-term residences. Stabling for horses and

carriages was provided at the many inns and elsewhere
for both overnighting tourists and those who came for
the day from London. Rocque's map of 1746 shows
Church Row extending westwards from the High
Street but not yet meeting up with the new church
completed in the following year.[63]

Even the central thoroughfare which led down to
the Wells, Flask Walk (where flasks of bottled water
were sold), was built in a vernacular idiom (fig. 106).
This was not due to any lack of custom. In 1755 it
was described as a place 'where a constant Assembly is
kept during the Summer, and frequently Balls and
Concerts of Musick'.[64] The gatherings, which included
tea, evening and card parties, as well as dances, took
place from Whitsuntide until October, a guinea subscription admitting a gentleman and two ladies to the
'Ball Room' every other Monday. Assemblies were
another of the new forms of leisure which challenged
established norms in being for both sexes, and often
organized by women, as well as admitting both the
upper and middle classes.[65] Bronze medallion season
tickets for Hampstead Wells and Marylebone Gardens
survive in the British Museum, but the Hampstead one
is particularly notable for its architectural imagery (fig.
107). It shows a possibly idealized view of the first Ball
or Long Room in a similar idiom to surviving houses
of the time such as Burgh or Fenton House but with

the addition of an imposing portico (see fig. 133).[66]
This building was replaced in the 1730s with a plain,
two-storey building (fig. 108). The first one had been
closed *c.*1720 as it was attracting too many disreputable
elements and ironically reopened as a chapel-of-ease.
It was the second Long Room on which Fanny Burney's eponymous heroine in *Evelina* of 1778 appositely
commented, 'This room seems to be very well named,
for I believe it would be difficult to find another
epithet which might with propriety distinguish it, as
it is without ornament, elegance, or any sort of singu-
larity, and merely to be marked by its length.'[67] Far
from being an aberration, the Long Room was in
keeping with the rest of the surrounding environment,
which was traditional in character and style, as can still
be seen in the surviving eighteenth-century architecture and layout of Hampstead and its close neighbour
Highgate, the subject of the following chapter. At
Hampstead, as at Islington, the approach deployed at
Vauxhall Gardens of utilizing modern art and architecture in the service of commercial success and increased
respectability was eschewed. Instead, in the case of
these existing villages the reverse strategy seems to
have been employed, and the vernacular with its associations of continuity, stability and permanence was
used to enhance an atmosphere of rusticity and infor-
mality, thus perpetuating an alternative environment to
that of the centre.

Jean Baptist Claude Chatelain's *Prospects of Highgate
and Hampstead* (1745, reissued 1750 and 1752), was the
first major series of views of Hampstead (figs 108 and
109). It created a new classicizing, genteel image for
the spa very different from that of the 1730s prints of
the Islington resorts. The 'rural' still provides the dominant theme, but under the hand of the Frenchman the
rustic has been replaced by the elegant pastoral. His
Prospects of Highgate and Hampstead comprised eight
views and were promoted in the *General Advertiser* of
1745 as being available at five shillings for the set from
W. H. Toms at Union Court, Holborn.[68] Chatelain
revitalized the depiction of the spa by a careful elimi-
nation of any actual details of its operations and clientele and a concentration instead on the magnificent
landscape in which Hampstead was situated. He shifted
the focus to the Heath, which with its walks, fine
views and scattered hostelries had become an attraction in itself. The built environment was used to

106 Flask Walk, Hampstead, early eighteenth century.

This shows the low building line, prominent roofscape and broad proportions which resulted in a townscape different in feel and scale from that of the city centre.

107 Bronze medallion season ticket for Hampstead Wells Ball Room, 1701–33, British Museum.

The inscription reads: 'This Admits Two Ladys into the Ball Room.'

provide eye-catching landmarks or operated as a generalized backdrop of pleasingly irregular architectural scenography. Unlike in his later series *Fifty Views* (1750), where the semi-rural zone was depicted as a social melting pot, in the *Prospects* we have an idealized vision of a resort populated exclusively by well-dressed representatives of polite society. These elegant figures are set against a background rustic chorus of 'peasants', who are scattered artfully about the Heath tending their herds while their makeshift hovels are kept firmly out of view. A comparison with his *View of St Mary's Church, Islington* (see fig. 76) demonstrates the differing approach between the two series. The one transforms the Northern Heights into a British campagna for the privileged classes dotted with the odd animal contentedly grazing, while in the other sheep are driven en masse to slaughter past buildings and locations delineated in detail. The contrast is further highlighted by the superior quality of the drawing and engraving of the Hampstead *Prospects* compared to the sketchy rough feel of the Islington *View* with its stick-like figures; even the very title of the former is grander. In eschewing the crude representational devices with which the middle classes were often saddled in satirical prints derived from the Hogarthian *Evening* genre, Chatelain provided an alternative means of figuring these new spaces as genteel and urbane. He reflected back to Hampstead's bourgeois residents an idealized image of themselves at their most polite, at leisure in their rustic suburban retreat.

108   J. B. C. Chatelain, 'A Prospect of the Long Room at Hampstead from the Heath', from *Prospects of Highgate and Hampstead*, 1745, etching, British Museum.

The Ball Room is to the right, the Long Room to the left. Behind the latter can be seen Burgh House, the residence of the spa doctor.

109   J. B. C. Chatelain, 'A Prospect of Part of Hampstead from the Top of Pond Street looking down to the Bottom', from *Prospects of Highgate and Hampstead*, 1745, etching, British Museum.

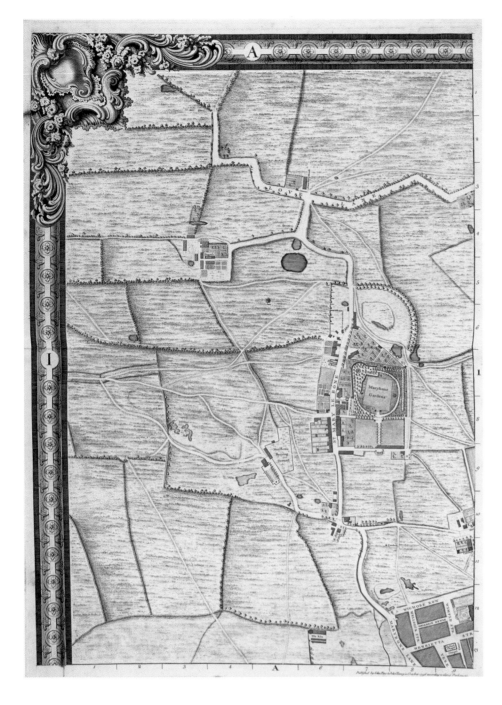

such as Tottenham Court Road and on a larger scale with the development of the Cavendish-Harley estate in the 1720s, which pioneered genteel housing above what was then the generally accepted northern limit of London, Oxford Street. Opposite the estate's centrepiece of Cavendish Square there was a coldbath and the basin. The latter was a less grand version of the great basins and canals in the royal parks, notably the Long Water in St James's Park and Kensington Basin to the west. Such water features were utilitarian as well as ornamental, providing reservoirs for the city.

Marleybone offered a mixture of types of venues and experiences finely calibrated to the pockets and expectations of different social groups. The *Tricks of the Town* (1747) related: 'The number of Bowling Greens that we have in and near this Town are unaccountable' but those at Marylebone 'having in these latte Years gain'd a kind of Preheminence [*sic*] and Reputation above the rest, and thither most of the Noblemen and Gentlemen about the Town, that affect that sort of Recreation, generally resort'.[69] Many of the bowling greens were attached to inns, such as the one at the Rose, a notorious gaming house and haunt of highwaymen and thieves, which featured in Gay's *Beggar's Opera* (1728). J. T. Smith wrote of the perils for 'Londoners in their walks through the green lanes to Mary-le-bone', which included 'highwaymen who committed nightly depredations . . . the pickpockets who attended the thousands of Sunday friends who congregated in Mary-le-bone-fields'.[70] Criminals were indiscriminate in their prey, not distinguishing between gamblers and Nonconformists, the area being a popular preaching spot for the latter. These outdoor meetings of Dissenters combined the spiritual with the possibility of more secular pleasures, as the author of *A Trip from St James's to the Royal-Exchange* (1744) cynically observed:

In my Peregrinations through the City, I could not help observing that the Dissenters are much degenerated from their former way of keeping the *Sabbath*. . . . To have refresh'd the Joints with a Walk, or the Countenance with a Smile, would have been as bad as Sacrilege or Murder, it would have been prophaning the Day, and closing with the Temptation of the Devil: But now also the Case is quite otherwise with too many of them, who can on the

110   John Rocque, *An Exact Survey of the City's of London, Westminster ye Borough of Southwark and the Country near Ten Miles Round*, 1746, London Metropolitan Archives.

MARYLEBONE FIELDS: BOWLING GREENS AND GARDENS

As London spread westwards, for those living in the Westminster suburbs the most convenient and nearest place for entertainment was Marylebone. Rocque's map of the area in the mid-eighteenth century (fig. 110) shows the major places of entertainment and the slow spread of development north of Oxford Street. This took place both incrementally along routeways

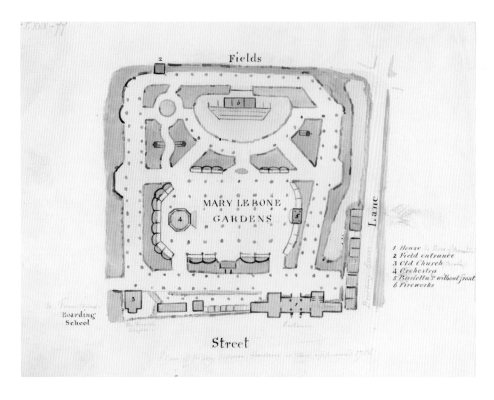

In the image, labels read:
Fields

MARY LE BONE
GARDENS

Lane

1 House
2 Field entrance
3 Old Church
4 Orchestra
5 Burletta? without front
6 Fireworks

Boarding
School

Street

The gardens could be entered either
through the old Rose Tavern from
Marylebone High Street (1) or from
Marylebone Fields to the north (2).
In the centre of the gardens was an
orchestra (4) with what may be
supper boxes arranged around it.
Opposite was a stage for the
performance of burlettas, miniature
comic operas (5), while the pièce de
résistance was the fireworks placed at
the far end (6), for which the
gardens were famed.

Lord's Day prefer *Saddler's Wells* to *Salter's Hall*, and
a *Bottle* to the *Bible*.[71]

The vogue for the peculiarly 'English preoccupation
with walking as a leisure activity' is another phenomenon, like landscape views, usually traced to the late
eighteenth century and the Romantic fascination with
the rural.[72] But there is plenty of evidence for the
middle classes, Dissenters and otherwise, indulging
in the pastime from the early eighteenth century:
an activity which had previously been purely the
unwanted lot of the poor. Laura Williams has shown
how perambulation was another phenomenon arising
from the ideas about health and movement discussed
in the Introduction. It was thought to be one of the
best ways to stimulate the necessary circulation of the
fluids in the body. This was deemed to be particularly
important for urban dwellers, whose lives were more
physically circumscribed than was 'natural'. Walking
and taking the air became the two essential activities
in order to maintain a healthy constitution.[73] The
extent to which walking in the rural hinterland had
become identified as the primary activity for a Sunday
is evidenced by the anonymous guidebook, *A Sunday
Ramble: Or, Modern Sabbath-Day Journey; In and about
the Cities of London and Westminster*, which went

through four editions between 1774 and 1780. The
book offered a guide to 'the various interesting
scenes ... of this Metropolis and its Environs', which
included mineral wells, coffee houses, places of public
worship, taverns, public gardens, Sunday routs and
bagnios.[74] The author observed: 'The innocent amusement of walking in the fields and publick gardens
about town, after divine service, and partaking of
moderate refreshment at those places; ...[is] highly
necessary [for] those whose business will not conveni-
ently permit them to leave the metropolis on any
other day[; they] should then endeavour to receive a
little wholesome air, were it only for the preservation
of their health.'[75]

Marylebone Fields was one such space for fresh air
and strolling, while more organized leisure pursuits
could be found at Marylebone Gardens (1737), which
grew out of the gardens of the Rose and became a
mini-Vauxhall with its walks, concerts, balls and fireworks for a largely polite clientele (fig. 111). John
Donowell produced a suitably refined depiction of it
in his print of 1755, in which the garden bears a striking resemblance to Vauxhall with its two-storey pavilions and grand central avenue (fig. 112). Very late in
the day, in 1773, mineral waters were discovered on
the site. Often such a 'discovery' was a ruse to revive
the fortunes of a flagging enterprise, but in this case
it is plausible as the Bayswater area was riven with
springs.[76] However, ultimately this was not successful,
and the by now 'Marylebone Spa' closed in 1778.
Marylebone Fields was too close to the expanding
suburbs of Westminster to survive beyond the end of
the eighteenth century. J. T. Smith reminisced about
how the orchestra at Marylebone Gardens where he
had stood as a boy was now 17 Devonshire Place, and
a 1793 print shows cricket being played behind the
new housing of the very same terrace (fig. 113).[77]
The Marylebone Cricket Club played in the adjacent
fields, having been established in 1787 on ground
belonging to one Thomas Lord, on the site of what is
now Dorset Square.[78]

In his book *Nollekens and his Times* Smith provides
a wonderfully vivid portrait of the use made of Marylebone Fields in the everyday life of those who lived
nearby. He was apprenticed to Nollekens in Mortimer
Street, just off Cavendish Square, and his account
shows how finely calibrated to the pockets and expec-

112 John Donowell, *A View of the Orchestra with the Band of Music, the Grand Walk &c. in Marybone Gardens*, published by John Tinney, 1755, etching and engraving, British Museum.

The orchestra pavilion is on the right with what is presumably the burletta building shown opposite. The print has dual English and French titles and positions Marylebone as a rival to Vauxhall.

tations of various social groups were the different venues and the offerings within them. Nollekens, although wealthy, was notoriously parsimonious, and Smith's text reveals a form of self-catering that was permitted at some premises:

Sometimes in the evening, when they had no engagements, to take a little fresh air, and to avoid interlopers, they would, after putting a little tea and sugar, a French-roll, or a couple of ruskes into their pockets, stray to Madam Caria's, a Frenchwoman,

113 Samuel Hieronymus Grimm, *View in Marylebone with Cricket Match*, 1793, drawing, British Library.

The view looks towards the rear elevation of the recently built Devonshire Place on the Portland Estate.

114 George Morland, *St James's Park*, 1790, oil, Yale Center for British Art, Paul Mellon Collection.

The milk seller's counter in the park with a family and a soldier, possibly one of those who patrolled the park, as also depicted in fig. 80.

who lived near the end of Marylebone-lane, in what were at that time called the French Gardens, principally tenanted by the citizens, where persons were accommodated with tea equipage and hot-water at a penny a-head. . . . Mrs Nollekens made it a rule to allow one servant, – as they kept two, – to go out on alternate Sunday; for it was Mr. Nollekens opinion, that if they were never permitted to visit the Jew's Harp, Queen's Head and Artichoke, or Chalk Farm, they never would wash 'theirselves'.[79]

Another example of the do-it-yourself nature of outdoor catering, as well as some highly imaginative

marketing, is found in the following advertisement from the *London Evening Post* of 2 July 1772 in which a walking milk bar, with a suitably grand Latin title, is presented as a new attraction:

The New Lactarium
Elizabeth Hannever presents her grateful respects to the public . . . and begs leave to inform them that her new Lactarium, near the Obelisk in St George's Fields, is just finished, where Ladies and Gentlemen may be supplied with new milk from the cow; likewise whey made fresh every day.
A daily paper taken in

115   George Morland, *A Tea Garden*,
1790, oil, Tate.

Three generations of a middle-class
family take tea at Bagnigge Wells.
They are waited on by a servant
filling a silver tea-pot which matches
the silver cream jug on the table, the
accoutrements of gentility supplied
by the gardens.

Syllabubs anytime, if customers bring their own
wine
NB Due attendance paid to carriages, in which
quality may sit and be supplied.
Wine may be had next door.[80]

Whether the Lactarium had any physical form beyond
the cow is unclear, but it shows how any assets, even
a humble cow, could be repackaged and commodified
for public consumption, notwithstanding that a large
part of the infrastructure seemed to be supplied by the
customers themselves. There was a similar 'Lactarium'
at St James's Park, of which the *London in Miniature*

guide wrote: 'At each end of the Mall there are stands
of cows, from whence the company at small expence,
may be supplied with warm milk.'[81] George Morland
painted the scene along with a companion piece, *A
Tea Garden*, which depicts a middle-class family taking
tea in the gardens at Bagnigge Wells (figs 114 and 115).
Tea drinking had been introduced to Britain in the
mid-seventeenth century as an elite activity, but had
overtaken coffee and chocolate in popularity by the
eighteenth century.[82] The purchasing of a tea set was
a considerable expense but also a status symbol, as the
many paintings of 'conversation pieces' grouped around
a tea table demonstrate.[83] Mr and Mrs Nollekens's

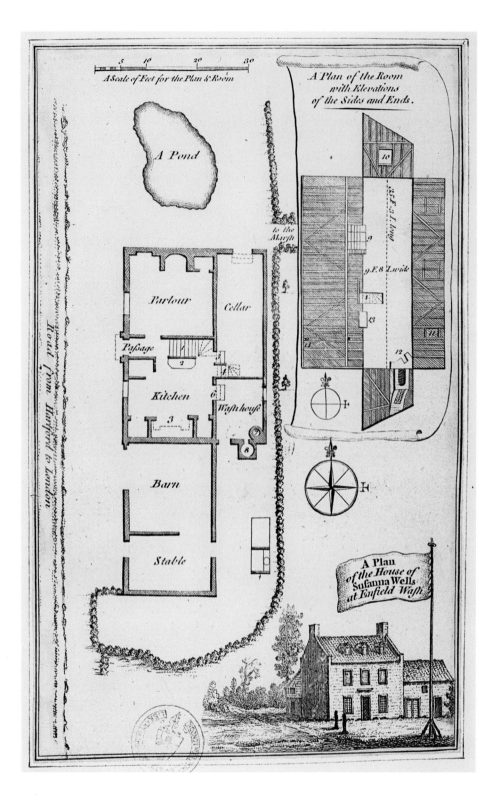

116 Anon., *View of Susanna Wells's house at Enfield in Middlesex*, n.d., etching, London Metropolitan Archives.

in an individual tea set, only the tea and sugar. The taking of tea by the middle classes became another object for abuse. *The Gentleman's Magazine* wrote of Islington in 1791: 'Despise it not, because the plodding cit there seeks to inhale a little fresh air, or his holiday prentice and sweetheart regale with tea and hot rolls at White Conduit House.'[84] Morland's sympathetic painting provides a powerful corrective to such satirical accounts, showing the tea garden as a space for family relaxation and quiet enjoyment rather than for frenetic social competition.

Tea gardens ranged greatly in scale and clientele. Some were combined with spas and provided mineral water as well, while others were simply a garden attached to an inn or even a house. Susanna Wells's house in Enfield seems to be a residential house with a long room, which is little more than a glorified timber shed, along one side (fig. 116). The addition of a Long Room was a standard means of providing a place for assemblies, concerts and other gatherings, and thus transforming a simple tavern or garden into a more varied attraction by tacking a lightweight wooden structure onto an existing building with upper-floor access (see fig. 95). As James Stevens Curl notes, there was a large degree of overlap in the battery of features deployed: 'So spurious Spas copied real ones; places of entertainment that were really only Gardens with a few buildings emulated Spas and spurious Spas; humble public-houses with Gardens attempted to follow fashion . . . and establishments with only the vaguest connection with health and pleasure latched on to the fashion of the day, no matter how mean and primitive were the facilities on offer.'[85]

The social geography of the Marylebone complex hinged on the gardens and the basin, and Nollekens was aghast one time when he was near to being spotted on the wrong side of the water at one of the three more plebian inns in the area (fig. 117). The following quote reveals the fine gradations that even a fairly ordinary inn might impose, with an outside placement reserved for those of inferior dress – cheap clothing being another eccentricity adopted by the affluent and socially well-connected artist:

Mr. Nollekens was returning from a bench placed in front of the Queen's-head and Artichoke as a seat for those persons whose dress did not appear to

taking of tea in the French gardens demonstrates that such public facilities enabled the transference of a private indoor ritual to the more democratic outdoor realm of the tea garden. The provision of the 'tea equipage' also meant that it was not necessary to invest

117 J. Findlay, *View of the Queen's Head and Artichoke*, 1796, drawing, British Museum.

entitle them to acommodation [*sic*] withinside the house. On spotting a friend he said to his man Dodimy – Nollekens. 'What! My old friend, Noel Jennings? What the devil does he do on this side of the water, in Marybone-fields? Does he look this way?' – 'No, Sir,' was the reply. 'Ah! Well then, walk on this side; don't let him see me.'[86]

118 George Cruikshank, *Mr Cripps encountering his Master in Mary-le-bone Gardens*, 1820, engraving, British Museum.

The master and mistress are the couple to the left looking shocked as they see their fashionably dressed servant consorting with the extravagantly attired lady on the right. The orchestra pavilion is visible behind.

A similar scene of social confusion is played out in Cruickshank's *Mr Cripps encountering his Master in Mary-le-bone Gardens*, in which the oft-repeated problem of distinguishing gentlefolk and servants is played out in this socially ambiguous public arena (fig. 118). These issues of social insecurity and competitiveness lead us to our last section, which brings many of the themes of this chapter together with a cautionary tale from Hampstead.

✳

119 Mounted fan-leaf with a view of the house of Thomas Osborne at Hampstead, recto, 1754, hand-coloured etching, British Museum.

The house with the tent for dancing that was hastily erected in the courtyard.

A MODERN MORALITY TALE: THOMAS OSBORNE'S HAMPSTEAD HOUSE-WARMING

Two fans survive in the Schreiber collection in the British Museum which form a wonderful Hogarthian parable on the costs (in all senses of the word) of social ambition and vanity in the rootless and highly competitive world of the outer London spa resorts (figs 119 and 120). The scene is set on the suburban mini-estate of the City bookseller Thomas Osborne, who is throwing a party at his newly acquired second house. The fans – one is black and white and unmounted and the other (reproduced here) is coloured and mounted – both show the same scene at the house of Thomas Osborne in Hampstead. The mounted fan has an inscription written along the side which tells us that its owner

'went to an entertainment with Duckhunting their [sic] 10 of September 1754'. The fan is a souvenir of a house-warming party of which we know a great deal thanks to a manuscript account written by the fan-owner's daughter:

My mother, who was then 16, was present at this housewarming, as part of the family of her uncle Mr Betts of Church Row Hampstead and as a visitor had a fan sent her the 5th of October following, which has been carefully preserved and is perhaps the only one left. From her I desire this information. I have no recollection of the situation of the house, which it is evident by the print stood on the right hand of the road, placed sideways to it, and very near the heath.[87]

140

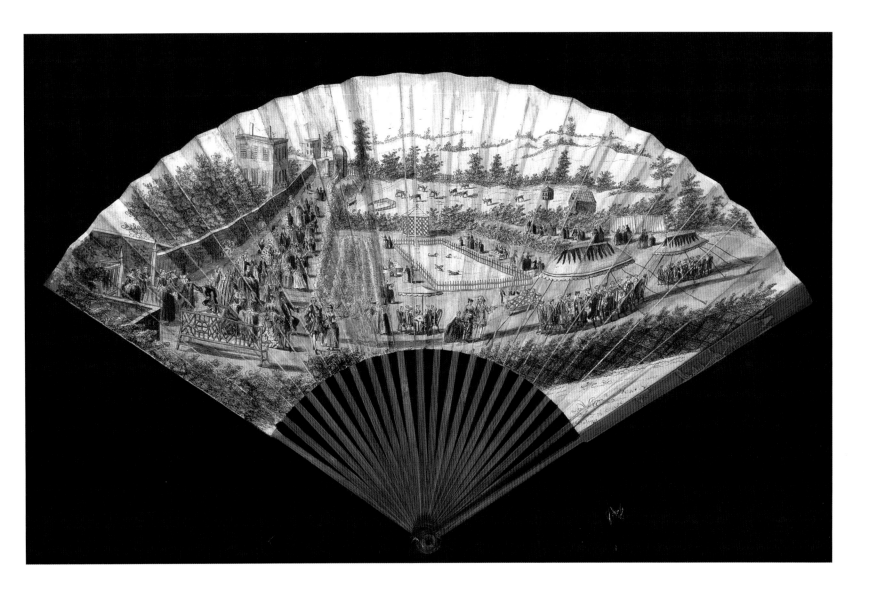

120 Mounted fan-leaf with a view of the house of Thomas Osborne at Hampstead, verso, 1754, hand-coloured etching, British Museum.

The garden showing the public breakfast and the duck hunting with annotations for the 'park', 'pond' and 'duck hunting'.

In fact, the house stood on the east side of the High Street behind Flask Walk and was called Norway or Burford House. This area was developing rapidly at the time, with a terrace of shops built at Flask Walk in the early eighteenth century (see fig. 106) and the neighbouring house of Thomas Gardnor, which was named after him, c.1736.[88] The house was typical of the new brick mansion houses in the Hampstead and Highgate area, some of which sat at the centre of what were effectively mini-estates (fig. 121). The fan is annotated in the same hand as the inscription, with the 'park', 'pond' and 'duck hunting' all delineated. The area where the duck-hunting and entertainments took place was actually the garden, while the miniature park beyond housed deer and a dovecot, all part of the signification of the traditional landed estate here reduced to a sub-

urban scale with a neighbouring house and inn for company. The view to the Heath in the distance increases the sense of scale and rurality. Similar houses, such as Fenton and Burgh, were built nearby to take advantage of the prospect over the Heath and the landscape that it provided (see fig. 133). The field where the duck-hunting was held is notable for its fretwork trellises, furniture and octagonal gazebo, which were probably installed temporarily.[89] They are reminiscent of the type of flamboyant ornamentation found in pleasure grounds, often themselves little more than fields. The most notable feature of all is the company parading in the grounds, dancing in front of the house and feasting under the tented pavilions. The duck-hunting is the physical and metaphorical centrepiece of the event, speaking as it does of the country pursuits

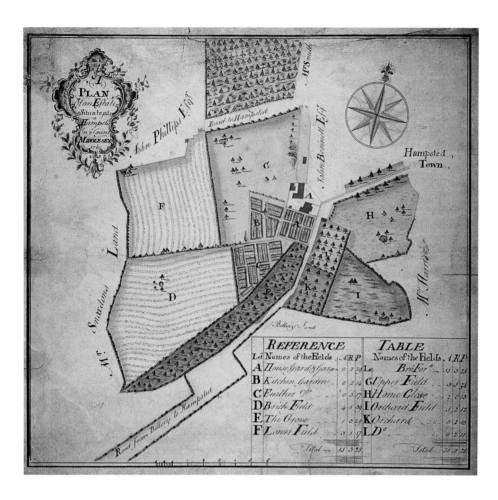

In 1754 he had a house at Hampstead whether he had lived there before, or not is now uncertain. Hampstead was then a watering place, and very gay. A Captain Pratten constituted himself Master of the Ceremonies at the Assembly in the Long Room, Flask Walk.

Amongst the fixed residents at Hampstead, was Mr Scarlet, a celebrated optician of Macclesfield Street Soho, whose microscopes for viewing opake [opaque] objects is still in use. [Following section crossed out – Capt Pratten was illegible illegible in his attention to Mrs Scarlett than to any other lady, and was her illegible companion in her walks and visits. He also dined almost constantly at her houses. As Mrs Scarlett illegible considerably plain in her person, the voice of scandal asserted that this attention was illegible by the use of her fortune, and that the Captain was supported by her. – end crossing out]

When Mr Osborne had settled himself in his new house, Capt. Pratten proposed to him that he should ingratiate himself with the families of Hampstead by giving a public breakfast for the ladies, and a duck hunting for the gentlemen; this gives room to suppose that he was then a newcomer to the place. Tommy Osborne though very successful in business, was not esteemed very acute in private life. He fell into the scheme and left the whole management to Capt. Pratten. Invitations were accordingly issued to all the genteel families in the place. Marquees were pitched in the adjoining field, for the breakfast, and ducks provided for the hunt.

The day 10th of September came, the company assembled, and were so happy that they were loath to depart. Capt. Pratten was everywhere, and finding things went on so smoothly suggested to Mr Osborne that the company seemed inclined to stay, [crossed out – would be offended if they were dismissed immediately while in the height of pleasure,] and that he had better continue the entertainment by a cold collation. The larders of the different taverns were accordingly put on requisition, and the collation appeared: still the company lingered on the spot, and Capt. Pratten and Mrs Scarlet circulated in whispers that if they staid they would have a

121 Plan of an estate in Hampstead, 1762, London Metropolitan Archives.

The key gives an idea of what a small suburban estate might include: (A) House Yard and Garden; (B) Kitchen Garden; (C) Further Gardens; (D) Brick Field; (E) The Grove (a plantation); (F) Home Close; (I) and (K) Orchards; the rest are fields. It is also noteworthy that the rent for the brick field is far higher than that for any of the other land or property.

of the landed gentry, although by this point in the proceedings only two ducks remain to be chased by two dogs (in the black and white version thirteen ducks are still alive). The passivity of the 'hunt', in which the ducks were tied to the ground rather than being pursued across a large estate, echoes the manufactured and miniaturized nature of the event and its setting.

The social significance of the duck-hunting is the key to the drama, as is revealed in the accompanying manuscript, which is quoted from in full:

Mr. Thomas Osborne, or as he was more commonly called Tommy Osborne was a very considerable bookseller and publisher in Gray's Inn Gate Holborn.

He bought the Harleian Collection of Printed books, and published a sale catalogue of them in [blank] which is still valuable as affording a classed list of the printable books respecting English History and Literature in which it was particularly rich. Dr Samuel Johnson has been said to be the compiler of this catalogue.

dance to conclude the day. The company took the hint, smiling at their host's vanity and expence; and Capt Pratten persuaded him that as the day was so far advanced he had better send to one of the taverns for their dancing tent and a band, and make a good finish to the day's pleasure. [crossed out illegible 'house warming'] No sooner was this suggested than it was done. The long dancing tent was set up in the court yard in the front of the house, and the younger part of the company tripped on the light fantastic toe until bed time.

To prolong the memory of this day enjoyment Capt. Pratten further persuaded Mr Osborne to have a fan engraved, and presented to each of his lady visitors: which was done. On one side appeared the field with the breakfast marquee and duck pond, with Hampstead Heath in the distance. Capt. Pratten appears just entering the field with Mrs Scarlet and her little daughter. On the other side is a view of Osborne's house, with the dancing tent and band as it appeared in the evening. Capt. Pratten with his two companions stand as spectators of the dance. On the left hand is the gate opening on the Hampstead road, and on the right, the entrance into the field where the festivities commenced. The etching of the fan is well executed.[90]

This tale could stand comparison with one of Hogarth's 'Modern Moral Progresses' in its depiction of greed, manipulation, social ambition and insecurity all posited around the recent purchase of a suburban estate. Osborne (?1704–1767) was one of the most successful booksellers of his day; as John Nichols related in his *Literary Anecdotes* of the period, 'Tom Osborne, who filled one side of Gray's Inn with his lumber, and, without knowing the intrinsic value of a single book, contrived such arbitrary prices as raised him to a country house and dog-and-duck huntings.'[91] It is likely that the great effort and expense that Osborne expended in attempting to ingratiate himself with his Hampstead neighbours was in vain. He only owned or leased the Hampstead house for a short period, and he later moved to Islington, where he was buried at St Mary's church in 1767. Whether he moved out of pique or by preference is impossible to know, but what his rather desperate party so clearly demonstrates is the essentially metropolitan nature of the ephemeral, competitive and rootless suburban 'company' of the Northern Heights in the mid-eighteenth century.

5

LANDSCAPES OF MOBILITY
1 6 6 0 – 1 7 7 0

THE RETREAT FROM 'SIN AND SEACOAL'

> *If Heav'n the grateful Liberty wou'd give,*
> *That I might chuse my Method how to live;*
> *And all those Hours propitious Fate shou'd lend,*
> *In blissful Ease and Satisfaction spend.*
> *Near some fair Town I'd have a private Seat,*
> *Built Uniform, not little, nor too great:*
> *Better, if on rising Ground it stood,*
> *Fields on this side, on that a Neighb'ring Wood.*
> *It shou'd within no other Things contain,*
> *But what are Useful, Necessary, Plain:*
> *Methinks 'tis Nauseous and I'd ne'er endure*
> *The needless Pomp of gawdy Furniture:*
> *A little Garden, grateful to the Eye,*
> *And a cool Rivulet run Murmuring by*
>
> .   .   .   .   .   .
>
> *At the end of which a silent Study plac'd,*
> *Shou'd with the Noblest Authors there be grac'd.*
>
> *The Choice: A Poem, By a Person of Quality,* 1700

The Choice by John Pomfret (1667–1702) was one of the most popular poems of the eighteenth century. It was an instant success on publication in 1700, and Samuel Johnson wrote in his *Lives of the English Poets* (1779–81) that it had been 'oftener perused' than any other poem in the English language.[1] Pomfret based the work on classical precedents, but through its refrain for modesty and restraint rather than excess – 'That I might live Genteelly, but not Great' – he re-envisaged the seventeenth-century epicurean royalist poetry of retreat for a new middle-class audience. Johnson commented that he was 'the favourite of that class of readers, who without vanity or criticism seek only their own amusement. His *Choice* exhibits a system of life adapted to common notions and equal to common expectations.'[2] It is these widely shared expectations and desires for a place of genteel but modest retreat 'near some fair Town' by the middling sort that this chapter explores.

Daniel Defoe opened letter Six of his *Tour* with an account of the northern 'villages round London', which, as he wrote, 'partake of the influence of London, so much, that it is observed as London is increased, so they are all increased also, and from the same causes'.[3] 'There is not any thing more fine in their degree, than most of the buildings this way; only with this observation, that they are generally belonging to the middle sort of mankind, grown wealthy by trade, and who still taste of London; some of them live both in the city, and in the country at the same time, yet many of these are immensely rich.'[4] We have already discussed in the Introduction the equation made by Defoe between social and spatial mobility and the rapid spread of 'villadom' in the outskirts. This chapter will examine that phenomenon in greater depth in relation to the area that he singled out as having the highest concentration of new residences for commercial families: the northern villages. Defoe began his account with Hackney, the City commuter suburb par excellence, a town, he wrote, 'so remarkable for the retreat of wealthy citizens, that there is at this time near a hundred coaches kept in it'; it had swallowed up 'no less than 12 hamlets or separate villages'.[5] Jacob Sawbridge was an example of one of these wealthy citizens. He was one of the directors of the South Sea Company, who were a byword for extravagance, and listed Hackney as his main and indeed only address.[6] Defoe went on to outline the great increase in building northwards of Hackney in Stoke Newington, Tottenham, Edmonton and Enfield, so that 'they seem to the traveller to be one continued street' along the Hertford Road (see fig. 42).[7] He also reported on the northern spa towns of Hampstead and Barnet, and their neighbour Highgate, before heading out west via Edgware to Kensington and Chelsea. The popularity of the northern suburbs with the City elite was overwhelming in the mid-seventeenth to mid-eighteenth centuries, with only a small number of merchants choosing to base themselves in the outer London villages to the south and east. The south and

south-west were more popular with the gentry, as Defoe wrote: 'The ten miles from Guilford to Leatherhead make one continued line of gentlemen's houses, lying all, or most of them, on the west side of the road, and their parks, or gardens, almost touching one another.'[8]

This chapter will look at one of these northern middle-class suburbs, Highgate, to examine the impact of this new City money in the outer areas in the first half of our period and the type of environment that it produced. But before we turn to one specific case study, let us consider the evidence more broadly for merchants and tradesmen having a foot in both the city and the country, as Defoe observed. The building of new properties by self-made men in the outer London areas was a well-established trend before the mid-seventeenth century. As early as the fourteenth century the great City magnate Sir John de Pulteney had both a London mansion and a grand country house at Penshurst in Kent. In 1595 121 of those living in the City also possessed country seats, although not all of them were merchants.[9] Stow's fellow antiquarian John Norden (c.1547–1625), who lived on the outskirts of London for most of his life, at Hendon and Walham Green, wrote of Middlesex in 1593:[10]

> This shire is plentifully stored, and as it seemeth beautified with manne faire and comely buildings, especially of merchants of London, who have planted their houses of recreation, not in the meanest places, which also they have cunningly contrived and curiously beautified with divers devices, neatly decked with rare invencions, invironed with orchards of sundrie delicate fruties, gardens with delectable walks, arbers, allees, and great variety of pleasing dainties.[11]

The sixteenth century saw the building of significant numbers of large houses on the outskirts, such as Sutton House in Hackney c.1535 (see fig. 5) or Eastbury Manor House, Barking, built by Clement Sysley, a City merchant, c.1556–73 (fig. 123). London became ringed during the 1630s by a series of substantial homes of the brick classical-vernacular style, which established a new type of suburban domestic form. Nicholas Cooper has suggested that the precursors for such metropolitan houses might be found in the lodge, a secondary house built in the grounds of great estates

123 Eastbury Manor House,
Barking, c.1556–73, National Trust.

A Tudor H-shape plan mansion with
courtyard.

as a place of recreation and retreat, with a new emphasis on individual rather than communal spaces.[12] Eschewing the rambling plans of Tudorbethan country houses based on hierarchy and the spatial articulation of status, a distinctive compact brick house, often built by self-made men, became the norm on the London fringes. Cooper has identified the salient characteristics of such houses as consisting of compactness and regularity, a plan of two or three ranges deep, few external projections, an entrance at the centre of the principal front, and a hall and staircase used purely for circulation rather than for entertaining.[13] Furthermore, John Archer has associated this plan with the growth of notions of privacy and private individuation within the bourgeois home.[14] Well-known surviving examples, built for an increasingly wealthy and assertive mercantile elite, include the 'Dutch House' at Kew (1631) for Samuel Fortrey, a City merchant; Swakeleys, Ickenham, Middlesex (1638), for Edmund Wright, another merchant and subsequently Lord Mayor of London; and Forty Hall, Enfield, Middlesex (1629–32),

for Nicholas Rainton, a haberdasher and also a Lord Mayor (fig. 124).[15]

However, these were for the most part very substantial houses built by the top civil servants, financiers and tradesmen of their day. The financial and commercial revolution of the late seventeenth century led to a huge increase in the numbers of those with the wherewithal and desire to build, lease or temporarily rent second homes in the outskirts or Home Counties. As Perry Gauci writes: 'It is clear that many active merchants based themselves just outside the City jurisdiction, particularly in Hackney or Stepney, attracted no doubt by cheaper rentals and an escape from the suffocating bustle of life within the walls.'[16] Or as Defoe put it in the quote below, a retreat from 'sin and seacoal':

These fine houses . . . are not, at least very few of them, the mansion houses of families, the ancient residencies of ancestors, the capital messuages of the estates, nor have the rich possessors any lands to a considerable value about them; but these are all

The new semi-classical rectangular box house of the seventeenth century.

houses of retreat...gentlemen's mere summer-houses, or citizen's country houses; whither they retire from the hurries of business, and from getting money, to draw their breath in a clear air, and to divert themselves and families in the hot weather; and they...are shut up, and as it were stripped of their inhabitants in the winter, who return to smoke and dirt, sin and seacoal...in the busy city.[17]

Samuel Lee's *A Collection of the Names of the Merchants living in and about the City of London* of 1677 reveals 7 per cent of merchants (138 out of a total of 1,953) living outside the City, with the most significant groupings being Hackney 23, Southwark 12, Wapping 11, Hoxton 10, Clerkenwell, Spitalfields and Mile End all 9, and Islington 8.[18] It was not just the City's elite – that is, the international merchant traders – who were attracted to the outparts. Samuel Tuffnell, master mason to Westminster Abbey, remodelled a house in Essex in the 1740s, while Great Hundridge Manor House, Bucks, was built in the late seventeenth century for a London apothecary.[19] The newspapers were filled with advertisements for houses to rent or buy around the capital. The *Daily Journal* of Friday, 13 March 1730 contained four classified ads for houses in Hackney, Acton, Epping Forest and Lee respectively:

To be Lett,
    For a Term of Years, at Lee near Blackheath
    A good House, or the Lease of upwards of 50 Years to come, to be sold: The House, Outhouses extraordinarily well supplied with Spring Water, large Barns, Coach-houses, and Stables for six Horses, in good Repair, Gardens well-planted with Fruit-Trees, and about five Acres of Meadow Ground.
    Inquire at the said House, or at London Stone Coffee-house in Canon-Street.[20]

The *Daily Courant* of Tuesday, 18 March 1718 featured the following advertisement. It is typical in stressing the outdoor amenities of the house rather than the interior, and particularly its location with the potential for either private or public commuting:

To be LETT
    A House fit for a small Family, with Conveniences of Coach-house and Stable, situate near the Church at Hanwell in the County of Middlesex. It is in very good Air, and has a pleasant Prospect. It is within Nine Miles of London two of Acton and Brentford; and Uxbridge Coach goes every Day within Half a Mile of the House. Inquire of Mr. Rogerson at Hanwell.

It seems that as a very broad generalization the new rich of the metropolis were more outwardly than upwardly mobile. Perry Gauci has argued that the merchant class was remarkably politically and socially unambitious given its immense wealth and power as the major servicers of the national debt.[21] The new elites intermarried with the gentry and were happy to accept titles and preferments. But they did not challenge the landed classes for a greater share in the running of the country until the nineteenth century, and they remained a remarkably confident but self-contained and self-defining group throughout our period. The mobility the majority of them sought was not upwards into the ranks of the landed elite but outwards into creating a more diversified economic base than their trading and financing activities alone could provide. The acquisition of property outside the City was a major form of investment for all levels of merchants and tradesmen. This ranged from suburban second homes to rental properties and land in counties near and far. Defoe itemized the estates bought

Table 3   Outer London Residence of City Office Holders, 1660–89 (based on Woodhead, 1965)

	Number	Per cent
Middlesex	93	7
Surrey	73	5
Essex	40	3
Kent	16	1
Hertfordshire	10	1
Total	232	

Table 4   Residence within counties (except Herts), 1660–89 (based on Woodhead, 1965)

Middlesex	
Hackney	18
Islington	14
Highgate	11
Edmonton/Enfield	8
Bethnal Green and Bow	5
Kensington and Chelsea	5
Hammersmith and Chiswick	5
Other SW riverside	5
Stepney	4
Saint Pancras	3
Tottenham	3
Stoke Newington	2
Other	10
Total	93
Surrey	
Clapham	11
Mortlake	9
Battersea/Wandsworth	6
Other SW riverside	6
Putney	5
Richmond	5
Newington Butts	4
Tooting	4
Peckham/Camberwell	4
Stockwell	3
Other	16
Total	73
Essex	
Woodford	6
Plaistow/West Ham	6
Romford	2
Upminster	3
Havering	2
Theydon Bois	2
Walthamstow	2
Other	17
Total	40
Kent	
E. Greenwich and Lewisham	8
Other inc. Bexley	8
Total	16
Grand Total	222

by London merchants in Essex in order to 'observe how the present increase of wealth in the city of London, spreads it self into the country, and plants families and fortunes, who in another age will equal the families of the ancient gentry, who perhaps were bought out'.[22]

If one examines the entries in J. R. Woodhead's *The Rulers of London 1660–89: A Biographical Record of the Aldermen and Common Councilmen of the City of London* (1965), evidence of second homes and land holdings across a range of occupations is widespread. Woodhead's list, in comparison to Lee's, covers a wider range of people: 'men of eminence in the worlds of trade, commerce, finance and politics along with more modest merchants, craftsmen and shopkeepers'.[23] The breakdown by county is given in Table 3 according to my calculations. It provides a figure of 17 per cent of City office holders living outside the City (compared with Lee's 7 per cent), a total of 232 out of 1,361 entries. Table 4 further analyses these figures within each county.

City–country and city–suburban links are evident throughout Woodhead's sample group. James Paul of the Linen Drapers' Company, for example, inherited an estate from his brother Sir William Bray at Bray in Berkshire and also owned lands in Oxfordshire and Essex.[24] He was one of a significant number of merchants who came from landed families. The ownership of land in more than one county and beyond one's own county of residence or family's county was commonplace, as was the possession of land without a country residence being listed. In some instances this was due to lack of documentation; in others no doubt the land was purely an investment. Thomas Polhill owned land in Otford, Kent, where his family was based, plus two houses in Clapham. In other cases they

featured in possessing land or property beyond those of his residences: in his case in the City, Essex, Kent and Middlesex.[28] In Greenwich, besides his own house, The Grange on Croom's Hill, he also owned three other houses in the road and built an elegant gazebo in his garden sited to take advantage of views over the Royal Park (fig. 125).[29] Although the majority of outer addresses in Woodhead's sample are in the London environs and Home Counties, a significant minority of merchants are listed with addresses in other counties, sometimes those from which they originated. Such was the case of William Crow, who became successful enough to list both Caister Castle in Norfolk as his residence as well as a house on the quay at Yarmouth where his family's original business was located. It was not uncommon for those with second properties to elect still to be buried in the City. Richard Meynell, for instance, owned a house at Stratford in Essex but chose to be buried in his City church of St Dunstan-in-the-East, 'where I have lived ever since I came to Apprenticeship'.[30] He was the brother of Francis Meynell, a banker and 'corner stone of government finance' according to Woodhead, who owned a suburban property in Tooting where, unlike his brother, he chose to be laid to rest.[31]

A late seventeenth-century painting of a house and estate at Belsize just to the south of Hampstead shows the type of medium-sized house that such entrepreneurs might build for themselves (fig. 126 and see fig. 122).[32] Although the exact identity and location of the house is unknown, it is thought to be the second most important house in the manor of Belsize after Belsize House itself. The latter was a larger building erected by Colonel Daniel O'Neil at 'vast expense' before his death in 1664, which subsequently became a notorious public house of entertainment from 1717.[33] The house depicted in the painting was probably built c.1686 by a goldsmith called John Coggs, who is listed by Lee as being at the sign of the King's Head in the Strand. He also owned a farm at Denham, Bucks, where he was born and buried and where his family lived. Coggs and his partner Dann were financiers to the establishment: bankers for Queen Anne and appointed to receive subscriptions towards the building of Greenwich Hospital in 1696. This is the same year that Coggs commissioned Jan Siberechts, the fashionable painter of great country estates, to depict his suburban estate in

125   Robert Hooke?, Gazebo, The Grange, 52 Croom's Hill, Greenwich, 1672, English Heritage.

(facing page) 126   Jan Siberechts, *View of a House and its Estate in Belsize, Middlesex*, 1696, oil, Tate.

The tranquillity and healthy surroundings of this suburban estate are set against the smoke of the city, which can be seen on the horizon along with Westminster Abbey, the landowners of the area. The road in the foreground is Rosslyn Hill, along which a coach passes towards Hampstead.

were purely second homes, such as that of Geoffrey Thomas, a merchant who had a house in Highgate 'in the summertime' and was buried in the chapel there when he died.[25] Unlike the Lee list, which provides a snapshot for a particular year, Woodhead covers a much longer timescale, and therefore in many instances both inner and outer London addresses are given. Thomas Gardner, an apothecary, lived at Richmond but had 'lodgings in London', while Giles Blooer is recorded as living at Cornhill, St Mary, Woolnooth, 'whilst I followed my calling' but moved out to Low Leyton in Essex thereafter.[26] Isaac Brand, a stockbroker, lived in a 'mansion house' in Tooting 'where I have lived many years' as well as owning land in Middlesex and Essex.[27] Sir William Hooker, grocer, is listed as having retired from Cornhill to East Greenwich, while in the Lee list of 1677 his address is given as Crown Court, Gracechurch Street. Hooker was typical of many of those

a suitably majestic portrait. The building of such out-of-town residences is one of the most potent symbols of the wealth of the middle classes in the late seventeenth and eighteenth centuries as they sought both to participate in a new form of rustic living, previously limited to the gentry, and to diversify their investment portfolios into property and land. The grand houses of London's hinterland as surely and prominently represented the unparalleled wealth of its citizens as the City church steeples and the gleaming suburbs of

Westminster. A few magnates, such as Sir William Scawen and Sir John Fellowes, built truly magnificent houses, in their cases both at Carshalton, Surrey. Defoe wrote of the area that the houses hereabouts 'are built with such a profusion of expence, that they look rather like seats of the nobility, than the country houses of citizens and merchants'.[34] This is confirmed by the *Inventories of the South Sea Directors* (1721), of whom Fellowes was one, which show that unlike most of his peers he lavished more money on his Surrey than his

City house.[35] The South Sea inventories form an important source for assessing ownership of property holdings and interior goods among the business elite; of the thirty-three directors the majority had houses in the London countryside.[36] Most City retiring houses were built on a more modest scale than these showy exceptions, and the willingness of their owners to part with them or rent them out shows that there was 'no inherent social strategy behind such ownership'.[37] They represented welcome retreats and worthwhile investments rather than an attempt to imitate the landed gentry lifestyle and economy, a leisured existence which would have been very alien to those accustomed to working in the hubbub of the City heartland. Nicholas Rogers writes of the City bourgeoisie: 'By and large they went in for riverside villas or medium-sized mansions within close proximity of the capital.'[38] As he comments, such houses were not emulative of landed culture; rather they formed part of urban genteel culture in the same way as pleasure gardens, spas and other suburban phenomena.

Besides the general increase in trading activity and the creation of a new consumer economy, a set of particular circumstances, namely the Great Fire of 1666 and the mid-century plagues that preceded it, prompted a pattern of relocation outside the centre for those who could afford it. The number of casualties in the Fire was greatly reduced by the fact that it started at the weekend when, as Strype wrote, 'many of the most eminent citizens, merchants and others were retired into the country, and none but their servants left to look after their City houses'.[39] Some who fled the City due to the Fire never came back; in 1672 it was related that Richard Chiverton of Clerkenwell had 'not lived in London...since the Fire'.[40] Those such as Pepys who were able to do so left the City during the plague, although one had to go a reasonable distance from the centre to escape the worst concentrations of the disease. It has been shown by Paul Slack that by the mid-seventeenth century there were in fact more deaths in the extramural inner suburban parishes than in the City itself.[41] Even then there were deaths among those who had fled to the outskirts. William Proctor, a tavern keeper of the Mitre in Wood Street and supplier to the royal household, was one such victim who (as Pepys recorded) 'died of plague at Islington' on 31 July 1665.[42] The family of Sir Robert

Clayton, one of the leading City financiers, spent 1665 outside London to escape the plague, including a stay with Sir Robert Vyner, that other great City magnate, at his house in Swakleys, Ickenham. We know this as one of Clayton's children was born there but died soon after.[43] The baby is poignantly commemorated in Ickenham church sculpted as a tiny bundle in swaddling clothes. The statue, as Pevsner and Cherry write, is 'now on a windowsill in the chancel, and in its accidental loneliness all the more pathetic'.[44] Following these experiences Clayton bought an estate at Marden in Surrey and built a house on the land in 1677. He also acquired the neighbouring manor of Bletchingley, and repaired the church there having acquired a burial space for his family. Besides this he was a major landowner in the Henley area along with several other City merchants who had owned wharves and other property there.[45] From the 1670s Clayton bought up land around Henley and in 1696 became the owner of Hambleden Manor. He never lived there himself, but his nephew was brought up there and groomed as heir to the family banking business. Laura Wortley has shown how Henley became 'the most prosperous trading centre on the non-tidal Thames' and was defined by City money. Even Cliveden, the Duke of Buckingham's stupendous mansion a few miles downstream, was 'financed largely through Clayton's deft administration of the accounts and [is] a testament to his, as much as to the Duke's power'.[46]

A NOTE ON VILLAS

There was, then, a long history of retirement to the metropolitan outskirts for either permanent or intermittent respite from city life. In the late seventeenth and early eighteenth centuries we find for the first time in England these patterns of living being discussed in relation to the classical tradition of retreat, exemplified in architectonic terms by the villa. The villa has had a long history in Europe from antiquity to modern times, as has been elegantly traced by James Ackerman.[47] We can first find evidence of the genre coming to the attention of English travellers with architectural interests in the seventeenth century. The newness of the term for John Evelyn is evident from an entry in his diary of 1645 from Rome: 'In these faire parks or Gardens called Villas, being only places of Recesse & pleasure, at some distance from the Streetes, yet all within . . . the Walls.'[48] As Nicholas Cooper, John Archer and others have established, the word was being used in England from the early seventeenth century.[49] However, it was recognized that the contemporary English milieu was far removed from that of classical Rome or the seventeenth-century Veneto of Palladio. Palladio's villas, with a couple of notable exceptions, were situated at the centre of agricultural estates in a similar manner to the English country house.

From the beginning in England the term 'villa' was applied to modest suburban homes around London, as well as to larger rural retreats. Henry Aldrich, an Oxford don, made the distinction between the two clear, writing *c.*1700: 'The term villa, taken in its full sense, means a country house with a farm annexed; but we shall here understand no more by it than a house built for rural retirement.'[50] Roger North emphasized the novelty of the 'suburb villa' in 1698, commenting that it was compact 'alla moderna' and was intended 'to retire to injoy and sleep, with out pretence of enterteinement of many persons'.[51] Up until the 1750s, then, the term could be equated broadly with the lesser kind of house, according to the *OED*: 'any residence of a superior type, in the suburbs of a town or in a residential district, such as is occupied by a person of the middle-class; also, any small better-class dwelling house, usually one which is detached or semi-detached'.[52] This confusing etymology has misled many social and cultural historians into dating the smaller villa only from the early nineteenth century when the term and the type become widespread.[53] The early phase of high-brow architectural interest in the villa, sparked by Robert Castell's *Villas of the Ancients* (1728), produced some exemplary elite neo-Palladian villas in the south-west of London at Chiswick House (1727–9) and Marble Hill (1724–9) (see fig. 23). The historiography, following Rudolf Wittkower's lead, has focused on these as the prototypically English exemplars at the expense of more modest non-Palladian designs.[54] Henry Aldrich, although the designer of the pioneering Anglo-Palladian Peckwater Quad (1706–14) at Christ Church, Oxford, was also aware of the increasing prevalence of these smaller kinds of suburban houses. He wrote that they were

of a middle nature, between the town house and the villa. . . . In the construction of it neatness should be attended to, but retirement more; its principal requisites are ease and repose. Its appearance is neater than the country house, and not so splendid as one in the city. It neither boasts of pastures, or sumptuous dining rooms; content with a study, a garden, and extensive walks. It will be conducive to health if it be placed somewhat on an eminence, and to pleasure if it has a view of the city you have left behind.[55]

This description of the modest retreat is very close to that in Pomfret's poem at the beginning of this chapter. It is clear that at the turn of the eighteenth century such houses were firmly embedded in the culture and that for increasing numbers of people they represented an attainable ideal. Aldrich and Pomfret could well have had in mind a place such as Highgate, a hill-top town which overlooked London from the north and was full of middle-class urbanites residing in just such houses of 'a middle nature'.

MANSIONS, MOBILITY AND THE MIDDLE CLASSES: A CASE STUDY OF HIGHGATE

But if not history itself, there are testimonies of history scattered all over Highgate, in its old mansions.

William Howitt, *The Northern Heights of London*, 1869

Highgate provides a wonderful example of the eloquence of architecture to speak to a development pattern thus far generally overlooked by social and economic historians. It is arguably the best place in London to be able to see and get a feel for the outer 'villages' as they existed prior to large-scale development in the late eighteenth and nineteenth centuries. Furthermore, it underwent remarkably little of the latter type of development on its western and southern slopes, so that it maintains today its seventeenth- and eighteenth-century scale both in the centre and when viewed at a distance from Hampstead Heath. Even the major modern interloper in the centre, Lubetkin's Highpoint I and II (1933–8), plays to eighteenth-century whimsicality with its famous caryatids.

In Highgate we can see the intersections of social, economic and physical mobility in the northern metropolitan villages. It sits five miles from the centre

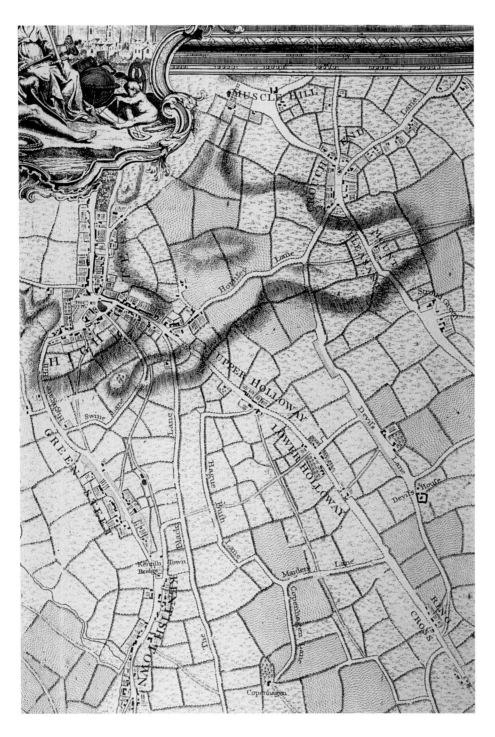

of the air but its circulation, so that 'the high ground' was just that: the peak of healthiness, civility and morality by virtue of its purging effects.[56] As early as 1593 Norden in his *Speculam Britannica* noted: 'Upon this hill is most pleasant dwelling, yet not so pleasant as healthful, for the expert inhabitants there report that divers who have long been visited by sickness not curable by physicke, have in a short time repayed their health by that sweet salutary air.'[57] Of course, such elevation was not always a benefit, and in 1679 the *Domestick Intelligence* reported that 'the late Stormy and Tempestuous Weather' had had very severe effects in Highgate and Hampstead.[58] Living on a hill was not for the faint-hearted, as Defoe's comments on Hampstead only being fit for 'a race of mountaineers' made evident.[59] Highgate was not simply a retreat for the leisured; it also had an important commercial function due to its position as a critical transport hub at the junction of two of the metropolis's main arterial routes northwards, one from the City and the other from Westminster (fig. 127 and see fig. 164). The land was owned by Bishop of London as part of his large Middlesex estate, which stretched northwards to Finchley where his outer London palace was situated. Toll roads were cut across the area in the fourteenth century with gates at the eponymous Gatehouse Inn in the village and the Spaniards Inn on the edge of the Heath (fig. 128). The presence of these major roads through the town and a more fragmented property structure led to Highgate developing an identity as 'more bustling and attractive to commercial men' than the nearby and geographically very similar pleasure resort of Hampstead.[60]

Highgate began to develop as an outer London resort from the sixteenth century when the nobility settled in the area. The lack of a local aristocratic land-owner or resident gentry in Highgate allowed for immense fluidity in the property market, and by 1600 at least six mansions had been erected in the village. These fashionable houses clustered around the ponds on the green for easy access to water, a particular issue in a hill-top location, creating a greater density of dwelling than in many of London's villages. The mansions included Dorchester House, Dartmouth House, Lauderdale House and Arundel House, the home from 1610 to 1630 of Thomas, 2nd Earl of Arundel, the well-known connoisseur (see fig. 141). These grand houses were surrounded by the much smaller dwellings

127 John Rocque, *An Exact Survey of the City's of London, Westminster ye Borough of Southwark and the Country Near Ten Miles Round*, 1746, London Metropolitan Archives.

feet high on the sandy ridge of Howitt's 'Northern Heights', which also includes Highgate's close neighbours discussed in the previous chapter, Hampstead to the west and Islington to the south. These hill-top settlements developed a distinctive identity as healthy retreats isolated from 'sin and seacoal', the moral and physical pollution below. Contemporary theories of 'airiness' stressed the importance of not just the purity of the village, and this architectural melange was to set the pattern for the subsequent two centuries. However, from the mid-seventeenth century the nobility began to move out of the area as it became an increasingly middle-class destination. Highgate's position just over five miles to the north of the centre made it particularly attractive for Dissenters following the Five Mile Act of 1665 – which banned Nonconformists from preaching within five miles of the centre – and it became known as 'a nest of Puritans'.[61] 1665 was also a peak plague year, which again prompted flight from the City to the more salubrious outparts. Highgate's position as a Nonconformist stronghold was strengthened under the Coventicle Acts of 1664 and 1670, as there was no parish church to report to the authorities on Dissenting activity. The town came within the parish of Saint Pancras at that date. In the late seventeenth century a wave of development led to the demolition of all the old aristocratic mansions and their division into smaller plots for middle-class properties, a pattern which occurred elsewhere – at Greenwich and Chelsea, for instance.[62] The willingness of the aristocracy to part with their outer London residences forms part of a broader picture of exceptional fluidity in the property market after the Restoration. In the late seventeenth century the nobility disposed of their houses both suburban and central (such as their Thames-side palaces) to property speculators while relocating themselves in the new suburbs of Westminster.[63]

Highgate Hill was the legendary spot where the pauper Dick Whittington, that epitome of upward mobility in the fourteenth and fifteenth centuries, heard Bow bells chiming 'Turn again Whittington, Thrice Lord Mayor of London-town' before he returned to the City to fulfil his destiny.[64] The spot was marked by a stone monument which formed a significant feature in the area's mythologizing and which had to be speedily replaced after its removal by the parish authorities in 1795 following strong public protests.[65] It is particularly apt that this signifier of social mobility should mark the entranceway to Highgate, and it was incorporated by Chatelain into his 'Prospect of Highgate from Upper Holloway' where its large triangular-looking base – the only part that existed at this date – can be seen beyond the rickety fence in the foreground (fig. 129). A plaque still marks the spot today, while the nearby Whittington Hospital

provides a more substantial reminder of the legend. The mythology of Dick Whittington was promoted from the late sixteenth century onwards on stage and in print as a fable of the transformative possibilities of City riches. A typical title from 1788 is the anonymous *Famous History of Sir Richard Whittington and his Cat: Shewing how from a poor country boy destitute of parents or relations, he attained great Riches, and was promoted to the high and honourable Dignity of Lord Mayor of London*. Whittington's story also featured prominently in London urban histories from Stow onwards. Noorthhouck in his *A New History of London* (1773), which concentrated on the City, related how the statue of Liberty on the gate at Newgate Prison had a cat lying at her feet, a homage to Whittington, who had funded the rebuilding of the prison in 1407.[66] James Boswell marked his first entry into London on Friday, 19 November 1762 with a joyous contemporary version of Whittington's vision: 'When we came upon Highgate Hill and had a view of London, I was all life and joy. I repeated Cato's soliloquy on the immortality of the soul, and my soul bounded forth to a certain prospect of happy futurity.'[67]

A remarkable number of subsequent Lord Mayors and other City grandees were to go on to make their homes in Highgate, literally within sight and sound of their domain below. Defoe wrote that from the summit the view was so good 'that they see the very ships passing up and down the river for 12 or 15 miles below'.[68] The visual links between City and 'village' were evident at every turn in Highgate due to its sweeping vistas, omnipresently representing the symbiotic commercial and social relationships which bound core and periphery together. Highgate's panoramic aspect was often depicted, stretching from Greenwich in one direction along the river to Westminster in the other (fig. 130). Equally, the Northern Heights themselves were visible from the town below, so that to those in the centre Highgate appeared as a beacon not just of rural airiness but also of social and commercial success (see fig. 71).

Laura Williams, commenting on the association between elevated sites, healthiness and social prestige, writes, 'In this environment, social climbing meant exactly that, to clamber above the urban scrum and flag one's elevated status.'[69] However, Henry Hunter in his *History of London and its Environs* said he had to

128   J. B. C. Chatelain, 'South-East View of Highgate Chapel', from *Fifty Views*, 1750, etching, London Metropolitan Archives.

This shows the chapel of ease in the centre of the town with the Gatehouse Inn and toll point spanning the road to the left.

129   J. B. C. Chatelain, 'Prospect of Highgate from Upper Holloway', from *Prospects of Highgate and Hampstead*, 1745, etching, British Museum.

Even in this classicized image the weight of drovers' traffic and the deep ruts on the steep road are prominent.

130 T. M. Baynes, *View down Highgate Hill*, 1822, lithograph, London Metropolitan Archives.

The City lies at the bottom of the hill, with the cupola of Cromwell House just showing on the left and the gates to Lauderdale House on the right.

make several journeys to Highgate to see the view as it was so often obscured by smoke: 'By experience it was found that the best time for viewing London was about three o'clock in the afternoon, of a bright, clear summer's day, with little haze, and a northerly wind.

131 Flask Tavern, West Hill, early eighteenth century.

At this hour the people of the middle class have dressed their dinners, and the cooks of the rich have not yet begun to make their fires.'[70]

If visibility remained variable, physical mobility throughout the century increased. The process began with the erection of turnpikes on two of the main roads through Highgate at Dartmouth Park Hill and Highgate Hill in the early eighteenth century. Defoe labelled Highgate a town as early as 1725, and by 1664 it contained 161 houses.[71] The population at this date was probably around 1,000, and by 1841 it had reached 4,302.[72] Its numbers were continuously swelled by the large number of travellers who stopped for the night in the many coaching inns before or after tackling the steep and rutted hill to London. Many of these inns remain in rebuilt form although there are some exceptional survivors, such as the Flask Tavern of the early eighteenth century (fig. 131).[73] Besides travellers and drinkers, the roads also had to accommodate the thousands of animals being driven on a one-way journey down to Smithfield, the main meat market in the City. The impact of this agricultural activity can still be seen in the width of the main roads, the exceptionally high pavements designed to keep animals off them, and the alleys and yards running off the High Street, behind which there used to be pens and grazing. Animals would also feed on the 'strays' at the side of the road. These were areas of waste land which were used for droving stock along the main routes into and out of the capital. Although the turnpike money improved the road, it still remained a formidable obstacle, particularly up Highgate Hill. This eventually led to the cutting of the Archway tunnel through the hill in 1813 and the later improvements of the new Archway Road as a bypass around the town. The impact of the animal traffic should not be underestimated. Joseph Massie in *An Essay on ... the City and Suburbs of London* (1754) commented on the dangers posed by driving live bullocks through the streets leading to 'broken Limbs, and sometimes the loss of Lives'.[74] He called for a place 'without the Town' to be found for their slaughter, a plea echoed by John Gwynn in his *London and Westminster Improved* (1766). Gwynn wanted new livestock markets to be sited at Islington, Southwark and to the west and east to prevent the dangers of cattle, in particular, being driven through the centre.[75] This idea finally reached fruition in 1855 with the building of the Metropolitan Cattle Market in Islington on the site of the old pleasure garden at Copenhagen House.

Dangers of a different type could be encountered on the roads, where highwaymen and thefts were common, as newspapers of the time attest. In July 1702 the *English Post with News Foreign and Domestick* reported that 'a Gang of dissolute Fellows ... are suspected of having lately committed several Robberies in the Night on the Roads near Highgate'.[76] By 1782 the situation had become so bad that the Highgate and Hampstead Roads Trust employed its own foot and horse patrols in the area, paid for from an additional toll.[77] Such disorder on the highways remained common throughout the eighteenth century, resulting in plaintive advertisements promising rewards for stolen property. This even extended to pets or hunting dogs: a ten shilling reward was offered in 1701 for a spaniel lap bitch which had been spirited away from Highgate by 'some Gentlemen in a Hackney Coach', while in 1706 another owner was keen to trace a dog taken from the Angel Inn while passing through the town.[78]

Highgate town or village consisted of a mix of small vernacular buildings interspersed with mansions and substantial middling-sized residences, a remarkable proportion of which survive to this day.[79] Amongst this melange there existed some highly innovative architecture which proclaimed its presence with startling novelty. The first modern classical building in the area was Cromwell House built in 1637–8 for Richard Sprignell, a trained band captain for the Parliamentarians.[80] He was one of a significant number of Cromwellians in the area, including General Ireton's brother at Lauderdale House and Andrew Marvell (1621–1678), the poet and radical MP, who is thought to have lived in a cottage on Highgate Hill for a time. Sprignell built a brick double-pile plan house notable for its symmetry and block-like form, emphasized by the use of the parapet rather than gables, which was to become the dominant type in the area (fig. 132). It has a fine staircase with newels carved in the shape of Commonwealth soldiers, alluding to the owner's profession: a boldly assertive refiguring of traditional familial emblems. It is one of the best surviving examples of the City-influenced houses which could once be found throughout the environs.[81] These took the rectangular brick mansion houses of the London financiers, such as Sir John Houblon's house or Sir Robert Viner's house in Lombard Street, as their models.[82] Yet despite its undoubted central origins, its generosity of scale and particularly its rooftop cupola with balustraded terrace proclaim its extramural location and the importance of vista. A similar surviving example of a merchant house with hill-top location and a partially railed roof terrace can be seen at Fenton House in Hampstead of the late seventeenth century, owned by the National Trust (fig. 133). In this way the links between the City and the outer areas were embedded in bricks and mortar, while the visual connection was maintained and displayed prominently as the houses' crowning feature. In 1675 Cromwell House was bought by the Da Costas (resident 1675–1749), the first Jewish family to own land in England since the medieval period.[83] Defoe observed of Highgate: 'The Jews have particularly fixed upon this town for their country retreats, and some of them are very wealthy; they live there in good figure, and have several trades particularly depending on them, and especially butchers of their own to supply them with provisions killed their own way; also, I am told, they have a private synagogue here.'[84]

132 Cromwell House, Highgate
Hill, 1637–8.

133 Fenton House, Hampstead,
1693, English Heritage.

The balustraded 'flats' at attic level
are visible here with the peculiarity
of the chimney stacks rising behind
them. The Doric loggia was added
in the early nineteenth century
when this was made the main
entrance.

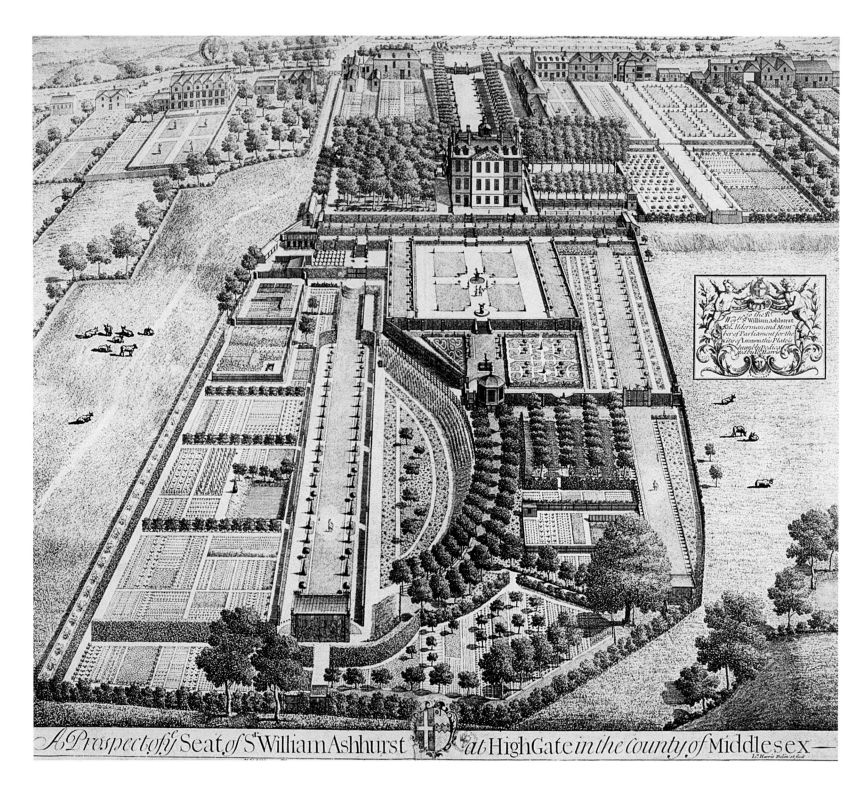

A Prospect of y.e Seat of S.r William Ashhurst ✠ *at High Gate in the county of* Middlesex —

The synagogue was installed by the Da Costas in Cromwell House, probably in the large front room subsequently used as a chapel. They had found royal favour, having lent money to Charles II during his exile. They then established what was to become a common pattern for successful Jewish immigrants, by leaving east London and moving northwards. Besides Cromwell House they bought a number of other properties in the village in the 1710s to 1730s, but had moved away by the mid-eighteenth century.[85] The *London in Miniature* guidebook gave their subsequent address as being a villa in Totteridge (see fig.

(facing page) 134 John Harris, *A Prospect of the Seat of Sir William Ashurst at Highgate*, 1720, engraving, London Metropolitan Archives.

The surviving part of Arundel House, now called Old Hall, can be seen to the right of the building along with other mansions in the centre of the village.

64).[86] Cromwell House provided an assertive symbol of a newly rich and powerful class acquiring the status that second-home ownership conferred. But these were houses without land and therefore generically villas, as opposed to country estates, and as such supremely suburban.

Another ambitiously modern and visible new residence was Ashurst House (1694), an elegant retreat with substantial grounds in a Dutch-influenced style (fig. 134). This was built in the grounds of Arundel House as part of the redevelopment there, and was either an adaptation or a complete rebuilding of the former banqueting house on the site.[87] The remodelling of existing buildings was a common trend even among the wealthy in the outskirts, where properties were predominantly leasehold. It was built by Sir William Ashurst, a hugely successful merchant and financier who served as Lord Mayor of London and was Director of the Bank of England for five terms between 1697 and 1714. Like Cromwell House, its modernity was essentially derived from its compact plan, rectilinear form and finely modulated brickwork, and also the careful integration of house and grounds.

Defoe commented favourably on the view down to the Thames. It was this type of garden that he had in mind when he chronicled the recent fashion for Dutch gardening with its emphasis on parterres, topiary and geometricity: the garden's box-like nature echoing that of the house behind.[88] Defoe wrote of such 'charming gardens' and their attendant dwellings as being particularly prevalent in the Thames-side villages, inspired by the royal exemplars at Hampton Court and Kensington both of the early 1700s (see fig. 4). We can gauge the level of the formality of the grounds at Ashurst House if we compare them to the less intricate arrangement of the Belsize estate (see fig. 126). Although differing in tone and effect, they also share many features in common in terms of their overall layout and composition, such as the axial gated avenue approach, the tree plantations, the sequence of rectangular bounded spaces, and the off-centre long allée to the rear.

The most startlingly piece of modern architecture in Highgate before 1700, at least to our eyes, was not an individual house but rather a development of six houses called The Grove (fig. 135). The Grove's novelty came from its layout as three pairs of large semi-

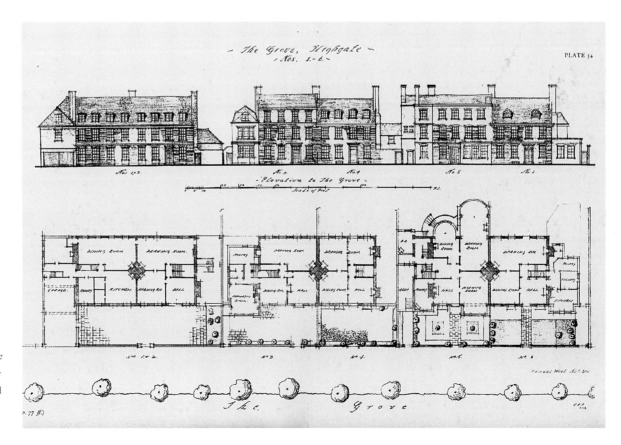

135 1–6 The Grove, Highgate, c.1688, from SOL, *The Parish of St. Pancras, Part 1: Highgate*, 1936, English Heritage / Survey of London.

This survey was taken c.1936 and shows later adaptations to the terrace including the rebuilding of No. 5 by C. H. James in the 1920s. Nos 4 and 6 are the nearest to their original appearance.

136 Englefield House, Highgate High Street, 1710.

137 Ivy and Northgate Houses, Highgate High Street, late seventeenth century.

traditional means of winning social and religious acclaim. He had originally intended to use Dorchester House himself as 'a Summer's recess from London'. However, 'having that great and noble city, with its numerous Childhood under view, gave the first thoughts to him of a great Design' subsequently outlined as 'The State and Case . . . for the Better Education of Thousands of Parish Children Successively in the Vast Northern Suburbs of London'.[90] This must be a unique case of a philanthropic act being ascribed to the persuasive presence of the metropolitan vista. The Grove became famous in the eighteenth century as the refuge and death-place of Samuel Coleridge, who lived there from 1823 to 1834 in the care of Dr James Gilman and his family. He was visited there by many of his circle, which may have contributed to the later popularity of the area among the younger Romantics such as Keats, Leigh Hunt and Constable, who established it as an artistic centre.

The Grove was sited both to take advantage of the nearby ponds and to provide a magnificent prospect to the rear over Hampstead Heath looking down towards the western side of London. However, the importance given to the semi-detached house as one of the hallmarks of the suburb by Summerson and subsequent architectural historians has helped to obscure the extent to which earlier patterns of development from the mid-seventeenth century onwards might also be labelled as suburban. The abandonment of uniform terrace housing was certainly one of the features that distinguished the outer suburbs from the inner ones, although this was less the case for cheaper suburban development. It also became less true as the eighteenth century progressed and the line between inner and outer suburbs inexorably expanded. In actuality there was a much broader and more creative range of approaches to the issue of attachment and detachment than architectural historians have allowed. In the dichotomy between the individual and the group one can easily find examples of houses in Highgate situated in rows but which self-consciously present themselves to the street as distinct entities. Others became semi-detached by default as later buildings or developments were added to them or when single houses were later subdivided. The early eighteenth-century Ireton and Lyndale Houses on Highgate Hill were originally one building, for example, while

detached houses, the first known use of the semi-detached formula in the capital. This led Sir John Summerson to label them as the proto-typical suburban house, which was to become inextricably linked with the semi-detached form.[89] The Grove was built as a speculative development on the site of Dorchester House c.1688 reusing some of the materials. It was built by William Blake, a City woollen draper, in order to fund a new charity school – an interesting combination of new investment approaches being applied to

more important. The end result was a variegated building line both in height and depth. Clearly suburbanites were happy to occupy houses resulting from this mix and match approach to architecture, which was the outcome of small irregular plots and an essentially ad hoc development process.[91] One can still find an astonishingly rich range of house types in Highgate village. The Grove, although exceptional in its attempts to combine a number of semi-detached houses into a coherent whole, was not the only semi-detached houses either in Highgate or elsewhere.[92] Another example can be found in the High Street at Ivy and Northgate Houses of the late seventeenth century, which maintain taller, more standard urban proportions but which were conceived as a pair (fig. 137).

Elsewhere on the High Street more conventional city-style terraces can be found, as was common along arterial routes in particular. However, such runs of terraces in this early period tended to be short in length as they were usually speculative developments carried out on small plots of land. They were interspersed with newly built brick cottages such as those at 33–37 High Street and 1–6 Pond Square, both of the earlier eighteenth century, as well as older timber cottages housing working people and/or industrial premises. Off the main road ran a series of yards and alleys in which various tradesmen were located. The physical evidence for these survives at Townsend Yard, named after a local building family, and at Kent's Yard, 58–60 High Street, which was a corn merchant's premises dating from around the turn of the eighteenth century. It was one of several in the locality which were established to take advantage of the passing traffic to Smithfield (fig. 138). Another trade serving a dual local and visiting clientele was the blacksmiths, of which there were several in the town. The Old Forge in the High Street demonstrates how ramshackle wooden buildings existed only feet away from the regular frontages of the main roads (fig. 139). Along the High Street there were plenty of other local shops and businesses essential to the supplying and running of the town. Richardson gives a list of traders from an admittedly rather later directory of 1805 which runs to ninety-five entries. Besides the expected occupations such as the large number of innkeepers, farriers and other services for horses, school proprietors, builders, farmers, doctors and shopkeepers of all kinds, there are also two bell-hangers,

138 Kent's Yard, 58–60 Highgate High Street, late seventeenth or early eighteenth century.

139 Old Forge, Highgate High Street, nineteenth-century photo, English Heritage

Englefield House (1710) in the High Street was originally detached but became part of a terrace as the adjoining plots were developed on either side (fig. 136). The architecture of the London villages was characterized above all by diversity, suggesting that a greater variety of forms were considered acceptable in such outer city locations, where more generous plot sizes were available and considerations of topography were

a tobacco pipe manufacturer, a dealer in earthenware, a jeweller and an auctioneer.[93]

The presence of the timber cottages and working premises among the new brick houses of the gentry and middling sort is a reminder of the mixed vernacular-classical tradition from which all the buildings in the area sprang. Although some of the houses in the area were startlingly new in their severe geometricity, all of them developed out of the red-brick classicism of the seventeenth century, which combined a new interest in proportion and regularity with traditional forms and construction techniques. The brick exterior of Ivy and Northgate Houses hid a timber frame, for example, as did other comparable houses in Hampstead and elsewhere.[94] And 17–19 North Road, erected in the early eighteenth century, has the long low proportions and look of an earlier seventeenth-century house with its brick gables and casement windows. Rock House, Pond Square, of c.1777 is another charming suburban vernacular composition (fig. 140). Its prominent oriels once more demonstrate the importance of the outward gaze, even though in this case the view would have been primarily of the pond area rather than down the hill, which by this date would have been largely obscured by the intervening buildings. This shows that even small houses might employ devices to frame the prospect, whether of the foreground or a more distant view, as can also be seen at Greenwich and Peckham.[95]

The house that perhaps best represents this history of adaptation and renewal is in fact the best surviving mansion from Highgate's earliest period of elite development. Lauderdale House was built in 1582 probably by its first occupant, City goldsmith Richard Martin (fig. 141). Its owners are representative of the cross-section of the elite attracted to the area and the short-term nature of their residency there. In the 1660s it was the home briefly of the Duke of Lauderdale, who had inherited it through his wife in 1644. He went on to rebuild Ham House in Richmond in spectacular fashion, which came to him courtesy of his second wife, the Countess of Dysart. It was Lauderdale who let the Highgate property to John Ireton, an MP, Lord Mayor and brother of Cromwell's general, Henry Ireton. From 1688 it belonged to another Lord Mayor of London, Sir William Pritchard, and for most of the eighteenth century it was inhabited by leaseholders, declining in social status to a series of schoolkeepers 1794–1837.[96] One of its most flamboyant owners in terms of social mobility was the property speculator and financier John Hinde, who lived at Lauderdale House 1680–85. He was a partner with Nicholas Barbon, the most notorious developer of his day, in many of his building schemes and his Fire Insurance Office.[97] He was one of the new breed of speculators who attracted intense fascination and opprobrium in equal parts. Hinde overreached himself and was declared bankrupt in 1685, dying in the Fleet Prison. After his death the *London Gazette* in 1687 advertised Lauderdale House as a 'capital messuage' for sale in Highgate, as well as '6 closes of Pasture; As also two other Messuages, near the aforesaid Capital Messuage, with their Appertunances; and the 2 parcels of waster Ground near the said Messuage'.[98] An inventory of his possessions at Highgate taken when he was declared bankrupt is immensely revealing both of the layout of the house and the immensely opulent fashion in which it was furnished.[99] Hinde's household goods included such valued luxury items as two Turkey carpets, sixty-nine pictures, six lengths of tapestry (c.500 square feet), two Japan lacquered cabinets, one Japan table and eighteen Japan chairs 'with redd damaske cushions', looking glasses and a pendulum clock. He also owned at least five other sets of tables and chairs spread throughout the house. These were all items of the highest value and fashionability, particularly the new 'exotic' wares, demonstrating that this was Hinde's principal residence and the immense dis-

posable income available to him when he fitted up the house. The total value of goods was estimated at £230 18s., although this was probably an underestimate as bankruptcy valuations were usually on the low side. The list of items above confirms Philippa Glanville's comment in relation to the bankruptcy inventories of the directors of the South Sea Company that 'expenditure on art encompassed a wide range of products in many media'.[100]

This history of continuously changing owners is reflected in the mixture of styles visible at Lauderdale House. It was one of the few houses that William Howitt was indifferent to in Highgate, remarking that 'it has no architecture about it'.[101] It was substantially updated and extended in 1640, and the authors of the definitive study of the house have speculated that the ceiling done at this time may have been similar to those which still survive at Cromwell House over the road.[102] It later received a classical lantern and cupola over the main stair in around 1715. The house was

further classicized c.1760 when three sides of the exterior were stuccoed and the existing oriel and casement windows replaced by modern sashes. Pediments were placed over the gables in the roof and a colonnade created on the south-east front underneath the original overhanging timber-frame jetty (fig. 142). Indeed, the oak frame remained intact throughout the house, and the placement of windows and other features was not therefore wholly symmetrical. Such a history of adaptation and reinterpretation is typical of outer London leasehold properties which were not principal seats. A similar pattern could be found down the road in Islington at Canonbury House, an early sixteenth-century building which at one time belonged to Thomas Cromwell.[103] In the early seventeenth century it came into the ownership of the Earl of Northampton, who divided his time between London and Castle Ashby. For most of the seventeenth and eighteenth centuries the property was let out to a miscellaneous succession of tenants including Francis Bacon and

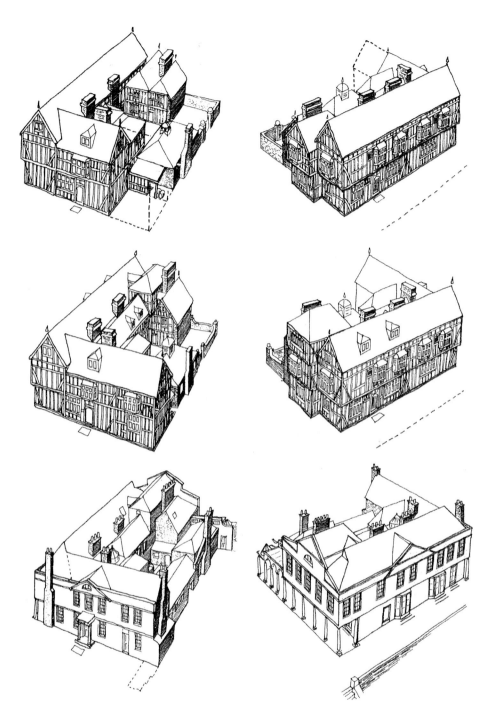

ment where it was moved in 1926: recycling taking a more drastic and mobile form in the twentieth century.[106] In 1599, Spencer carried out a substantial remodelling of Canonbury House including on the first floor, in what was probably his Great Chamber, where he commissioned a plaster-work ceiling with emblems of trading ships in roundels representing his trading interests stamped upon it (fig. 143).[107] Most studies on the East India and other trading companies have focussed on country houses, generally of a later date, but in fact the first and most crucial property investment for such traders were their town and sub-urban houses, on which far more research is needed.[108] This ornate ceiling brings us full circle back to the beginnings of the interpenetration of core and periph-ery in the early sixteenth century. It provides a suitably flamboyant gesture symbolizing the links not just between the greater London region and the City but with overseas trading and colonialism as well. The con-nections between America, the Caribbean and Asia ran from where the cargoes unloaded Thames-side up to the City and right along the great arterial routeways into the drawing rooms of Islington, Highgate and Hackney. The new suburbs built by London merchants and tradesmen were as much the outcome of the international economy and imperialism as the city centre itself.

CONCLUSION

Robert Fishman in his *Bourgeois Utopias* acknowl-edged these early eighteenth-century retreats as a dis-tinct phase of pre-suburban development in which wealthy London merchants built weekend villas in the London countryside. He considered that this was not true suburban development, as these were secondary not primary residences, but nevertheless emphasized their importance as the 'crucial intermediate stage' in peripheral metropolitan growth.[109] However, as we have seen, there were many people – women, the retired, gentry and others who did not need to travel to the City daily – who were living in the outer vil-lages while many of the merchants commuted. John Archer, by contrast, saw the development of elite villas in the late seventeenth and early eighteenth centur-ies in the Twickenham area as the beginnings of

142 Lauderdale House, axonometric, showing the house's transformation from its timber-framed origins in 1582 and 1649 to its recladding and classicizing in 1760.

Oliver Goldsmith. It was rented by John Short *c.*1688–9, who was a merchant and investor in the East India Company.[104] The house had previously been substan-tially remodelled in 1599 by Sir John Spencer, a Lord Mayor and enormously wealthy merchant as one of the founders of the Spanish Company, the Levant trade and the East India Company.[105] He also owned Crosby Place in Bishopsgate, a magnificent fifteenth-century City mansion, now to be seen on the Chelsea Embank-

143 Canonbury House, Islington, first floor chamber, 1599.

The badge and motto are those of the Levant Company (of which Spencer was a member), although carved in reverse.

suburbia.[110] However, as this chapter has shown, the south-western suburbs were far from unique in experiencing profound growth at this time. Furthermore, to limit definitions of the 'villa' to a particular style or form of dwelling is to ignore both contemporary etymologies and the widespread evidence of non-Palladian villas across the environs which constituted the majority of new buildings for the middling sort on the London fringes.

Highgate, and indeed north London as a whole (plus Hackney), offers a corrective to the existing narratives of early suburban morphologies. Highgate was very far from being simply a sleepy resort for the retired. Its mixture of commercial and residential functions is one of the distinguishing hallmarks of the early modern suburb which differentiates it from its later nineteenth- and early twentieth-century counterparts. Its identity was forged by communications and circulation – of roads, coaches, travellers and inns – the very sinews of the modern commercial nation. Spitalfields provides the extreme example at one end of the spectrum of the industrious inner suburb where work and living where inextricably intertwined.[111] But the outer suburbs, too, often contained a mixture of functions, as here at Highgate, or in the riverside villages of the Thames and the Lea. Defoe called it a town, and like all towns once it grew to a particular size it needed to develop its own services and food supplies. There was no single landowner or property holding, nor a parish church, so that two of the bastions of traditional society were absent, creating a lacuna in which the middling sort could forge their own identity in the area. They created a vibrant centre with its inns and businesses set among a plethora of types of small domestic buildings plus a fair number of new mansions for the wealthy. The background landscape provided plenty of opportunities for pleasure and recreation, with Hampstead Heath, Highgate Ponds and pleasure grounds such as the Spaniards Inn all contributing to the rustic ambience of the area. This provided a quite different and distinctive environment from that of the centre, one that we might call the first modern suburbs.

6

LANDSCAPES OF SELECTIVITY
1770–1840

THE CIT'S BOX AND THE GENTLEMAN'S COT

Suburban villas, highway-side retreats,
That dread the encroachment of our growing streets,
Tight boxes neatly sash'd, and in a blaze
With all a July sun's collected rays,
Delight the citizen, who, gasping there,
Breathes clouds of dust, and calls it country air.

William Cowper, *Retirement*, 1781

In this chapter we will consider the development of ideas about the suburban in the second half of our period. In the late eighteenth and early nineteenth centuries both the style of architecture adopted in the outskirts and the density of development changed considerably. Above all, the landscape began to be regularized and controlled as fresh ideas about visual order and a new emphasis on social and spatial differentiation in architecture made its impact. The environs increasingly became a designed landscape as, in a new departure, architects busied themselves with medium-sized housing. The thinking behind these interventions can be traced in a torrent of architectural publications which offered for the first time a significant written attempt to engage with the terrain of the suburban.

This novel environment emerged in response to the continued expansion of the capital and its rising prosperity. By 1750 London's population had reached 600,000–675,000 and was to rise to 900,000 by 1801.[1] Following a period of stagnation c.1738–63, the capital's economy boomed in the 1760s and building took off, maintaining a high level of activity until the early 1790s, excluding some intermittent short-term troughs.[2] The greatest area of new growth was to the south of the Thames, where the opening of Westminster Bridge in 1750 followed by that of Blackfriars Bridge in 1769, both with attendant major road networks, allowed for the development of what previously had been open farmland (fig. 145). Notable middle-class enclaves were built in places like Clapham, which Fishman cites as the paradigmatic residential suburb of

the late eighteenth century.[3] At the same time existing southern villages expanded, such as Putney and Roehampton, which have been studied by Dorian Gerhold. He is one of the few social historians to have paid attention to the spread of villa building, and it is to be hoped that more research of this kind could establish a firmer evidential base for understanding its locales and impact.[4] The most intensive area of activity in the inner suburbs of Westminster was on the Portland, Portman and Bedford estates, which were all developed in this period.[5] The outer areas continued to expand

due to improvements in the road network and an increasingly frequent public carriage system of coaches for commuters. Cary's map shows the extensive turnpike network which spread in all directions by 1790 (see fig. 49). According to Dyos, by the 1770s a total of eighty coaches left the City and Westminster each evening for the outer areas, a number which had increased fourfold by 1805.[6] There were daily coach services to residential suburbs such as Barking, Bromley, Camberwell, Clapham, Highgate and Hampstead, and by 1779 an hourly service was running from the City to Hackney.[7] Thompson recorded the steady rate of increase in the number of daily return journeys to Hampstead: 1740–1, 1763–5, 1770–14, 1793–18, 1799–43, 1815–43.[8]

These improvements in public transport enabled an increasing number of the middle classes to move their main residences out of the crowded conditions of the city. The first phase of commuting had been limited to those wealthy enough to own their own carriages, and while the fares charged still demanded a significant income, for the first time non-'carriage folk' could embrace the joys of suburban life. The growing emphasis on the nuclear family and the removal of middle-class women from the workplace also contributed to the increasing split between work and home.[9] As early as 1748, Pehr Kalm commented in disbelief on how well dressed middle-class English women were and how little work they did:

> Nearly all the evening occupations which our women in Sweden perform are neglected by them, but, instead, here they sit round the fire without attempting in the very least degree what we call hushails-syslor, household duties. But they can never be deprived the credit of being very handsome and very lively in society. In pleasant conversation, agreeable repartie, polite sallies, in a word, all that the public calls ... politeness and savoir vivre, they are never wanting. ... The mistresses and their daughters are in particular those who enjoy perfect freedom from work.[10]

Fishman links the development of this bourgeois ideology with Nonconformism in particular. Part of his identification of Clapham as the first 'true' suburb rests on the group, centred around William Wilberforce and Henry Thornton, who settled there and created a godly retreat based on Christian values.[11] Thornton bought an estate there in 1792 and peppered the west side of Clapham Common with large houses for his fellow evangelicals, 'the chummery' as he called them, most of whom commuted to the centre from their suburban enclave.[12] Indeed, it was the evangelical poet William Cowper who first captured the essence of this new split lifestyle in his poem *Retirement* (1781).[13]

'Tis such an easy walk, so smooth and straight,
The second milestone fronts the garden gate:

A step if fair, and, if a shower approach,
They find safe shelter in the next stage-coach.
There prison'd in a parlour snug and small,
Like bottled wasps upon a southern wall,
The man of business and his friends compress'd,
Forget their labours, yet find no rest;
But still 'tis rural — trees are to be seen
From every window and the fields are green:
Ducks paddle in the pond before the door,
And what could a remoter scene shew more?

Evangelical though he was, Cowper's poem betrays a strong ambivalence to the new dormitory settlements. He provides one of the earliest uses of the term 'suburban' with its modern derogatory connotations of having a narrow outlook or limited horizons.[14] Cowper's sympathies were strongly biased towards the rural; he was, after all, the author of those well-known lines: 'God made the country, and man made the town' (*The Task*, 1785, Bk 1, l. 749). But in *Retirement* although the viewpoint shifts continuously throughout the poem, and the merits and demerits of life in town and country are both evaluated, only the suburbs come in for an entirely negative assessment. The separation of work and residence became commonplace throughout British cities in the later eighteenth and early nineteenth centuries and was enthusiastically embraced by the middle classes.[15] But Cowper's lines are a reminder that not everyone saw this as a welcome phenomenon, and protests against the environmental despoilation created by the new suburbs were frequently voiced, as the following section explores.

JOHN GWYNN AND THE SHAPING OF THE SUBURBS

We saw in the last chapter that the architecture of the environs, if it was characterized by anything, displayed variety up until the 1770s. Large residences rubbed shoulders with semi-detached houses, cottages and terraces in the villages of outer London, while the connecting roads between them might also contain any and all of the same list of dwellings in a fairly random mixture. Just as some of the norms of social behaviour seem to have been suspended in the suburban areas, so were the accepted architectural hierarchies in terms of the planning and placement of buildings. However, from around 1770 this haphazard approach became less acceptable to architectural commentators and urban theorists. Increasingly the ideal was individual detached dwellings, and while many rows of terraces continued to be built for cheaper housing, for those who could afford it, the detached house became the suburban form par excellence. John Gwynn, author of *London and Westminster Improved* (1766), wrote in relation to Chelsea: 'The houses built in country places should always be detached, for the benefit of air, light and prospect, and not built in rows according to the present taste, nor should they be suffered to project one before the other; if this method was observed, every house would be situated in a garden, and the whole would be cheerful and pleasant.'[16] The problem of how such 'country places' just outside the city might be shaped and managed became an increasingly acute one as the centre expanded remorselessly. The issue of the edge, as we have seen, was not a new one in the nineteenth century. In the seventeenth and eighteenth centuries there was also a strong discourse concerning London's seemingly uncontrollable growth and its consequences. Anxieties coalesced around the irregular shape that such development produced in contravention of classical architectural ideals, the poor environment that rapid development created, its impact on the surrounding landscape and agriculture, and a fear that London might grow disproportionately to the rest of the nation.[17] From Stow's *Survey* to Defoe's *Tour* and onwards, the theme of the monster city devouring the countryside was a well-established trope.[18] Stow wrote of Whitechapel: 'Also without the bars, both the sides of the street be pestered with cottages and allies, even

up to Whitechapel church; and almost half a mile beyond it into the common field; all of which ought to be open and free for all men.'[19] He particularly singled out cottages for criticism here, and this again was a familiar theme, one which we will return to later in the chapter. John Evelyn made similar comments in *Fumifugium* where he argued that 'poor and nasty *Cottages* near the City, be prohibited, which disgrace and take off from the sweetness and amœnity of the Environs of *London*' (fig. 146).[20] This type of cheap row housing was often labelled as 'cottages' alongside the more familiar use of the term for individual small rural dwellings. John Gwynn opened his polemical work with a quote from Dr Johnson on this very theme: 'like an entrance into a large city, after a distant prospect. Remotely, we see nothing but spires of temples, and turrets of palaces, and imagine it the residence of splendor, grandeur, and magnificence; but, when we have passed the gates, we find it perplexed with narrow passages, disgraced with despicable cottages, embarassed with obstructions, and clouded with smoke.'[21]

Gwynn's target, however, was both more wide reaching and more profound, his aim being nothing less than harmonization of all the parts of the metropolis. He wrote of the random nature of development in the outskirts:

Whenever any buildings either in a city, town or village go to decay the proprietor (if able) should be obliged to rebuild in a regular uniform manner. The villages about London, in particular, such as Chelsea, Kensington, Knightsbridge, Paddington, Islington, &c. should be subject to a law of this kind; they are all capable of vast improvements, and might very

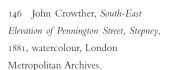

146 John Crowther, *South-East Elevation of Pennington Street, Stepney*, 1881, watercolour, London Metropolitan Archives.

A view of a speculative development in Wapping built *c.*1680 which survived until after the First World War.

easily be made delightful spots, worthy the neighbourhood of so rich and opulent a city as London.[22]

And he went on to attack 'the fraternity of builders' responsible for this chaos:

> If they are permitted to proceed at their accustomed rate, we may expect to find that the neighbouring hills of Hampstead and Highgate, will soon become considerable parts of the suburbs of London; and when the limbs extend themselves too fast, and grow out of proportion to the body which is to nourish and sustain them, it may very rationally be supposed, that a consumption will be the consequence.... And if these quacks in building can be called in and be made any way serviceable towards restoring and repairing the decayed parts of the body, they may then be allowed ... [to] make atonement for the wretched operations they have already performed upon its mangled limbs.[23]

Gwynn's comparison of London to the human body was another long-standing metaphor through which ideas of proportionality, sickness and circulation were presented. It was essential not just for metropolitan but for national well-being that the balance between London and its region be maintained. In order to keep goods, people and services flowing through the city, its physical shape and form must be kept in harmony.[24] Increasingly attention turned to the outer parishes and their integration with the centre. Urban reformers no longer saw it as acceptable to have a designed core surrounded by a chaotic and unplanned periphery; the two must be brought together in some way to create a harmonious physical entity.

Gwynn's desire for wholeness was not new; rather the novelty lay in the level of attention he gave to exactly how buildings might be orientated and organized along the city–country fringe. What was also innovative in terms of city planning was the prominence given to the relationship between the architecture and the surrounding landscape, although as a broader cultural concern this had a long pedigree in literature and art, as we have seen. It was not just the hovels which embarrassed Gwynn and others but also their inhabitants, the cottagers and squatters, who were deemed to cause particular problems on the urban fringes (see fig. 83). As John Middleton

wrote in the Board of Agriculture report for Middlesex in 1798:

> Cottagers who live on the borders of commons, woods and copses, are a real nuisance, from the circumstances of a considerable part of their support being acquired by pilfering.... The erecting of a cottage, and placing a poor family on the waste, and close to a wood, is a certain means of relieving the parish, at the expence of the proprietors of such property. This kind of grant, made in the front of other land, in the vicinity of London, or any other increasing town, is a serious loss to the owners of such land, as much of its value depends on its fronting a road or a green, and also in not having an unsightly cottage close to it.[25]

The appropriation of common land by cottagers had been a long-standing practice. Pressure for land intensified under the numerous Enclosure Acts passed from Tudor times onwards but with increasing regularity from the second half of the eighteenth century.[26] Daniel Lysons reported how agricultural land was rapidly being enclosed in the metropolitan area. In Lambeth there were 250 acres of 'land now inclosing from common' and only 30 acres of 'land to remain in common'. The rush to enclose was fuelled around the capital by the consequent rise in land values. In Lambeth the average rent for unenclosed garden-ground was £4 per acre and for enclosed land around £5.[27] The squatters hoped in time to become copyholders, who paid a fine for life to the lord of the manor, which provided him with an income and was cynically used, according to John Middleton, to help reduce the parish's provision for the poor. Those who established such squatter settlements used the common land to graze their animals and cut turf and peat for fuel. They also caused a problem by grazing their animals on the verges or 'strays' at the side of the road. In so doing they often spilled over onto the highway, increasing congestion as well as reducing the available fodder for drovers bringing their livestock to the London markets.[28] Cottagers' dwellings could be found on all the major open areas around London, and it was these properties that were depicted by J. T. Smith in his *Picturesque Views* of Epping Forest and Hampstead Heath (see figs 84 and 85). It was not just cottagers who appropriated common land, of course. At Hampstead Thompson wrote: 'It seems that virtually the entire town was built on encroachments and enclosures from the manorial waste, that is the Heath.' He estimated that by *c*.1800 100 of the 340 acres which were known to exist in 1703 had been enclosed or built over.[29] Cary's maps of the Enfield area vividly chart the progress of 'emparkment', the creation of gentry park from common land, at the turn of the nineteenth century (see figs 41 and 42).

DESIGNING THE SUBURBS: ARCHITECTS AND BUILDERS

John Gwynn was one of the few writers in the later eighteenth century to engage with the suburban. There was a torrent of architectural publications produced from the 1780s onwards largely concerned with domestic dwellings, but direct references to 'the suburban' or 'the suburbs' in this literature are few and far between. Rather, the issue of designing a new type of residential environment was addressed not at the macro but at the micro-scale through the more familiar territory of individual building types, principally the villa and the *cottage orné*. The writers of the time worked outwards from the individual dwelling to consider the garden and grounds that surrounded it, and in this incremental fashion a notion of a distinct suburban landscape came into being heavily dependent on prevailing picturesque theories.

This section will focus principally on these theoretical writings about suburban building types to explore shifts in the perception of the outer London landscape in the 1770–1840 era. This publishing boom has largely been studied to date in relation to its place in the literature of architectural theory and its advancement of the picturesque, most authoritatively and comprehensively by John Archer in *The Literature of British Domestic Architecture 1715–1842*.[30] Here, instead, we will concentrate on the production of such works within the context of professionalization: that is, the professionalization both of architects themselves and of their clients, among whom the professions formed a growing constituency.

Let us begin by considering the major themes of these architectural publications, notably the individual building types of the villa, mansion and cottage from which so many of them derived their titles. It is noteworthy that Gwynn did not use the word 'villa' to describe the detached houses that he was advocating in the suburbs, for even by the 1760s the term was still relatively uncommon. From that date a second wave of villa building took place around the metropolis which helped to establish the term. The renewed interest in the villa came particularly out of the work of Sir Robert Taylor (1714–1788), who re-established the form as a significant type with works such as Asgill House, Richmond, Surrey (1760–65), for Sir Charles Asgill, a banker and Lord Mayor of London (1757–8), and Danson House, Bexley, Kent (1762–6), for John Boyd, a notable trader in West Indian slaves and sugar (fig. 147).[31] Taylor himself came from a City background. He was born in a villa in Essex which his mason father had built. Taylor remained close to his roots and, as Colvin writes, for his extensive City clientele 'he designed offices in London and villas in the country.'[32] He transformed the rather austere layouts of the earlier elite neo-Palladian villas into comfortable modern suburban homes for plutocrats, which were copied across the metropolitan middle-class commuter belt. His main innovations were the introduction of canted bays to break up the rectangular block; compact plans with few corridors; interconnecting rooms revolving around a central staircase on the main floor suitable for the more informal entertaining of the later eighteenth century; the incorporation of the service areas at ground and basement level; and at Asgill the

147   W. B. Cooke after Samuel Owen, *Villa at Richmond*, 1814, engraving, London Metropolitan Archives.

View of Asgill House, Richmond, Surrey (1760–65), by Robert Taylor for Sir Charles Asgill.

to come with the scope of this publication, which partakes more of the useful than the grand....Those who apply columns to such a building, give to a Villa the dressings of a mansion, and run into an equal absurdity with those who give to a garden building the form, the ornaments, and embellishments of a Cathedral![36]

The primary new building type of the suburbs became these cuboid or at least regular small houses, whether semi-detached or detached, frequently designated as villas. It is important to remember that at the same time the terrace house remained an equally dominant form, particularly in less affluent areas and on arterial roads (fig. 148).[37] However, as the terrace house was not a new phenomenon it received relatively little attention from contemporary writers, who, following Gwynn, favoured the detached house for the outer metropolitan areas.[38] James Elmes (1782–1862) wrote of the suburban villa as benefiting 'from *situation* as to the town, and from *position* as to rural beauty'.[39] This dual aspect of suburban living was pinned down more precisely by J. B. Papworth (1775–1847): 'The roads by which it is surrounded, and the communication with a city, a town, or large village, should be such as will afford pleasant rides and walks, and allow the supply of necessaries, which small grounds cannot produce in themselves, and for which there is frequent need.'[40]

J. C. Loudon (1783–1843) went further and claimed that the produce available in the London suburbs was of a superior quality to that 'of any private individual in the country' and that 'the suburbs of towns are alone calculated to afford a maximum of comfort and enjoyment and at a minimum of expense.'[41] Papworth wrote that the location should not be far from medical aid and no more than a mile from a church, unless the family owned a carriage. Papworth was the architect of a suburban estate at Brockwell in Dulwich, south London (1825–30), which does not survive. He also designed Park Hill, Streatham (c.1830–41), the only remaining example of a large villa in its original parkland grounds still facing Streatham Common.[42] It is noteworthy that Papworth does not assume carriage ownership among his readers, and indeed most writers in this period went out of their way to stress that their designs were suitable for a wide range of budgets and sizes of dwelling.

148 Kennington Park Road, Lambeth, 1770s arterial housing, London Metropolitan Archives.

descent of the *piano nobile* to ground floor level connecting with the garden, a feature which later became the norm.[33] As villas became more widespread, there was a concomitant attempt in the architectural literature to define them more precisely and especially to distinguish between them and other building types.

The problem with such attempts at definition, according to Archer, was that anything from a mansion to a one-room shooting box might be deemed a villa.[34] A mansion indicated a more substantial house, often a permanent residence rather than a secondary one. Humphry Repton, for example, boasted that he would turn Kenwood from a 'villa' to a 'mansion' with his improvements and additions in the 1790s. Robert Lugar (c.1773–1855), the county architect for Essex, in his *Architectural Sketches* (1805) stated that the villa should be simple, light and unornamented; other-wise it would look like a 'mansion'.[35] He went on to outline the advantages of the villa's compactness for 'Persons of Genteel Life and Moderate Fortune':

It may be stated as a maxim, that a house which partakes in form much of the cube will be more compact in the plan and elevation, afford more conveniences within less cost, than any other form. Houses of large extensive fronts require much architectural decoration, and can scarcely be considered

149 R. St George Mansergh, *Timothy Tallow, and his Wife, going to Graves Hall, on a Sunday*, 1772, engraving, London Metropolitan Archives.

The title at the top of the print translates as 'The English Caper' while 'The Buggy' refers to the modesty of their horse and 'carriage'. St Paul's is framed in the apex of the man's whip, while a 'For Sale' sign, indicating the transitory nature of property holding in the suburbs, can be seen outside the 'cockney villa' with its bare grounds.

Besides villas the other main middling-sized dwelling types were the *cottage orné* and the 'box'. It is to the latter much maligned and misunderstood category of dwelling that I want to turn first. The term 'box' originally meant either a small country house or a residence for temporary use while following a particular sport, as in a hunting-box, shooting-box, fishing-box, etc.[43] From around the 1760s it began to be applied to the increasing numbers of small detached houses being built in places like Clapham and labelled citizen's or more derogatively 'cit's' boxes. James Elmes wrote of 'merchants' and sugar-bakers' boxes which croud the sides of Clapham Road and Kennington Common'.[44] As such houses began to be built in numbers around the capital, the discourse of rural despoliation and social pretension became increasingly shrill. A cartoon from 1772 lampoons 'Timothy Tallow' with his domineering wife, a symbol of petit bourgeois respectability, visiting his country house in Essex on a Sunday (fig. 149). The scene almost perfectly illustrates the opening lines of Robert Lloyd's 'The Cit's Country

Box', first published in the *Connoisseur*, a publication that specifically pitted itself as a 'Town' mouthpiece against the 'Cits':[45]

> The wealthy Cit, grown old in trade,
> Now wishes for the rural shade,
> And buckles to his one-horse chair,
> Old Dobbin, or the founder'd mare:
> While wedged in closely by his side,
> Sits Madam, his unwieldy bride,
> With Jacky on a stool before 'em,
> And out they jog in due decorum.
> Scare past the turnpike half a mile,
> How all the country seems to smile!

Lloyd's outcry grew out of an anxiety that the industrious middle classes, who made the nation wealthy, might cease their activities and retire to their estates not just on a Sunday but all week round to the detriment of the economy. One of the best-known images of the satirical genre is *A Common Council Man of Candlestick Ward, and his wife, on a visit to Mr*

Deputy – at his Modern Built Villa near Clapham (*c.*1750, fig. 150). The scene depicted echoes the architectural confusion of Mr Deputy Dumpling and his family's visit to Bagnigge Wells, where the architecture is also utilized to create a *mise-en-scène* of social confusion and ridicule (see fig. 100).[46] The Clapham print mocks the attempts of City folk to individualize their homes through exuberant architectural embellishment and to turn what were essential large gardens into mini-country estates through cramming in a plethora of features. While such an architectural melange might be acceptable for a commercial pleasure garden, where it could be considered as playful eclecticism, the deployment of such a range of styles in a domestic situation was seen as betraying a lack of taste and discrimination. Lloyd's poem has been said to mark 'the unmistakable beginning of the Betjeman tradition, the poetry of the English suburbs, a landscape, physical and mental, that thankfully still survives'.[47] Yet while Betjeman was affectionate towards the suburbs, Lloyd's critique was harsh and unyielding against a phenomenon which to him broke all the norms of accepted taste:

Now bricklay'rs, carpenters, and joiners,
With Chinese artists, and designers,
Produce their schemes of alteration,
To work this wond'rous reformation.
The useful dome, which secret stood,
Embosom'd in the yew-tree's wood,
The trav'ler with amazement sees
A temple Gothic, or Chinese,
With many a bell, and tawdry rag on,
And crested with a sprawling dragon;
A wooden arch is bent astride,
A ditch of water, four foot wide,
With angles, curves and zigzag lines,
From Halpenny's★ exact designs.

★ William Halfpenny produced a number of works of exotic designs, such as *New Designs for Chinese Temples* (1750), *Chinese and Gothick Architecture Properly Ornamented* (1752), and *Rural Architecture in the Gothick Taste* (1752).

Jeremiah Sago's garden in Islington, a byword for small-scale suburban retreats by this date, typifies this eclectic mix (fig. 151). The walled garden is dominated by a flamboyant gazebo, in this case previously sur-

150 Anon., *A Common Council Man of Candlestick Ward and his Wife, on a Visit to Mr Deputy – at his Modern Built Villa near Clapham*, *c.*1750, engraving, London Metropolitan Archives.

The villa combines classical, Gothic and Chinese elements à la Halfpenny topped by a griffin on the roadside-viewing pagoda with its fretwork glass panels.

WHEREAS my New Pagoda has been clandestinely carried
off & a new pair of DOLPHINS taken from the top of the
GAZEBO by some blood-thirsty Villains. & whereas
a great deal of TIMBER has been cut down & carried
away from the Old GROVE That was planted last Spring
& PLUTO & PROSERPINE thrown into my BASON. from
henceforth Steel-Traps & Spring Guns will be constantly
set for the better extirpation of such a nest of Villains
by me JEREMIAH SAGO.

THE DELIGHTS OF ISLINGTON.

Publish'd as the Act directs April 30.1772 By J.Bretherton N.° 134 New Bond Street

151 Charles Bretherton after Henry
William Bunbury, *Delights of Islington*,
1772, etching, British Museum.

earlier (see fig. 125). The use of steel traps to defend such houses, where no retainers were present when they were empty, was another common device for mocking the pretentions of those aspiring to country estates, but lacking the income to support such a lifestyle in the form of carriages and servants.

The problem with Anglo-Palladianism's essential mutability – in which mansions, villas, boxes and cottages all derived from the same basic model – arose as a desire for greater social differentiation began to become more pronounced from the late eighteenth century onwards. It was as the environs became more crowded that a desire for spatial and social distinction arose, and the 'cit's box' became an easy target for snobbish satire. However, it is important to remember that positive images of this new landscape continued to far outweigh the negative ones in both image and text. The author of *London in Miniature* praised Mr Turner's modern house on Hampstead Heath as a 'handsome square-built Brick Edifice...that has a most extensive and delightful View over all the circumjacent Country'.[48] Visual images such as Boydell's prints of Denmark Hill (see fig. 145) or his view of Richmond (see fig. 89) show how representations of the new landscape followed the development pattern while at the same time reinforcing its suburban ideology. This was a new architectural ecology, to use Banham's term, which the middle classes had created in their own image and appropriated for their own purposes.[49]

While satirists might mock the small proportions and doll's house quality of the citizen's box, as the epitome of modern suburban living it had no equal. Not only was it relatively cheap to build, compact and fashionable, but it was also easy to maintain. As Edmund Bartell noted in his *Hints for Picturesque Improvements in Ornamented Cottages*: 'In size and convenience the ornamented cottage and the citizen's box are nearly on a par; and I confess, I could wish to see the former more generally in place of the latter...yet, as every one, perhaps the majority, may not be of my opinion, but prefer a house of brick and tile.'[50] The preference for the modern convenience and easier maintenance of a 'box' is understandable when it is remembered that many of these were secondary residences and therefore not necessarily seen as meriting equal attention to a family's main abode (see fig. 163). As J. B. Papworth lamented in *Rural Residences* (1818): 'The villas that sur-

mounted by dolphins rather than dragons, which epitomizes Lloyd's perverted pastoral. The gazebo was used both as an eye-catcher and display for passing traffic and as a point from which to view the prospect of St Paul's or other landmarks: thus continuing the tradition of viewing platforms, whether roof-top or in the grounds, but in a far more flamboyant fashion than the restrained Croom's Hill example of a hundred years round London, the country residences of the most wealthy of its inhabitants, not being designed by the architect, are little more than mere cases of brick, in which a certain number of apartments are injudiciously arranged, presenting to the eye a continuity of ill bestowed expense and tasteless absurdities, disgraceful to the proprietors and offensive to true taste.'[51] Papworth's rhetoric, however, was not just directed at the abominable taste of the wealthy; his principal target was the system under which such buildings were produced:

> There is much reason to believe that architecture in this country has failed to receive its proportion of public patronage, because the public has not distinguished it as a fine art ... but have rather considered it as a mechanical operation, in which the mere builder is fully competent to all its duties. ... In London, the speculative builder has generally superseded the labours of the artists, for the architect is there rarely called upon, unless it be to remedy the errors, or supply some of the deficiencies as well of art, as of practical sciences. The result of this system of building is an obvious perversion of true architecture.[52]

Gwynn had already noted the dominance of builders over architects in the outskirts, but from the late eighteenth century architects, under the leadership of Sir John Soane, began to seek ways to formalize their professional standing as separate from the building trades. J. B. Papworth was a founder member in 1834 of the Institute of British Architects (later the RIBA), the last and ultimately the most successful of a series of professional bodies beginning with the founding of the Royal Academy in 1768.[53] As architects became increasingly aware of the need to position themselves against developers in the highly competitive and deregulated house-building world, this resulted in increasing specialization in the design, and especially the marketing, of architecture. Daniel Abramson has traced the impact of segmentation in commercial buildings in this period, and similar trends can be identified in the domestic sphere.[54]

The shift towards the semi-detached and more individualized house, while evidently partially indebted to the impact of the picturesque and notions of the suburbs as architecturally distinct from the centre, was also the outcome of the creeping professionalization of architecture. By the early to mid-nineteenth century the one-shape-fits-all Palladian box, with mere scaling up or down in size to accord with social status, was no longer seen as appropriate for new housing. The architectural books of the time make it abundantly clear that what they were offering was not just architectural knowledge but the fine calibration of social distinctions translated into bricks and mortar. In their publications architects offered their services as specialists who could create individualized designs for every conceivable circumstance. This was essentially a means of creating differentiation through design in an increasingly fluid market socially and stylistically: what today we would call branding.

As architects created a growing range of domestic buildings from the cottage upwards, they sought to distinguish their products from those of builders. One of the things that architects could provide was personalized space planning, and there was a tremendous emphasis on internal arrangements as a specialized branch of knowledge in the literature of the period. As David Laing (c.1755–1856), a pupil of Soane, wrote in his popular work *Hints for Dwellings, Consisting of Original Designs for Cottages, Farm Houses, Villas, etc.* (1800):

> This Branch of the Architect's Profession is the most arduous. ... In the Plan ... will be shown the Skill, Taste, and Ingenuity of the Artist; here, his Address in surmounting Difficulties will evince itself; and here, the Conveniences to be combined and arranged, must render the Mansion inviting to the Master, and convenient to the Family: by a good Distribution also much Space is saved, or applied to useful Purposes, and the Expenses much abridged.[55]

In a further attempt to emphasize the bespoke nature of his houses, as opposed to the off-the-shelf speculative variety, he says that he has not included costs as each individual design had too many variables, but that he would willingly answer enquiries about financing.[56] In the search for a broader range of clients, architects began to produce a range of designs specifically for suburban situations, which entailed a move away from individual houses to paired and multiple-form arrangements. David Laing produced the first metropolitan version of the theme (figs 152 and 153). In this design Laing seeks to demonstrate the range of options that the architect might offer in the suburbs, from paired

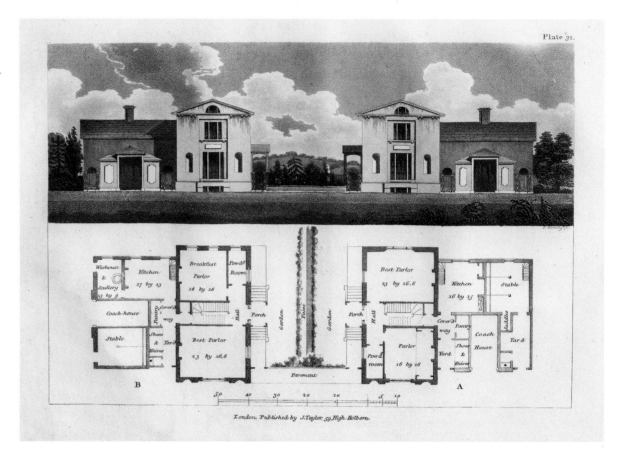

152 David Laing, 'Plans and Elevations for Two Houses, with Coach-houses and Stables attached, calculated for the Neighbourhood of the Metropolis', Plate 31 from *Hints for Dwellings*, 1800, British Architectural Library.

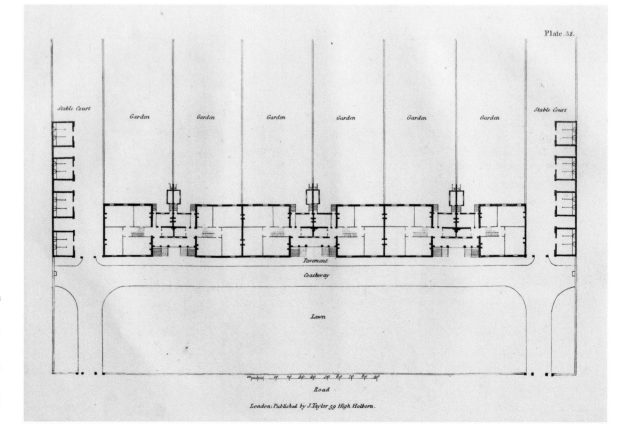

153 David Laing, 'Plan of a Design for Six Houses in a Row, with Stabling, Coach-house &c. for each; suitable for Situations similar to the Foregoing, but on a more Extensive Scale', Plate 32 from *Hints for Dwellings*, 1800, British Architectural Library.

houses – which he wrote might also be built as detached ones – to a six-house terrace block incorporating a combination of single and double houses along its length. The terrace dwellings were linked by lower-level entrance blocks set back from the main pavilions at a height of two rather than three storeys. The gardens were to be separated by post and rail fences with 'a low Shrubbery' planted on each side to preserve privacy, while the six-house terrace is carefully set back from the road behind a curving entrance drive and lawn. The importance of commuting is evident in the care accorded to the provision of stabling and coach houses. This was the first published design of this type of layout, although terraces were already in existence in Bristol and around London.[57] Early examples were built at Kingsland Place, Hackney, and Kennington Road, Lambeth, in the 1770s, contemporaneous with the traditional terrace (see fig. 148), but the form did not really become popular until later in the century.[58] The best-known metropolitan terrace of paired houses with interconnections is the Paragon, Blackheath (1793), by Michael Searles (1751–1813), often wrongly called the first of its type.[59] The format spawned many copies and variants, such as the simplified example at the eponymously named Paragon Road, Hackney, of 1809–13

(fig. 154). The boom in architectural publications in the late eighteenth and early nineteenth centuries presents powerful evidence of the anxious attempts by architects both to find employment in the economic depression of the 1790s and the 1810s and to create a market for themselves as designers of houses for a middle-class audience. As J. C. Loudon, the landscape architect, declared in 1835: 'The surest foundation on which [architects] . . . can found their hopes of future employment is on the taste of the middling classes. The time for building palaces, castles and cathedrals is gone by, or nearly so.'[60] It is to those middling-class clients and their changing lifestyles that we now turn.

LANDSCAPES OF PROFESSIONALISM:
CREATING SOMETHING 'OUT OF NOTHING'

Hackney'd in business, wearied at that oar,
Which thousands, once fast chained to, quit no more,
But which, when life at ebb runs weak and low,
All wish, or seem to wish, they could forgo;
The statesman, lawyer, merchant, man of trade,
Pants for the refuge of some rural shade

William Cowper, *Retirement,* 1781

Cowper's poem associates the suburbs not just with wealthy businessmen, as had been the case in the preceding century or so, but also with the growing ranks of the professional classes such as architects, doctors and lawyers. These were all groups whose most successful practitioners had the potential to earn large sums, who were self-employed, and as such had some flexibility over where and how they chose to operate. As Coleridge observed in 1832, a 'silent revolution' had occurred in Britain 'when the Professions fell off from the Church'.[61] Jeremy Boulton has drawn attention to the increase in the number of professionals in seventeenth-century London, particularly lawyers, due to an immense expansion in the volume of legal business.[62] About a third of all attorneys and doctors in England and Wales were based in 'Greater London' (London, Westminster, Southwark and Middlesex) in the 1780s.[63] However, most of them continued to live outside the centre, only staying in London during the law terms, and so there developed legal enclaves in the environs. In Boyle's *City and Court Guide* for 1798, for example, T. Smith is listed at 3 Gray's Inn Square and Tottenham, while John Smith can be found at 1 New Inn and Highgate.[64] In Hampstead for the later eighteenth century F. M. L. Thompson concluded that there were no resident nobility and gentry, considerable numbers of businessmen, but that it was above all the home of professionals and 'a lawyer's nest'.[65] Stephen Daniels has mapped this Hampstead grouping where a number of lawyers lived along the top edge of the Heath.[66] Its most famous member was Lord Mansfield (1705–93), the Lord Chief Justice, whose country villa was at Kenwood, while just down the road was Evergreen Hill, the house of Thomas Erskine (1750–1832), the most famous barrister of his day and later Lord Chancellor. Howitt in his *Northern Heights* commented on the phenomenon: 'As Caen Wood [Kenwood] yet exists, it is an example of the magnificent rewards of law in this country. . . . Everywhere we run against the broad lands and aristocratic abodes of the lawyers in this law-loving England. Literati and artists in general may inherit large fortunes, but lawyers are every day creating them out of nothing. Lord Mansfield won Caen Wood and infinitely more, out of nothing.'[67] Creating something out of nothing is an apt metaphor for the process whereby the fortunes of those who made their living through their skills and knowledge

transformed the semi-rural outskirts into a suburban landscape for both the aspirant and the established middle classes. But Howitt's quote also reveals the sense of bafflement at the speed and comprehensiveness with which the London countryside was being transformed by forces that were neither obvious nor controllable. In this way the unplanned development of the environs continued as those with funds bought up land and property as and where they could.

We will now turn to one particular case study to see what kind of houses wealthy professional men might build for themselves and why they might locate to the outskirts of town. John White (c.1747–1813) was Surveyor to the Duke of Portland and a successful architect and developer.[68] He seems to have trained as a carpenter, being cited as such on an early Portland Estate lease, and then with the passing years is referred to in turn as 'surveyor' and 'architect', although at this date the latter two terms were interchangeable.[69] Indeed, White's practice reflected this mixture of land surveying and architectural design work. He laid out the Portland Estate in Marylebone from 1787, making a fortune in the process. He was married to the daughter of Thomas Farnolls Pritchard, the Shrewsbury architect and designer of the Coalbrookdale iron bridge (1777–9). White was the architect for a number of projects outside the capital besides extensive work in the Marylebone area, where he lived, including the new Parish Workhouse in 1775–6. In 1791 White built a house for himself and his family on the far side of the New Road on land owned by the Portland Estate just south of Marylebone Park (see fig. 177). The New Road, which opened in 1756, was built to facilitate east–west movement along the edge of the built-up area. It linked the City with the rapidly developing suburbs of Islington, Marylebone and Paddington, and it became the key northern commercial and commuting axis. Effectively it was London's first bypass, aimed at unblocking the chronic stasis that the development of the West End estates had created with their private roads barred to outside traffic. In so doing it created a definable edge to the north of London for the first time since the demolition of the old City walls. It was the first of many attempts to limit London's growth through the creation of an arterial routeway which at the same time defined the city's parameters: the most recent and probably equally doomed being the M25.

155 Samuel Henry Grimm, *Looking North to New Road*, drawing, 1793, British Library.

A view from Devonshire Street on the site of what is, on the left, now Park Crescent showing John White's villa and its smaller next-door neighbour belonging to the Duke of Hamilton. On the right are farm buildings and cottages and the Jew's Harp and Queen's Head and Artichoke inns.

A view by Samuel Grimm shows how undeveloped the area was in 1793, when White's house (on the left of the picture) was first built (fig. 155). Even that symbol of modernity, the New Road, which can be seen running across the middle of the picture, was little more than a fenced track. This was still very much *terra incognita*, as the many later comments on the remoteness of Regent's Park for residential settlement indicate. Lysons wrote of neighbouring Paddington: 'The situation is ... so uncommonly retired, that a person residing there could scarcely conceive himself to be in a parish adjoining to that of St. George, Hanover-square.'[70] This was an edge location, and indeed John Gwynn paid it particular attention in his attempts to transform London's outskirts. Writing in 1766 – by which time the road had been open for ten years

– Gwynn was not impressed by the landlords' efforts on either side of the road:

One inconvenience deserves particular notice. Some streets that would naturally open into the country are shut up and darkened by houses built cross them at the end next the fields. This ought to be avoided ... in the streets which shall be raised on the ground yet unoccupied, between the present buildings and the new road from Paddington to Islington, which in this work has always been considered as the great boundary or line for restraining or limiting the rage of building. A stop ought also to be put to the practice of erecting irregular groups of houses at the extremeties of the town, an evil which if continued will make this metropolis more

183

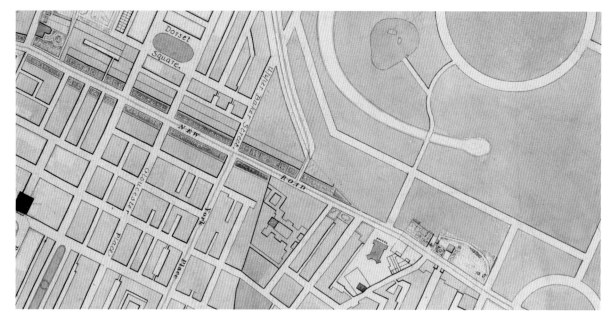

156 John White, *Plan of the Parish of St Marylebone with the Improvements proposed on the Marylebone Park Estate*, 1809, The National Archives (MPE 1/913/001).

This survey shows the gardens along the New Road and White's house and grounds above it on the right.

irregular if possible than it is. The act of parliament directs, that no building be erected for the future within fifty feet of the New-Road, but some people, in order to evade this judicious clause, have ingeniously contrived to build houses at that distance, but then to make themselves amends they take care to occupy the intermediate space, which was intended to disencumber the road, by a garden, the wall of which comes close upon it, and entirely defeats the original intention. This practice, and the mean appearance of the backs of the houses, offices and hovels, will in time render the approaches to the capital so many scenes of confusion and deformity, extremely unbecoming the character of a great and opulent city. Certainly the fronts of all buildings should be as conspicuous as possible, and therefore the before-mentioned practice is absurd; on the contrary, if the environs were properly regulated by a judicious disposition, a most elegant line would be formed round the metropolis; and the adjacent fields compose a beautiful lawn, and make an agreeable finish to the extream parts of the town.[71]

Grimm did a number of drawings of the area, and his view of the rear of Devonshire Place shows the ragged edge effect that Gwynn abhorred (see fig. 113). Gwynn's solution was to tear down the existing houses and set them back substantially in order to allow enough room for a proper footpath and regular grass plots in front of each house, thus creating the garden setting that he felt appropriate for such an edge of city location rather than the current 'confusion' (fig. 156).

Although White's house was pioneering in being on the northern side of the New Road, this was largely down to the ownership of the freehold of this small patch of ground by the Duke of Portland. Beyond lay Marylebone Park, currently leased by his employer until 1811 but with the ground ownership belonging to the Crown Estate. This was a situation White hoped to profit from, as we will see in the next chapter, either as a developer or through the rise in property values that would result benefiting his own house. Despite its seeming remoteness, in fact White was one of a significant number of architects, surveyors and artists who chose to base themselves on the edge of town. London was the undisputed centre of the art world, as John Sell Cotman proclaimed: 'London with all its fog and smoke is the only air for an artist to breathe in.'[72] A 1793 directory of London artists – a category which stretched from engravers and printers through painters of all types to architects, surveyors and even builders – lists fifty entries in the suburbs out of a total of approximately 400. These figures suggest that while the majority still agreed with Cotman's verdict, a significant number were eager to seek refuge from the smoke. Of those in the outskirts, the highest concentrations of artists were to be found in Chelsea, Clerkenwell and Islington, but a further eight entries were along or

157 Paul Sandby, *Evening View near Bayswater*, 1791, watercolour, private collection.

This is a companion piece to a *Morning View* of the same scene, one looking west and one east along the boundary wall of Hyde Park. This is taken by the Swan Inn near the turnpike with a similar mixture of figures and conveyances to Rowlandson's satirical scene in fig. 50.

immediately adjacent to the New Road alone. They included Charles Townley, 'Engraver to the King of Prussia'; Charles Peart and Frederick Breamer sculptors; and John Carter 'Designer and Draughtsman of Gothic Architecture'.[73] While highly successful artists and architects such as Vanbrugh, Hogarth, Chambers and Reynolds had long kept second homes around London, the trend to favour outer city locations as a permanent base seems to have been a new one. Paul Sandby (1731–1809) was one of the earliest, moving to 4 St George's Row, Hyde Park, Bayswater, in 1772, where he combined his studio and household. He drew and painted many views of his new suburban surroundings, clearly fascinated by their conjunction of urban and rural (fig. 157 and see fig. 16).[74] Prior to this Sandby

had lived in Woolwich from 1769 to 1772 during part of his tenure as Drawing Master at the Royal Military Academy there (1768–96).[75] He drew the view from the front of his isolated semi-detached 'villa' along with many other scenes from the surrounding landscape, such as the *Lime Kilns* at Charlton in Kent (see fig. 15). Once he had acquired his Bayswater property, he stayed at lodgings in Charlton when undertaking his two days' teaching a week at the Academy.

Such moves to the margins were no doubt prompted by cheaper rents on the periphery but also perhaps as an increasingly visible way of signifying difference and artistic identity. The 'House for an Artist' began to become a specific type in the architectural publications of the time, with Soane, Plaw and Papworth all offer-

ing designs on the theme.[76] While many artists (despite Howitt's surprising characterization of them as wealthy) could not afford to employ an architect, the idea of creating an identity 'out of nothing' through a combined residential and work environment – whether for solicitors, doctors or artists – was becoming established.[77] J. C. Loudon built a famous example of what he called a 'double detached villa' at Porchester Terrace in Bayswater for himself and his mother (1823–5): 'two small houses which should appear as one'.[78] The fiction of the sanctity and typology of the individual house was maintained by having a single block with independent access at each end of the building. Loudon's home was primarily residential, although it did also house the office of his *Gardener's Magazine*. He recommended the semi- or double-detached type as especially suitable for professionals, being well 'adapted for a person wishing the one house to be occupied as his office, and as the residence of his principal clerk, and the other to be retained as his own residence'.[79] He included a design by E. B. Lamb, who provided the illustrations for *The Suburban Gardener and Villa Companion*, which transplanted the long-standing town house tradition of a combined house and shop to a

suburban villa location (fig. 158): 'This plan was designed by Mr. Lamb for a suburban bookseller and stationer who proposes to occupy the one house with his family, and to use the front room of the other as a shop, the back room as a public reading-room, and the apartments under and over for book-binding, for containing part of his stock of books, and as sleeping-rooms for his apprentices and his shopmen.'[80]

John Plaw (1744/5–1820) produced a design for a combined work–home accommodation in his 1796 publication *Rural Architecture* (figs 159 and 160). Plaw was a prolific architect-writer who lived near to John White at Paddington from 1788 to 1795 and designed the new St Mary's church there (1788–91).[81] Significantly, he calls this design a 'house' not a villa, the latter suggesting a purely leisured lifestyle, while the church steeple and houses shown to the right indicate its suburban location. But while the nomenclature of the building is relatively transparent, the design is a smoke-screen intended to disguise the structure's dual function. Plaw deployed end pavilions, with two separate entrances attached to a central block, in an early usage of what was to become a common feature in many semi-detached layouts. In his design the emphasis on

159 John Plaw, 'Design for a Small House in the Environs of a Town or Village, suitable for a Family or a Genteel Profession', Plate 16 (plan) from *Rural Architecture*, 1796, British Architectural Library.

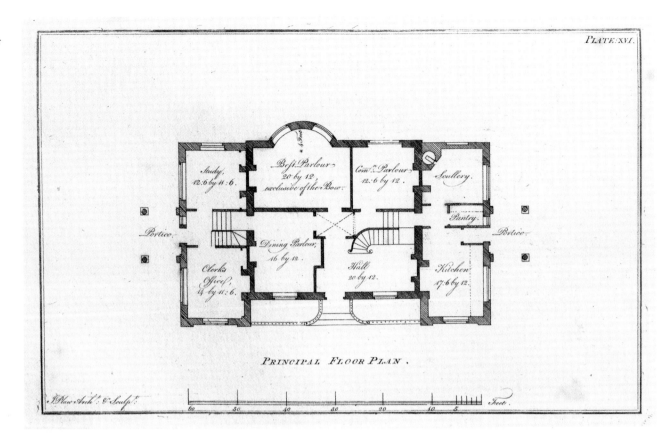

160 John Plaw, 'Design for a Small House in the Environs of a Town or Village, suitable for a Family or a Genteel Profession', Plate 17 (elevation) from *Rural Architecture*, 1796, British Architectural Library.

161 T. H. Shepherd, *View of the of House John White . . . on New Road, opposite Devonshire Place, Marylebone, as it appeared in 1794,* 1820–50, watercolour, British Museum.

This is based on a drawing by Samuel Hieronymus Grimm of 1794 from his Marylebone portfolio; see BL Add MSS 15542, fol. 139.

162 T. H. Shepherd, *View of the House John White . . . on New Road, opposite Devonshire Place, Marylebone, with the Addition of the Smaller House built by his Son John White Junior,* 1850, watercolour, British Museum.

the body of the house is further reinforced by a central doorway, which is in fact the main entrance. The two pavilions, in the traditional style of grand Palladian mansions, house the 'offices' or service areas: domestic at one end and commercial at the other. The business area is divided into a 'clerks' office' and a 'study' for the master, the latter term once again an etymological distancing device from its true business function.

White's Marylebone house, although on a grander scale, is very much in this genre. This was his town residence; he also owned a country house at Two Waters, Hemel Hempstead, Hertfordshire, which he designed himself. However, 2 Devonshire Place, to give the building its official address, was not just a home but also a workplace in the tradition of combined architectural practices and dwellings, of which Sir John Soane's is now the most famous example.[82] By virtue of his position and by being willing to breach the accepted building line, White was able to acquire a large plot and create a substantial villa and gardens. It provided a hugely visible sign of his material and social success, further reinforced by his charitable activities in the area: serving as a parish vestryman, donating a design for Marylebone Parish Workhouse and its attached infirmary in 1775, and through his close involvement in the plans for a new parish church. T. H. Shepherd (1784–1862) produced a view of White's house from the corner of Devonshire Place based on a drawing by S. H. Grimm showing the house as it was in 1794, just three years after it was completed (fig. 161).[83] The house is an unostentatious late eighteenth-century brick neoclassical three-bay box with prominent round-arched windows which provide the principal focal points. Its main impact derives from its spacious setting in substantial grounds clearly delineated by the prominent encircling wall. A plan of the property, drawn up by White himself, includes seemingly embryonic landscaping, certainly compared to the much smaller but more finished garden layout of the neighbouring property of the Duke of Hamilton (see fig. 156). The simple detached stable block is a highly visible status symbol, and considerable attention was given to the placement and design of stabling by architectural writers. Bartell wrote on the importance of keeping the coach house separate from the main dwelling: 'This is certainly a good method of telling the country that the owner keeps a carriage; and that

he has no objection to it being known.... And sometimes in order to separate the out-buildings from the house, a high wall, forming a garden or court yard before it, disgustingly bounds the view.'[84] White follows Bartell's approved method with regard to the former if not the latter requirement. In such a literally edgy position a high boundary wall was imperative, as Grimm's view of Marylebone Fields demonstrated. J. T. Smith related that the area was plagued by 'highwaymen who committed nightly depredations in the adjacent lanes' and that 'before the New-road was made from Paddington to Islington ... the public newspapers announced an inhabitant of the city to have arrived safely at his house in Mary-le-bone!'[85] Shepherd was a leading topographical illustrator with a specialism in metropolitan views. He was employed by Frederick Crace consistently between 1809 and 1859 to produce watercolours of London buildings.[86] Often these consisted of paired 'before' and 'after' views, such as those he produced of White's house as it appeared in 1794 and in 1850 at the time of his son's death (figs 161 and 162). White's son was also called John and followed in his father's profession. He is known to have been active from 1807 and worked with his father from 1809 until the latter's death in 1813, spending some of his time thereafter at the Marylebone house.

What, then, of White's other residence, Two Waters in Hertfordshire (fig. 163)? The illustration shows the house to be a tripartite regular classical villa, like 2 Devonshire Place, although this time with an added clerestory window. The latter was no doubt included to take advantage of its position 'on a pleasant brow ... overlooking the vale in every direction', as John Hassell reported in his account of 1819 on the 'villa of Mrs White' (by then a widow).[87] The building might look like the country home of a self-made man, but as the inscription below the print reveals, the seeming legibility of the structure in fact masks other purposes and activities. The caption reads: 'Mr White's new built house at Two Waters near Hemel Hempstead this mansion has been erected since the cutting the Grand Junction Canal (near where it stands) the House and grounds were open fields before that time: not far from this pleasant residence Mr White has established a Timber yard on a very extensive scale, the situation is well adapted for inland traffick.' This was no simple rural retreat. It was business not leisure that had drawn

the ambitious and energetic White to this spot in particular. The Grand Junction Canal reached Two Waters in 1798 on its route between Braunston in Northamptonshire and Brentford in west London where it joined the Thames. This was to be the vital artery linking White's timber yard with the centre of his operations in the capital. Brentford, however, was not very convenient for Marylebone, as any timber to be used on the Portland Estate or to the north would have to be transported across London. However, a branch canal to Paddington had been authorized in 1795. Paddington was just along the New Road from Marylebone, about a mile and a quarter away, the perfect location at which to unload White's timber. Paddington's significance as a distribution centre increased even further from 1820, when it was joined up to the new Regent's Canal, allowing goods to be transported by barge from west to east London and down to the Thames avoiding the traffic congestion of the centre. At this date canals were the future, something that Hassell (1767–1825) latched on to eagerly. He was an entrepreneurial publisher and printmaker

of a by now familiar type. He produced a weekly drawing magazine from 1809 to 1811 as well as various drawing manuals and topographical and antiquarian works illustrated with his own sketches. He published *Picturesque Rides and Walks with Excursions by Water, Thirty Miles round the Metropolis* (1817–19), and in his *Tour of the Grand Junction, Illustrated in a Series of Engravings* of the following year he wrote: 'Inland navigation to a manufacturing country, is the very heart's blood and soul of commerce, nor can we easily estimate the utility and importance of this mode of conveyance in obviating the expense and tediousness of land carriage, or the more protracted delays invariably attendant on opposite winds and tides.'[88]

White seemed to be perfectly placed to take advantage of the new opportunities that the canal offered to diversify his business interests into land, timber supply and possibly forestry as well. Hassell had noted the abundance of timber along the course of the canal in the Hertfordshire region as well as the variety of industries that had been established along its banks, including colleries, copper-works, plate-glass manufactories and paper mills.[89] The fact that White opened a timber yard 'on a very extensive scale' would support the evidence that he started out as a carpenter, the most successful of whom often operated as timber merchants.[90] However, White did not stop there. In 1801, the year the Grand Junction reached Paddington Basin, White was listed by Paddington vestry as one of a number of encroachments on Westbourne Green.[91] He leased Westbourne Farm, which sat just above Paddington Basin alongside the canal, and he obviously saw this as an opportune moment to purchase what would become highly valuable prime building land. In 1810 he was able to buy some more land there from the lessors, thus extending his freehold possession.[92] Westbourne Farm in Paddington therefore provided a third leg to White's operations, all situated in the environs but with the northern base about twenty-five miles away. No doubt Westbourne Farm was purchased as an investment, but at the same time the farm would have provided ample space for another timber yard, from whence orders could be dispatched across London using the fast link of the New Road. Another development on Westbourne Farm's land was Desborough Cottage, the home of Mrs Siddons, subsequently known as Desborough House (see fig. 168).[93]

In 1805 White junior married and built himself a small house – Bridge House – on the north side of the canal at Westbourne Green opposite Westbourne Farm.[94] In his later years he is listed at that address by the *Dictionary of Surveyors*, although he certainly used the Devonshire Place address for most of the period after his father died up until 1844.[95] John White junior was less successful than his father and ran into financial difficulties in the economic downturn of the mid-1820s when working on the Eyre Estate, now St John's Wood (see fig. 178).[96] He did, however, become District Surveyor for St Marylebone parish from 1807 to 1850. When he was appointed to the post there was some initial opposition, until the benefits of the family connections were pointed out to the appointing panel of magistrates: 'They have seen that he is perfectly qualified for the situation; and they have seen also, the benefit which would arise in the management of the Buildings in the District to which he is appointed, from the circumstances of having the experience and the knowledge of his Father to resort to, whenever he might have occasion to do so.'[97] John junior's son, John

Alfred, succeeded him as District Surveyor in turn. Family connections obviously still held considerable sway, despite the increasing reliance by architects and surveyors on public posts rather than private patronage for their employment.

Let us return now to Shepherd's second view, which shows the Devonshire Place house in 1850, the year White junior died (fig. 162).[98] By this date the dual purpose of what has become almost a complex is far more evident. A new block has been added at the side for 'Miss White' according to the old paper Crace catalogue, although its reliability is questionable. Already in the 1809 plan a new structure had been erected next to the stable block (see fig. 156), which by the date of Shepherd's later drawing seems to have abandoned its original purpose altogether. It now sports a chimney, a doorway to the street and another door into the courtyard where previously one could only see a fanlight. The perimeter wall is less like a barrier with the section nearest the extension replaced by railings in the upper sections on two sides and another door, inserted next to the old stable block, now presumably the office, giving direct access from the street. In order to distinguish this side office door, the residential front door is given additional emphasis with a new columned portico.

White's London house provided a suitable frame for his practice and a powerful proclamation of his family's success and dominance in the local building world. It was built to look like a villa, but in fact its position right at the junction of town and country meant that White could operate in both directions. White designed his houses to look like leisured retreats, while in reality they were built to achieve maximum commercial advantage both for his present operations and for future development, positioned in what he knew to be prime sites. In the earlier period, 1660–1760, we discussed houses which did not fit the traditional architectural typology of villas but most certainly had the villa's function as a suburban residence or retreat. By the turn of the nineteenth century, we have houses that look like the accepted prototype and are labeled villas but with a commercial or dual residential and business function. It seems that if we look at the middle-class rather than the elite villa, a very different history of this particular building type emerges, one that it is intrinsically tied to the development of the suburbs as multifunctional entities. If we accept a redefinition of the suburb in this period as both commercial and residential, we must be wary in how we read the architectural evidence; even prosperous looking villas, the very epitome of leisure and luxury, were not just the fruits of enterprise; they might also house entrepreneurial activities themselves.

VIEWING THE VILLA

Appearances and prospect were important, of course, for all types of domestic buildings, not just those that incorporated a business function. Another notable trend in the later eighteenth and early nineteenth centuries was a new interest in seclusion and privacy.[99] Indeed, the evident visibility of White's two new-built properties emphasizes their purpose as more than simply domestic retreats. This cultural shift has usually been discussed in relation to changing ideas of domesticity and the interior life of the 'home'.[100] However, it is also visible at the macro scale in suburban layouts and landscape design. As the London countryside became subject to intense development pressures, the more exclusive villa owners sought to shield themselves from the public gaze, with strategic screening replacing an earlier emphasis on visibility and presence. The satirical attacks on the 'box' frequently lampooned its bare grounds and the citizen's interest in displaying himself and his property. In a 'Letter, on the Villas of our Tradesmen' published two years before his famous poem Lloyd had written: 'Their Boxes, (as they are modestly called) . . . which stand single, and at a distance from the road, have always a summer-house at the end of a small garden: which being erected upon a wall adjoining to the highway, commands a view of every carriage, and gives the owner an opportunity of displaying his best wig to every one that passes by.'[101] The desire for openness and visibility began to take on new connotations once it became associated with a lack of discrimination in distinguishing between appropriate decorum in town and country. To return to 'The Cit's Country Box', Lloyd shows how the new suburban landscape was a creation of City expectations brought to bear on a previously rural location, in this case those of the City wife, the standard butt of gender- as well as a class-based satire:

Although one hates to be expos'd,
'Tis dismal to be so inclos'd;
One hardly any object sees –
I wish you'd fell those odious trees.
Objects continual passing by
Were something to amuse the eye,
But to be pent within the walls –
One might as well be at St. Paul's.
Our house beholders would adore,
Was there a level lawn before,
Nothing its views to incommode,
But quite laid open to the road:
While every trave'ler in amaze,
Should on our little mansion gaze,
And pointing to the choice retreat,
Cry, that's Sir Thrifty's Country Seat.

The impact of these mini-Brownian parks of open lawns and prospects on landscape debates has been little explored in the secondary literature to date. However, it is questionable that the late eighteenth-century reaction against Brown's so-called 'smooth style' in favour of a more rugged rusticity was a phenomenon borne purely out of shifts in elite taste and country parks, as it has tended to be presented. It might be that it also developed as a reaction against the new kind of suburban landscape emerging around the metropolis. If the open lawn, visibility and indeed the villa itself were now associated with middle-class vulgarity and ostentation, then the elite would certainly be receptive to an alternative strategy which provided the necessary distancing and social differentiation. Another impetus behind the desire for seclusion was as a response to the inventive and expanding literature of domestic tourism. Not only were increasing numbers of guides and prints produced of the environs in the late eighteenth century, but they became ever more detailed and specific in their information. John Cary's *Survey of the High Roads from London* (1790), for example, sought to provide travellers with information on the turnpike routes as well as the location of taverns, milestones, road junctions, parks and commons (see fig. 49). The large number of inns on the roads leading directly out of the Tottenham Court and Battle Bridge turnpike gates, as well as around North End on the far side of Hampstead Heath, are noticeable (fig. 164). However, the *Survey* stated that its 'principal object' was to convey

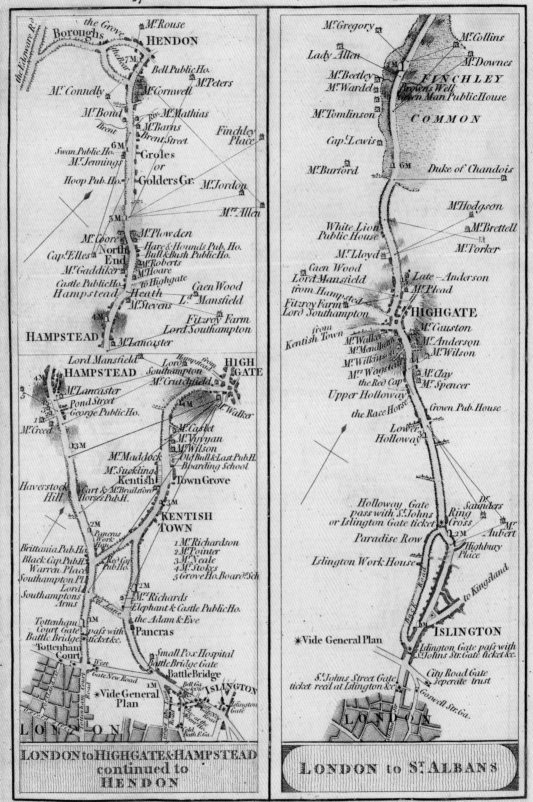

27   28

LONDON to HIGHGATE & HAMPSTEAD
continued to
HENDON

LONDON to St. ALBANS

Published by J. Cary, July 1st. 1790.

'to the traveller that kind of information which will give him pleasure in his peregrinations'. Its chief novelty in this respect lay in the attempt to provide sight lines for the 'numberless Villas ... which are situate on, or within sight of the Road'.[102] Cary concentrates on these dwellings in this plate, with many of the sightlines converging on Highgate due to its many wealthy residents, elevated position and visibility from multiple directions.

Foremost among those villas was Lord Mansfield's residence at 'Caen Wood', which can be seen on Rocque's map between Hampstead and Highgate (see fig. 104). It originated as the home of a tradesman, John Bill, the king's printer in the seventeenth century, and it came to prominence as the home of William Murray, the most famous lawyer of his day. Murray purchased the house in 1754 as a second home to complement his town house in Bloomsbury Square. He later became the Lord Chief Justice and Earl of Mansfield, and as such in 1764 commissioned the Adam brothers to extend and remodel the existing house. The Adams transformed the red brick box into a white Anglo-Palladian villa through the application of a stuccoed pedimented temple front to the south, the creation of a new library to balance the existing orangery as flank-

ing wings, splendid interiors and a grand portico to the north (fig. 165). Kenwood was yet another in the long tradition of remodelled houses on the London fringes, and it is interesting to note that Lauderdale House on the other side of the Heath was also redesigned around the same time, again by refronting rather than rebuilding. Here we are mainly concerned with the siting and landscaping of the house. What is interesting about Kenwood in terms of landscape scenography is how it was refashioned over the course of the eighteenth century to adapt to the changing suburban environment around it. Julius Bryant has written of the deliberate showcasing of the villa arising from its inherent nature — as a second home — as an object of excess consumption. Villas, particularly those near the capital, were positioned for display. This encompassed both the view out for the owners and the view in for passers-by of the villa in its surroundings. As Bryant discusses in his 'Villa Views and the Uninvited Audience', this necessarily, in such a suburban situation, meant consumption by the broad mass of the public as well as by the landowning elite. This was particularly true in Kenwood's case, due to its proximity to Hampstead Heath, which was a noted site for excursions for all levels of society.[103] Paradoxically, this both created the illusion of social inclusivity, whereby all classes might seem to participate in the enjoyment of the same landscape, and at the same time reinforced social distinctions, as the hours and terms on which they might do so varied considerably. These social contradictions were brought to a head most dramatically in the case of Kenwood in 1780 when the anti-Catholic Gordon rioters set Mansfield's town house in Bloomsbury on fire and then marched to Kenwood intent on doing likewise. They were prevented, so the story goes, by the landlord of the Spaniards Inn raising the alarm in time for the militia to be called.

At Kenwood in the 1760s Adam had visually reorientated the house to place the main emphasis on the south front with its views over the landscape park and down the hill towards London. The actual entrance was on the north front where he erected a great portico which now sits at the apex of a sweeping carriage drive. Up until the 1790s the house was very close to the main road, in a similar fashion to Chiswick House, and thus rather than being secluded was an integral part of the everyday landscape and suburban traffic (fig. 166).[104] John Gywnn had criticized Chiswick for a similar 'fault' due to its closeness to the road rather than addressing the Thames, as he felt it should.[105] The road at Kenwood was moved in 1793, and similar measures took place at Danson House and

Strawberry Hill to protect the seclusion of their occupants. At Danson, which sat right by the London–Dover road, the open view from the main entrance to the carriageway was closed off and intensive screening undertaken in the early nineteenth century.[106] At Strawberry Hill in order to extend his villa and maintain his privacy, Walpole planted trees extensively and rerouted the highway to Hampton Court which ran across his land. Indeed, the proximity of the road to the house was a major determining factor in the evolution of its design.[107]

The changes at Kenwood were part of Humphry Repton's commission to improve the grounds in 1793 once Lord Stormont, Mansfield's heir, made the property his main residence. Repton wrote in his Red Book:

Kenwood has hitherto been considered only as a Villa, but notwithstanding its proximity to the Capital, yet the command of property by which it is surrounded entitles it to a much higher degree of importance. . . . I shall therefore beg leave to consider the subject not merely as a Villa, but as a superb and elegant Mansion, surrounded by a sufficient extent of landed property, to give all the importance, convenience and even privacy, of many situations in more distant parts of the Kingdom.[108]

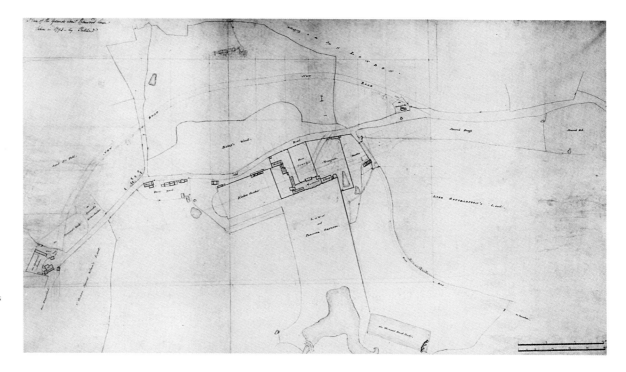

166   Pritchard and J. Prickett, *Plan of the Grounds about Kenwood House*, 1793, drawing, British Museum.

The plan shows the new road running to the north above 'Bishops Wood' and the position of the farm and outbuildings prior to remodelling by Humphry Repton.

Repton was promising to provide Kenwood with an appropriate landscape context and at the same time to transform it from a 'villa' to a 'mansion'. But rather than the overt public display that Adam contrived, the emphasis was now on privacy and exclusion.[109] Repton created a layered landscape to minimize the impact of the users of Cary's map, who might try to spot the villa from the road. Earlier picturesque theorists had decried unnatural boundaries such as fences and masonry walls which interfered with the view and recommended natural planting instead. Gilpin, for example, commended the Bishop of Salisbury, who 'has exchanged the disagreeable appearance of a long straight wall, for a very grand boundary to his garden'.[110] Repton introduced 'belts' of planting to create screens around the perimeter of an estate or garden. At Kenwood Repton moved the road away from the house and repositioned the farm and outbuildings (fig. 166). Two lodges were formed as entrances to the estate and a new stable and office block created with a carriage drive cut through the grounds between them. The farm was remodelled as a *ferme ornée* with an octagonal central building and adjacent picturesque dairy and dairy cottage. Lord Mansfield, his wife and his son were keen amateur dairy farmers, which led to a rivalry with the adjacent aristocratic herd at Fitzroy House (or Farm as it was sometimes designated).[111] The changes introduced by Repton reflect the shift in the late eighteenth century from an organic landscape, which had accommodated suburban growth within a

primarily agricultural context, to a self-consciously tasteful 'rustic' landscape in which the growing of produce was contingent upon the harvest from property and rising land values. At nearby Fitzroy Park a similar process of pastoralism took place. Fitzroy House was newly built *c.*1774, not for a professional man, but for Charles Fitzroy, 1st Baron Southampton, as an out-of-town retreat with grounds landscaped by Capability Brown.[112] Fitzroy House was very much a Palladian box – 'the architecture of a modern character' as the Highgate historian Frederick Prickett described it – with extensive outbuildings and stabling (fig. 167).[113] Like his neighbour at Kenwood, Southampton too managed to divert the course of Hampstead Lane further away from his house, giving him greater privacy and an additional four acres of farmland. The house was remodelled by Henry Holland in the 1790s and Humphry Repton consulted about improvements to the park around the same time.[114] But notwithstanding these improvements, it was demolished in 1828. The Southampton Estate was put up for sale in the 1840s and plans were drawn up for large-scale villa development, although in the end only five substantial houses were built.[115]

This shift from display and openness to privacy and concealment led to a major shift in the look and texture of the environs. Plantations, fences and belts of perimeter shrubs and trees sprouted to screen the grander houses in the area from prying eyes. This marks the change from Morris's all-encompassing view which sought to embrace the whole of culture and society to a privatized and necessarily selective view. As Loudon observed in *The Suburban Gardener and Villa Companion* (1838), 'The truth is that the modern style is essentially calculated for solitude and retirement.'[116] He went on to examine the Kenwood landscape; what had previously been acclaimed for its open aspect and views over the metropolis was by contrast praised by Loudon for its seclusion: 'This is, beyond all question, the finest country residence in the suburbs of London; in point of natural beauty of the ground and wood. . . . All exterior objects are excluded; and a stranger walking around the park would never discover that he was between Hampstead and Highgate, or even suppose that he was so near London. It is indeed, difficult to imagine a more retired or romantic spot, and yet of such extent, so near a great metrop-

167   Robert Sayer, *Lord Southampton's Lodge at Highgate, Middlesex*, 1792, engraving, British Museum.

olis.'[117] J. B. Papworth wrote: 'If a house be viewed as it usually is when some distance from the public road, it may be assumed as a rule, that the base line should be in part concealed by intervening plantations.'[118] The concern for privacy was echoed in smaller suburban houses with their individual front and back gardens surrounded by hedges and gates to shut them off from the road. The 'garden gate' featured in Cowper's poem as a symbol of the suburban home, while as Michael Read concludes of residential development overall in this period in the *Cambridge Urban History*, 'Privacy was all-important.'[119]

The establishment of a garden setting for suburban dwellings was partly the outcome of picturesque principles, in which taste shifted from classical symmetry and proportion to rustic variety and the natural, but it was also due to changes in concepts of privacy, property and seclusion. The notion of enclosure became applied not just to common land but to all land as the environs became more bounded and controlled. As the suburbs increased in density, the rich retreated behind their high hedges and large lawns, while the middle classes created their own green

shields at whatever scale they could afford. The suburban ideology of the sanctity of private individual space had arrived.

GENTRIFICATION AND THE LANGUAGE OF COTTAGES

considering the regular gradation between the plan of the most simple hut and that of the most superb palace . . . a palace is nothing more than a cottage IMPROVED; and that the plan of the latter is the basis as it were of plans for the former.
John Wood the younger, *A Series of Plans for Cottages or Habitations of the Labourer*, 1781

The newest building type to be introduced into the suburbs from the late eighteenth century onwards was the *cottage orné* or 'gent's cot', which existed in contradistinction to the 'cit's box'. The *cottage orné* was a genteel version of an idealized rural cottage usually distinguished by picturesque ornamentation in the form of barge boards, weather-boarding and other 'rustic' detailing (fig. 168). Many felt that it was little more than a highly decorated and picturesque alterna-

168   John Hassell, *Westbourne Farm, Middx., the Residence of Mrs Siddons*, 1812, aquatint, London Metropolitan Archives.

The actress lived here from 1805 to 1817.

tive to the villa. Architectural publications of the time gave alternative designs for villas and ornamental cottages both based on the same underlying rectangular structure: or in other words a disguised box. The cottages of the poor meanwhile had a long pedigree in the metropolitan hinterland. It might be thought that the polite and vernacular variants of the cottage may be seen as two separate strands in the development of the form, but in fact there were connections between the two and uneasy social and cultural relationships can be traced between them at this time.[120]

John Wood the younger, as the quote at the head of this section demonstrates, had highlighted the essential continuities between cottage and palace in *A Series of Plans for Cottages or Habitations of the Labourer* (1781). This was the first investigation into the cottages of the labouring classes in the eighteenth century. He wrote: 'The greatest part of the cottages that fell within my observation, I found to be shattered, dirty, inconvenient, miserable hovels, scarcely affording a shelter for beasts of the forest.'[121] Nathaniel Kent in his 1775 *Hints to Gentlemen of Landed Property* gave a harrowing description of these places with a powerful plea for improvement:

The shattered hovels which half the poor of this kingdom are obliged to put up with, is truly affecting to a heart fraught with humanity. Those condemned to visit these miserable tenements, can testify, that neither health nor decency can be preserved in them. The weather frequently penetrates all parts of them: which must occasion illness of various kinds; which more frequently visit the children of cottages than any others, and early shake their constitutions.[122]

None of these shacks still exist, but there are a few instances of more substantial cottages surviving in the London area, such as Collins Square, Blackheath, and Pond Cottages, Dulwich, the former of the late and the latter largely of the early eighteenth century. The Dulwich cottages were built opposite the village pond and are presumed to have been used as housing for the adjacent brickmaking clay pits (fig. 169).[123] Such timber-framed buildings had their disadvantages; as John Wood the younger outlined, they were 'hot in summer and cold in winter; their being too liable to fire, and their being continually in want of repairs'.[124] However, they were far cheaper to build than their

198

brick equivalents and a significant step up from the miserable hovels that Kent had described. Wood included a large number of plans for semi-detached pairs of cottages as well as rows of four. 'It is an easy matter to imagine a continuation of them to any number,' he wrote, and they were 'proper for large towns or cities'.[125] This shows that experiments with the semi-detached were not limited to the villa at the time, and also demonstrates that Wood's idea of a continuum between domestic buildings might also be applied to the semi-detached house and the terrace.

Towards the end of our period we have some visual evidence of what the homes of the poorest might have looked like through the Romantic interest in localism and dilapidation. J. T. Smith's work discussed in Chapter 3 came out of a picturesque aesthetic whereby the irregular and informal in architecture began to be celebrated for the first time. Joshua Reynolds had written:

It may not be amiss for the architect to take advantage sometimes of that to which I am sure the painter ought always to have his eyes open, I mean the use of accidents; to follow when they lead, and to improve them, rather than always trust to a regular plan. It often happens, that additions have been made to a house, at various times, for use or pleasure. As such buildings depart from regularity, they now and then acquire something of scenery by this accident, which I should think might not unsuccessfully be adopted by an architect, in an original plan, if it did not too much interfere with convenience.[126]

The debate over the merits of regularity or 'beautiful variety' extended across all types of cottage 'whether for a gentleman or a peasant', as Lugar wrote.[127] This is not the place to outline this debate in any detail but merely to note its impact on the London environs.[128] The *cottage orné* became another favoured building type along with the villa for those who could afford an individual house. If anything the *cottage orné* was in reality further up the social scale, as it was not suitable for semi-detachment due to its irregularity and, also unlike the villa, required the services of an architect if picturesque variety was the object. Papworth recommended the *cottage orné*, comparing it favourably with the geometric box: 'It is essential that this building should be small . . . that it should combine properly with the surrounding objects, and appear to be native

to the spot, and not one of those crude rule-and-square excrescences of the environs of London, the illegitimate family of town and country.' He went on to highlight the novelty of the type and its association with types of enterprise, encompassing even the scientific: 'The cottage orné is a new species of building in the economy of domestic architecture, and subject to its own laws of fitness and propriety. It is not the habitation of the laborious, but of the affluent, of the man of study, of science, or of leisure.'[129] In their desire to achieve the variety and distinctiveness that Reynolds had advocated, architects went to great extremes. Lugar even went so far as to illustrate a *cottage orné* with ruins: 'built at the express desire of a gentleman in the neighbourhood of town. . . . The idea to be conveyed was an abbey mutilated, and to shew the cottage as if dressed out of the remains.'[130]

The surroundings and garden of the cottage were critical in sustaining the image of a rustic *genius loci*, and a strict social hierarchy pertained in its landscaping. Lugar warned against planting common creepers or honeysuckle: 'Their province is to shade and enrich the peasant's cot.'[131] At the same time the grounds must be proportionate to the architecture: 'Great attention should be given that its true character of a garden be not lost. Ha! Ha! Fences, by extending a lawn too far, give it the air of a park in miniature, a thing equally ridiculous with a flower garden, in the entrance front of a mansion.'[132] The ha-ha was also pilloried by Lloyd in his 'Cit's Country Box': 'By whose miraculous assistance / You gain a prospect two fields distance.' The state of the garden provided an equally important indicator of social propriety in working people's cottages. Gardens were barometers of social health and morality. The provision of a small amount of ground that could be tended was deemed essential in order to keep the man of the family purposefully occupied at leisure and out of the ale house, to the benefit of family life and prosperity.[133] A row of cottages was erected by the Hampstead Water Company in 1777 at the optimistically named Vale of Health, where a bog was drained and dammed to form a new reservoir (fig. 170).[134] In Sarjent's print these cottages are depicted as models of industry and virtue. Their regular and well-kept appearance establishes an image of order and industriousness. The washing on the lines, taken in by the women as a means of employment, and the tidy gardens where

170 F. Jukes after F. J. Sarjent,
*View on Hampstead Heath, looking
towards London,* 1804, aquatint
etching, British Museum.

food might be grown and animals tended, are all
markers of a healthy domestic economy. This view is
far removed from the usual ramshackle, picturesque
cottages favoured by artists at this date. It provides a
sharp contrast to the nearby cottage on the Heath
drawn by J. T. Smith showing a non-industrious cot-
tager puffing on his pipe outside his barely upright
hut (see fig. 84). The Hampstead Water Company cottages are significant for another reason. Although they
were built for the parish poor, within ten years they
were beginning to be inhabited by figures such as
Leigh Hunt, becoming the centre for his bohemian
circle. This was part of a much longer process of colonization by incomers as they took over what had

previously been humble dwellings both in the villages
and the countryside around. The problem became so
bad that 'Waste Land Funds' were established specifically to channel money from the sale of enclosed land
back into housing for the poor, as at Highgate where
'Waste Land Cottages' were erected at Southwood
Lane in 1806.[135]

The process of gentrification in the environs took
place at several levels. Small cottages and houses might
be taken over by artists or other members of the
middle classes on limited budgets. But architects also
were quick to adapt to this trend and began to proffer
their services as experts in renovation and extensions
alongside new-build properties. J. C. Loudon in *The*

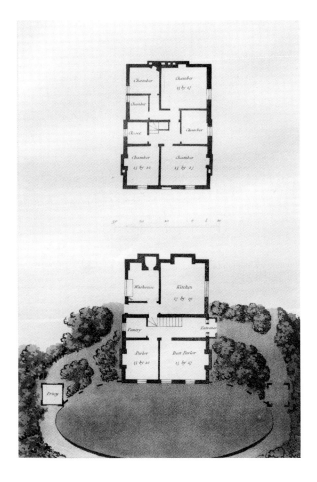

Suburban Gardener and Villa Companion included a
section on 'Additions and Alterations', writing that in
suburbs, 'It is not unusual in building a house to keep
in view probable additions.'[136] John Plaw even made a
series of designs intended to turn the ramshackle com-
moners' cottages into habitable dwellings (figs 171 and
172). He did add, with a transparency that contrasts
with Lugar's on financial matters, that the cost of the
conversion was 'very little short of a building of the
same magnitude raised from the ground, which would
amount to 500l. or thereabouts'. However, in another
similar adaptation he remarked: 'I say nothing of
expense as much depends on the condition of the old
building.'[137] Another common practice was the refronting of old manors or farmhouses with new classical
facades. William Cobbett railed against such gentrification, complaining of a farmhouse in Reigate, Surrey:
'One end of the front of this once plain and substantial
house had been moulded into a "parlour", and there
was the mahogany table, and the fine chairs, and the
fine glass, and all as bare-faced upstart as any stock-
jobber in the kingdom can boast of.'[138] Plaw showed
a design for Selsdon House near Croydon where
he employed this technique of transmogrification

173 John Plaw, 'Plan of Selsdon House, Croydon, Surrey', 'being an addition made to the old Farm House, which with the wing walls, serve as a façade before the old Buildings and Farm Yard', Plate VIII from Plaw, *Rural Architecture*, 1796, British Architectural Library.

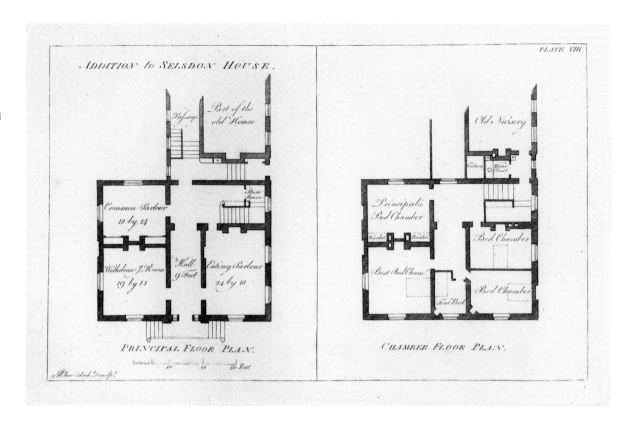

(figs 173 and 174). His design effectively created a mini-Palladian villa frontage screening the older remnant of agricultural activity behind. This is particularly ironic when one remembers that one of the key features of Palladio's own villas in the Veneto was the integration of the domestic and agricultural functions. Surviving examples are numerous and include Walton Hall, Bucks, where a stuccoed Palladian front block,

174 John Plaw, 'Elevation of Selsdon House, Croydon, Surrey', Plate IX from Plaw, *Rural Architecture*, 1796, British Architectural Library.

by Charles Pinfold, was added to a late seventeenth- or early eighteenth-century farmhouse in 1830.[139] Other architects offered designs for houses that might be built in stages, for a central block with optional wings, or gradations in the level of ornament that might be applied.

Such conversions and devices to maximize impact on relatively small sites are revealing of the enormous pressure on land around urban areas. As the suburbs began to spread ever wider, their architecture became increasingly regularized and commercialized, and the accidental arrangement of the village and arterial routeway was replaced by an artfully planned variety increasingly orchestrated by architects rather than just builders. The common land and farm land around the capital had previously been seen as an urban playground open to all. In the late eighteenth century it began to be shaped and 'improved' by the cumulative effect of multiple acts of enclosure, large and small, to create a landscape which was increasingly formalized and controlled. Although specifically suburban large-scale planning and development was still largely absent, in this incremental and atomized fashion a notion of a particular green territory of individual buildings with demarcated grounds and gardens began to emerge in which privacy and the protected prospect – both out and in – were paramount. As Loudon wrote in his Introduction to the *Suburban Gardener and Villa Companion*, a suburban ideology was now extant, and furthermore it was no longer seen as a compromise between city and country, as Cowper had presented it, but rather the pinnacle of civilized bourgeois society: 'Such residences may be considered as the ultimatum [*sic*], in point of comfort and enjoyment, of the great mass of society; not only at present, but even after society has advanced to a much higher degree of civilisation, and to a comparative equalisation of knowledge, wealth and taste.'[140]

TOPOGRAPHICAL SURVEY
of the
Borough
of
ST. MARYLEBONE,
as incorporated & defined by Act of Parliament 1832
Embracing & Marking the Boundaries of the Parishes of
St. Marylebone, St. Pancras & Paddington;
also the extent & limits of the
PRINCIPAL LANDED ESTATES
WITHIN THE BOROUGH
and Plans & Elevations of the Public Buildings.

Engraved by B. R. Davies, from Surveys & Drawings by W. A. Bartlett, under the direction of John Britton, F.S.A. &c. &c. &c.

Inscribed to the Dukes of Bedford, Portland & St Albans, The Marquis Camden,
The Lord Bishop of London, Lords Mansfield and Southampton,
E. B. Portman, Esq & other Landed Proprietors.

7

LANDSCAPES OF TRANSITION
1790–1840

ENDINGS AND BEGINNINGS

The fields from Islington to Marylebone,
To Primrose Hill and Saint John's Wood,
Were builded over with pillars of gold,
And there Jerusalem's pillars stood.

. . . . .

Pancras & Kentish-town repose
Among her golden pillars high,
Among her golden arches which
Shine upon the starry sky.

The Jew's-harp-house & the Green Man,
The Ponds where Boys to bathe delight,
The fields of Cows by Willan's farm,
Shine in Jerusalem's pleasant sight.

William Blake, *Jerusalem*, 1804–20

Jerusalem, William Blake's epic poem, provides an apt conclusion for a chapter which looks back to the past and forward into the future simultaneously. Blake provided an apocalyptic vision of the new Britain in which its landscape, particularly that of the metropolis, played a central role in providing both a structural framework for the poem and an abundance of architectonic imagery. Blake (1757–1827) grew up in Golden Square, Soho, but spent much of his time roaming the fields to the north. He lived in Lambeth from 1790 to 1800 for the happiest and most prosperous period of his life, a place which became a metaphor for tranquillity and stability in the poem. In the section quoted above, he drew strongly on his childhood remembrances of Marylebone Fields as a prelapsarian paradise and reimagined it as the site of the perfection of the new Jerusalem yet to come. At the same time the poem is grounded in the realities of contemporary phenom-

176 John White, *Wellins [sic] Farm, Marylebone*, 1789, watercolour, British Museum.

A view of Willan's Farm to the right of the pond which accords with Blake's image of the Marylebone Fields as a sylvan paradise.

ena, as this area was undergoing the most public and visible development of all London's fringes in the early nineteenth century. The inns Blake mentions and Willan's Farm were all to disappear from 1811 onwards with the transformation of its pasture land into the new creation of Regent's Park (fig. 176). Past and present were fused in Blake's imagination, with the northern edge of the city representing an idealized landscape of pastoral perfection just at the moment it was being snatched away irrevocably by the march of bricks and mortar. Cruickshank's famous engraving of 1829 depicts the scene, which shows the northern fields under attack from speculative builders (see fig. 11). This chapter will focus on the Marylebone area, a place which has become of immense national and international significance over the succeeding two hundred years due to its characterization as the birthplace of the garden suburb. Like Blake, however, it will also simultaneously consider how that future was rooted in the past. And it will ask to what extent did the newly self-conscious green suburb come out of the unplanned suburban hinterland that we have looked at thus far?

*

DANIEL LYSONS AND THE TOPOGRAPHY OF CHANGE

No one gives us a better or more comprehensive account of the rapid changes that the outer parishes were undergoing in the early nineteenth century than the Reverend Daniel Lysons. We have already encountered his pioneering history of greater London, *The Environs of London, Being an Historical Account of the Towns, Villages and Hamlets, within Twelve Miles of that Capital with Biographical Anecdotes* (1792–6). In 1811 he produced a *Supplement* to the work in which he updated his entries to include accounts of new building during the intervening time. Given that this was only a period of fifteen to nineteen years Lysons's additions are surprisingly numerous in some parishes. His earlier volumes do contain a strong sense of an area under siege, but in the *Supplement* the full impact of the building and industrial boom of the first decade of the nineteenth century can truly be felt. The rate of change was not always related to distance from centre. Indeed, economic growth itself was by no means constant in this difficult period of the successive French Wars (1793–1815). Following a trough in the late 1790s, there was a great deal of building throughout London in the 1800s. This growth was abruptly halted by a severe financial crash in 1811–12, the date at which Marylebone Park reverted to the Crown, ripe for development. Lysons's commentary is therefore made just at the point at which there had been a ten-year boom. After victory at Waterloo things slowly recovered until by the 1820s building was flourishing once more.[1] The introduction of the census in 1801 produced reliable household figures for the first time. These show that London's population as a whole rose from c.900,000 in 1801 to just over a million in 1811 and to c.1.5 million by 1831.[2] As Leonard Schwarz writes: 'The nineteenth century population explosion took place largely in the new "outer" London.' It is worth quoting his commentary on this phenomenon at some length, as the areas he discusses are precisely those with which this chapter and the preceding one are concerned:

> From Marylebone to Hackney in the north, from Richmond to Lambeth in the south, this ring contained some 300,000 inhabitants in 1700, over half a million a century later, and nearly 1,900,000 in 1851. After 1800, when the population of London was increasing at the rate of 20 per cent a decade, Westminster's expansion of some 50 per cent during the first half of the century paled by comparison with St Pancras, which expanded more than four-fold, Marylebone, which grew from 64,000 in 1801 to 158,000 in 1851, or Paddington, which increased from less than 2,000 to over 46,000.[3]

Lysons made use of the 1801 Census in his *Supplement* of 1811 to update the population figures given for each parish in the original volumes. He provides a sense of a shifting centre as London rapidly expanded, with great increases in building remarked upon for many parishes, for example Kentish Town, which had ballooned by a third since 1795 according to Lysons.[4] Further out parishes, such as Stanmore, had grown little by comparison. Overall, his figures show Middlesex and Surrey as the most populous counties, with Kent, Essex and Hertfordshire expanding at a far less dramatic rate.[5] The creation of new forms of transport led to the development of areas such as Camberwell and Paddington for the first time.[6] The first horse-bus ran four times a day from 1829 from the Yorkshire Stingo on Marylebone Road to the Bank for a fare of one shilling, including a newspaper, for the journey.[7] London spread not just due to residential development but also through new industrial and other initiatives, particularly to the east. The military complex at Woolwich was greatly expanded from 1801 onwards, while the building of the West India Docks (1799–1806) on the Isle of Dogs, the East India Docks at Blackwall (1803–6) and St Katharine Docks (1825–9) in Wapping created the first enclosed secure docks along the river. In some places, paradoxically, the new developments actually led to a decline in the number of dwelllings. At St George-in-the-East, where the London Dock Company was established in 1800, forty-eight acres of land were required for their commercial activities, leading to a decline in the number of houses from 4,138 in 1801 to 3,800 in 1809–10.[8] However, the population of the parish had actually increased due to the building of many small 'cottages' to the north, as Lysons wrote, and the fact that 'the houses have been occupied by a much greater proportion of families than before'.[9] Lysons is using 'cottages' here in the sense of small terraced houses for working people. This type of overcrowding was common in previously more expansive areas where they became absorbed into the inner core. He wrote that a special barracks had to be erected at Shadwell to house the Indians and Chinese 'hired to navigate the East India Company ships to this country', with a thousand plus lodged there.[10] The building of large factories replacing previously small-scale production, such as the new silk mills at Hackney Wick (the largest in the country), created similar short- and long-term housing pressures.[11] This area is now part of the Olympic Park and so has recently undergone a similarly dramatic transformation of equal intensity and rapidity.

This suburban and industrial expansion naturally affected the surrounding farms and landscape. Lysons carefully observed its impact on the natural world with his usual meticulous fieldwork. In his recording of the growth of the trees at Fulham Palace, for example, he duly noted which had been lost and which grown, and by how much, measuring their girth in feet and inches.[12] Agricultural enterprises had suffered substantially, for example at Hammersmith, where 'a considerable portion of what was garden-ground has been converted into brick-fields'.[13] He expanded on this in his account of the 'State of Market Gardens, Nursery

Grounds within Twelve Miles of London': 'The quantity of ground occupied by market gardeners in the immediate vicinity of London has been considerably diminished since 1795, (perhaps as much as 300 or 400 acres) in consequence of the various improvements, and the increase of buildings.'[14] He estimated that only 1,600 acres were now occupied by nurserymen and seedsmen around the capital.[15] In Lambeth, for example, which had been one of the centres of the nursery business, out of a total of 4,000 acres only 80 were now used for market gardens and 40 for nurseries, while 1,390 were built over and 415 were covered by private and pleasure gardens (including Vauxhall).[16]

The *Supplement* traces the cycle of development and expansion on the urban fringes. Lysons charts changes in land use and ownership with new uses for old buildings, redevelopment of existing sites, as well as new-build schemes and numerous transfers of property. He laments the loss of many large estates, such as Gunnersbury House, which were pulled down and redeveloped with clusters of villas built in their grounds.[17] Indeed, villas and the spread of villadom is a recurring theme: a disruption in Lysons's view to the established order. Other losses are also chronicled, such as the poignant account of the closure of Ranelagh, where the contents and furniture were auctioned off far and wide. The organ, for instance, went to the recently rebuilt early Gothic Revival church at Tetbury, Gloucestershire (1781) by Francis Hiorn.[18] Lysons's topographical illustrations of subsequently demolished buildings are in many instances the only ones known and have become a considerable source in their own right. The expansion of the civic infrastructure is another notable feature of the *Supplement* with new workhouses, poor schools and asylums much in evidence, the latter two often taking over existing large houses, as at Marylebone where the Manor House became an educational establishment. This growing population required an ever-greater infrastructure to service its needs, and thus new cemeteries, transport links and other amenities are all documented in the text. Reservoirs were opened at Kensington and Hammersmith by the West Middlesex Water-works Company in 1806.[19] Early railways make an appearance, such as the Surrey Iron Railway which opened in 1803 and ran from Wandsworth to Croydon.[20] Lysons struggled to keep up with the changing terrain

around him as strips of urbanization began to encroach on what had been a suburban Elysium. The major new transport, industrial and residential developments of the 1790–1840 period were mainly situated in the semi-urban and rural areas of the capital where there was room for growth. Their impact was thus felt disproportionately in the suburban zone. This can be seen most clearly in relation to the building of London's railway stations from the 1840s onwards in a ring, particularly to the north, marking a new outer–inner – or inner–outer – edge to the city. Lysons's measured, scholarly lament for the lost Arcadia was echoed in a more polemical fashion by Cobbett's *Rural Rides* of the 1820s, in which the malignant impact of the Great Wen on the surrounding counties is transmuted into a powerful social and economic critique.

THE EDGE LANDSCAPE OF MARYLEBONE FIELDS AND THE NEW ROAD

The rest of this chapter will focus on the northern fringes of the city, principally the area of Marylebone. Here we can see how the edge of the city morphed and changed from the time when Gwynn was writing in the 1760s through to the 1820s and 1830s with the completion of Regent's Park. It is not the intention of this chapter to rehearse the well-known history of the park, but rather to consider the specifics of the topography in which it was located and the environmental context from which it was created.[21] It has been argued throughout this work that the long-entrenched idea of Regent's Park as London's first suburb can be well and truly scotched. Nor do I want to dwell on whether it was London's and the world's first true garden suburb, although that question cannot be ignored entirely. What I am more concerned with here is exploring the extent to which Regent's Park came out of existing ideas about the suburbs, as John Gwynn had propounded, and out of developments on the London hinterland more broadly over the preceding century and a half.

We saw in the previous chapter that Marylebone in the late eighteenth century was still a tranquil landscape of farmland and isolated buildings (see fig. 155). Marylebone Park was owned by the Crown but let on a lease which had been bought at auction by the Duke of Portland for the remainder of its term until 1811.

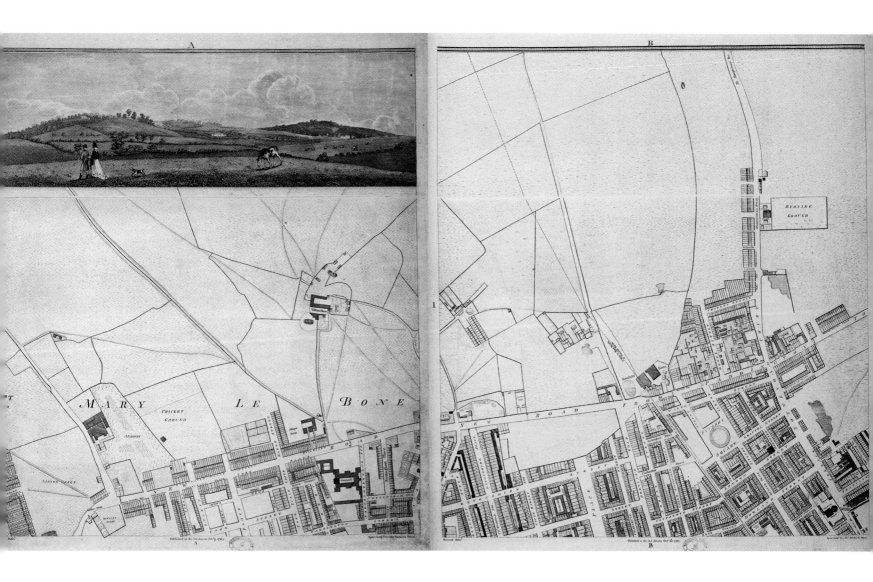

A

177 Richard Horwood, *Plan of Parish of St Marylebone*, in *Plan of Cities of London and Westminster*, 1792–9, engraving, London Metropolitan Archives.

The Marylebone area just prior to the development of Regent's Park with Willan's Farm prominent in the centre of the fields. John White's house can be seen at the top of Devonshire Place with a timber yard next door, suggesting that this may have been a further part of his operations.

The main tenant was John Willan of Marylebone Park Farm, who farmed some 500 acres producing hay and milk for the lucrative London market (figs 176 and 177).[22] The more rustic buildings to the right of John White's house in Grimm's view of Marylebone Fields (see fig. 155) include the Jew's Harp and Queen's Head and Artichoke inns, discussed in Chapter 4 (see fig. 117). Most of the cottages in Marylebone Park were let to the farm labourers, but a few were rented out as weekend or summer houses. J. T. Smith gives a vivid description of the robustness with which these retreats were defended, while also providing yet another dig at 'Cockney taste': 'On the south of the tea-gardens a number of summer-houses and gardens, fitted up in the truest Cockney taste; for on many of these castellated edifices wooden canons were placed; and at the entrance of each domain, of about the twentieth part

of an acre, the old inscription of "Steel-traps and spring-guns all over these grounds," with an "N.B. Dogs trespassing will be shot".'[23]

If we look at Horwood's map of 1792–9 we can see that the building of the New Road had led to infilling between it and London's previous northern boundary of Oxford Street over the intervening thirty years (fig. 177).[24] The two principal landowners, the Portman and Portland estates, had been busily building long terraces of new houses in a largely grid system up to the bypass. The Duke of Portland through his acquisition of the lease of Marylebone Park was currently in possession of land stretching all the way from Oxford Street to Primrose Hill in one uninterrupted sweep. This put him in an unrivalled position to exploit London's inexorable movement northwards. John Gwynn, as we have seen, was not impressed by the developers' efforts on either side of the New Road, and he was not alone in his concerns. Leigh Hunt later welcomed the arrival of Regent's Park as 'it has checked in that quarter the monstrous brick cancer that was extending its arms in every direction and has prevented Harley and Wimpole Street from going further.'[25] Gwynn wrote that unity between the centre and the edge might be achieved 'if attention was paid to the widening rather than the lengthening the town'.[26] He added that in so doing it was necessary to create a social mix, ensuring that wholeness would be social and moral as well as physical:

> In setting a plan of large streets for the dwellings of the rich, it will be found necessary to allot smaller spaces contiguous, for the habitations of useful and laborious people, whose dependence on their superiors requires such distribution; and by adhering to this principal [sic] a political advantage will result to the nation; as this intercourse stimulates their industry, improves their morals by example, and prevents any particular part from being the habitation of the indigent alone, to the great detriment of private property.[27]

The road remained as it was, but Gwynn's ideal of individual houses set in gardens remained potent. When the area began to be developed in the early nineteenth century, the notion was already ingrained that a different type of environment should be created beyond the New Road, distinct from the urban terraces of the West End. The first major development was on the Eyre Estate, in what is now known as St John's Wood. The history of the area has been recently and comprehensively detailed by Mireille Galinou in her book *Cottages and Villas: The Birth of the Garden Suburb*.[28] Galinou shows how the estate was developed from the 1800s onwards in the form of individual houses rather than terraces, set in a suburban green landscape, in line with Gwynn's ideas. However, her claim that St John's Wood rather than Regent's Park should be seen as the first garden suburb is put in context by Lysons's comments on the scheme. He reported, referring to the first small houses on the estate known as Alpha Villas, that nearly one hundred new 'cottages' had been built to the north of the Tyburn turnpike housing *c*.600 people (fig. 178).[29] This suggests a less genteel interpretation of the develop-

ment, at least in its initial phases, than its proponents and indeed historians have suggested. St John's Wood was indeed new in consciously providing a green environment for its residents; what it did not do is experiment with new forms of architecture or layouts for the suburb. The houses themselves were neoclassical Italianate and the roads laid out in straight lines.

It was the area between Oxford Street and the New Road that J. T. Smith described so vividly in his account of life in Mortimer Street from the 1770s to the 1820s. In Smith's writing the pull of the open spaces of Marylebone Fields just beyond the building line is tangible. Nollekens used to resort there regularly after work in the evenings and weekends. The coming of the New Road changed the character of Marylebone from an old village to a new suburb. Horwood's map shows the trappings of modernity that emerged in the nearly half century following the opening of the New Road but which predated the Regent's Park development. The new parish church and cemetery, the charity school, workhouse and infirmary were all built in the 1790s and 1800s to meet the needs of a rapidly expanding population. The 1801 Census listed 7,209 inhabited houses with a further 555 uninhabited houses, mainly new built.[30] Following the New Road a second major communications network ran through the area with the opening of the Grand Union Canal from Uxbridge to Paddington in 1801, creating a novel type of urban infrastructure and a new type of landscape. The Grand Junction Canal branch line from Hemel Hempstead also joined up with the Grand Union, terminating at Paddington Basin.

It would be wrong to see the canal as simply introducing a modern and unwelcome industrial corridor into previously pastoral surroundings. We have already seen how Hassell wove the rural and commercial together in his account of the Grand Junction and that the environs had long consisted of a mixture of industrial, residential and leisure functions often side by side. The usual building-related industries were prominent on the northern fringes with brick-making taking place in the fields. In Marylebone Park itself there were two small factories, one making varnish for coaches and the other hair powder. The park also housed a wheelwright's yard, a sculptor's yard and a carpentry workshop owned by James Wyatt, architect to George III.[31] The New Road contained a mixture

178   John Seguier, *View of the Alpha Cottages near Paddington*, 1812, oil, private collection.

Evidence of the processes behind the newly built houses is evident in this picture, with a smoking kiln visible in the centre and timber planks piled up under a shelter to the right.

of commercial and domestic buildings. The Grand Union Canal seems to have been embraced in this spirit as a new attraction which was rapidly appropriated into the discourses and leisure practices of the suburban realm. Lysons wrote in 1811: 'Passage-boats go five times a week, during the summer season, from Paddington to Uxbridge, to carry passengers and goods.'[32] Benjamin West's painting *The Paddington Passage-Boats returning from Uxbridge in the Evening* (fig. 179 and see fig. 144) depicts such a trip. A commentary was provided by the ever-observant Smith:

> It was customary for so much company to visit Uxbridge by the barge drawn by horses gaily decked out with ribands.... Mrs Nollekens actually tired her friends with letters upon their canal adventures from Paddington to Uxbridge, and from Uxbridge to Paddington. In these epistles, she most poetically expiated upon the clearness of the water,

the fragrance of the flowers, the nut-brown tints of the wavy corn, and the ruddy and healthful complexions of the cottagers' children, who waited anxiously to see the vessel approach their native shores.... The pleasures of a similar excursion induced the late venerable President West to paint a picture of the barge he went by, on the crowded deck of which he has introduced his own portrait, and also those of several of his friends who were that day on board.[33]

Writing in the 1820s Smith goes on to say that such canal trips were soon no longer fashionable. A similar fate had also befallen air balloons and steamboats, 'since a steam stage-coach is about to start without horses'.[34] However, the novelty of the canal continued to be felt when it was extended to Limehouse in 1814–20 and it became a water feature alongside Regent's Park. T. H. Shepherd's engravings powerfully convey the

thrill of the industrial sublime (fig. 180). Only the edge zone could offer such a mixture of a new leisure activity, a fascinating new industrial landscape and the joys of innovative forms of transport. This combination of the traditional pastoral enjoyment of the suburban countryside plus new visitor attractions and a strong emphasis on circulation was to be central to the later development of Regent's Park.

THE EMERGING LANDSCAPE OF REGENT'S PARK, 1809–12

Galinou's detailed chronicling of the Eyre Estate has provided one recent challenge to the existing historiography which places John Nash's Regent's Park as the first consciously landscaped suburban villa settlement. However, there is also another challenge to Nash's crown as the pioneer of the garden suburb, and that is from those who worked on the Regent's Park plans prior to his involvement in the scheme from 1811. As J. M. Crook has written, Nash arrived 'late on the scene of metropolitan improvements' and inherited 'a body of thinking on the subject dating back thirty years'.[35] Indeed, it was only a series of 'accidents' that put Nash in charge of such a major development at all.[36] He was appointed to the Office of Woods and Forests in 1806, along with that prophet of the picturesque Uvedale Price. It would have been expected that the Surveyor General James Wyatt might have taken charge of the project, but he died in 1813 and responsibility for Marylebone Park then fell to Woods and Forests where Nash was now securely installed. In Crook's analysis Nash should be seen 'less as London's master-planner, more as an opportunist of genius, responding pragmatically to the pressures of political circumstances and the fluctuations of urban economics'.[37]

Lysons's *Supplement* once more provides us with an interesting perspective on how matters stood in 1811, the same year that the park's lease expired. By then plans for major change were already underway, as the Crown sought to maximize the park's potential as soon as possible after its release. Lysons relates that the Crown, in its desire to raise revenue from its whole estate, first looked to Hyde Park and Kensington Gardens as a place for new exclusive housing. This may have come from John Gwynn's idea that the two parks should form the site for a new royal palace. Even more directly influential was John Fordyce, Surveyor General of H. M. Land Revenue, who transformed the running of the Crown lands into an up-to-date, efficient operation fit for the coming century. He had originally suggested the formation of new park rides and an ornamental garden by Park Lane with villas in the centre. However, as Lysons relates, the 'plan [was] abandoned in consequence of a considerable popular clamour . . . from the apprehension that it might lead to the further extension of buildings, and might eventually exclude the public from their accustomed resort to the park for air and exercise'.[38] However, the royal parks in general provided plenty of precedents for villas in semi-rural parkland settings, as at Windsor, Kew and Richmond in particular, where residences for the royal

family had been built throughout the eighteenth century. Besides these royal retreats all the parks contained cottages and houses for employees, notably their custodians, the Rangers. The Ranger's House at Green Park (1768) by Robert Adam was particularly grand, and views of it peeking through the trees prefigure those of the Regent's Park villas.

The idea of a parkland setting for villas was therefore already extant in official thinking prior to the decision to develop Marylebone Park and was laid down in Fordyce's 1793 strategic plan for its redevelopment. The remoteness of Marylebone Park was continually stressed, and it was certainly a second choice to what were perceived as far better known and situated locations. Lysons, drawing on Fordyce's fourth Land Revenue report of 1809, commented that it was presumed that the proposed buildings 'although so remote from the central part of the metropolis will eventually be very numerous'.[39] Lysons then outlined the proposals for Marylebone Park as they stood in 1811:

> Mr White of Devonshire-place, has suggested a plan to the surveyor-general of the crown-lands, by which he proposes that only the lower part of the site of Marybone-park should be built on; that the buildings should terminate northward with a grand crescent half a mile in span, in the centre of which, fronting the end of Harley-street, should be erected the new parish church of Marybone, to which there should be an approach from a street continued from Harley-street; that the remainder of the ground, which is ill-adapted for building on, by its clayey soil and want of water, should be restored to its original state and converted into a park (which would be three miles in circumference) with walks and drives, a plan certainly highly conducive to the ornament of that part of the metropolis and the recreation of its inhabitants. Nothing has yet been determined as to the appropriation of this estate.[40]

'Mr White' was the same John White senior who, as we have seen, lived on the New Road and as Surveyor to the Portland Estate had been intimately involved with the Marylebone area, including the park. Lysons provides an admirable summary here of White's plans in 1811. His scheme was produced in response to a competition established by Fordyce in 1809 in order to seek designs for the improvement of Marylebone

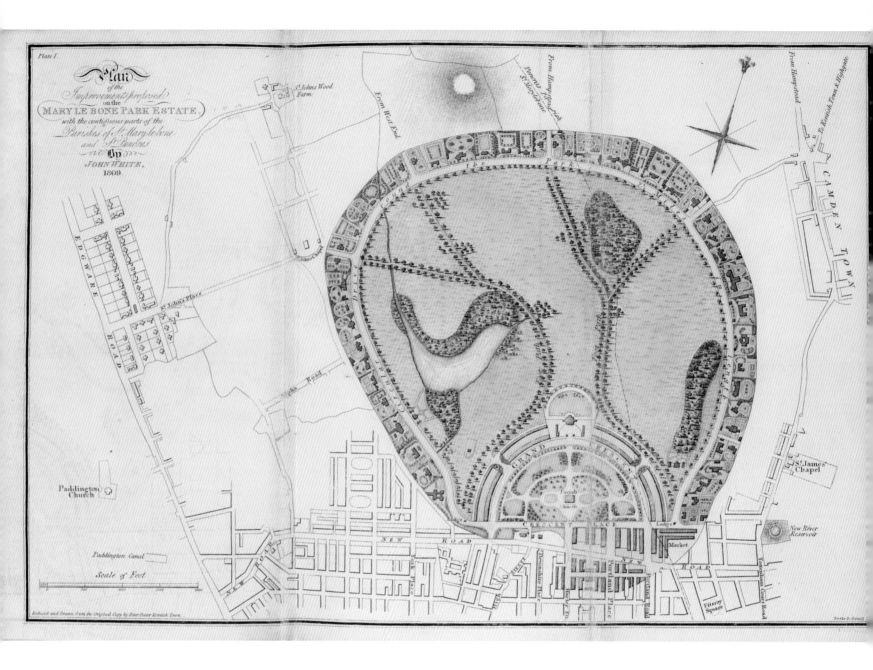

Plan of the Improvements proposed on the MARYLEBONE PARK ESTATE with the contiguous parts of the Parishes of St. Marylebone and St. Pancras By JOHN WHITE, 1809.

181   John White junior, 'Plan of the Improvements proposed on the Marylebone Park Estate with the Contiguous Parts of the Parishes of St Marylebone and St Pancras by John White, 1809', Plate 1 from White, *Some Account of the Proposed Improvements of the Western Part of London*, 1814, British Library.

Park once it should revert to the Crown. In fact, White was the only entrant to the competition, for which he produced three designs (fig. 181 and see image on p. viii). White's plans were not adopted, but they played an important part in the scheme's genesis and were published by his son in *Some Account of the Proposed Improvements of the Western Part of London* (1814) after his father's death. White's scheme essentially combined two interests: those of the Portland Estate and those of his family. The Duke of Portland, the owner of the park lease up until 1811, had hoped to buy it from the Crown and develop the land himself. The centring of

the plan on Harley Street, the creation of a new parish church and the clear lines of communication established across the New Road were all long-cherished ambitions of the Portland Estate. As James Anderson has shown, White had entered into a financially advantageous agreement with the duke whereby he would share the profits of any development 50/50 once full rents had been achieved.[41] He was therefore to be the duke's partner in any subsequent scheme.

White was also a prominent local resident and as such would naturally have been anxious to protect both his own property and the amenity of the neigh-

214

bourhood. His plan shows his villa and its neighbour remaining *in situ* with a new road, Crescent Place, created to the north.[42] Under an agreement of 1811 reached between the Crown Estate and the Duke of Portland, one of the conditions stated: 'No development would take place in the Park opposite the houses of John White and the Duke of Hamilton on the southern edge of the Park, lying just to the north of the New Road.'[43] Summerson, who strongly resisted any claims that might dilute sole authorship for Nash's scheme, thought that White junior's 1814 *Account* arose out of a desperate attempt to avoid the destruction of his own property: 'His father's design for the development of the Park had been set aside and his own house on the New Road was now to be swept away.'[44] But all subsequent plans, including Nash's, left the existing villas intact, which in any case were built on Portland Estate freehold land and not Crown property.

John White junior's *Account* provided a posthumous publication of his father's 1809 plan and betrays a justifiable anger at the way that he had been treated. As White junior acknowledged in his concluding remarks: 'A love for the neighbourhood of the place of his nativity, and an affection for local objects, may perhaps have induced the Writer ... to express his feelings too strongly.'[45] White senior's plan was likewise firmly rooted in the topography of the area and took account of the dual aspect that the new landscape had to address. On the one hand, the linkages to the south were well embedded, enabling access from the existing built-up areas of town. On the other, the new park was to be a contained entity in its own right. White, unlike Nash, limited through traffic to the existing footpaths, which he presented as providing public access to green space:

> The interior of the park is intersected by foot-paths, which appear to be meant as substitutions for the ancient tracks to Hampstead and Highgate, Kilburn and Kentish Town, long the favourite promenades of the inhabitants of the metropolis. ... By some persons it may be said that the foot-paths would be extremely objectionable, and that it would be proper to confine the public to the external drive. But in answer to this we may surely ask, whether it is right to take away what Mr Windham has so emphatically called the lungs of the metropolis? or

whether it is legally justifiable to destroy foot-paths used for centuries without forming others nearer or more convenient?[46]

White's emphasis on open access predates the switch in official policy in 1812, as identified by Crook, which changed the conception of the park from an enclosed elite development to a far more permeable space for public as well as private enjoyment.[47] The politicians rightly saw that a private enclave of exclusive houses and a barracks would be hugely unpopular with the public at a time of economic crisis and civil unrest. So it is interesting to see White deploying this argument in favour of his scheme, which draws on long-established notions of rights of access to green space around the capital.[48] What he was seeking to create, White wrote, was 'a great pomaerium [the open space running inside and outside the wall of a city left free of buildings] for the public health and recreation, and which the daily extension of the town is making increasingly necessary. ... Should the opportunity now be lost of thus providing for the public accommodation, it will be irreparable, as no land favorably circumstanced, either as to its proprietor or its situation for an open park, is any where to be found in the vicinity of the metropolis.'[49] Indeed, White's vision seems to have been a formalization of the existing park landscape so that its inherent qualities were maintained, including the tradition of dairy production, which he assumed (wrongly) would continue as happened in St James's Park: 'The highest possible rental for land, to be used for pasture, would be obtained for that which forms the interior of the park, as every inhabitant would readily pay a full price for the admission of cows to supply their families with milk, and they might be wintered without difficulty or inconvenience in the range of offices forming the external boundary of the crescent.'[50]

The circular carriage drive with villas was perhaps the most radical part of the scheme. It simultaneously formed a boundary to the park and created a series of villas arranged in a continuous sequence to maximize views both across and within the park itself:

> Another feature of this plan is, a circular road or drive, surrounded by a border of villas with the interior of the park wholly exposed to view. ... The length of this drive, between the two lodges, is

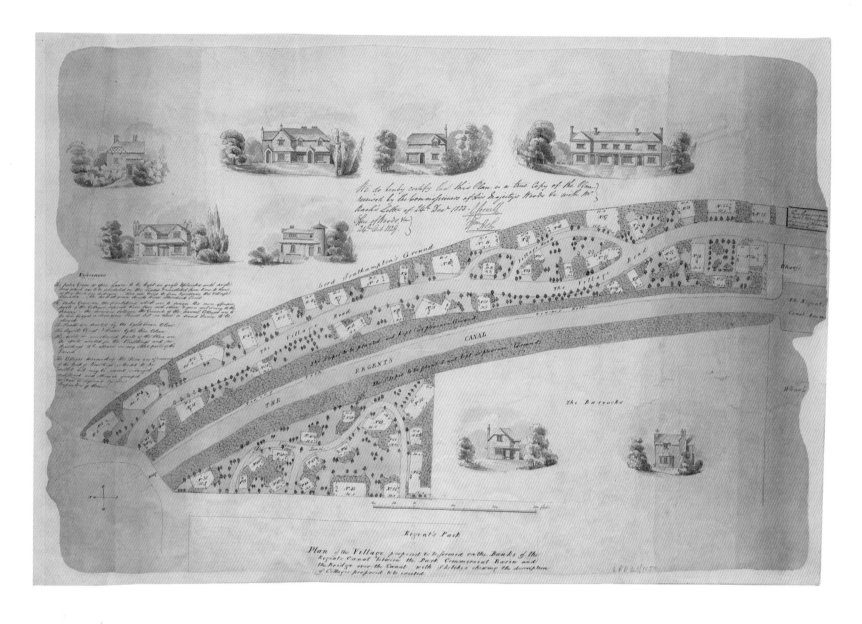

182 John Nash, *Plan of the Villages proposed to be formed on the Banks of the Regent's Canal*, 1823, The National Archives (MPE/911).

nearly two miles and three-quarters. A crescent, of nearly half a mile in diameter, is situated on the north side of the New Road, to be composed of first rate houses, and taking advantage of a gradual rise of the ground, which naturally favours this disposition, every house would be possessed of a complete view of the area of the crescent, and an entire command of the interior of the park, bordered with villas and surmounted by the beautiful hills of Hampstead and Highgate.[51]

White's arrangement of variegated villas with equally distinctive individual landscaped grounds in a parkland setting prefigures Nash's original design for Park Villages East and West of 1823 (fig. 182). Nash's plan has been widely credited as the first truly suburban layout in the world by Fishman and Tyack among many others.[52] Unlike Nash, White did not provide elevations, and it is unlikely that White, lacking his rival's background in neo-vernacular design (notably at Blaise Hamlet), would have produced such an innovative array of elevational treatments. White's plan is, however, perhaps the first suburban villa layout in which the demands of the individual house to privacy and prospect have been combined with a landscaped parkland setting to create a sustainable model for large-scale middle-class villa development. The Eyre Estate, while adopting a less dense form of development based on the individual dwelling, did not experiment with picturesque layouts or forms. A number of scholars, including Crook, have suggested, however, that the germ of the Regent's Park plan is to be found in White's scheme.[53] Anne Saunders more forthrightly comments: 'It was a good design with a number of exciting ideas, some of which Nash borrowed without acknowledgment.'[54] Nash had to modify his cottage development – which he had originally intended for houses 'of the smallest class' – when it became evident that such people could not afford these mini-*cottage ornés*, while at the same time they proved too small for middle-class occupation.[55] So he redesigned the village again in 1823 with a less rustic and more spacious series of Italianate and neo-Tudor houses (fig. 183). The suburban village arrangement for Regent's Park began, then, with a local architect who drew on his own experience as an established villa dweller in this fringe location to draw up a plan which addressed the specifics of the terrain while at the same time providing radical ideas for its redevelopment. The concept of the suburban estate was writ large in White's plan for the first time. It is not accidental that it sprang from someone with a long and intimate knowledge of living and working in the London environs.

If we turn now to the other two schemes reproduced in White's *Account*, the first by Leverton and Chawner of 1811 – which was rejected – can be quickly dispatched. Their grid-based plan, which looks as if a bit of the West End has crossed the New Road and established itself in the park, is devastatingly dismissed by White as a plan that 'would certainly produce an immense revenue, which indeed seems to have been the main object of its authors'.[56] The other scheme illustrated was Nash's second design of 1812, in which we can see the elements Nash took from White's scheme – principally the curving lake, the crescent and the villas in the park (fig. 184). Nash's plan at this date still had some unhappy conjunctions between the fluid – the sinuous lake and circus with villas in the interior – and the geometric – the water basin, the square and above all the disjointed perimeter road. White wrote acutely of the latter: 'What in this plan is rather amusingly called a circular road round the park, is an awkward combination of straight lines with right and obtuse angles; and what is meant for the interior of the park, is an appropriation of the ground to villas, interspersed with trees very cleverly drawn.'[57]

If we compare the plans of Nash's and White's schemes, the latter was the more rural and traditionally picturesque of the two. It was also the more conservative, replicating as it did a conventional park landscape, albeit with public access via footpaths. However, these two plans do not tell the whole story. Nash's first

183   T. H. Shepherd, 'Park Village East, Regent's Park', 1828, from J. Elmes, *Metropolitan Improvements or London in the Nineteenth Century*, 1827–30, private collection.

Showing the 'village' as built with the canal in front.

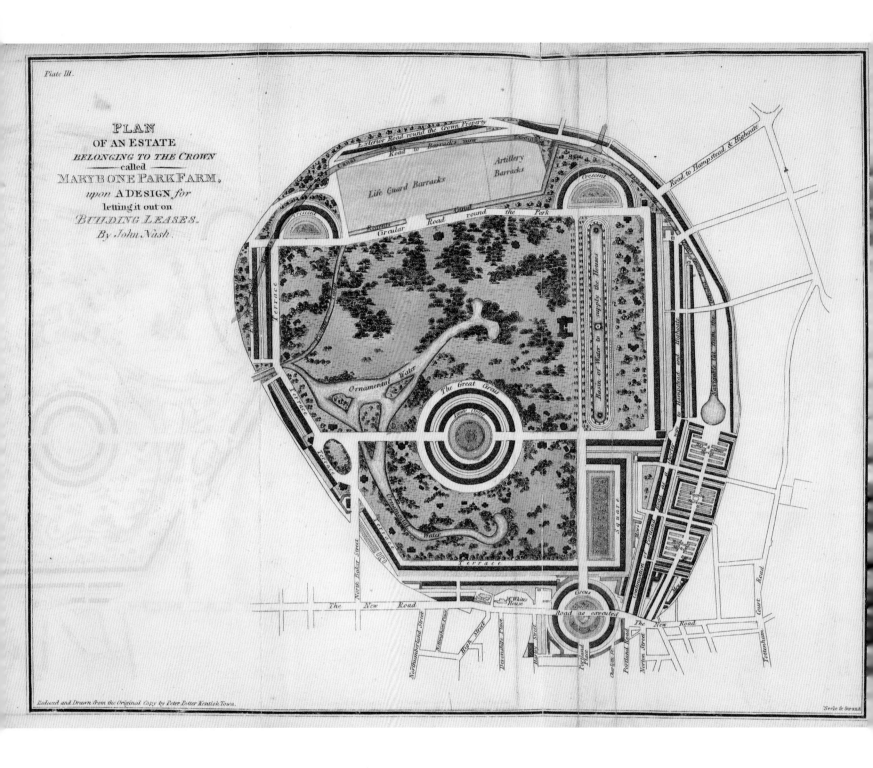

surviving plan dates from March 1811, and in order to bring its bald outlines to life, in a well-established architect's technique, he plied his prospective patron with accompanying seductive perspectives. These were produced in the modish format of two panoramas that he had drawn up by an unknown artist. The drawings, which tellingly White did not reproduce, depict the park as a highly stylized vision of a classical idyll with architectural features such as villas, arches and bridges set within a heavily wooded Arcadian landscape. The artist, if not Nash himself, was returning here to the mid-eighteenth-century heavily French-influenced depiction of the environs as a pastoral Elysium in the Claudean manner. As Summerson comments, the panoramas demonstrate that, despite the incorporation of more formal elements in Nash's plan, it is clear that (facing page) 184 John White junior, 'Plan of an Estate belonging to the Crown called Marylebone Park Farm upon a Design for letting it out on Building Leases by John Nash, 1811/12', Plate 3 from White, *Some Account of the Proposed Improvements of the Western Part of London*, 1814, British Library.

Nash's second design of 1812, which, as White observed, provides an indication of the spread of villas proposed but little clue as to their design.

from the beginning he envisaged the park in picturesque terms. Their purpose, he writes, was 'to demonstrate the picturesque beauties of Nash's proposals as distinct from the economic benefits arising from the built-up areas shown on the plan and quantified in his estimates'.[58] By the time of Nash's involvement, the brief had expanded to include modern features such as a barracks, canal and markets which White did not need to consider. The finished park was framed by monumental terraces linked by triumphal arches around its perimeter and increasingly filled with a variety of leisure buildings, learned societies and other miscellaneous institutions. There was even a small quasi-commercial area to the east where the market, canal and barracks were situated alongside some workers' housing intended for those servicing the new estate. Nash grasped the essential change in character that such features would demand, and produced a more radical design than White's which moved beyond the existing Romantic landscape model to genuinely embrace the urban elements and location of the scheme. Nash's final design triumphantly combines the rural parkland and suburban villas with an urban aesthetic of grand terraces which together constituted a new form of urban picturesque. As he wrote, above all, 'The buildings and even the Villas should be considered as Town residences and not Country Houses.'[59] It is this perhaps, rather than the pre-existing suburban aesthetic, which should be seen as Nash's greatest achievement (see fig. 186).

THE TRANSITIONAL LANDSCAPE OF REGENT'S PARK, 1812–40: 'NOT SO MUCH A CHANGE AS A RESTORATION'

When we first saw that the Mary-le-bone-fields were enclosed, and that the hedge-row walks which twined through them were gradually being obliterated, and the whole district artificially laid out, we underwent a painful feeling or two, and heartily deplored the destructive advances of what goes by the name of improvement....

A few years, however, have elapsed, and we are not only reconciled to the change alluded to, but rejoice in it. A noble park is rapidly rising up ... and a vast space, close by the metropolis, not only preserved from the encroach-

ment of mean buildings, but laid out with groves, lakes, and villas, with their separate pleasure grounds, while through the whole place there is a winding road which commands at every turn some fresh features of an extensive country prospect....

The noble appropriation of the district of which we are now speaking, is not so much a change as a restoration. It was formerly a park ... it passed into the hands of other possessors, till, at length it has reverted to the crown, by whose public spirit a magnificent park is secured to the inhabitants of London.... There will be nothing like it in Europe....

In the centre of the park ... you are in a perfect Arcadia. The mind cannot conceive any thing more hushed, more sylvan, more entirely removed from the slightest evidence of a proximity to town. Nothing is audible there, except the songs of birds and the rustling of leaves.... We cannot recommend a better thing to our readers, than a day spent wandering amidst the union of stately objects and rural beauty which constitute the charm of Mary-le-bone Park.
   Charles Ollier, *Literary Pocket Book*, 1823

Regent's Park as completed can be seen in a map by Benjamin Davies (fig. 185 and see fig. 175). By 1837, the date of Davies's map, the new borough of St Marylebone had been created incorporating a number of parishes, including St Pancras. It was one of four new metropolitan boroughs formed in 1832 to reflect the changing nature of the metropolis and bring the outer parishes administratively within the bounds of a single authority.[60] Nash's plans had morphed, partly through economic pressures, into a less densely residential and more varied scheme functionally than that originally envisaged. As the illustrations alongside the map make clear, there had been a rash of church building in connection with the new suburb following the Church Building Act of 1818 (the Commissioners' Act). These contributed significantly to the creation of viewpoints across the New Road in a fashion that John Gwynn would have applauded. We can see on the map that instead of villas dotted throughout the park only eight were eventually built. The canal has been pushed to the far edges, and the zoo now sits where the barracks were originally intended. There are other changes which are less obvious from the plan to do with the use and character of the park, and in outlining these

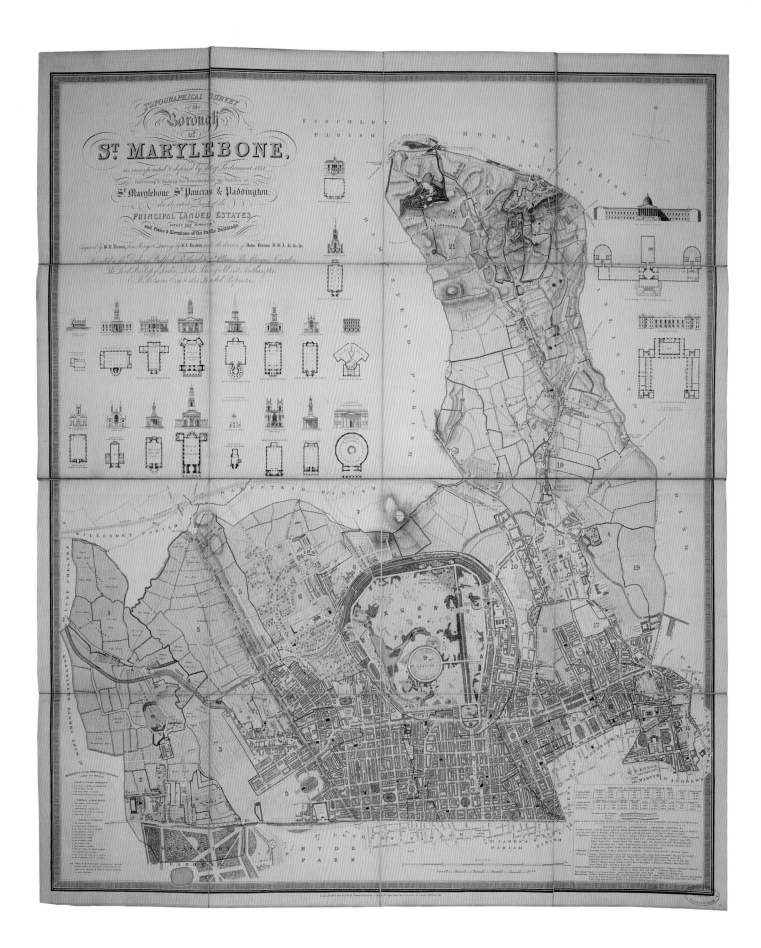

(facing page) 185 Benjamin R. Davies (engraver), F. A. Bartlett survey under direction of John Britton, *Topographical Survey of the Borough of St Marleybone, as Incorporated and Defined by Act of Parliament 1832....and Plans and Elevations of the Public Buildings*, 1837, Bodleian Library, University of Oxford.

The map shows Marylebone as fairly intensively developed with Regent's Park completed and the Eyre Estate in St John's Wood well underway. The old boroughs of St Pancras and Paddington remain substantially untouched apart from their southern ends. Among the buildings depicted is the Toxophilite Society, also seen in figs 188 and 192.

we need to draw on other types of evidence, particularly prints and accounts of the park. The best guide to the park's architecture at the time is to be found in James Elmes, *Metropolitan Improvements or London in the Nineteenth Century: Being a Series of Views of the New and Most Interesting Objects in the British Metropolis and its Vicinity* (1827–30). Elmes (1782–1862) was an architect and writer based in Greenwich. He produced the first biography of Wren and was part of the Romantic literary circle of Haydon and Keats.[61] *Metropolitan Improvements* was illustrated by T. H. Shepherd, the same artist who drew the two views of White's London house, and his steel engraved illustrations were central to the success of the work. They combined for the first time topographical accuracy with an animated and populated urban scene of bustling people, animals and carriages (fig. 186)[62] In this section we will consider to what extent Regent's Park as a whole – not simply its domestic architecture – represents a new type of environment on the London fringes and how far it maintains many of the trends outlined in the preceding chapters.

The first and most obvious continuity is that the old royal hunting park remained parkland, but in a reinvented form for the new century. Its royal nomenclature, as the Regent's Park, was purely an honorific title; the Prince Regent himself played no role in its development beyond lending his general support.[63] The park no longer had any agricultural function as White had envisaged, and Mr Willan moved his dairy farm out to West Twyford in Middlesex. There he became lord of the manor and built a Gothic house by the architect William Atkinson on the proceeds of the sale.[64] Initially only the roads through the park were open to the public, but with the reduction in the number of villas eighty-eight acres of open parkland were eventually made available for public usage in 1833. This was further increased in 1841 when Primrose Hill was acquired by the Crown from Eton College in a swap for land at Windsor.[65] As White had hoped, the park continued to function as the 'green lungs' for the northern part of the city in the time-honoured fashion of open space around the urban fringes. The difference was that the land was not open fields and that it had been self-consciously fashioned in the style of a country seat. This was not a new departure for royal London parks, all of which were based on the landed estate model, but what the other royal parks did not do was to combine such an environment with private residential development.

186 T. H. Shepherd, 'The Coliseum, Regent's Park', 1827, from J. Elmes, *Metropolitan Improvements or London in the Nineteenth Century*, 1827–30, Bodleian Library, University of Oxford.

Note the flanking lodges, one of the triumphal arches and the monumental terrace visible behind.

The key element with regard to the domestic buildings was to maintain the open park-like aspect while at the same time providing sufficient architectural differentiation for the various types of residents. Regent's Park, as Gwynn had advocated, upheld the long-established norm in the environs of a socially mixed environment. The poorer dwellings were located east of Albany Street, next to the undesirable Somers Town, intended to house those servicing the new estate. Its socially intermediate zones lay in the 'Park Villages', home to the suburban cottages. The terraces that lined the Park were a very up-market version of the ribbon development that could be found on any of the arterial routes into and out of the capital. Here they were blown up to gigantic proportions, given eye-catching silhouettes and terminated by vast triumphal arches which screened the mews houses to the rear (fig. 186). At the top of the hierarchy were the individual villas inhabited by a few aristocrats such as the Marquis of Hertford but more typically by wealthy self-made men such as James Burton, the builder and developer of much of the park and Regents' Street, whose financing was central to the scheme's success (fig. 187).[66] Nash had to balance the competing demands of his mixture of residential types, ensuring privacy, particularly for the two wealthier groups, while at the same time creating views across the estate. He wrote: 'No Villa should see any other, but each should appear to possess the whole of the Park. . . . The Streets of the Houses which overlook the Park should not see the Villas, nor the Streets of the Houses overlook those of any other street.'[67]

At the same time, the villas in the centre of the park served as scenic features in their own right, as the numerous reproductions of them in publications, prints and maps demonstrate. These villas, like their predecessors such as Kenwood or the Ranger's Lodge in Green Park, were therefore both private and public simultaneously. They continued the tradition of cat-and-mouse viewing, being both open and closed to viewing, following his erstwhile collaborator's Humphry Repton's principle of 'apparent extent'. This was an idea derived from Gilpin which was employed to create an illusion of space. Repton's success in modest landscape parks (as well as grand ones) was in large part due to his belief that 'one of the fundamental principles of Landscape Gardening is to disguise the real boundary'.[68] He created vistas through to 'borrowed' elements outside the park, such as distant hills or church steeples, which were thus appropriated and made to seem part of the designed landscape. The impression of space at Regent's Park was increased by following Repton's practice of designing imposing drives and lodges to increase the sense of scale and significance.

The canal, which many thought a controversial part of the scheme, was successfully absorbed into the pastoral landscape as the Paddington canal had been previously. Nevertheless, it was felt necessary to create a 'precipitous bank' to protect the park from the 'incursions of the bargemen' who might otherwise encroach from the towpath.[69] Nash had originally meandered the canal through the centre of the park, but it too, like the housing, was pushed to the edges. He wrote: 'Many persons would consider . . . Boats and Barges passing along the Canal as enlivening the Scenery.'[70] In reality the areas closest to the canal did become the least desirable, but as Crook makes clear, they still remained resolutely bourgois and respectable.[71] In *Metropolitan Improvements* they are presented as a triumphant harmonization of the commercial and the domestic. Elmes wrote of Park Village East: 'We next arrive at . . . a few detached villas of tasteful beauty. Behind their plantations that beneficial stream, the Regent's Canal, enters the northern circuit of the park, and conveys the produce of the inland part of our island, in a beautiful dell, to the bosom of old father Thames' (see fig. 182).[72] He even went so far as to paint the Islington tunnel of the canal in the language of the sublime: 'The western aperture in White Conduit

Fields appears reduced to a point of great brilliancy, resembling a star surrounded by a halo of Rembrandtish darkness' (see fig. 180).[73]

The commercial and service sector was located east of Albany Street by the cheaper housing. This area included the Opthalmic Hospital, a riding school and stables, barracks, the canal basin and markets. Only one market of the planned three was eventually built, Cumberland Market, the successor to the more central Haymarket which relocated there in 1830.[74] The Jew's Harp and the Queen's Head were also located in the new eastern tradesmen's sector. John White was disapproving of their inclusion and of Nash's opening up of roadways through the park to Hampstead and Highgate, which he said will only 'furnish custom to the two public houses already built, but which ought never to have been tolerated in a royal or ornamental park'.[75] The existing inns were demolished as early as 1811 to make way for the new development and then were rebuilt almost as rapidly. Their landlords, as Summerson wrote, were no doubt 'anxious to take advantage of their licences in an area soon to be invaded by thirsty bricklayers'.[76] However, the provision of public houses also underlines how far the shift in thinking had gone towards this being a people's park rather than a royal or exclusive domain. In 1814 Joseph Farington noted in his diary, 'the multitudes of respectably dressed people, men with their wives and families . . . walking in . . . the Regency Park, or quietly sitting with Pipes and Ale in the open air at small taverns'.[77] The park itself continued to serve as an urban playground of mock-rusticity in which the old inns and pleasure grounds were recreated in new architectural guises; the Botanical (1839) and Zoological (1828) gardens replaced the old Marylebone pleasure gardens as an extramural parade ground. Some early plans even featured a royal 'guinguette', a French word for a tea garden or place of entertainment in the suburbs, suggesting the spirit in which the park was intended to be consumed.

The playful architectural approach of the park was derived from the pleasure garden idiom, although there were limits as to how far this levity might be taken. Anderson cites the commissioners rejecting one of Burton's designs for a villa in the form of a *cottage orné* with a portico formed of tree trunks: 'Although buildings of this character, if formed with taste, may be appropriate and picturesque in certain situations, remote from London, the commissioners do not consider them fit to be adopted in the Crown's Estate of Marybone.'[78] However, as the non-residential, institutional and commercial aspects of the park developed in the 1820s and 1830s, the official stance changed. The Toxophilite Society was built in 1832 on a five-acre site as the centre of the royal archery club. The residents complained at the extreme rusticity of the building, which was defended by the commissioners, suggesting that their views had softened in the intervening period (fig. 188).[79] The society was founded in 1781 as an amateur group which grew out of the Finsbury Archers. They had practised since medieval times on the fields outside the walls. The rustic archers' hall was therefore intended to conjure up the society's proud lineage stretching back to the medieval companies of archers who used to practise all around the City in its defence.[80] In Pierce Egan's *Life in London* (1821), 'our heroes' have a day out at an archery competition in the capital held at what is almost certainly the Toxophilite Society, although it is not named as the venue. Archery, Egan relates, had declined 'till about forty years ago, when it was revived with increased splendour'. Its particular attraction according to the man-about-town Corinthian Tom was 'that it is equally open to the fair sex' (fig. 189).[81] The friends have a great day out trying their hand at archery while being accompanied by music and partaking of refreshments from the marquees. Jerry, the countryman, declares that

it was the most enjoyable thing he had done while in London. A one-time military activity of the citizenry had been transferred from Finsbury Fields and recreated for the relaxation and enjoyment of the leisured bourgeoisie in the sylvan surroundings of a make-believe royal park. Past and present were linked together here in an uneasy alliance but not in the way that Blake had envisaged.

The old suburbs underpinned both the spirit and form of Regent's Park. The crowds still flocked to the area, as they had to Marylebone Gardens, for all the old pleasures with some new ones thrown in besides. Pierce Egan's *Life in London: The Day and Night Scenes of Jerry Hawthorn Esq. and his Elegant Friend Corinthian Tom, accompanied by Bob Logic, the Oxonian, in their*

Rambles and Sprees through the Metropolis, an instant hit from its first appearance in 1821, featured Regent's Park as one of the most sought-after sights of the new improved city. As Bob Logic commented of the new diversion: 'The situation is altogether delightful; it is a pleasant walk, or a fine drive for the gentry and a most agreeable lounge into the bargain' (fig. 190).[82] Nash grasped the opportunity provided by the public nature of the park to orchestrate a thrilling landscape of visual spectacle with its flamboyant gestures, lavish scale and breath-taking theatricality. He tamed the essentially heterogeneous and unplanned nature of the suburban landscape and forged it into a scenographic whole for the first time. Nash wrote that the park and its surroundings were intended to be viewed as a visual

ensemble: 'The leading object is that of presenting from without one entire Park complex in unity of character and not an assemblage of Villas and Shrubberies like Hampstead, Highgate, Clapham Common.'[83] The importance of viewpoints and vicarious viewing, as one of the primary means of experiencing the environs, was highlighted in the previous chapter, and the visual remained equally the primary mode of consumption for Regent's Park. Just as urban tourists had visited the outskirts in their droves and been helped to appreciate its essential qualities and sights by guides and maps, so Elmes and others directed Londoners around this new attraction.

Elmes was explicit in praising Nash's picturesque approach, which he said derived from his association with Humphry Repton, the landscape gardener, with whom he had worked extensively at the beginning of his career.[84] Moreover Elmes's text itself is also highly visual as befits an architect. He employed what he called the 'pictorial eye' to viewing the compositional devices of the park, making constant reference to art and architectural precedents and allusions.[85] He pre-

sented the park as a sequence of multidirectional viewpoints and aesthetic experiences, an unfolding panorama to equal or even outdo that housed in the Colosseum: 'If we cross over to the pavement of the terrace, and turn our backs upon the houses, we shall enjoy one of the most pleasing views in the park. Look at the beautiful expanse of the lake before us! See the exquisite diversity of the scene. . . . Such power has the artist of pure taste, who looks to nature as his guide, in the formation of living pictures like the scene that we are now enjoying.'[86] This scenographic experience of 'living pictures' came out of the long tradition of landscape appreciation and urban tourism. This was the culmination of Robert Morris's vision which brought architecture and landscape into a scenic whole, here given its latest incarnation in which the trinity of the rural, urban and suburban were encompassed as one for the first time.

Like the environs the park could be appreciated at a number of levels and through a variety of modes of transport of differing speeds. The views inside the park were constructed for the appreciation of strolling visitors and boaters on the lake as much as for the residents themselves. Elmes was quite specific that for a properly detailed examination the park was best visited on foot.[87] The carriage drive around its perimeter, first proposed by White, appropriated a standard feature of country estates and brought it to the suburban environment. Hyde Park also had long-established carriage drives, including Rotten Row, but the novelty at Marylebone was the architectural drama which the carriage occupant was invited to survey. At Hyde Park and St James's, by contrast, the focus was firmly on human displays of form and fashion. The views along the New Road catered for the mobile visitor or simply passing commuter traffic speeding along the edge of the park. Elmes imagined guests enjoying the unfolding scene on their way to dinner in St John's Wood.[88] Sandy McCreery has drawn attention to the impact which the new age of faster road travel had on architectural design, and has suggested that Regent's Park and Regent Street were the first major developments designed for such circulatory vision.[89] The streets in Shepherd's drawings are thronged with a variety of carriages both public and private, ranging from racy broughams to large stage coaches, as well as individual horse riders and pedestrians on the pavement (see fig. 186).

The architectural heterodoxy of the park, and particularly its leisure buildings, can be related to the tradition of garden architecture in the suburbs which sanctioned experimental or unorthodox architecture for buildings of pleasure, whether public or private. Of those in Regent's Park it is the Colosseum which has been the most discussed as offering a new form of urban viewing experience.[90] The building housed a panorama of the view from St Paul's from the top of its dome drawn by Mr Horner, a surveyor (fig. 191). Its great merit lay in combining 'the *unusual* interest of picturesque effect with the most scrupulous accuracy'.[91] The long history of viewing the city from external eminences was given a new, modern form recreated for a paying public in a purpose-built structure on the edge of the city.[92] The advantages of viewing the city here, rather than from St Paul's itself, were that – unlike the outlook from the real dome – the facsimile would not be obscured by smoke and dust. As one commentator wrote: 'The only period at which London can be seen, is at sun-rise on a fine summer morning. . . . This must be before the many

thousand fires are lighted – exactly the period at which it is impossible to gain admittance to the cathedral. In the Panorama of the Colosseum, therefore, alone it is that we can see the "mighty heart" of the town we inhabit.'[93] A true vision of London could now only be experienced vicariously not at first hand; the constant cycle of reproducing and copying the city as an image in its own right had reached its apogee.

The city that the panorama depicted was not just confined to the centre but covered the 'Greater London' with which this book has been concerned. Elmes in his description of the panorama writes of the distant prospects to the Home Counties in all directions. In the long tradition of metropolitan viewing, the vista, continued until 'it stretches away beyond the busy haunts of industry, to the rural beauties of Richmond, and the castellated splendour of Windsor. . . . The representation of the environs is delightfully picturesque, and the distances are admirably executed; while the whole forms an assemblage of grandeur, unparalleled in art.'[94] In order to aid the viewing of the hills of Surrey or Epping Forest there were explanatory panels, and glasses were placed in the gallery 'by which houses at the distance of ten or twelve miles from the city may be easily discerned'.[95] The *Picturesque Guide to the Regent's Park* of 1829 wrote that 'every inch of the vast circumference abounds with subject for reflection,' and it was this circularity of viewing that was both traditional and novel.[96] The panorama can also be understood as the next step in the transference of the seventeenth-century tradition of bird's-eye viewing via the circular maps of the environs to a new three-dimensional representation. The essentially holistic and circular view of the city in which centre and periphery were bound together in a sphere was revivified in the panorama. An earlier example, the *Eidometropolis* by Thomas Girtin, was exhibited at Spring Gardens in 1802 (see fig. 33) and itself followed on from Roger and Henry Barker's panorama of London from Albion Mills (1792).[97] It would not be long before the railways broke this circular vision of the London region with their radial spokes extending across the country, but here its compelling centrifugal force is seen at the height of its powers.[98]

In 1823 an equally radical building opened, the Diorama, the exterior of which gave no clue as to an interior which 'has nothing in common with any thing

else in the metropolis'.[99] It housed an exhibition of architecture and landscape scenery painted on stage flats and lit to produce the impression of three-dimensionality: 'These paintings are lighted from behind by large windows as big as the pictures, and by sky-lights over and in front of them; and by the aid of opaque and transparent screens and curtains of various colours and degrees of transparency, the various effects of light, shade and gradations of colour are produced.'[100] The audience sat in a circular theatre which rotated mechanically so that 'all are moved imperceptibly round, from the Mary Chapel of Canterbury Cathedral to the lake of Lausanne, or from the city of Rouen in France, to the interior of Rosslyn Chapel in Scotland.'[101] The Diorama employed the same rotational viewpoint as in the panorama and as in the actual park itself, but with the viewpoint now expanded to encompass not just the metropolis but the whole of Europe. One of the exhibits was of the 'Valley of Sarnen, in the canton of Underwald, one of the most delightful spots in Switzerland'. This forms an interesting link with our final and concluding example in a parade of astonishingly innovative scopic experiments

housed in Regent's Park, the Colosseum.[102] Gradually a number of the buildings in the park, particularly those of the Zoological Gardens, began to deploy an eclectic range of styles to counterpoint the stuccoed classical forms of the first wave of buildings. The *Picturesque Guide* wrote of the Zoological Society grounds: 'Several of the dens and houses in these gardens are not a whit less picturesque than the villas and mansions which we have elsewhere noticed from Mr Burton's designs' (see fig. 190).[103] The anonymous author cited the 'Gothic House for Llamas' with its outsize curving roof and paired ogee-arched doors as a particular illustration of this trend.[104] Nash's urban picturesque composition was increasingly been asked to accommodate a rustic romanticism which pulled the park back towards its origins and created a more traditionally suburban idiom.

The two most radical buildings in the park in this respect were the Toxophilite Society and the Colosseum, brought together in a view by T. M. Baynes of *c.*1830 (fig. 192). The architectural connection between these two very different buildings is not immediately obvious except scenographically. What could a rotunda, traditionally an icon of neoclassical rationality, have in common with a rustic archers' hall? The answer even more elliptically can be found in alpine architecture, which became fashionable following the publication of P. F. Robinson's *Rural Architecture* in 1823. The Toxophilite Society can be seen as a prototypical Swiss chalet. It was not labelled as such, but its overhanging eaves and pronounced gables and balconies certainly show it to be of the chalet style. The Colosseum, on the other hand, unlikely as it may seem, was also home to a Swiss Chalet of 1827 designed by Robinson (1776–1858), who had become infatuated with Swiss design during his travels there on his return from the more traditional sites of the Grand Tour.

The promoters of the Colosseum found that they needed to diversify into other attractions besides the panorama. The *Picturesque Guide* expiated on what it considered 'the *bijou* of the whole . . . a suite of small chambers representing a Swiss cottage':

> One of these rooms is . . . carved in imitation of the fanciful interior of the dwellings of Swiss mountaineers. . . . The illusion is not a little enhanced by the prospect from the windows, consisting of rocks and caverns, among which a cascade is to fall from an immense height into a lake, which is to spread

immediately beneath the windows. . . . The exterior of the dwelling, with its broad eaves, &c. is beautifully picturesque; and the interior, supplied with a suite of rustic furniture, of unique and *recherché* taste.[105]

From the windows of the chalet the visitor could contemplate waterfalls with running water against the background of the Mer de Glace and Mont Blanc, as painted by Mr Danson (fig. 193). A plan of 1855 shows the building when it was put up for auction, the Diorama having previously closed in 1848 (fig. 194).[106] It shows that the illusionism extended to the main building itself, so that what appears from the front as a perfectly regular neoclassical rotunda was in fact subverted by the addition of extraneous irregular elements around its edges. The Swiss Cottage grows out of the side of the rotunda like some monstrous miscegenetic graft. The boundaries of inside and outside are then further complicated by the construction of the fake lake and mountains in the grounds seen through the windows of the chalet. This merging of interior and exterior, of the facsimile and the real, was taken one step further with the final removal of the chalet from the Colosseum and its placement in the park outside.

The watercolour of the chalet in the park by Edmund Marks dates from 1837 so the structure must have been shifted sometime before this date (fig. 195).[107] The similarity of the building, at least in this view, to the Queen's Head and Artichoke and other old inns of the area is striking, and we are reminded of the leisure landscapes of Hampstead and Islington but this time as vernacular revival not survival, to return to Howard Colvin's phrase (see fig. 117).[108] The stage architecture of the interiors of the Colosseum and Diorama here became an equally theatrical reassertion of the park's enduring rusticity in the face of the monumental terraces which can be seen in the background of the picture. The intertextuality between image, text, building and landscape which we have seen interweaved throughout this work is now given its ultimate and final twist as the ephemeral becomes real. Intermateriality now stretched from print to image to stage-set to bricks and mortar and back again, and so was ushered in a new age of stylistic, historical and technical eclecticism.

This book has argued that the first modern suburbs were to be found scattered around London's fringes

193 Edmund Marks, *View of the Swiss Cottage in Regent's Park*, 1837, watercolour, London Metropolitan Archives.

194 George Frederick Sargent,
Swiss Cottage and Alpine View at the
*Colosseum, Regent's Park, c.*1847,
watercolour, London Metropolitan
Archives.

from the late seventeenth century onwards rather than in the early nineteenth-century landscape of Regent's Park. However, as the prototype of the new manufactured historicism which was to find one of its most significant and enduring expressions in the architecture of the suburbs, Regent's Park had no equal. London provided a model which was to be adopted not just in the rest of Britain but across the Anglo-American world. William Howitt wrote in the 1860s of the by now at least partially planned landscape created by this process on the Northern Heights:

> Turning back to look at Highgate itself, the aspect of it is singularly beautiful and picturesque. The white villas amid their trees and pleasant grounds running up the hill ... green uplands and noble scattered trees, with the waters flashing at their feet, compose a picture that has no peer anywhere immediately round London and reminds one rather of a foreign than an English suburb. ... With their green swells and slopes, and their trees dispersed in park-like order, they remind me of hundreds

of miles of such lands that I have traversed in Australia.[109]

Howitt, in a surprising echo of modern historiography, links this metropolitan landscape to the suburbs of the New World. London was the first suburban city and regional conurbation. It provided a model not just for America, as Fishman and Archer have shown, but throughout the Anglophone world, particularly in Australia.[110] The latter today is arguably the suburban culture par excellence. From Highgate to Hobart, from Sydenham to Sydney, from Mortlake to Montreal and from Bayswater to Boston, the story continues to the present day, and as far as one can see is likely to do so for many years to come. We might argue that the twenty-first century suburb is coming full circle back to its roots in the amorphous and uncontrolled landscapes of the London environs. As working patterns and workplaces increasingly shift out of city centres, aided by modern technology, it looks like the wheel is coming full circle and the suburb will return to its seventeenth- and eighteenth-century

195 James Basire, *Ground Plan of the Royal Colosseum, Regent's Park, London*, 1855, British Library.

As well as the Swiss Cottage with its attendant scenery which disrupted the regularity of the plan, on the other side of the rotunda were the Stalactite Caverns with wraparound corridors and conservatories beyond.

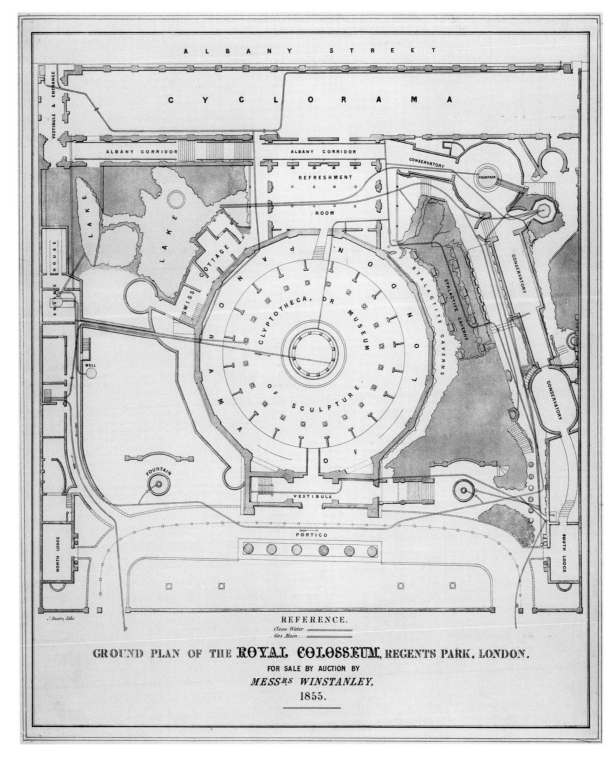

roots as a working as well as a residential and leisure landscape. The 'Plains of Id', as Banham called the suburban psychology and landscape of Los Angeles, still seem to appeal as strongly to the Western and increasingly to the global collective unconscious – or perhaps one should say consciousness – as ever.[111] London in the long eighteenth century was the forerunner of this fractured modern city. It was not just the first suburban metropolis but also a modern-style multivalent, spatially discontinuous conurbation.

NOTES

ABBREVIATIONS

BL   British Library, London
BM   British Museum, London
BOD   Bodleian Library, Oxford
ODNB   *Oxford Dictionary of National Biography*
OED   *Oxford English Dictionary*
TNA   The National Archives, Kew
SOL   Survey of London
VCH   Victoria County History

PREFACE

1   De Certeau, 1984, p. 97.
2   Thompson, 1974, p. 1.
3   In this I am using Lefebvre's idea that space is socially produced and culturally conditioned: Lefebvre, 1991.
4   For the literature on the post-metropolis see Soja, 2000, Ch. 8, 'Exopolis: The Restructuring of Urban Form'. The term 'edge city' comes from Garreau, 1992.
5   Fishman, 1987, Ch. 7.
6   For a good introduction to centre-place theory and the problems of applying it historically, see Ballantyne, 2010, pp. 5–7.
7   Venturi, Scott Brown and Izenour's *Learning from Las Vegas* (1972), rev. ed. 1977, was another powerful corrective with its analysis of form and order on the Strip.
8   Banham, 1971, p. 203.
9   Hoskins, 1992, p. 219.
10 Fabricant, 1987, p. 273.
11 Hoskins, 1992, pp. 219, 224.
12 Barrell, 1980, 1990; Brewer, 1997, Ch. 16.
13 Hoskins, 1992, p. 18.
14 Keats, 1978, 'On the Grasshopper and the Cricket', 30 December 1816.
15 For a particularly fine example of the latter, see the series of publications produced by the East London History Society on early modern suburbs: Morris, 2007, 2011; Morris and Cozens, 2009.
16 Bryant, 1996; Solkin, 1982; Archer, 2005.
17 Guillery, 2004; Summerson, 1988; also see Boulton, 1987; Power, 1978a and b.
18 Thompson, 1974, p. 3.
19 Abramson, 2005, p. 3.
20 Girouard, 1978.
21 Knight, 2009.
22 Guillery, 2004, pp. 1–3.
23 Fishman, 1987, p. 14.
24 Davidoff and Hall, 1987; and for a critique Vickery, 1993.
25 Williams, 1984, p. 7.
26 MacLean, Landry and Ward, 1999, p. 4; also see de Bolla, 1995; Ballantyne, 2010.
27 Warf and Arias, 2009.
28 Arnold, 2005.

INTRODUCTION

1   Rasmussen, 1982, p. 36.
2   Ibid., appended to this revised edition, pp. 405–62.
3   Ibid., p. 431.
4   Ibid., p. 62.
5   On speculative development see Summerson, 1988; McKellar, 1999a.
6   Finlay and Shearer, 1986; Clark, 2001; Schwarz, 2000.
7   On suburban development see Summerson, 1988, Ch. 20; Miele, 1999. On West End growth see Olsen, 1982; Thorold, 1999.

8 Dyos, 1954, 1966; Summerson, 1995.

9 On London's modernity see Lubbock, 1995; Ogborn, 1998.

10 Hebbert, 1988, p. 208.

11 Bradley and Pevsner, 1997, p. 46.

12 Boulton, 2000, pp. 316–17.

13 Ibid., p. 317.

14 Brett-James, 1935; Smuts, 1991.

15 Bradley and Pevsner, 1997, p. 57.

16 Stow, [1598] 1987, p. 376.

17 As memorably depicted in Danny Boyle's film *Slumdog Millionaire*, 2008.

18 Stow, [1598] 1987, p. 381.

19 Ibid., pp. 381–2.

20 Power, 1978a.

21 Earle, 1989.

22 Florio, 1578, p. 18.

23 Knight, 2009, p. 161.

24 It was previously thought that the terrace was erected specifically for the Maids of Honour, but Sally Jeffrey has shown that it began as a speculative development in 1717–21: Jeffrey, 2010.

25 Defoe, [1724–6] 1971, p. 173.

26 Anon., *London in Miniature*, 1755, p. 292.

27 Bold, 2000.

28 For more on Greenwich see McKellar, 2011.

29 Saint, 1999, p. 11.

30 Stevenson, 2000.

31 Massie, 1754, p. 27.

32 Allen, 1987.

33 Dodsley, 1761, p. 116, directly lifting some of Ralph, 1734, p. 5.

34 Stone, 1980; Beier and Finlay, 1986; Wrigley, 1978.

35 Clark, 2001, p. 251.

36 Anon., *London in Miniature*, 1755, pp. 257, 285.

37 For more details see Guillery, 2004, p. 20.

38 Harding, 2001, p. 139.

39 Defoe, [1724–6] 1971, p. 287.

40 Schwarz, 2000, pp. 644, 647.

41 Ibid., pp. 645–7.

42 Ibid., p. 648.

43 Clark, 2000, p. 4.

44 Anon., *A Trip from St James's to the Royal-Exchange*, [1744] 1927, p. 220.

45 Thompson, 1974, pp. 40–41.

46 Anon., *The London and Westminster Guide*, 1767, p. 5.

47 Anon., *The Foreigner's Guide*, 1729, p. 2.

48 Maitland, 1756, vol. 2, p. 718.

49 Ibid., vol. 2, p. 750.

50 Ibid., vol. 2, p. 752.

51 Defoe, [1724–6] 1971, p. 306.

52 Howell, 1657, p. 345. For other instances see Ward, 1999, pp. 26, 28.

53 Thomas Nashe, *Christs teares ouer Jerusalem*, London, 1593, as referenced in the *OED*. However, Ward, 1999, p. 26, shows that Nashe implicated the whole metropolis in corruption, not just the suburbs, and argues that a more positive image of the suburbs existed in Elizabethan and Stuart London.

54 Archer, 2005, p. 83.

55 Cobbett, [1830] 1912.

56 Everitt, 1990, p. 112.

57 Langford, 1989, Ch. 3 'The Progress of Politeness', provides a good introduction.

58 Defoe, *Review*, 25 June 1709, as quoted in Guillery, 2004, p. 12.

59 Schwarz, 1992, p. 57. These figures are based on the male working population as many of them derive from sources that only list men, although Schwarz is at pains to point out that a considerable percentage of London's workers were female; 43 per cent of women aged ten and over were listed as being employed in the 1851 census.

60 Clark 2001, pp. 251–2.

61 Habermas, 1989.

62 Borsay, 1989.

63 Hall, 2002; Brookes, 1999.

64 Estabrook, 1998, has argued that town and country remained two different spheres in Bristol in 1660–1780.

65 Bull, 1956a and b.

66 Hunter, 1811, vol. 2, p. 3.

67 Ibid., vol. 2, p. 3.

68 Bull, 1956a, p. 3.

69 Atkins, 1977.

70 Ibid., p. 396 n. 8, quoting a parliamentary Select Committee report into Smithfield in 1828.

71 Richardson, 1988, p. 9.

72 Foot, 1794, p. 84.

73 Hunter, 1811, pp. 10, 22.

74 Atkins, 1977, p. 384.

75 Hunter, 1811, vol. 2, p. 3.

76 Ibid., vol. 2, p. 3.

77 Ibid., vol. 2, p. 4.

78 Kalm, 1892, p. 22.

79 Hunter, 1811, vol. 2, p. 4.

80 Shesgreen, 2002.

81 Kalm, 1892, pp. 19, 33.

82 Ibid., p. 80.

83 Ibid., p. 219.

84 Hunter, 1811, vol. 2, p. 4.

85 Kalm, 1892, p. 49.

86 Atkins, 1977, p. 385.

87 Hunter, 1811, vol. 2, p. 5.

88 Ibid., vol. 2, pp. 9, 14, 27.

89 Ibid., vol. 2, p. 15.

90 Maitland, 1756, vol. 2, pp. 717–18.

91 Estimates from Ralph Davis, *The Rise of the English Shipping Industry in the Seventeenth and Eighteenth Centuries*, 1962, p. 390, as quoted in Schwarz, 1992, pp. 8–9.

92 Guillery, 2004, p. 24 and especially Ch. 6.

93 Defoe, [1724–6] 1971, p. 284.

94 Ibid., p. 277.

95 On the transport of stone and on the wider issue of links between the Oxfordshire mason dynasties of the Stones and Kempsters and their involvement in the rebuilding of London after the Fire, see Mobus, 2012.

96 Schwarz, 1992, p. 9.

97 For more on Spitalfields see SOL, 1957; Guillery, 2004; McKellar, 2012.

98 Curl, 2011, Ch. 7, gives market buildings, exchanges, banks and shops as the exceptions, where varying degrees of architectural differentiation from the domestic model were employed.

99 For more on industrial suburbs see George, 1976; Guillery, 2004.

100 Guillery, 2004, p. 8.

101 Schwarz, 1992, p. 32.

102 Kalm, 1892, p. 54.

103 London had *c*.100,000 horses by 1811; see Thompson, 1976, p. 80.

104 Evelyn, 1661, p. 4.

105 Ibid., p. 9.

106 Williams, 1985.

107 Kalm, 1892, p. 77.

108 Jenner, 1995.

109 Evelyn, 1661, pp. 25–6.

110 Williams, 2001.

111 Sennett, 1994, pp. 256–63.

112 Lysons, 1792–6, vol. 3, p. 628.

113 VCH, 2004, p. 129.

114 Lysons, 1792–6, vol. 3, p. 628.

115 Smith, 1828, p. 17.

116 McKellar, 1996, p. 17.

117 Gwynn, 1766, p. 131.

118 *ODNB*.

119 Anon., *A Trip Through the Town*, [1735] 1927, p. 162.

120 *Morning Herald*, 27 February 1802. From Daniel Lysons, 'Collectanea', BL, C.191.c16 vol. 1.

121 Lysons, 1811, p. 243.

122 Ibid., p. 39.

123 Harris and Simon, 1997.

124 *ODNB*.

125 Ward, 1700, p. 16.

126 Colsoni, 1693, p. 19.

127 For more on crime see Shoemaker 2004; Hitchcock, 2004; and *The Proceedings of the Old Bailey 1674–1913* website: www.oldbaileyonline.org.

128 *Flying Post or The Post Master*, 14–16 December, 1699.

129 Pennant, 1791, p. 124.

130 Seal, 1996.

131 Wrigley, 1978; Pearl, 1979.

132 Power, 1978a; Stone, 1980.

133 See McKellar 1999a; Guillery, 2004; and Power, 1978b.

134 Defoe, [1724–6] 1971, pp. 440–41.

135 Ibid., p. 176.

136 Ibid., p. 174.

137 Ibid., p. 176.

138 Boulton, 2000, p. 344.

139 Ibid., pp. 344–5.

1 MAPPNG THE LANDSCAPES OF LONDON

1 Harley, 1988.

2 The best introduction to the subject is the editor's introduction in Cosgrove, 1999, pp. 1–23.

3 Matless, 1999, p. 194.

4 Brewer, 1997, p. 450.

5 Harley, 1988, pp. 290–92.

6 De Certeau, 1984, p. 97.

7 Information on London maps is drawn from the following: Howgego, 1978; Glanville, 1972; Barker and Jackson, 1990.

8 Bradley and Pevsner, 1997, p. 57.

9 For a good summary of London's development see Keen, 2001.

10 See Harding, 1990b.

11 Glanville, 1972, p. 17.

12 Howgego, 1978, pp. 8, 13.

13 Scouloudi, 1953; Bold, 2010.

14 See, for example, de Certeau, 1984, pp. 122–45. See Foucault, 1979, for his writing on Jeremy Bentham's Panopticon.

15 Charlesworth, 1996. He argues that panopticism creates an all-seeing eye whose gaze controls those it surveys, whereas in panoramic viewing the subjects are rarely aware that they are being viewed at all and therefore the element of power is absent.

16 George, 1976, p. 15.

17 Howgego, 1978, p. 1.

18 Glanville, 1972, p. 30.

19 Sinclair, 2002.

20 Defoe, [1724–6] 1971, pp. 50–51.

21 Defoe, [1724–6] 1971, p. 171.

22 Aubrey as quoted in *Diary of Samuel Pepys*, Latham and Matthews, eds., 1978, vol. 3 i, pp. xvi–xvii.

23 Shoemaker, 2001, pp. 149–50.

24 *ODNB.*

25 Nead, 2000, Part I, 'Mapping and Movement'.

26 Dodsley, 1761, Preface.

27 Howgego, 1978, pp. 18–19.

28 Glanville, 1972, pp. 32–3.

29 *ODNB*; Howgego, 1978, p. 19. Also see Phillips, 1952.

30 Rocque, 1741.

31 Ibid.

32 Ibid.

33 Ibid.

34 Ibid.

35 Massie, 1754, p. 44.

36 Fordham, 1925, p. ix.

37 Fordham, 1925, p. xiv; *ODNB.*

38 Cary, 1786, 'Advertisement'.

39 De Laune, 1681, pp. 356–7.

40 Ibid., p. 312.

41 Anon., *Foreigner's Guide*, 1729, p. 78.

42 Fordham, 1929, p. 71.

43 Foxell, 2007, p. 164.

44 For more on transport history see, among many others, Albert, 1972; Fairman, 1911; Pawson, 1977.

45 Defoe, [1724–6] 1971, p. 438.

46 Ibid., pp. 430–31.

47 Pawson, 1984; Freeman, 1993.

48 Defoe, [1724–6] 1971, pp. 439–40.

49 Chalkin, 2000, p. 50; Schwarz, 2000, p. 647.

50 Pawson, 1977, p. 136.

51 Smith, 1828, p. 169.

52 Clark, 2001, pp. 242–3.

53 Charles Booth's *The Descriptive Map of London Poverty* (1889) provided a detailed social survey of London with four levels of poverty differentiated.

54 Bull, 1956b, p. 25.

55 Ibid., pp. 28–30.

56 Bull, 1956a, p. 4.

57 Hall, 1966.

58 *ODNB.*

59 Baynton-Williams, 1994, p. 7.

60 Barron, 1990, p. 11.

61 Moule, 1837, p. iv.

62 Moule, 1830, Prospectus, n.p.

63 Ibid.

64 Baynton-Williams, 1994, p. 7.

65 Moule, 1837, notes to *Middlesex* plate.

66 Moule, 1837, notes to *Environs* plate.

67 Moule, 1837, notes to *Environs* plate.

68 See Bermingham, 1986, Ch. 4.

2 WRITING THE LANDSCAPES OF LONDON

1 There were a few earlier sixteenth-century Roman examples, for which see Godfrey, 1951, 'Ancestry of town guide books', pp. 54–5. The other standard accounts are Webb, 1990, and Harris, 1984.

2 Hobhouse, 1994.

3 Merritt, 2001, p. 53; also Merritt, 1998.

4 Pearl, 1987, p. vi.

5 Howell, 1657, 'To the Reader'.

6 Ibid.

7 *ODNB.*

8 Cotgrave and Howell, 1650; Howell, 1660.

9 Howell, 1657, p. 341.

10 Ibid., p. 345.

11 Ibid., p. 341.

12 Ibid., p. 404.

13 Merritt, 2001, p. 71.

14 Colsoni, [1688] 1972.

15 Colsoni, 1699b, advertisement for 'Books Printed and Sold by the Author', n.p.

16 Colsoni, 1699b, title page.

17 He may have come from one of the Italian regions absorbed into the Swiss Confederation where Protestantism was practised, such as the Grisons cantons, or he could have been from Geneva, which, although technically not part of Switzerland at this date, formed the centre of Swiss Protestantism.

18 For a more extensive discussion of Colsoni see McKellar, 2013, (forthcoming).

19 Sweet, 1997, pp. 14–15. The relation between language texts and urban literature is explored in McKellar, 2013, (forthcoming).

20 Anon., *A Trip from St. James's*, [1744] 1927, 'The Contents'.

21 Ibid., p. 190.

22 See Godfrey, 1951, p. 54.

23 Colsoni, 1693, pp. 18–22.

24 Ibid., p. 22.

25 Ward, 1709. On Ward's modernity see Ogborn, 1998, pp. 104–14.

26 Colsoni, 1693, p. 24.

27 For more on Brice see Wittman, 2007.

28 Hatton, 1708, vol. 1, 'Preface'.

29 Cherry, 2001.

30 Strype, 1720.

31 Ibid., vol. 2, p. 69.

32 Ibid., vol. 2 , p. 47.

33 Merritt, 2001, p. 87.

34 Defoe, [1724–6] 1971, 'Preface to the First Volume', pp. 43, 45.

35 His early poem *The Pacificator* deals with the controversy; see *ODNB.*

36 Andrews, 1960; Rogers, 1998.

37 One of his more successful commercial ventures was a brick and pantile factory which had contracts with Greenwich Hospital and other major projects; see *ODNB*.

38 Defoe, [1724–6] 1971, 'Preface to the First Volume', p. 45.

39 In *The Expedition of Humphry Clinker* (1771) Smollett makes Edinburgh the pinnacle of civilization and London the nadir.

40 Defoe, [1724–6] 1971, p. 337.

41 Ibid., p. 288.

42 Ibid., p. 301.

43 Ibid.

44 For more on this see Byrd, 1978, Introduction and Ch. 1; McKellar, 1999a, Ch. 1.

45 Clark, 2001.

46 *ODNB*.

47 Defoe, [1724–6] 1971, pp. 288–94.

48 Ibid., p. 286.

49 Ibid., p. 337.

50 For example, Defoe's text on Spittlefields (ibid., p. 298) is very similar to Strype's entry in the *Survey*, 1720, vol. 2 pp. 48–9.

51 Defoe, [1724–6] 1971, pp. 47–8.

52 Ibid., p. 49.

53 Ibid., p. 118.

54 Ibid., p. 287.

55 Ibid., p. 173.

56 Anon., *The Foreigner's Guide*, 1729, Preface.

57 *ODNB*.

58 Longstaffe-Gowan, 2001, pp. 105, 113–14.

59 Adams, 1983, p. 105.

60 Dodsley, 1761, Preface.

61 Tinniswood, 1998, p. 91.

62 Bryant, 1996, pp. 14–16; Tinniswood, 1998, pp. 96–9; Snodin, 2009, Ch. 2.

63 Anon., *The Ambulator*, 1792, p. 21.

64 Anon., *The Ambulator*, 1774, Preface.

65 Anon., *The Ambulator*, 1792, Preface.

66 Andrews, 1989; Victoria and Albert Museum, 1984; Fabricant, 1987.

67 Burke, 1757.

68 It was first published as *An Account of London* in 1790, but the second and subsequent editions are the ones more commonly used.

69 Pennant, 1791, 'Advertisement', p. iii.

70 Ibid., pp. iv–v.

71 Ibid., pp. 25, 35.

72 Ibid., p. 259.

73 Ibid., p. 328.

74 Adams, 1983, p. xvii. For its relation to antiquarianism and for the approaches to antiquarian illustration, see the two articles by Lucy Peltz (both 1999).

75 Adams, 1983, p. xviii.

76 *ODNB*.

77 Sweet, 1997, pp. 74–7, although she argues that this can in fact be traced back earlier than the eighteenth century in the survey tradition of Stow and the compilation of annals and recording lists.

78 Lysons, 1800, 'Advertisement', p. iii.

79 Sweet, 1997, pp. 143–58; Sweet, 2004.

80 Lysons, 1800, 'Advertisement', p. v. On these historiographical debates see Sweet, 1997, pp. 143–58; Sweet, 2004.

81 *Gentleman's Magazine*, vol. LXXII, as quoted in Alexander Chalmers, *General Biographical Dictionary*, 1812–17, vol. 18, p. 316. Also see *ODNB*.

82 Bod G. Pamph. 1960 (2) John Stockdale, 'Proposals for Publishing by Subscription a Description of London and the Circumjacent Country', 1797.

83 Compare, for example, the two writers, entries on Leyton: Lysons, 1792–6, vol. IV, pp. 158–82, and Hunter, 1811, vol. 2, pp. 449–52, where the information is identical but reduced down to about a quarter of its original length.

84 See for example, Hunter, 1811, vol. 2, p. 167, on Eltham.

85 Ibid., p. 2.

86 Baird, 1793; Boys, 1796.

87 Clark, 2001, p. 242.

88 Harding, 2001, p. 143.

3 PICTURING THE LANDSCAPES OF LONDON

1   Habermas, 1989.

2   Adams, 1983.

3   The two most sustained accounts are Solkin, 1982, Ch. 4; Bryant, 1986.

4   Bryant, 1996, p. 14.

5   Lippincott, 1983; Clayton, 1997. On the commercialization of art more broadly, see Solkin, 1993.

6   Clayton, 1997, pp. 129–34.

7   Lippincott, 1983, pp. 28, 61–2.

8   Griffiths, 1998, pp. 248–51. Winstanley did produce two views of the Earl of Danby's house in Wimbledon in 1678, although it seems that these were speculative rather than commissioned by the earl. British Musuem online catalogue: www.britishmuseum.org – BM 1881,0611.353/354, accessed 25/09/2012.

9   Clayton, 1997, p. xiii.

10 Ibid., p. 11.

11 Clark, 2001, p. 246, Table 14.1. As Clark acknowledges, his figures can only be indicative and there is probably a weighting towards City images, given the institutional base of the survey.

12 Ibid., p. 248.

13 Clayton, 1997, p. 140.

14 H. W. Foote, *John Smibert, Painter*, New York, 1969, p. 91, as quoted in Lippincott, 1983, p. 143.

15 Clayton, 1997, pp. 261–2.

16 For Hollar see Godfrey, 1995; and on prints in seventeenth-century England, Griffiths, 1998.

17 There are some earlier isolated examples such as van Dyck's pioneering view of Greenwich; see Smith, 2011, p. 43, no. 4. Strangely, the location is given as unidentified in the catalogue, although it is clearly Greenwich and includes the distinctive cupola of Robert Osboldston's house in Croom's Hill (1638), which was depicted in many Greenwich views.

18 *ODNB*.

19 Clark, 2001, p. 246.

20 Anon., *London Described*, 1731; Adams, 1983, no. 29. For more on squares see Longstaffe-Gowan, 2012.

21 Adams, 1983, no. 37.

22 For more on this see Hebbert and McKellar, 2008.

23 Among many other see Dixon Hunt and Willis, 1975; Andrews, 1989; Jacques, 1983.

24 Bermingham, 1986, Chs 1 and 2.

25 Harris, 1990, pp. 214, 317–24; Leatherbarrow, 1985.

26 Colvin, 1995.

27 Harris, 1990, p. 321.

28 Morris, 1739, p. 20.

29 Barrell, 1990, p. 33.

30 Craske, 2009, p. 53.

31 Morris, 1739, p. 15.

32 Ibid., pp. 15–16.

33 On topographical viewing in the eighteenth century see Craske, 2000.

34 Howard, 1728.

35 Baker, 1706, 'Prologue'. He also wrote another dramatic comedy, *Tunbridge Walks* (1703), which seems to have achieved greater success, being reprinted at least nine times up until 1758.

36 Brewer, 1997, pp. 428–9.

37 Wilkes, 1747.

38 Cleland, 1760, pp. 5–6.

39 Morris, 1739, pp. 16–17.

40 Knight, 1794; Price, 1794.

41 Morris, 1739, p. 31.

42 Ibid., p. 35.

43 Defoe, [1724–6] 1971, p. 176.

44 Wricklemarsh (*c.*1724–7) was Sir Gregory Page's great Palladian mansion designed by John James, while Vanbrugh Castle (1718–26) was seen as bizarre at this date for its pioneering use of a mock-castle idiom.

45 On issues of defining community and neighbourhood in the period see Everitt, 1990.

46 SOL, 2012, pp. 135–7.

47 Monks, 2006.

48 Royal Collection online catalogue: www.royal-collection.org.uk – RCIN 405166, 401526, 405165, 401543, 405164, accessed 06/02/2013.

49 Grove Art Online, www.oxfordartonline.com, accessed 22/10/2010.

50 *ODNB.*

51 See Hyde, 1994.

52 Curl, 2011, p. 67.

53 Macaulay, 1975, p. 59.

54 Snodin, 2009, pp. 107, 112.

55 R. de Piles, *The Principles of Painting*, 1743, from Dixon Hunt and Willis, 1975, p. 113.

56 Ibid., p. 117. David Leatherbarrow discusses how Morris adapted de Piles's notion of 'situation' to architecture (1985, pp. 50–51).

57 His name is given as both Chatelaine and Chatelain, and his original surname was Philippe: *ODNB.* Also see Bryan, 1886; Strutt, 1785.

58 Hyde, 1994, pp. 27–8.

59 Bryan, 1886.

60 Lippincott, 1983, p. 137.

61 Ibid., pp. 135–8.

62 The inscription on the prints advertised that they were sold by Preist himself 'near the ferry at Chelsea' and W. H. Toms at Union Court, Hatton Garden, Holborn. They were reissued by John Bowles in 1742.

63 British Museum online catalogue: www.british-museum.org – BM 1919,0712.1-97, accessed 21/05/2008.

64 Redgrave, 1878.

65 Chatelain's design for the cover and four landscapes survive among the Chatelain prints in the British Museum.

66 Clayton, 1997, pp. 140–41.

67 Friedman, 2011; Clarke, 1966.

68 Clayton, 1997, pp. 157–61.

69 Bryan, 1886.

70 Later prints no longer bear Chatelain's name plus there is an anonymous oil painting of *c.*1750 based on Chatelain's *Fifty Views*; see Galinou and Hayes, 1996, p. 77.

71 Clayton, 1997, p. 163.

72 Bermingham, 1986, p. 84. On the creation of identity through prospect also see Williamson, 1995.

73 Raeburn, 1995, p. 136.

74 Ibid., p. 141, and ex-cat entries G45–6, 88–9, 117–31.

75 Ibid., p. 144, and ex-cat entries G211–17. Howitt lists twenty-seven views of Hampstead and Highgate from the Frog Service catalogue from Chatelain and other sources (Howitt, 1869, pp. 275–6).

76 Clayton, 1997, p. 100.

77 British Museum online catalogue: www.british-museum.org – BM 1923,0611.5.CR, accessed 06/02/2012.

78 Baker, 1995.

79 Dodsley, 1761, Preface.

80 Ibid.

81 Adams, 1983, p. 106.

82 Ibid., p. 106.

83 Fabricant, 1987, p. 259.

84 Bermingham, 1986, pp. 166–7.

85 On theories of the picturesque see Bermingham, 1986, Ch. 2; on tourism Andrews, 1989.

86 Gilpin did not publish a theory of the picturesque until his *Three Essays* in 1792.

87 Bermingham, 1986, p. 63.

88 *ODNB.*

89 Smith, 1797, p. 10.

90 Ibid., pp. 5–6.

91 Ibid., p. 6.

92 Ibid., pp. 8–9.

93 Ibid., p. 23.

94 Ibid., p. 12.

95 Galinou and Hayes, 1996, p. 168.

96 Bermingham, 1986, pp. 105–6. Constable sent several drawings of cottages that he had made on his walks in the London countryside to Smith for the project. None of them were included in the final volume, although Smith used a couple as the basis for his own engravings.

97 For the relationship between representations of landscape and enclosure see Barrell, 1980; Bermingham, 1986. For the political aspects of cottage design, particularly after the French Revolution the following year, see Ballantyne, 2004.

98 *ODNB.*

99 Boydell, *Autobiography*, p. 84, as quoted in *ODNB.*

100 Clayton, 1997, p. 198.

101 Ibid., p. 209.

102 The British Library copy (744 g.10) of Boydell, 1790 is from the royal bequest and has a note from Boydell pasted into the flyleaf: 'Mr Boydell's Respectful Compliments to Miss Banks . . . only Book that had the Honour of Marking a Lord Mayor of London'. 29 May 1792.

103 Lippincott, 1983, p.147.

104 Clayton, 1997, p. 262.

105 Ibid., p. 285.

106 Boydell, 'Advertisement', 1790, p. 4.

107 Boydell, 1790.

108 Clark, 2001, p. 247, Table 14.2. Other subject matter for which data are given include interiors, public and private buildings and open spaces.

109 Boydell, 'Advertisement', 1790, p. 4.

110 Clayton, 1997, p. 284.

111 Combe, 1794–6, Preface, vol. 1, p. ix.

112 Ibid., p. x; Burke, 1757.

113 Combe, 1794–6, vol. 1, p. xii.

114 Hunter, 1811, vol. 2, p. 54.

115 Bryant, 1996, pp. 15–18.

116 *ODNB*; Jacques, 1983, pp. 176–7.

117 Combe, 1794–6, vol. 1, p. xiii.

118 Hunter, 1811, vol. 2, p. 54.

119 De Bolla, 1995, p. 186.

120 For more on 'high' and 'low' definitions of landscape see Barrell, 1990.

121 Clayton, 1997; Lippincott, 1983, pp. 158–9.

122 Brewer, 1997, p. 459.

4 LANDSCAPES OF PLEASURE

1 De Certeau, 1984, p. 97.

2 Pennant, 1791, p. 251.

3 Habermas, 1989.

4 Borsay, 1989.

5 For Vauxhall see, among others, Borg and Coke, 2011; Ogborn, 1998; Solkin, 1993.

6 Wroth and Wroth 1896; Curl, 2010 and 2011, Ch. 8.

7 The standard books on the commodification of culture in the period include McKendrick, Brewer and Plumb, 1982; Brewer and Porter, 1993; Bermingham and Brewer, 1995; Brewer, 1997; Berg and Clifford, 1999.

8 Fabricant, 1987, p. 256.

9 Stow, [1598] 1987, p. 374.

10 Clark and Houston, 2000, p. 578.

11 Baker, 1736, p. 16.

12 Anon., *Foreigner's Guide*, 1740, pp. 10–12.

13 SOL, 2008, pp. 24–7; Curl, 2010, pp. 32, 77–9.

14 Curl, 2010; Barton, 1992, pp. 13–15.

15 Defoe, [1724–6] 1971, p. 287.

16 Anon., *Foreigner's Guide*, 1740, p. 148.

17 On the Islington spas see Wroth and Wroth, 1896; Curl, 2010; and SOL, 2008. Information on Islington from Nelson, 1811; Pinks, 1865; Richardson, 1988; VCH, 1988; Willats, 1988; SOL, 2008.

18 Nelson, 1811, p. 272.

19 The definitive account of Sadler's Wells's origins and building history is in SOL, 2008, Ch V. The theatrical history is covered in Arundell, 1965.

20 Elmes, 1827–30, p. 54.

21 Bermondsey Spa, for example, copied the lamps; see Curl, 2010, p. 180.

22 Wroth and Wroth, 1896, p. 62.

23 Donald, 1989.

24 *ODNB*.

25 Clayton, 1997, pp. 118–19.

26 Anon., *Islington*, 1733, pp. 4–5.

27 Langford, 1998, p. 3.

28 Barrell, 1990, pp. 20–21.

29 Girouard, 1978, p. 189.

30 Anon., *Tricks of the Town*, [1747] 1927, p. 27.

31 Ibid., p. 15.

32 Ibid., p. 53.

33 Ibid., Letter X, pp. 60–61.

34 Anon., *A Trip from St James's*, [1744] 1927, p. 229.

35 Clark and Houston, 2000, p. 582.

36 Baker, 1706, pp. 4, 59.

37 For more on this outer London development, particularly in relation to housing, see McKellar, 1996.

38 Anon., *Foreigner's Guide*, 1740, p. 146.

39 Arundell, 1965, p. 16.

40 As suggested by Forcer's insurance policy for 1732 (SOL, 2008, p. 12).

41 Arundell, 1965, pp. 10–11.

42 Quoted ibid., 1965, p. 15.

43 SOL, 2008, pp. 145–7. The Survey suggests that this wooden theatre may have been a reduced version of a more ambitious scheme, for which a drawing survives.

44 Wordsworth, 1850, BK VII, 'Residence in London', lines 267–72.

45 Quoted in Arundell, 1965, p. 31.

46 Colvin, 1948.

47 Information on Hampstead from VCH, 1989; Barratt, 1912; Farmer, 1984; Jenkins and Ditchburn, 1982; Park, 1814.

48 Thompson, 1974, p. 126.

49 Soame, 1734, pp. 26, 29.

50 Ibid., p. 48.

51 Ibid., p. 37.

52 Ibid., p. 27.

53 Defoe, [1724–6] 1971, p. 339.

54 Baker, 1706, p. 4.

55 Ibid., p. 16.

56 Ibid., p. 4.

57 Anon., *London in Miniature*, 1755, p. 250.

58 Curl, 2010, p. 127.

59 Thompson, 1974, p. 21.

60 Dodsley, 1761, p. 134.

61 Smith, 1828, p. 52.

62 Thorne, 1876, p. 285.

63 Port, 1995.

64 Anon., *London in Miniature*, 1755, p. 250.

65 Clark and Houston, 2000, p. 582.

66 Surviving images of the first Long Room, which was later converted to a chapel-of-ease, do not show a portico; see J. P. Emslie's watercolour of 1879 from the Camden Local Studies Collection.

67 Burney, [1778] 1903, p. 268.

68 Reference kindly provided by Timothy Clayton.

69 Anon., *Tricks of the Town*, [1747] 1927, Letter X, p. 55.

70 Smith, 1828, pp. 64–5.

71 Anon., *A Trip from St James's*, [1744] 1927, p. 246.

72 MacLean, Landry and Ward, 1999, p. 14.

73 Williams, 2001, pp. 194–6.

74 Anon., *A Sunday Ramble*, 1774, Title page.

75 Ibid., Introduction.

76 Curl, 2010, p. 149.

77 Smith, 1828, p. 17.

78 Lord later obtained land further west to which the club moved in 1811 before settling in its present home in St John's Wood in 1814.

79 Smith, 1828, p. 40.

80 Lysons, Collectanae, BL C.191.c.16, vol. II, p. 33.

81 Anon., *London in Miniature*, 1755, p. 181.

82 Snodin and Styles, 2001, pp. 252–3.

83 On conversation pieces see Retford, 2006; Solkin, 1993.

84 *The Gentleman's Magazine*, 1791, Part I, pp. 216–17, as quoted in Gomme, 1905, p. 222.

85 Curl, 2010, p. 144.

86 Smith, 1828, p. 143.

87 British Museum online catalogue: www.british-museum.org – BM 1891,0731.73, accessed 27/04/2012.

88 VCH, 1989, pp. 15–33.

89 Longstaffe-Gowan, 2001, pp. 173–81, discusses how gardens and rooms were transformed with hired plants and furniture for parties and balls.

90 BM 1891,10731.73.

91 *ODNB*.

5 LANDSCAPES OF MOBILITY

1 *ODNB*; MacLean et al., 1999, pp. 5–6.

2 Fairer and Gerrard, 1999, p. 1.

3 Defoe, [1724–6] 1971, p. 337.

4 Ibid., p. 338.

5 Ibid., p. 337.

6 Anon., *The Particulars and Inventories of the Estates of . . . South Sea Company*, 1721. The inventory reveals that Sawbridge also owned property in the City, farms in Hendon and the manor of Harty in Kent. For the latter see Hasted, 1798, vol. 6, pp. 276–83.

7 Defoe, [1724–6] 1971, p. 337.

8 Ibid., p. 159.

9 Bradley and Pevsner, 1997, pp. 61–2.

10 *ODNB*.

11 Norden, as quoted in Lloyd, 1888.

12 Cooper, 1999, pp. 109–28.

13 Ibid., p. 141.

14 Archer, 2005, Ch. 3, p. 94.

15 For more on this group see Cooper, 1999; Worsley, 1995, Ch. 1; Knight, 2009; Prosser and Worsley, 2007; Harwood, 2007; Peats, 2008.

16 Gauci, 2001, p. 23.

17 Defoe, [1724–6] 1971, p. 177.

18 Lee, 1677. Figures from Lee based on Gauci, 2001, p. 23.

19 Lippincott, 1983, p. 62; Tyack, 1982, p. 130.

20 *Daily Journal*, Friday, 13 March 1730, no. 2865.

21 Gauci, 2001.

22 Defoe, [1724–6] 1971, p. 57.

23 Woodhead, 1965.

24 Ibid., p. 127.

25 Ibid., p. 161; Lysons, 1792–6, vol. 3, p. 69.

26 Ibid., pp. 75, 33.

27 Ibid., p. 36.

28 Ibid., p. 92. Also see Strype, 1720, Bk 5, p. 148.

29 TNA MPE 1/245, pp. 50–51; see McKellar, 2011, p. 56.

30 Woodhead, 1965, p. 115.

31 Ibid., pp. 114–15.

32 Hearn, 2004.

33 VCH, 1989, pp. 91–111.

34 Defoe, [1724–6] 1971, pp. 167–8.

35 Anon., *The Inventories and Particulars of the Estates of . . . South Sea Company*, 1721. The contents of Fellowes' London house were valued at £604 and his Carshalton house at £753. See Galinou, 2004, p. 39.

36 Glanville and Glanville, 2004, p. 12 and Appendix 1.

37 Gauci, 2007, p. 93.

38 Rogers, 1990, p. 282.

39 Strype, 1720, as quoted in Gauci, 2007, p. 10.

40 W. J. Pinks, *The History of Clerkenwell*, London, 1865, p. 11, as quoted in Woodhead, 1965, p. 46.

41 As quoted in Harding, 2001, pp. 133–5.

42 Pepys, 1970–83, 31 July 1665.

43 Hotson, 2004, p. 140.

44 Cherry and Pevsner, 1991, p. 338 and fig. 23.

45   Wortley, 2004.

46   Ibid., p. 100.

47   Ackerman, 1990.

48   Evelyn, *Diary*, 1645, II, 401, as quoted in the *OED*.

49   Cooper, 2007; Archer, 1985; Archer, 2005, Ch. 2; Airs and Tyack, 2007.

50   As quoted in Archer, 1985, p. 60.

51   Colvin and Newman, 1981, p. 62.

52   *OED*, giving a date of 1755 for this quote.

53   For example, Clark and Houston, 2000, pp. 603–4, write of the first suburban villas being discovered by the urban elite c.1800.

54   Wittkower, 1974. For a discussion of this seminal work see McKellar, 2004.

55   Henry Aldrich, *The Elements of Civil Architecture*, London, 1789, pp. 63–4, as quoted in Archer, 1985, p. 178.

56   Williams, 2001, pp. 196, 198–9, 210.

57   Norden, as quoted in Prickett, 1842, p. 11.

58   *Domestick Intelligence or News Both from City and Country*, Friday, 8 August 1679, no. 10.

59   Defoe, [1724–6] 1971, p. 339.

60   Thompson, 1974, p. 27.

61   Varley, 1933, p. 9. Also see Thompson, 2001.

62   On Chelsea see VCH, 2004, 'Landownership', pp. 107–45; on the shift in Greenwich from a royal to a middle-class suburb see McKellar, 2011.

63   McKellar, 1999a, Chs 1–3; Stone, 1980.

64   Barron, 1969.

65   Thorne, 1876, p. 355.

66   Noorthhouck, 1773, p. 615.

67   Boswell, 1950, pp. 70–71. After this high-minded start, Boswell's thoughts turn to the sexual promise of the city with a typically earthy ditty.

68   Defoe, [1724–6] 1971, p. 338.

69   Williams, 2001, p. 199.

70   Hunter, 1811, vol. 2, p. 86.

71   Defoe, [1724–6] 1971, p. 338.

72   VCH, 1980, pp. 122–39.

73   Guillery, 2001.

74   Massie, 1754, p. 15. For more on this in the early nineteenth century see Donald, 1999.

75   Gwynn, 1766, pp. 18–20.

76   *English Post with News Foreign and Domestick*, 15–17 July 1702. Also see *Flying Post or The Post Master*, 14–16 Dec. 1699.

77   Lloyd, 1888, p. 199.

78   *Post Man and the Historical Account*, 23–26 August 1701; *Daily Courant*, Monday, 20 May 1706.

79   For examples, see SOL, 1936; Richardson, 1983, pp. 43–148; McKellar, 1999a, pp. 182–3. Guillery, 2004, pp. 244–7.

80   SOL, 1926.

81   Summerson, 1983, p. 163.

82   This is still an understudied type, on which see Summerson, 1988, Ch. 4; McKellar, 1999a, pp. 174–80; Cherry, 1993; Galinou, 2004.

83   Richardson, 1983, pp. 194–5.

84   Defoe, [1724–6] 1971, p. 338.

85   Richardson, 1983, pp. 194–5.

86   Anon., *London in Miniature*, 1755, p. 253.

87   Richardson, 1983, p. 47 and p. 71 for a drawing of c.1688 which shows the original building before Ashurst transformed it.

88   Defoe, [1724–6] 1971, pp. 175–6.

89   Summerson, 1995.

90   William Blake, *The State and Case of a Design for the Better Education of Thousands of Parish Children Successively in the Vast Northern Suburbs of London*, c.1688, as quoted in Thorne, 1876, pp. 349–50.

91   For a similar process in relation to Hoxton, see McKellar, 1996.

92   For other early eighteenth-century examples elsewhere, principally Southside House, Wimbledon, see Miele, 1999, p. 48.

93   Richardson, 1989, pp. 124–5.

94   McKellar, 1999a, pp. 180–3; Guillery, 2004, especially Chs 4 and 7.

95   For examples see McKellar, 2011, on Greenwich; Guillery, 2004, pp. 258–61, on 56–8 Peckham High Street.

96   Barber, Cox and Curwen, 1993, pp. 10–11.

97   McKellar, 1999a, p. 52.

98   *London Gazette*, 27–30 June, 1687.

99   PRO C54/4661/10/4/no. 31. Reproduced in Barber, Cox and Curwen, 1993, pp. 62–4, plus a plan of the house based on the inventory, pp. 32–3.

100 Glanville, 2004, p. 13.

101 Howitt, 1869, p. 382.

102 Barber, Cox and Curwen, 1993, p. 21.

103 Knight, 2009, pp. 208–10.

104 Woodhead, 1965, p. 148.

105 *ODNB*.

106 Saint, 1991.

107 Information kindly supplied by Claire Gapper; see Gapper, 1998, Chs 4 and 5.

108 For example, the East India Company at Home project covers country houses and the period 1757–1857; see, www.warwick.ac.uk/go/eastindiacompanyathome.

109 Fishman, 1987, Ch. 2, p. 39.

110 Archer, 2005, pp. 87–92.

111 Guillery, 2004, Ch. 3; McKellar, 2012; George, 1976, pp. 176–95.

6 LANDSCAPES OF SELECTIVITY

1   Schwarz, 2000, p. 650.

2   Sheppard, Belcher and Cotterell, 1979.

3   Fishman, 1987, Ch. 2.

4   Gerhold, 2009.

5   Summerson, 1988, Ch. 12, 'Great Estates: I'.

6   Dyos, 1954, p. 70.

7   Rogers, 1990, p. 285.

8   Thompson, 1974, p. 56.

9   Davidoff and Hall, 1987, Ch. 8.

10   Kalm, [1892] 2010, p. 174.

11   Fishman, 1987, pp. 51–62.

12   For the architecture of these houses and a wealth of information on south London villa development more broadly, see SOL, 2013, especially Ch. 17. I am grateful to Peter Guillery for letting me see manuscript copies of the relevant chapters prior to publication.

13   Confusingly Cowper wrote two poems both titled 'Retirement', the second in 1782.

14   *OED*.

15   Clark and Houston, 2000, p. 613.

16   Gywnn, 1766, p. 118.

17   See McKellar, 1999a, Ch. 1.

18   Byrd, 1978; Lindsay, 1978.

19   Stow, [1598] 1987.

20   Evelyn, 1661, p. 25.

21   Gwynn, 1766, frontispiece.

22   Ibid., p. 14.

23   Ibid., p. 16.

24   Jenner, 1995; Sennett, 1994.

25   Middleton, 1798, pp. 42–3.

26   Bowden, Brown and Smith, 2009, p. 8.

27   Lysons, 1811, p. 447.

28   Lloyd, 1888, pp. 6–7.

29   Thompson, 1974, p. 13.

30   Archer, 1985.

31   Asgill, however, did not envisage maintaining his new villa as a family estate and anticipated its sale or rental in his will. PROB 11/1169/423, as quoted in Rogers, 1990, p. 284.

32   Colvin, 1995.

33   Lea, Miele and Higgott, 2011, pp. 16–20. Danson House was restored by English Heritage with recreated eighteenth-century interiors and is one of the best places to see a second generation Palladian villa. It is opened and run by the Bexley Heritage Trust.

34   Archer, 1985, p. 65.

35   Lugar, 1805, p. 15.

36   Ibid., pp. 4, 15.

37   See Guillery, 2004, Ch. 5, on the Mile End Road and the Kingsland Road, both in east London.

38 See Archer, 1985, pp. 71–7, for its 'scant' treatment in the contemporary literature.

39 Elmes, 1827, p. 26.

40 Papworth, 1818, p. 29.

41 Loudon, 1838, pp. 9–10.

42 Cherry and Pevsner, 1983, p. 393.

43 *OED*.

44 Elmes, 1827–30, p. 26.

45 Lloyd, 1756.

46 Donald, 1989, p. 761.

47 Fairer, 1999.

48 Anon., *London in Miniature*, 1755, p. 250.

49 Banham, 1971.

50 Bartell, 1804, p. 63.

51 Papworth, 1818, pp. v–vi.

52 Ibid.

53 Colvin, 1995, pp. 34–45; Wilton-Ely, 1977.

54 Abramson, 2004.

55 Laing, 1800, p. vii.

56 Ibid., p. v.

57 Archer, 1985, pp. 5, 75.

58 For Kingsland Road see Guillery, 2004, pp. 184–8, and for Kennington Road, Miele, 1999, pp. 48–9.

59 Searles produced earlier, less polished versions at the New Kent Road, Southwark, from 1788 and Gloucester Circus, Greenwich, c.1791; see Bonwitt, 1987.

60 Loudon, 1835, p. 472.

61 Corfield, 1995.

62 Boulton, 2000, pp. 326, 346.

63 Corfield, 1995, pp. 82, 217, Tables 4.2 and 8.2.

64 Boyle, 1798, p. 123.

65 Thompson, 1974, pp. 29–30.

66 Daniels, 1999, pp. 213–28.

67 Howitt, 1869, p. 331.

68 Colvin, 1995; Bendall, 1997; Galinou, 2010, p. 482.

69 Westminster archives, D/Wh/18, refers to him as a carpenter; for subsequent leases see D/Wh/1–3.

70 Lysons, 1792–6, vol. 3, p. 330.

71 Gwynn, 1766, pp. x–xi.

72 As quoted in Clark and Houston, 2000, p. 583.

73 Wakefield, 1793, 'Alphabetical List of the Artists'. The directory was originally to cover only ten miles but was extended.

74 Bonehill and Daniels, 2009, p. 48.

75 SOL, 2012, pp. 245–7.

76 Archer, 1985, pp. 109–10.

77 For the longer history of such combined dwellings see Hollis, 2011.

78 Loudon, 1838, pp. 325–49; Simo, 1988, Ch. 15.

79 Ibid., p. 351.

80 Ibid., p. 352.

81 *ODNB*.

82 The bulk of his practice correspondence in the Westminster archives is headed with his Devonshire Place address with the occasional letter from Two Waters.

83 The Grimm drawing can be found at BL Add mss 15542 fol. 139.

84 Bartell, 1804, p. 61.

85 Smith, 1828, p. 65.

86 *ODNB*.

87 Hassell, 1819, p. 30.

88 Ibid., p. 1.

89 Ibid., p. 3.

90 For a discussion of this practice see McKellar, 1999a, pp. 75–8.

91 VCH, 1989, pp. 198–9.

92 Ibid., p. 231.

93 Ibid.

94 Colvin.

95 Galinou, 2010, p. 482, citing a letter of 1844 from that address in the Eyre archives. She also suggests that he may have had an office in Bedford Row at some point (p. 59).

96 Ibid., pp. 142, 147, 451, 474, 480, 482.

97 19 April 1807, Correspondence John Heaton (solicitor to the Duke of Portland) and John White, Westminster archives, D/Wh/70–71.

98 Colvin, 1995 says that the house was demolished in 1820 but seems to have been unaware of the Shepherd views, citing only the Grimm drawing in the British Library.

99 For an alternative view locating the beginning of privacy in the late seventeenth-century urban environment, see Heyl, 2002.

100 Aries, 1962; Rybczynski, 1986.

101 Lloyd, 1754.

102 Cary, 1790, 'Advertisement'.

103 Bryant, 1996.

104 As Bryant, 1986, p. 101, outlines, the artist Joseph Farington was one of the last to record a ride around the Heath which incorporated views of Kenwood as part of the normal route. See Garlick and Macintyre, 1978, p. 97.

105 Gwynn, 1766, pp. 117–18.

106 Lea, Miele and Higgott, 2011, p. 68.

107 Guillery and Snodin, 1995, pp. 117–23.

108 As quoted in Daniels, 1999, p. 220.

109 Leach, 2008.

110 Gilpin, 1798, p. 68.

111 Bryant, 1986, p. 122, relates how Lady Mansfield and Lady Southampton had several fallings out due to their rivalry over their respective dairy herds.

112 Farmer, 1982.

113 Prickett, 1842, p. 79.

114 Richardson, 1983, p. 84.

115 Ibid.

116 Loudon, 1838, p. 653.

117 Ibid., pp. 661–2.

118 Papworth, 1818, p. 67.

119 Read, 2000, p. 620.

120 For a discussion of these themes in a different location see Abbott, 2010.

121 Wood, 1781, p. 2.

122 Kent, 1775, pp. 242–3.

123 For the plan see Guillery, 2004, p. 257.

124 Wood, 1781, p. 17.

125 Ibid., p. 30.

126 Reynolds, Thirteenth 'Discourse on Art', as quoted in Bartell, 1804, pp. 125–6.

127 Lugar, 1805, p. 5.

128 For more on cottages see Archer, 1985, pp. 67–71; Darley, 1975; Ballantyne, 2004, 2011.

129 Papworth, 1818, p. 25.

130 Lugar, 1805, p. 21.

131 Ibid., p. 11.

132 Ibid., p. 12.

133 Papworth, 1818, pp. 12, 22–3. On the moral and political context of cottages see Ballantyne, 2004.

134 Farmer, 1984, pp. 30–2.

135 Lloyd, 1888, p. 102.

136 Loudon, 1838, p. 349.

137 Plaw, 1800, Plate XI.

138 Cobbett, 1830, as quoted in Bermingham, 1986, p. 74.

139 Walton Hall is now the home of the Open University.

140 Loudon, 1838, p. 10.

7 LANDSCAPES OF TRANSITION

1 Sheppard, Belcher and Cotterell, 1979.

2 Schwarz, 2000, p. 650.

3 Schwarz, 1992, p. 8.

4 Lysons, 1811, p. 259.

5 Ibid., 'General View of the Increase of Population within 12 Miles of London, from Fifteen to Eighteen or Twenty Years Past', p. 449.

6 Dyos, 1966.

7 VCH, 1989, p. 177.

8 Lysons, 1811, p. 449.

9 Ibid., pp. 158–61.

10 Ibid., p. 286.

11 Ibid., p. 163.

12 Ibid., p. 146.

13 Ibid., p. 153.

14 Ibid., p. 446.

15 Ibid., p. 447.

16 Ibid., p. 447.
17 Ibid., p. 128.
18 Ibid., p. 120.
19 Ibid., pp. 157–8.
20 Ibid., p. 92; Fox, 1992, no. 156.
21 For the history of Regent's Park see Saunders, 1969; Summerson, 1977 and 1980; Crook, 1992 and 2013; Tyack, 1993 and 2013. I am extremely grateful to Geoffrey Tyack for his helpful comments on this chapter in draft and for allowing me to read the relevant chapters in manuscript from his 2013 collection on Nash prior to publication.
22 Saunders, 1969, pp. 48, 90–1.
23 Smith, 1845, p. 23.
24 Laxton, 1999.
25 Glanville, 1972, p. 167.
26 Gwynn, 1766, p. viii.
27 Ibid.
28 Galinou, 2010.
29 Lysons, 1792–6, vol. 3, pp. 336–7.
30 Lysons, 1811, p. 228.
31 Saunders, 1969, pp. 64–6.
32 Lysons, 1811, p. 241.
33 Smith, 1828, pp. 188–9.
34 Ibid., p. 189.
35 Crook, 1992, p. 79.
36 Crook, 2013, p. 76. For Wyatt's possible early contribution and for another variant of White's 1809 schemes, see Anderson, 2001.
37 Crook, 2013, p. 75.
38 Lysons, 1811, pp. 123–4.
39 Ibid., p. 225.
40 Ibid., pp. 225–6.
41 Anderson, 2001, p. 107.
42 TNA MPI 1/575/5 C.1814, 'Mr White and Duke of Hamilton's House and Proposed Plantation between them and New Road to North', and associated documents show White's attempts to negotiate with the Crown to create a green barrier between his property and the new scheme.

43 TNA CRES 2/746, as quoted in Anderson, 1998, p. 258.
44 Summerson, 1980, p. 72.
45 White, 1814, p. 98.
46 Ibid., pp. 20, 23.
47 Crook, 2013, pp. 78–9.
48 See McKellar 1999a, Ch. 9; Lubbock, 1995, Ch. 1.
49 White, 1814, p. 25.
50 Ibid.
51 Ibid., p. 19.
52 Fishman, 1987, pp. 65–71; Tyack, 1993; Crook 1992, p. 87.
53 Crook, 2013, p. 77.
54 Saunders, 1969, pp. 72–7.
55 As quoted in Tyack, 1993, p. 68.
56 White, 1814, p. 29.
57 Ibid., p. 30.
58 Summerson, 1977, p. 61. In this article he reproduces the first plan and all the drawings for the panorama from the National Archives.
59 TNA CRES 2/742, as quoted in Crook, 1992, p. 81.
60 Howgego, 1978, p. 3.
61 ODNB.
62 Adams, 1983, p. xxii.
63 Anderson, 2009.
64 Saunders, 1969, pp. 48, 90–1.
65 Ibid., pp. 146–7.
66 For James Burton see Arnold, 1996 and 2005, Chs 1–3.
67 Crook, 2013, p. 82.
68 Repton, 1794, p. 1.
69 Elmes, 1827–30, p. 21.
70 As quoted in Crook, 2013, p. 82.
71 Elmes, 1827–30, p. 20.
72 Ibid., p. 20.
73 Ibid., p. 157.
74 Saunders, 1969, pp. 133–4.
75 White, 1814, p. 34.
76 Summerson, 1980, p. 73.
77 Crook, 2013, p. 83.

78 Anderson, 1998, p. 175.
79 Saunders, 1969, p. 145.
80 Longman and Walrond, 1894, Ch. XIV.
81 Egan, [1821] 1869, pp. 250–1.
82 Ibid., p. 253.
83 TNA CRES 3/742, as quoted in Crook 1992, p. 81.
84 Elmes, 1827–30, p. 11.
85 Ibid., p. 34.
86 Ibid., p. 47.
87 Ibid., p. 19.
88 Ibid., p. 29.
89 McCreery, 2005.
90 Arnold, 2000, Ch. 1, especially pp. 1–5.
91 Anon., *Picturesque Guide*, 1829, p. 33.
92 See Hebbert and McKellar, 2008.
93 Anon., *Picturesque Guide*, 1829, p. 33.
94 Ibid.
95 Ibid.
96 Ibid.
97 Fox, 1992, pp. 355–6.
98 For more on centrifugal viewing see Daniels, 1993.
99 Elmes, 1827–30, p. 80.
100 Ibid., p. 81.
101 Ibid.
102 Anon., *Picturesque Guide*, 1829, pp. 40–41.
103 Ibid., p. 18.
104 Ibid., p. 46.
105 Ibid., p. 38.
106 Saunders, 1969, pp. 149–51.
107 This building was distinct from the Swiss Cottage which was erected in the 1837 at the junction of Finchley and Avenue Roads and went on to give its name to the north-west London district that was built around it. See Galinou, 2010, p. 211.
108 Colvin, 1948.
109 Howitt, 1869, p. 327.
110 Fishman, 1987; Archer, 2005.
111 Banham, 1971, Ch. 8.

BIBLIOGRAPHY

MANUSCRIPT SOURCES

BL, C.191.c16, vols 1 and 2 Daniel Lysons, 'Collectanea'

BL Add mss 15542 Middlesex Drawings by Samuel Henry Grimm

Bod G. Pamph. 1960 (2) John Stockdale, 'Proposals for Publishing by Subscription a Description of London and the Circumjacent Country', 1797

D/Wh Westminster archives John White file

TNA MPI 1/575/1–7 Maps and Plans relating to Regent's Park and John White

TNA MPEE 1/57/1–4 Plans of Marylebone Park

TNA MR 1/11082/2 Plan of Marylebone Park, Leverton and Chawner, 1811

TNA MPE 1/913 Plan of Parish of St Marylebone with Improvements, John White, 1809

TNA MPE/911 Plans for Park Village, John Nash, 1823

TNA MPE 1/329 and 1/245 Survey of Crown Lands in the Royal Manor of Greenwich, Samuel Travers, 1695–7

CONTEMPORARY PRINTED SOURCES

Capitalization and italicization have been standardized to modern usage here and in the text.

Adam, R., and J. Adam, *The Works in Architecture of Robert and James Adam*, nos I–III, London, 1773–5.

Anon., *The Particulars and Inventories of the Estates of the Late Sub-Governor, Deputy-Governor and Directors of the South Sea Company*, London, 1721.

Anon., *The Foreigner's Guide: Or, a Necessary and Instructive Companion Both for the Foreigner and Native, in their Tour through the Cities of Westminster and London*, London, 1729, revised 1740.

Anon., *London Described or the most noted Regular Buildings both Publick and Private with the Views of Several Squares in the Liberties of London and Westminster*, published by John Bowles with engravings by Sutton Nicholls, London, 1731.

Anon., *Islington: Or, The Humours of New Tunbridge Wells*, London, 1733.

Anon., *A Trip Through the Town* (1735), reprinted in *Eighteenth Century Diversions: Tricks of the Town*, London, Chapman and Hall, 1927, pp. 111–82.

Anon., *A Trip from St James's to the Royal-Exchange* (1744), reprinted in *Eighteenth Century Diversions: Tricks of the Town*, London, Chapman and Hall, 1927, pp. 183–256.

Anon., *Tricks of the Town Laid Open: Or, a Companion for Country Gentlemen*, London (1747), reprinted in *Eighteenth Century Diversions: Tricks of the Town*, London, Chapman and Hall, 1927, pp. 1–110.

Anon., *London in Miniature: The Whole collected from Stow, Maitland . . . Intended as a Complete Guide to Foreigners*, London, 1755.

Anon., *The London and Westminster Guide, Through the Cities and Suburbs*, London 1768.

Anon., *The Ambulator: Or, The Stranger's Companion in a Tour round London, within the Circuit of Twenty Five Miles*, London, 1774 and later eds.

Anon., *A Sunday Ramble: Or, Modern Sabbath-Day Journey; In and about the Cities of London and Westminster*, London, 1774.

Anon., *A Picturesque Guide to the Regent's Park with Accurate Descriptions*, London, 1829.

Baird, T., *A General View of the Agriculture of the County of Middlesex: With Observations on the Means of its Improvement*, London, 1793.

Baker, T., *Tunbridge Walks: Or, The Yeoman of Kent; a Comedy. As it is acted at the Theatre Royal by Her Majesty's Servants*, London, 1703.

—, *Hampstead Heath: A Comedy. As it was acted at the Theatre-Royal in Drury Lane*, London, 1706.

—, *Tunbridge Walks: Or, The Yeoman of Kent. A Comedy*, London, 1736.

Bartell, E., *Hints for Picturesque Improvements in Ornamented Cottages*, London, 1804.

Boswell, J., *London Journal 1762–3*, ed. F. Pottle, Harmondsworth, Penguin, 1950.

Boydell, J., *A Collection of Views in England and Wales, Drawn and Engraved by John Boydell*, London, 1790.

Boyle, P., *Boyle's City Companion to the Court Guide for the Year 1798*, London, 1798.

Boys, J., *A General View of the Agriculture of the County of Kent: With Observations on the Means of its Improvement*, London, 1796.

Brice, G., *Description nouvelle de ce qui'il ya de plus remarquable dans la Ville de Paris*, Paris, 1684.

Burke, E., *A Philosophical Enquiry into the Origin of our Ideas of the Sublime and the Beautiful*, London, 1757.

Burney, F., *Evelina; Or, The History of a Young Lady's Entrance into the World* (1778), London, Macmillan, 1903.

Cary, J., *The Country Fifteen Miles Round London*, London, 1786.

—, *Survey of High Roads from London*, London, 1790.

—, *Cary's new itinerary, or, An accurate delineation of the great roads*, London 1798.

Chalmers, A., *General Biographical Dictionary*, 32 vols, London, 1812–17.

Cleland, J., *The Romance of a Day: Or, an Adventure in Greenwich Park*, London, 1760.

Cobbett, W., *Rural Rides* (1830), 2 vols, London, 1912.

Colsoni, F., *The New Trismagister* (1688), ed. R. C. Alston, Menston, Scolar Press, 1972.

—, *Le guide de Londres* (1693), London, 1693, ed. W. Godfrey, London, London Topographical Society, 1951.

—, *La clef-dor de la langue Angloise*, London, 1699a.

—, *The English Ladies New French Grammar*, London, 1699b.

Combe, W., *An History of the River Thames*, 2 vols, London, 1794–6.

Cotgrave, R., and J. Howell, *A French-English Dictionary, compiled by Mr Randall Cotgrave: With another in English and French; Whereunto are newly added the Animadversions, and Supplements &c. of James Howell Esquire*, London, 1650.

Crouch, N. (R.B.), *Historical Remarques and Observations of the Ancient and Present State of London and Westminster*, London, 1681.

Defoe, D., *A Tour through the Whole Island of Great Britain* (1724–6), ed. P. Rogers, Harmondsworth, Penguin, 1971.

De Laune, T., *The Present State of London: Or, Memorials, Comprehending a Full and Succinct Account of the Ancient and Modern State Thereof*, London, 1681.

Dodsley, R., *London and its Environs Described*, London, 1761.

Egan, P., *Life in London: The Day and Night Scenes of Jerry Hawthorn Esq. and his Elegant Friend Corinthian Tom, accompanied by Bob Logic, the Oxonian, in their Rambles and Sprees through the Metropolis* (1821), London, 1869.

Elmes, J., *Metropolitan Improvements or London in the Nineteenth Century: Being a Series of Views of the New and Most Interesting Objects in the British Metropolis and its Vicinity*, London, 1827–30.

Evelyn, J., *Fumifugium: Or, The Inconvenience of the Aer and Smoak of London Dissipated*, London, 1661.

Faulkener, T., *Historical and Topographical Description of Chelsea and its Environs*, London, 1810.

—, *Historical and Topographical Description of Fulham*, London, 1813.

Florio, J., *His Firste Fruites*, London, 1578.

—, *Florios Second Frutes*, London, 1591.

Foot, P., *General View of the Agriculture of the County of Middlesex: With Observations on the Means of their Improvement . . . Drawn up for the Consideration of the Board of Agriculture*, London, 1794.

Gilpin, W., *Three Essays: On Picturesque Beauty, Picturesque Travel, and on Sketching Landscape*, London, 1792.

—, *Observations on the Western Part of England, relative chiefly to Picturesque Beauty*, London, 1798.

Gwynn, J., *London and Westminster Improved*, London, 1766.

Hassell, J., *Tour of the Grand Junction, Illustrated in a Series of*

Engravings: With an Historical and Topographical Description, London, 1819.

Hasted, E., *The History and Topographical Survey of the County of Kent*, 12 vols, Canterbury, 1797–1801.

Hatton, E., A *New View of London; Or, an Ample Account of that City . . . Being a more Particular Description thereof than has hitherto been known to be published in any City in the World . . . A Book Useful not only for Strangers, but for the Inhabitants, and for All Lovers of Antiquity . . .*, 2 vols, London, 1708.

Howard, E., *Greenwich-Park: Humbly Inscribed to his Grace the Duke of Montagu*, London, 1728.

Howell, J., *Londinopolis: An Historicall Discourse or Perlustration of the City of London . . . whereunto is added another of the City of Westminster*, London, 1657.

—, *Lexicon Tetraglotton*, London, 1660.

Hunter, H., *The History of London and its Environs . . . Likewise an Account of all the Towns, Villages and Country, within Twenty-five Miles of London*, 2 vols, London, 1811.

Kalm, P., *Kalm's Account of his Visit to England: On his Way to America in 1748*, (1892) Memphis, General Books, 2010.

Kent, N., *Hints to Gentlemen of Landed Property*, London, 1775.

Knight, R. P., *The Landscape: A Didactic Poem*, London, 1794.

Laing, D., *Hints for Dwellings, consisting of Original Designs for Cottages, Farm Houses, Villas, etc.*, London, 1800.

Lee, S., *A Collection of the Names of the Merchants living in and about the City of London*, London, 1677.

Lloyd, R., 'Letter, on the Villas of our Tradesmen', *Connoisseur*, 33, 1754.

—, 'The Cit's Country Box', *Connoisseur*, 135, 1756.

Loudon J. C., *Architectural Magazine*, no. 2, 1835.

—, *The Suburban Gardener and Villa Companion*, London, 1838.

Lugar, R., *Architectural Sketches for Cottages, Rural Dwellings and Villas, in the Grecian, Gothic and Fancy Styles with Plans, Suitable to Persons of Genteel Life and Moderate Fortune*, London, 1805.

Lysons, D., *The Environs of London, Being an Historical Account of the Towns, Villages and Hamlets, within Twelve Miles of that Capital with Biographical Anecdotes*, 4 vols, London, 1792–6.

—, *An Historical Account of Those Parishes in the County of Middlesex, which are not described in The Environs of London*, London, 1800.

—, *Supplement to the First Edition of the Historical Account of the Environs of London*, London, 1811.

Maitland, W., *History and Survey of London from its Foundation to the Present Time*, 2 vols, London, 1756.

Massie, J., *An Essay on the Many Advantages accruing to the Community, from the Superior Neatness, Conveniences, Decorations and Embellishments of Great and Capital Cities: Particularly applied to the City and Suburbs of London, Renowned Capital of the British Empire*, London, 1754.

Middleton, J., *View of the Agriculture of Middlesex: With Observations on the Means of Their Improvement . . . Drawn up for the Consideration of the Board of Agriculture*, London, 1798.

Morris, R. (Anon.), *An Essay upon Harmony*, London, 1739.

Moule, T., 'Prospectus for The English Counties Delineated', *Berkshire* (individual series of county maps), 1830.

—, *The English Counties Delineated* (collected and bound series of county maps), London, 1837.

Mountfort, W., *Greenwich-Park: A Comedy; Acted at the Theatre Royal by Their Majesties Servants*, London, 1691.

Nelson, J., *History, Topography and Antiquities of St Mary's, Islington*, London, 1811.

Noorthhouck, J., *A New History of London, including Westminster and Southwark*, London, 1773.

Papworth, J. B., *Rural Residences*, London, 1818.

Park, J. L., *The Topography and Natural History of Hampstead*, London, 1814.

Pennant, T., *Some Account of London*, London, 1791.

Pepys, S., *The Diary of Samuel Pepys: A New and Complete Transcription*, ed. R. Latham and W. Matthews, 11 vols, London, G. Bell, 1970–83.

Plaw, J., *Ferme Ornée; or Rural improvements, a series of domestic and ornamental designs*, London, 1795.

—, *Rural Architecture; or Designs, from the simple cottage to the decorated villa*, London, 1796.

—, *Sketches for Country Houses, Villas and Rural Dwellings*, London, 1800, 1803.

Price, U., *An Essay on the Picturesque*, London, 1794.

Prickett, F., *The History and Antiquities of Highgate, Middlesex with Illustrations*, London, published by the Author, 1842.

Ralph, J., *A Critical Review of the Publick Buildings, Statues and Ornaments of London and Westminster*, London, 1734.

Repton, H., *Sketches and Hints on Landscape Gardening*, London, 1794.

Robinson, W., *The History and Antiquities of the Parish of Tottenham High Cross*, London, 1818.

—, *The History and Antiquities of the Parish of Edmonton*, London, 1819.

—, *The History and Antiquities of the Parish of Stoke Newington*, London, 1820.

Rocque, J., *Proposals . . . for Engraving and Publishing by Subscription a New and Accurate Map of the Country Adjacent to the Cities and Liberties of London, Westminster, and Borough of Southwark*, 1741.

Smith, J. T., *Remarks on Rural Scenery: With Twenty Etchings of Cottages from Nature and Some Observations and Precepts relative to the Picturesque*, London, 1797.

—, *Nollekens and His Times*, London, 1828.

—, *A Book for a Rainy Day: Or, Recollections of the Events of the Years 1766–1833*, London, 1845.

Smollett, T., *The Expedition of Humphrey Clinker* (1771), ed. J. L. Thorson, New York and London, W. W. Norton and Co., 1983.

Soame, J., *Hampstead Wells: Or, Directions for the Drinking of those Waters*, London, 1734.

Stow, J., *The Survey of London* (1598), ed. H. B. Wheatley, London and Melbourne, Dent, 1987.

Strutt, J., *A Biographical Dictionary: Containing an Historical Account of All the Engravers*, London, 1785.

Strype, J., *The Survey of London*, enlarged edn of John Stow, 2 vols, London, 1720.

Wakefield, R., *Wakefield's Merchant and Tradesman's General Directory for London, Westminster, Borough of Southwark and Twenty-Two Miles Circular from St Paul's*, London, 1793.

Ward, E., *A Frolick to Horn-fair: With a Walk from Cuckold's-Point thro' Deptford and Greenwich*, London, 1700.

—, *The London Spy Compleat in Eighteen Parts*, 4th ed., London, 1709.

White, J., *Some Account of the Proposed Improvements of the Western Part of London, by the Formation of the Regent's Park, the New Street, the New Sewer, &C. &C. Illustrated by Plans and Accompanied by Critical Observations*, London, 1814.

Wilkes, W., *Hounslow-Heath: A Poem*, London, 1747.

Wood, J., the younger, *A Series of Plans for Cottages or Habitations of the Labourer*, Bath, 1781.

Wordsworth, W., *The Prelude; Or, Growth of a Poet's Mind; An Autobiographical Poem*, New York, 1850.

SECONDARY SOURCES

Abbott, S., 'Urban meets Rural: A Study of Three Eighteenth-Century Retreats on the Isle of Wight', in A. Ballantyne (ed.), *Rural and Urban: Architecture between Two Cultures*, London and New York, Routledge, 2010, pp. 70–88.

Abramson, D. M., 'Commercialization and Backlash in Late Georgian Architecture', in B. Arciszewska and E. McKellar (eds), *Articulating British Classicism: New Approaches to Eighteenth-Century Architecture*, Aldershot and Burlington, Vt, Ashgate, 2004, pp. 143–61.

—, *Building the Bank of England: Money, Architecture, Society. 1694–1942*, New Haven and London, Yale University Press, 2005.

Ackerman, J. S., *The Villa: Form and Ideology of Country Houses*, London, Thames and Hudson, 1990.

Adams, B., *London Illustrated 1604–1851*, London, Library Association, 1983.

Airs, M. and G. Tyack (eds), *The Renaissance Villa in Britain 1500–1700*, Reading, Spire Books, 2007.

Albert, W. I., *The Turnpike Road System in England 1663–1840*, Cambridge, Cambridge University Press, 1972.

Allen, B., 'Topography or Art: Canaletto in London', in *The Image of London*, exh. cat., London, Barbican Art Gallery, 1987, pp. 29–48.

Anderson, J., 'Marylebone Park and the New Street: A Study of the Development of Regent's Park and the Building of Regent's Street, London, in the First Quarter of the Nineteenth Century', PhD thesis, Courtauld Institute of Art, 1998.

—, 'John White Senior and James Wyatt: An Early Scheme for Marylebone Park and the New Street to Carlton House', *Architectural History*, vol. 44, 2001, pp. 106–14.

—, 'The Prince Regent's Role in the Creation and Development of Regent Street and Regent's Park', *Georgian Group Journal*, vol. 17, 2009, pp. 107–14.

Andrews, J. H., 'Defoe and the Sources of his *Tour*', *Geographical Journal*, vol. 126, no. 3, 1960, pp. 268–77.

Andrews, M., *The Search for the Picturesque: Landscape, Aesthetics and Tourism in Britain, 1760–1800*, Aldershot, Scolar Press, 1989.

Archer, J., *The Literature of British Domestic Architecture 1715–1842*, Cambridge, Mass., and London, MIT Press, 1985.

—, *Architecture and Suburbia: From English Villa to American Dream House, 1690–2000*, Minneapolis and London, University of Minnesota Press, 2005.

Aries, P., *Centuries of Childhood: Social History of Family Life*, New York, Vintage, 1962.

Arnold, D. (ed.), *The Georgian Villa*, Stroud, Alan Sutton Publishing, 1996.

—, *Re-presenting the Metropolis: Architecture, Urban Experience and Social Life in London 1800–1840*, Aldershot and Burlington, Vt, Ashgate, 2000.

—, *Rural Urbanism: London Landscapes in the Early Nineteenth Century*, Manchester, Manchester University Press, 2005.

Arundell, D., *The Story of Sadler's Wells*, London, Hamish Hamilton, 1965.

Atkins, P. J., 'London's Intra-Urban Milk Supply, circa 1790–1914', *Transactions of the Institute of British Geographers*, vol. 2, no. 3, 1977, pp. 383–99.

Baker, M., 'A Rage for Exhibitions: The Display and Viewing of Wedgwood's Frog Service', in H. Young (ed.), *The Genius of Wedgwood*, London, Victoria and Albert Museum, 1995, pp. 18–27.

Ballantyne, A., 'Joseph Gandy and the Politics of Rustic Charm', in B. Arciszewska and E. McKellar (eds), *Articulating British Classicism: New Approaches to Eighteenth-Century Architecture*, Aldershot and Burlington, Vt, Ashgate, 2004, pp. 163–86.

—, *Rural and Urban: Architecture between Two Cultures*, London and New York, Routledge, 2010.

—, *Tudoresque: In Pursuit of the Ideal Home*, London, Reaktion, 2011.

Banham, R., *Los Angeles: The Architecture of Four Ecologies*, Harmondsworth, Penguin, 1971.

Barber, P., O. Cox, and M. Curwen, *'Lauderdale Revealed: A History of Lauderdale House; Highgate. The Building, its Owners and Occupiers: 1582–1993*, London, Lauderdale House Society, 1993.

Barker, F., and R. Hyde, *London: As It Might Have Been*, London, John Murray, 1982.

Barker, F., and P. Jackson, *The History of London in Maps*, London, Barrie and Jenkins, 1990.

Barnet, A., and R. Scruton, *Town and Country*, London, Jonathan Cape, 1995.

Barratt, T. J., *The Annals of Hampstead*, London, A. and C. Black, 1912.

Barrell, J., *The Dark Side of the Landscape: The Rural Poor in English Painting, 1730–1840*, Cambridge, Cambridge University Press, 1980.

—, 'The Public Prospect and the Private View: The Politics of Taste in Eighteenth-Century Britain', in S. Pugh (ed.), *Reading Landscape: Country–City–Capital*, Manchester and New York, Manchester University Press, 1990, pp. 19–40.

Barron, C. M., 'Richard Whittington: The Man Behind the Myth', in A. E. J. Hollander and W. Kellaway (eds), *Studies in London History: Presented to Philip Edmund Jones*, London, Hodder and Stoughton, 1969, pp. 197–248.

Barron, R., 'Introduction', in T. Moule, *English Counties Delineated*, London, Studio Editions, 1990, pp. 9–11.

Barton, N., *The Lost Rivers of London* (1962), London, Historical Publications, 1992.

Baynton-Williams, A. 'Introduction' in T. Moule, *The East and South-East of England*, London, Bracken, 1994, pp. 1–7.

Beier, A. L., and R. Finlay (eds), *London 1500–1700: The Making of the Metropolis*, Harlow, Longman, 1986.

Bendall, S. (ed.), *Dictionary of Land Surveyors and Local Map Makers*, London, British Library, 1997.

Berg, M., and H. Clifford, *Consumers and Luxury: Consumer Culture in Europe, 1650–1850*, Manchester, Manchester University Press, 1999.

Bermingham, A., *Landscape and Ideology: The English Rustic Tradition 1740–1860*, Berkeley, University of California Press, 1986.

Bermingham, A., and J. Brewer (eds), *The Consumption of Culture 1600–1800: Image, Object, Text*, London and New York, Routledge, 1995.

Bevan, A. B., *The Aldermen of the City of London*, 2 vols, London, 1908, 1913.

Bold, J., *Greenwich: An Architectural History of the Royal Hospital for Seamen and the Queen's House*, New Haven and London, Yale University Press, 2000.

—, 'Bird's-Eye Views: From Hollar to the London Eye', *London Journal*, vol. 35, no. 3, November 2010, pp. 225–35.

Bonehill, J., and S. Daniels (eds), *Paul Sandby: Picturing Britain*, exh. cat., London, Royal Academy of Arts, 2009.

Bonwitt, W., *Michael Searles: A Georgian Architect and Surveyor*, London, Society of Architectural Historians of Great Britain, 1987.

Borg, A., and D. Coke, *Vauxhall Gardens: A History*, New Haven and London, Yale University Press, 2011.

Borsay, P., *The English Urban Renaissance: Culture and Society in the Provincial Town, 1660–1770*, Oxford, Clarendon Press, 1989.

Boulton, J., *Neighbourhood and Society: A London Suburb in the Seventeenth Century*, Cambridge, Cambridge University Press, 1987.

—, 'London 1540–1700' in P. Clark (ed.), *The Cambridge Urban History of Britain: Volume II 1540–1840*, Cambridge, Cambridge University Press, 2000, pp. 315–46.

Bourdieu, P., *Outline of a Theory of Practice*, Cambridge, Cambridge University Press, 1997.

Bowden, M., G. Brown, and N. Smith, *An Archaeology of Town Commons in England: 'A very fair field indeed'*, Swindon, English Heritage, 2009.

Bradley, S., and N. Pevsner, *The Buildings of England, London, 1: The City of London*, Harmondsworth, Penguin, 1997.

Brandwood, G. K., N. Pevsner, and E. Williamson, *The Buildings of England: Buckinghamshire*, New Haven and London, Yale University Press, 2000.

Brett-James, N. G., *The Growth of Stuart London*, London, G. Allen and Unwin, 1935.

Brewer, J., *The Pleasures of the Imagination: English Culture in the Eighteenth Century*, London, HarperCollins, 1997.

Brewer, J., and R. Porter (eds), *Consumption and the World of Goods*, London and New York, Routledge, 1993.

Brookes, C., *The Gothic Revival*, London, Phaidon, 1999.

Bryan, M., *Dictionary of Painters and Engravers*, London, G. Bell and Sons, 1886.

Bryant, J., *Finest Prospects – Three Historic Houses: A Study in London Topography*, London, English Heritage, 1986.

—, *The Iveagh Bequest: Kenwood*, London, English Heritage, 1990.

—, 'Villa Views and the Uninvited Audience' in D. Arnold (ed.), *The Georgian Villa*, Stroud, Alan Sutton Publishing, 1996, pp. 11–24.

Bull, G. B., 'Introduction', in *Thomas Milne's Land Use Map of London and its Environs in 1800*, London, London Topographical Society, 1956a.

—, 'Thomas Milne's Land Utilization Map of the London

Area in 1800', *Geographical Journal*, vol. 122, no. 1, March 1956b, pp. 25–30.

Byrd, M., *London Transformed: Images of the City in the Eighteenth Century*, New Haven and London, Yale University Press, 1978.

Chalkin, C. W., 'South-East England', in P. Clark (ed.), *The Cambridge Urban History of Britain: Volume II 1540–1840*, Cambridge, Cambridge University Press, 2000, pp. 49–66.

Chancellor, E. B., and Sir M. M. Beeton (eds), *A Tour thro' London about the Year 1725: Being Letter V and Parts of Letter VI of 'A Tour thro' the Whole Island of Great Britain'; Containing a Description of the City of London, as taking in the City of Westminster, Borough of Southwark and Parts of Middlesex*, London, Batsford, 1929.

Charlesworth, M., 'Thomas Sandby Climbs the Hoober Stand: The Politics of Panoramic Drawing in Eigtheenth-century Britain', *Art History*, vol. 19, no. 2, June 1996, pp. 247–66.

Cherry, B., 'John Pollexfen's House in Walbrook', in J. Bold and E. Chaney (eds), *English Architecture Public and Private*, London, Hambledon Press, 1993, pp. 89–105.

—, 'Edward Hatton's *New View of London*', *Architectural History*, vol. 44, 2001, pp. 96–105.

Cherry, B., and N. Pevsner, *The Buildings of England, London, 2: South*, Harmondsworth, Penguin, 1983.

—, *The Buildings of England, London, 3: North West*, Harmondsworth, Penguin, 1991.

—, *The Buildings of England, London 4: North*, Harmondsworth, Penguin, 1998.

Clark, P., 'Introduction', in *The Cambridge Urban History of Britain: Volume II 1540–1840*, Cambridge, Cambridge University Press, 2000, pp. 1–24.

—, 'The Multi-Centred Metropolis: The Social and Cultural Landscapes of London, 1600–1840', in P. Clark and R. Gillespie (eds), *Two Capitals: London and Dublin 1500–1840*, Oxford and New York, British Academy and Oxford University Press, 2001, pp. 239–64.

Clark, P., and R. A. Houston, 'Culture and Leisure 1700–1840', in P. Clark (ed.), *The Cambridge Urban History of Britain: Volume II 1540–1840*, Cambridge, Cambridge University Press, 2000, pp. 575–614.

Clarke, B. F. L., *Parish Churches of London*, London, B. T. Batsford, 1966.

Clayton, T., *The English Print 1688–1802*, New Haven and London, Yale University Press, 1997.

Colley, L., *Britons: Forging the Nation 1707–1837*, New Haven and London, Yale University Press, 1992.

Colvin, H. M., 'Gothic Survival and Gothick Revival', *Architectural Review*, March 1948, pp. 91–8.

—, *A Biographical Dictionary of British Architects 1600–1840*, New Haven and London, Yale University Press, 1995.

Colvin, H. M., and J. Newman (eds), *Of Building: Roger North's Writings on Architecture*, Oxford, Oxford University Press, 1981.

Cooper, N., *Houses of the Gentry 1480–1680*, New Haven and London, Yale University Press, 1999.

—, 'The English Villa: Sources, Forms and Functions' in M. Airs and G. Tyack (eds), *The Renaissance Villa in Britain 1500–1700*, Reading, Spire Books, 2007, pp. 9–24.

Corfield, P. J., *Power and the Professions in Britain 1700–1850*, London, Routledge, 1995.

Cosgrove, D. (ed.), *Mappings*, London, Reaktion, 1999.

Cosgrove, D., and S. Daniels (eds), *The Iconography of Landscape: Essays on the Symbolic Representation, Design and Use of Past Environments*, Cambridge, Cambridge University Press, 1988.

Craske, M., 'Richard Jago's *Edge-Hill* Revisited: A Traveller's Prospect of the Health and Disease of a Succession of National Landscapes', in R. Wrigley and G. Revill (eds), *Pathologies of Travel*, Amsterdam, Rodopi, 2000, pp. 121–56.

—, 'Court Art Reviewed: The Sandbys' Vision of Windsor and its Environs', in J. Bonehill and S. Daniels (eds), *Paul Sandby: Picturing Britain*, exh. cat., London, Royal Academy of Arts, 2009, pp. 48–55.

Crook, J. M., 'Metropolitan Improvements: John Nash and the Picturesque', in C. Fox (ed.), *London: World City 1800–1840*, exh. cat., New Haven and London, Yale University Press, 1992, pp. 77–96.

—, 'John Nash and the Genesis of Regent's Park', in G. Tyack (ed.), *John Nash*, Swindon, English Heritage, 2013, pp. 75–100.

Curl, J. S., *Spas, Wells, and Pleasure-Gardens of London*, London, Historical Publications, 2010.

—, *Georgian Architecture in the British Isles 1714–1830*, Swindon, English Heritage, 2011.

Daniels, S., 'The Prince of Wales and the Shadow of St Paul's', in *Fields of Vision: Landscape Imagery and National Identity in England and the United States*, Cambridge, Polity Press, 1993, pp. 11–42.

—, *Humphrey Repton: Landscape Gardening and the Geography of Georgian England*, New Haven and London, Yale University Press, 1999.

Darley, G., *Villages of Vision*, London, Architectural Press, 1975.

Davidoff, L., and C. Hall, *Family Fortunes: Men and Women of the English Middle Class, 1780–1850*, London, Hutchinson, 1987.

De Bolla, P., 'Antipictorialism in the English Landscape Tradition: A Second Look at the Country and the City' in C. Prendergast (ed.), *Cultural Materialism: On Raymond Williams*, Minneapolis and London, University of Minnesota Press, 1995, pp. 173–87.

De Certeau, M., *The Practice of Everyday Life*, trans. Steven Rendall, Berkeley, Los Angeles and London, University of California Press, 1984.

Dixon Hunt, J., and P. Willis, *The Genius of the Place: The English Landscape Garden 1620–1820*, London, Paul Elek, 1975.

Donald, D., ' "Mr Deputy Dumpling and Family": Satirical Images of the City Merchant in Eighteenth-Century England', *Burlington Magazine*, vol. 131, no. 1040, November 1989, pp. 755–63.

—, ' "Beastly Sights": The Treatment of Animals as a Moral Theme in Representations of London *c*.1820–1850', in D. Arnold (ed.), *The Metropolis and its Image: Constructing Identities for London, c.1750–1950*, Oxford, Blackwell, 1999, pp. 48–78.

Dyos, H. J., 'The Growth of a Pre-Victorian Suburb: South London, 1580–1836', *Town Planning Review*, vol. XXV, 1954, pp. 59–78.

—, *Victorian Suburb: A Study of the Growth of Camberwell*, Leicester, Leicester University Press, 1966.

Earle, P., *The Making of the English Middle Class: Business, Society and Family Life in London, 1660–1730*, London, Methuen, 1989.

Estabrook, C. B., *Urbane and Rustic England: Cultural Ties and Social Spheres in the Provinces 1660–1780*, Manchester and New York, Manchester University Press, 1998.

Everitt, A., 'Country, County and Town: Patterns of Regional Evolution in England', in P. Borsay (ed.), *The Eighteenth Century Town: A Reader in English Urban History 1688–1820*, London and New York, Longman, 1990, pp. 83–115.

Fabricant, C., 'The Literature of Domestic Tourism and the Public Consumption of Private Property', in F. Nussbaum and L. Brown (eds), *The New Eighteenth Century: Theory, Politics, English Literature*, New York and London, Methuen, 1987, pp. 254–76.

Fairer, D., 'Eighteenth-Century Poetic Landscapes', *Coleridge Bulletin*, new seri. 13 (NS), Spring 1999, pp. 2–3.

Fairer, D., and C. Gerrard (eds), *Eighteenth-Century Poetry: The Annotated Anthology*, Oxford, Blackwell, 1999.

Fairman, O. T., 'Roads out of London: Being Photographic Reprints from Ogilby's "Britannia" 1675', *London Topographical Society*, vol. VIII, 1911.

Farmer, A., 'Colonel Fitzroy's Rustic Villa', *Camden History Review*, vol. 10, 1982, pp. 19–20.

—, *Hampstead Heath*, London, Historical Publications, 1984.

Finlay, R., and B. Shearer, 'Population Growth and Suburban Expansion', in A. L. Beier and R. Finlay (eds), *London 1500–1700: The Making of the Metropolis*, Harlow, Longman, 1986, pp. 37–59.

Fishman, R., *Bourgeois Utopias: The Rise and Fall of Suburbia*, New York, Basic Books, 1987.

Ford, M. (ed.), *London: A History in Verse*, Cambridge, Mass., and London, Harvard University Press, 2012.

Fordham, Sir H. G., *John Cary: Engraver, Map, Chart and Print-Seller and Globe-Maker 1734–1835: A Bibliography with an Introduction and Biographical Notes*, Cambridge, Cambridge University Press, 1925.

—, *Some Notable Surveyors and Map Makers*, Cambridge, Cambridge University Press, 1929,

Foucault, M., *Discipline and Punish: The Birth of the Prison*, Harmondsworth, Penguin, 1979.

Fox, C. (ed.), *London: World City 1800–1840*, exh. cat., New Haven and London, Yale University Press, 1992.

Foxell, S., *Mapping London: Making Sense of the City*, London, Black Dog Publishing, 2007.

Freeman, M., 'Popular Attitudes to Turnpikes in Early Eighteenth-Century England, *Journal of Historical Geography*, vol. 19, 1993, pp. 33–47.

Friedman, T., *The Eighteenth-Century Church in Britain*, New Haven and London, Yale University Press, 2011.

Galinou, M., 'Merchants' Houses', in M. Galinou (ed.), *City Merchants and the Arts 1670–1720*, London, Oblong for the Corporation of London, 2004, pp. 25–40.

—, *Cottages and Villas: The Birth of the Garden Suburb*, New Haven and London, Yale University Press, 2010.

Galinou, M., and J. Hayes, *London in Paint: Oil Paintings in the Collection of the Museum of London*, London, Museum of London, 1996.

Gapper, C., 'Plasterers and Plasterwork in City, Court and Country *c*.1530–*c*.1640', PhD thesis, Courtauld Institute of Art, 1998.

Garlick, K., and A. Macintyre (eds), *The Diary of Joseph Farington*, New Haven and London, Yale University Press, 1978.

Garreau, J., *Edge City: Life on the New Frontier*, New York, Anchor Books, 1992.

Gauci, P., *The Politics of Trade: The Overseas Merchant in State and Society, 1660–1720*, Oxford, Oxford University Press, 2001.

—, *Emporium of the World: The Merchants of London 1660–1800*, London and New York, Hambledon Continuum, 2007.

George, M. D., *London Life in the Eighteenth Century*, Harmondsworth, Penguin, 1976.

Gerhold, D., 'London's Suburban Villas and Mansions, 1660–1830', *London Journal*, vol. 34, no. 3, 2009, pp. 233–63.

Girouard, M., *Life in the English Country House: A Social and Architectural History*, New Haven and London, Yale University Press, 1978.

—, *The English Town*, New Haven and London, Yale University Press, 1990.

Glanville, G., and P. Glanville, 'The Art Market and Merchant

Patronage 1680–1720', in M. Galinou (ed.), *City Merchants and the Arts 1670–1720*, London, Oblong for the Corporation of London, 2004, pp. 10–24.

Glanville, P., *London in Maps*, London, The Connoisseur, 1972.

Griffiths, A., *The Print in Stuart Britain, 1603–1689*, London, British Museum, 1998.

Godfrey, R., *Wenceslaus Hollar: A Bohemian artist in England*, exh. cat., New Haven and London, Yale University Press, 1995.

Godfrey, W. (ed.), F. Colsoni, *Le guide de Londres (1693)*, London, London Topographical Society, 1951.

Gomme, G. L. (ed.), *English Topography, Part XVI, London, Volume II*, London, Elliot Stock, 1905.

Guillery, P., *The Buildings of London Zoo*, Royal Commission on the Historical Monuments of England, London, 1993.

—, 'On the Road to London: Coaching-Inn Lodgings in Highgate', *Georgian Group Journal*, vol. 11, 2001, pp. 203–19.

—, *The Small House in Eighteenth-Century London*, New Haven and London, Yale University Press, 2004.

Guillery, P., and M. Snodin, 'Strawberry Hill: Building and Site', *Architectural History*, vol. 38, 1995, pp. 102–28.

Habermas, J., *The Structural Transformation of the Public Sphere*, Cambridge, Polity Press, 1989.

Hall, M. (ed.), *Gothic Architecture and its Meanings 1550–1830*, Reading, Spire Books, 2002.

Hall, P., 'Introduction', *Von Thünen's Isolated State*, trans. Carla M. Wartenberg, Oxford, Pergamon Press, 1966.

Harding, V., 'The Population of London, 1550–1700: A Review of the Published Evidence', *London Journal*, vol. 15, no. 2, 1990a, pp. 111–28.

—, ' "Whither wilt thou build?": Gardens and Open Space in Tudor and Early Stuart London', in M. Galinou (ed.), *London's Pride: The Glorious History of the Capital's Gardens*, London, Museum of London and Anaya Publishers, 1990b, pp. 44–55.

—, 'City, Capital, and Metropolis: The Changing Shape of Seventeenth-Century London', in J. F. Merritt (ed.), *Imagining Early Modern London: Perceptions and Portrayals of the City from Stow to Strype 1598–1720*, Cambridge, Cambridge University Press, 2001, pp. 117–44.

Harley, J. B., 'Maps, Knowledge and Power', in D. Cosgrove and S. Daniels (eds), *The Iconography of Landscape: Essays on the Symbolic Representation, Design and Use of Past Environments*, Cambridge, Cambridge University Press, 1988, pp. 277–312.

Harris, E., *British Architectural Books and Writers 1556–1785*, Cambridge, Cambridge University Press, 1990.

Harris, M., 'London Guidebooks before 1800', in R. Myers and M. Harris (eds) *Maps and Prints: Aspects of the English Booktrade*, Oxford, Oxford Polytechnic Press, 1984, pp. 31–66.

Harris, R., and R. Simon (eds), *Enlightened Self-Interest: The Foundling Hospital and Hogarth*, exh. cat., London, Draig Publications and The Thomas Coram Foundation for Children, 1997.

Harwood, E., 'Forty Hall and Tyttenhanger', in M. Airs and G. Tyack (eds), *The Renaissance Villa in Britain 1500–1700*, Reading, Spire Books, 2007, pp. 206–22.

Hearn, K., 'Merchant Clients for the Painter Jan Siberechts', in M. Galinou (ed.), *City Merchants and the Arts 1670–1720*, London, Oblong for the Corporation of London, 2004, pp. 83–92.

Hebbert, M., *London More by Fortune than Design*, Chicester, John Wiley, 1988.

Hebbert, M., and E. McKellar (eds), 'Tall Buildings in the London Landscape', Special Issue, *London Journal*, vol. 33, no. 3, November 2008.

Heyl, C., 'We are not at Home: Protecting Domestic Privacy in Post-Fire Middle-Class London', *London Journal*, vol. 27, no. 2, 2002, pp. 12–33.

Hitchcock, T., *Down and Out in Eighteenth-Century London*, London, Hambledon, 2004.

Hobhouse, H., *London Survey'd: The Work of the Survey of London 1894–1994*, Swindon, Royal Commission of the Historical Monuments of England, 1994.

Hollis, F., 'From Longhouse to Live/Work Unit: Parallel Histories and Absent Narratives', in P. Guillery (ed.), *Built from Below: British Architecture and the Vernacular*, London and New York, Routledge, 2011, pp. 189–207.

Hoskins, W. G., *The Making of the English Landscape*, ed. C. Taylor, London, Hodder and Stoughton, 1992.

Hotson, A., 'Tomb Sculpture and Dynastic Ambition', in M. Galinou (ed.), *City Merchants and the Arts 1670–1720*, London, Oblong for the Corporation of London, 2004, pp. 132–44.

Howgego, J., *Printed Maps of London circa 1553–1850*, Folkestone, Dawson, 1978.

Howitt, W., *The Northern Heights of London: Or, Historical Associations of Hampstead, Highgate, Muswell Hill, Hornsey and Islington*, London, Longmans, 1869.

Hyde, R. (ed.), *A Prospect of Britain: The Town Panoramas of Samuel and Nathaniel Buck*, London, Pavilion, 1994.

Jacques, D., *Georgian Gardens: The Reign of Nature*, London, B. T. Batsford, 1983.

Jeffrey, S., 'The Building of Maids of Honour Row, Richmond', *Georgian Group Journal*, vol. 18, 2010, pp. 65–76.

Jenkins, S., and J. Ditchburn, *Images of Hampstead*, Richmond-upon-Thames, Ackermann, 1982.

Jenner, M., 'The Politics of London Air: John Evelyn's *Fumifugium* and the Restoration', *The Historical Journal*, vol. 38, no. 3, 1995, pp. 535–51.

Keats, J., *Poetical Works*, ed. H. W. Garrod, Oxford, Oxford University Press, 1978.

Keen, D., 'Growth, Modernisation and Control: The Transformation of London's Landscape, *c.*1500–*c.*1760', in P. Clark and R. Gillespie (eds), *Two Capitals: London and Dublin 1500–1840*, Oxford and New York, British Academy and Oxford University Press, 2001, pp. 7–38.

Knight, C., *London's Country Houses*, Chichester, Phillimore, 2009.

Langford, P., *A Polite and Commercial People: England 1727–1783*, Oxford, Clarendon Press, 1989.

Latham, R. (ed.), *Catalogue of the Pepys Library at Magdalene College, Cambridge*, 7 vols, Woodbridge, D. S. Brewer, 1978.

Laxton, P., 'The Evidence of Richard Horwood's Maps for Residential Building in London, 1759–1819, *London Journal*, vol. 24, 1999, pp. 1–22.

Lea, R., and C. Miele with G. Higgott, *Danson House: The Anatomy of a Georgian Villa*, Swindon, English Heritage, 2011.

Leach, P., 'The House with a View in Late Eighteenth-Century England', *Georgian Group Journal*, vol. 16, 2008, pp. 117–31.

Leatherbarrow, D., 'Architecture and Situation: A Study of the Architectural Writings of Robert Morris', *Journal of the Society of Architectural Historians*, vol. XLIV, March 1985, pp. 48–59.

Lefebvre, H., *The Production of Space*, trans. D. Nicholson-Smith, Oxford, Oxford University Press, 1991.

Lindsay, J., *The Monster City: Defoe's London, 1688–1730*, London and New York, Hart-Davis MacGibbon, 1978.

Lippincott, L., *Selling Art in Georgian London: The Rise of Arthur Pond*, New Haven and London, Yale University Press 1983.

Lloyd, J. H., *The History, Topography and Antiquities of Highgate, with Notes on Hornsey, Crouch End, Muswell Hill &c.*, London, Highgate Literary and Scientific Institute, 1888.

Longman, C. J., and H. Walrond, *Archery*, Badminton Library of Sports and Pastimes, London, Longmans, Green and Co., 1894.

Longstaffe-Gowan, T., *The London Town Garden 1740–1840*, New Haven and London, Yale University Press, 2001.

—, *The London Square: Gardens in the Midst of Town*, New Haven and London, Yale University Press, 2012.

Lubbock, J., *The Tyranny of Taste: The Politics of Architecture and Design in Britain, 1550–1960*, New Haven and London, Yale University Press, 1995.

Macaulay, J., *The Gothic Revival 1745–1845*, Glasgow and London, Blackie, 1975.

McClure, R., *Coram's Children: The London Foundling Hospital in the Eighteenth Century*, New Haven and London, Yale University Press, 1981.

McCreery, A., 'Turnpike Roads and the Spatial Culture of London, 1756–1830', PhD thesis, University College London, 2005.

McKellar, E., 'The City and the Country: The London Vernacular in the Late Seventeenth and Early Eighteenth Century', in N. Burton (ed.), *Georgian Vernacular*, London, Georgian Group, 1996, pp. 10–18.

—, *The Birth of Modern London: The Development and Design of the City 1660–1720*, Manchester, Manchester University Press, 1999a.

—, 'Peripheral Visions: Alternative Aspects and Rural Presences in Mid-Eighteenth Century London', *Art History*, vol. 22, no. 4, November 1999b, pp. 495–513.

—, 'Populism versus Professionalism: John Summerson and the Creation of "the Georgian" ', in B. Arciszewska and E. McKellar (eds), *Articulating British Classicism: New Approaches in Eighteenth-Century Architecture*, Aldershot and Burlington, Vt, Ashgate, 2004, pp. 35–56.

—, 'The Suburban Villa Tradition in Seventeenth and Eighteenth-Century London', in B. Arciszewska (ed.), *Baroque Villa: Suburban and Country Residences, c.1600–1800*, Warsaw, Wilanow Palace Museum, 2009, pp. 197–208.

—, 'The Villa: Ideal Type or Vernacular Variant?', in P. Guillery (ed.), *Built from Below: British Architecture and the Vernacular*, London and New York, Routledge, 2011, pp. 49–72.

—, 'The Metropolitan Urban Renaissance: London 1660–1760', in E. Barker (ed.), *Art and Visual Culture 1600–1850: Academy to Avant-Garde*, London, Tate Publishing with the Open University, 2012, pp. 101–40.

—, 'Guides, Guidebooks and Visitors to London, *c.*1650–1730: Metropolitan Literature in its Continental Context', in D. Arnold and J.-L. Cohen (eds), *Paris et Londres s'observent 1670–1970*, Institut national d'histoire de l'art and Infolio Editions, (forthcoming).

McKendrick, N., J. Brewer, and J. Plumb, *The Birth of a Consumer Society: The Commercialization of Eighteenth-Century England*, London, Europa Publications, 1982.

MacLean, G., D. Landry, and J. P. Ward (eds), *The Country and the City Revisited: England and the Politics of Culture, 1550–1850*, Cambridge, Cambridge University Press, 1999.

Matless, D., 'The Uses of Cartographic Literacy: Mapping, Survey and Citizenship in Twentieth-Century Britain', in D. Cosgrove (ed.), *Mappings*, London, Reaktion, 1999, pp. 193–212.

Merritt, J. F., 'Puritans, Laudians, and the Phenomenon of Church-Building in Jacobean London', *Historical Journal*, vol. 41, 1998, pp. 935–60.

—, 'The Reshaping of Stow's Survey: Munday, Strype, and the Protestant City', in J. F. Merritt (ed.), *Imagining Early Modern London: Perceptions and Portrayals of the City from*

Stow to Strype 1598–1720, Cambridge, Cambridge University Press, 2001, pp. 52–88.

Miele, C., 'From Aristocratic Ideal to Middle-Class Idyll: 1690–1840', in *London Suburbs*, London, Merrell Holberton and English Heritage, 1999, pp. 31–59.

Mobus, M., 'The Burford Masons and the Changing World of Building Practice in England, c.1630–1730', PhD thesis, Open University, 2012.

Monks, S., 'The Visual Economies of the Downriver Thames in Eighteenth-Century British Art', in S. Monks (ed.), *Visual Culture in Britain*, Manchester and New York, Manchester University Press, 2006, pp. 1–20.

Monteyne, J., *The Printed Image in Early Modern London: Urban Space, Visual Representation and Social Exchange*, Aldershot and Burlington, Vt, Ashgate, 2007.

Morris, D., *Mile End Old Town 1740–1780: A Social History of an Early Modern London Suburb*, 2nd edn, London, East London History Society, 2007.

—, *Whitechapel 1600–1800: A Social History of an Early Modern London Inner Suburb*, London, East London History Society, 2011.

Morris, D., and K. Cozens, *Wapping 1600–1800: A Social History of an Early Modern London Maritime Suburb*, London, East London History Society, 2009.

Nead, L., *Victorian Babylon: People, Streets and Images in Nineteenth-Century London*, New Haven and London, Yale University Press, 2000.

Ogborn, M., *Spaces of Modernity: London's Geographies 1680–1780*, New York and London, Guilford Press, 1998.

Olsen, D. J., *Town Planning in London: The Eighteenth and Nineteenth Centuries*, New Haven and London, Yale University Press, 1982.

Pawson, E., *Transport and Economy: The Turnpike Road of Eighteenth Century Britain*, London, Academic Press, 1977.

—, 'Debates in Transport History: Popular Opposition to Turnpike Trusts?', *Journal of Transport History*, 3rd ser., vol. 5, no. 2, 1984, pp. 57–65.

Pearl, V., 'Change and Stability in Seventeenth-Century London', *London Journal*, vol. 5, no. 1, May 1979, pp. 3–34.

—, 'Introduction', in J. Stow, *The Survey of London* (1598), ed. H. B. Wheatley, London and Melbourne, Dent, 1987.

Peats, R., 'Forty Hall, Enfield: Continuity and Innovation in a Carolean Gentry House', *Architectural History*, vol. 51, 2008, pp. 33–62.

Peltz, L., 'Aestheticizing the Ancestral City: Antiquarianism, Topography and the Representation of London in the Long Eighteenth Century', in D. Arnold (ed.), *The Metropolis and its Image: Constructing Identities for London, c.1750–1950*, Oxford, Blackwell, 1999a, pp. 6–28.

—, 'The Extra-Illustration of London: The Gendered Spaces and Practices of Antiquarianism in the Late Eighteenth Century', in M. Myrone and L. Pletz (eds), *Producing the Past: Aspects of Antiquarian Culture and Practice, 1700–1850*, Aldershot, Ashgate, 1999b, pp. 115–34.

Phillips, H., 'John Rocque's Career', *London Topographical Record*, vol. 20, 1952, pp. 9–25.

Pinks, W. J., *The History of Clerkenwell*, London, 1865.

Port, M. H., *Hampstead Parish Church: The Story of a Building through 250 Years*, London, St John-at-Hampstead Parochial Church Council, 1995.

Power, M. J., 'The East and West in Early-Modern London', in E. W. Ives et al. (eds), *Wealth and Power in Tudor England*, London, Athlone Press, 1978a, pp. 167–85.

—, 'Shadwell: The Development of a London Suburban Community in the Seventeenth Century', *London Journal*, vol. 4, no. 1, 1978b, pp. 29–46.

—, 'The Social Topography of Restoration London', in A. L. Beier and R. Finlay (eds), *London 1500–1700: The Making of the Metropolis*, Harlow, Longman, 1986, pp. 199–224.

Prosser, L., and L. Worsley, 'Kew Palace', in M. Airs and G. Tyack (eds), *The Renaissance Villa in Britain 1500–1700*, Reading, Spire Books, 2007, pp. 180–91.

Raeburn, M., 'The Frog Service and its Sources', in Young H. (ed.), *The Genius of Wedgwood*, exh. cat., London, Victoria and Albert Museum, 1995, pp. 134–48.

Rasmussen, S. E., *London: The Unique City* (1934), Cambridge Mass., and London, MIT Press, 1982.

Read, M., 'The Transformation of Urban Space 1700–1840', in P. Clark (ed.), *The Cambridge Urban History of Britain: Volume II 1540–1840*, Cambridge, Cambridge University Press, 2000, pp. 615–40.

Redgrave, S., *A Dictionary of Artists of the English School*, London, George Bell, 1878.

Retford, K., *The Art of Domestic Life: Family Portraiture in Eighteenth-Century England*, New Haven and London, Yale University Press, 2006.

Richardson, J., *Highgate: Its History since the Fifteenth Century*, New Barnet, Historical Publications, 1983.

—, *Islington Past*, New Barnet, Historical Publications, 1988.

—, *Highgate Past*, New Barnet Historical Publications, 1989.

Rogers, N., 'Money, Land and Lineage: The Big Bourgeoisie of Hanoverian London', in P. Borsay (ed.), *The Eighteenth Century Town: A Reader in English Urban History 1688–1820*, Harlow and New York, Longman, 1990, pp. 268–91.

Rogers, P., *The Text of Great Britain: Theme and Design in Defoe's 'Tour'*, Newark and London, University of Delaware Press and Associated University Presses, 1998.

Rybczynski, W., *Home: A Short History of an Idea*, Harmondsworth, Penguin, 1986.

Saint, A., 'Ashbee, Geddes, Lethaby and the Rebuilding of Crosby Hall', *Architectural History*, vol. 34, 1991, pp. 206–23.

— (ed.), *London Suburbs*, London, English Heritage, 1999.

Saunders, A., *Regent's Park: A Study of the Area from 1086 to the Present Day*, Newton Abbot, David and Charles, 1969.

Schama, S., *Landscape and Memory*, London, HarperCollins, 1995.

Schwarz, L., *London in the Age of Industrialisation: Entrepreneurs, Labour Force and Living Conditions, 1700–1850*, Cambridge, Cambridge University Press, 1992.

—, 'London 1700–1840', in P. Clark (ed.), *The Cambridge Urban History of Britain: Volume II 1540–1840*, Cambridge, Cambridge University Press, 2000, pp. 641–72.

Scouloudi, I., *Panoramic Views of London 1600–1666: With Some Later Adaptations; An Annotated List*, London, Library Committee of the Corporation of London, 1953.

Seal, G., *The Outlaw Legend: A Cultural Tradition in Britain, America and Australia*, Cambridge, Cambridge University Press, 1996.

Sennett, R., *Flesh and Stone: The Body and the City in Western Civilization*, London, Faber and Faber, 1994.

Sheppard, F., V. Belcher, and P. Cotterell, 'The Middlesex and Yorkshire Deeds Registries and the Study of Building Fluctuations', *London Journal*, vol. 5, no. 2, 1979, pp. 177–217.

Shesgreen, S., *Images of the Outcast: The Urban Poor in the Cries of London*, Manchester and New York, Manchester University Press, 2002.

Shoemaker, R., 'Gendered Spaces: Patterns of Mobility and Perceptions of London's Geography, 1660–1750', in J. F. Merritt (ed.), *Imagining Early Modern London: Perceptions and Portrayals of the City from Stow to Strype 1598–1720*, Cambridge, Cambridge University Press, 2001, pp. 144–65.

—, *The London Mob: Violence and Disorder in Eighteenth-Century England*, London, Hambledon, 2004.

Simo, M. L., *Loudon and the Landscape: From Country Seat to Metropolis, 1783–1843*, New Haven and London, Yale University Press, 1988.

Sinclair, I., *London Orbital: A Walk around the M25*, London and New York, Granta, 2002.

Smith, A. (ed.), *Watercolour*, exh. cat., London, Tate Publishing, 2011.

Smuts, M. R., 'The Court and its Neighbourhood: Royal Policy and Urban Growth in Early Stuart West End', *Journal of British Studies*, vol. 30, 1991, pp. 117–49.

Snodin, M. (ed.), *Horace Walpole's Strawberry Hill*, New Haven and London, Yale University Press, 2009.

Snodin, M., and J. Styles, *Design and the Decorative Arts: Britain 1500–1900*, London, V&A Publications, 2001.

Soja, E. W., *Postmetropolis: Critical Studies of Cities and Regions*, Malden, Mass. and Oxford, Blackwell, 2000.

Solkin, D. H., *Richard Wilson: The Landscape of Reaction*, exh. cat., London, Tate Gallery, 1982.

—, *Painting for Money: The Visual Arts and the Public Sphere in Eighteenth-Century England*, New Haven and London, Yale University Press, 1993.

Stevenson, C., *Medicine and Magnificence: British Hospital and Asylum Architecture 1660–1815*, New Haven and London, Yale University Press, 2000.

Stone, L., 'The Residential Development of the West End of London in the Seventeenth Century', in B. Malament (ed.), *After the Reformation*, Philadelphia, University of Pennsylvania Press, 1980, pp. 167–212.

Summerson, J., 'The Beginnings of Regent's Park', *Architectural History*, vol. 20, 1977, pp. 56–62 and 90–9.

—, *The Life and Work of John Nash, Architect,* London, Allen and Unwin, 1980.

—, *Architecture in Britain 1530–1830*, Harmondsworth, Penguin, 1983.

—, *Georgian London* (1945), New Haven and London, Yale University Press, 1988.

—, 'The Classical Country House in 18th-Century England', in *The Unromantic Castle and Other Essays*, London, Thames and Hudson, 1990.

—, 'The Beginnings of the Early Victorian Suburb', *London Topographical Record*, no. 27, 1995, pp. 1–48.

Survey of London (SOL), *Cromwell House, Highgate*, Monograph 12, London, Eyre and Spottiswoode, 1926.

—, *The Village of Highgate (The Parish of St Pancras, Part 1)*, vol. 17, London, London County Council, 1936.

—, *Spitalfields and Mile End New Town*, vol. 27, London, Athlone Press, 1957.

—, *Northern Clerkenwell and Pentonville*, vol. 47, New Haven and London, Yale University Press, 2008.

—, *Woolwich*, vol. 48, New Haven and London, Yale University Press, 2012.

—, *Battersea*, vols 49 and 50, New Haven and London, Yale University Press, 2013.

Sweet, R., *The Writing of Urban Histories in Eighteenth-Century England*, Oxford, Clarendon Press, 1997.

—, *Antiquaries: The Discovery of the Past in Eighteenth-Century Britain*, London, Hambledon and London, 2004.

Thompson, F. M. L., *Hampstead: Building a Borough, 1650–1964*, London and Boston, Routledge and Kegan Paul, 1974.

—, 'Nineteenth-Century Horse Sense', *Economic History Review*, 2nd ser., vol. 29, no. 1, 1976, pp. 60–81.

Thompson, J. H., *Highgate Dissenters: Their History since 1660*, Cambridge, Highgate URC, 2001.

Thorne, J., *Handbook to the Environs of London*, London, 1876.

Thorold, P., *The London Rich: The Creation of a Great City from 1666 to the Present*, Harmondsworth, Penguin, 1999.

Tindall, G., *The Fields Beneath: The History of One London Village*, London, Temple Smith, 1977.

Tinniswood, A., *The Polite Tourist: A History of Country House Visiting*, London, National Trust, 1998.

Tristram, P., *Living Space in Fact and Fiction*, London, Routledge, 1989.

Tyack, G., 'The Freemans of Fawley and their Buildings', *Records of Buckinghamshire*, Buckinghamshire Archaeological Society, vol. 24, 1982, pp. 130–43.

—, 'John Nash and the Park Village', *Georgian Group Journal*, 1993, pp. 68–74.

— (ed.), *John Nash*, Swindon, English Heritage, 2013.

Varley, F. J., *Highgate Worthies: Alderman John Ireton*, Highgate, Highgate Literary and Scientific Institute, 1933.

Venturi, R., D. Scott Brown, and S. Izenour, *Learning from Las Vegas* (1972), Cambridge, Mass. and London, MIT Press, 1977.

Vickery, A., 'Golden Age to Separate Spheres: A Review of the Categories and Chronology of English Women's History', *Historical Journal*, vol. 36, no. 2, 1993, pp. 383–414.

—, *The Gentleman's Daughter: Women's Lives in Georgian England*, New Haven and London, Yale University Press, 1998.

Victoria and Albert Museum, *The Discovery of the Lake District: A Northern Arcadia and its Uses*, exh. cat., London, Victoria and Albert Museum, 1984.

Victoria County History (VCH), *A History of the County of Middlesex: Friern Barnet, Finchley, Hornsey with Highgate*, vol. 6, Oxford, Oxford University Press, 1980.

—, *A History of the County of Middlesex: Islington and Stoke Newington Parishes*, vol. 8, Oxford, Oxford University Press, 1988.

—, *A History of the County of Middlesex: Hampstead and Paddington*, vol. 9, Oxford, Oxford University Press, 1989.

—, *A History of the County of Middlesex: Chelsea*, vol. 12, Woodbridge and Rochester, N.Y., Boydell and Brewer, 2004.

Ward, J. P., 'Imaging the Metropolis in Elizabethan and Stuart London', in G. MacLean, D. Landry, and J. P. Ward (eds), *The Country and the City Revisited: England and the Politics of Culture, 1550–1850*, Cambridge, Cambridge University Press, 1999, pp. 24–40.

Warf, B., and S. Arias, *The Spatial Turn: Interdisciplinary Perspectives*, New York, Routledge, 2009.

Webb, D., 'Guide Books to London before 1800: A Survey', *London Topographical Record*, vol. 36, 1990, pp. 138–52.

Willats, E. A., *Streets with a Story: The Book of Islington*, London, Islington Local History Education Trust, 1988.

Williams, L., ' "To recreate and refresh their dulled spirites in the sweet and wholesome ayre"; Green Space and the Growth of the City', in J. F. Merritt (ed.), *Imagining Early Modern London: Perceptions and Portrayals of the City from Stow to Strype 1598–1720*, Cambridge, Cambridge University Press, 2001, pp. 185–213.

Williams, R., 'Between Country and City', in S. Pugh (ed.), *Reading Landscape: Country–City–Capital*, Manchester and New York, Manchester University Press, 1990, pp. 7–18.

—, *The Country and the City* (1973), London, Hogarth Press, 1985.

Williamson, T., *Polite Landscape: Gardens and Society in Eighteenth-Century England*, Stroud, Alan Sutton, 1995.

Wilton-Ely, J., 'The Rise of the Professional Architect in England', in S. Kostof (ed.), *The Architect: Chapters in the History of the Profession*, New York, Oxford University Press, 1977.

Wittkower, R., *Palladio and English Palladianism*, London, Thames and Hudson, 1974.

Wittman, R., *Architecture, Print Culture and the Public Sphere in Eighteenth-Century France*, New York and London, Routledge, 2007, pp. 19–24.

Woodhead, J. R., *The Rulers of London 1660–89: A Biographical Record of the Aldermen and Common Councilmen of the City of London*, London, London and Middlesex Archaelogical Society, 1965.

Worsley, G., *Classical Architecture in Britain: The Heroic Age*, New Haven and London, Yale University Press, 1995.

Wortley, L., 'City Merchants' Landownership around Henley-on-Thames and the Paintings of Jan Siberechts', in M. Galinou (ed.), *City Merchants and the Arts 1670–1720*, London, Oblong for the Corporation of London, 2004, pp. 93–102.

Wrigley, E. A., 'A Simple Model of London's Importance in Changing English Society and Economy 1650–1750', in P. Abrams and E. A. Wrigley (eds), *Towns in Society: Essays in Economic History and Historical Sociology*, Cambridge, Cambridge University Press, 1978, pp. 215–43.

Wroth, W. W., and A. E. Wroth, *The London Pleasure Gardens of the Eighteenth Century*, London and New York, Macmillan, 1896.

ILLUSTRATION CREDITS

Tate Image / Digital Image © Tate, London, 2012: *frontis.*, 115, 122, 126; Photo © Christie's Images /The Bridgeman Art Library: *p. v*, 178; © Trustees of the British Museum: *p. vi*, 11, 12, 13, 14, 15, 16, 18, 24, 25, 27, 31, 32, 33, 50, 69, 70, 71, 73, 74, 75, 76, 79, 83, 84, 85, 88, *p. 109*, 91, 93, 94, 95, 96, 99, 100, 101, 102, 107, 108, 109, 111, 112, 117, 118, 119, 120, 129, 145, 151, 161, 162, 166, 167, 170, 176, 180, 187, 189; By permission of the British Library: *p. viii*, 9, 35, 37, 39, 44, 51, 52, 53, 54, 55, 56, 57a, 57b, 58, 59a, 59b, 61, 62, 63a, 63b, 64, 65, 66, 72, 87, 89, 113, 155, 181, 184, 195; © English Heritage: 2 (Andrew Donald), 23, 125, 133, 139; © Her Majesty Queen Elizabeth II 2012: 4; © National Trust Images: 5 (Geoffrey Frosh), 123 (A F Kersting); © The Courtauld Institute of Art, London: 6; © The Bridgeman Art Library: 7, 21, 68, 81, 86, 144, 179; © Photograph by Prudence Cumming Associates Ltd: 8; Courtesy Royal Geographical Society: 10; Author: 17, 20, 43, 46a, 46b, 60, 92, 106, 131, 132, 136, 137, 138, 141, 143, 154, 165, 169; © National Maritime Museum, Greenwich, London: 19; City of London, London Metropolitan Archives: 26, *p. 29*, 30, 77, 78, 104, 105, 110, 116, 121, 127, 128, 130, 134, 146, 147, 148, 149, 150, 168, 177, 188, 191, 192, 193, 194; © Look and Learn / Peter Jackson Collection /The Bridgeman Art Library: 28, 183; © The Pepys Library, Magdalene College, Cambridge: 29, 34, 36; The Bodleian Library, University of Oxford: 38, 40, 41, 42, 47, 48, 49, 67, 82, 158, 164, 175, 185, 186; © Royal Mail Group Ltd 2012, courtesy of The British Postal Museum & Archive: 45; Photograph © The State Hermitage Museum / Photo by Vladimir Terebenin, Leonard Kheifets, Yuri Molod-kovets: 80; David Coke: 90, 98; © Victoria and Albert Museum, London: 97; © English Heritage/Survey of London: 103, 135; Yale Center for British Art, Paul Mellon Collection: 114; Christine Matthews: 124; Estate of Oliver Cox: 142; RIBA Library Photographs Collection: 152, 153, 159, 160, 171, 172, 173, 174; Courtesy of Sotheby's Picture Library: 157

INDEX

Index created by Meg Davies (Fellow of the Society of Indexers)